# Lab Manual for
# A+ Guide to Managing and Maintaining Your PC

## SIXTH EDITION, COMPREHENSIVE

## Jean Andrews, Ph.D.

## Todd Verge

COURSE TECHNOLOGY
CENGAGE Learning™

Australia • Canada • Mexico • Singapore • Spain • United Kingdom • United States

## COURSE TECHNOLOGY
### CENGAGE Learning™

**Lab Manual for A+ Guide to Managing and Maintaining Your PC,**
**SIXTH EDITION, COMPREHENSIVE**
is published by Cengage Course Technology

Managing Editor: Larry Main

Senior Product Manager: Michelle Ruelos Cannistraci

Editorial Assistant: Jessica Reed

Marketing Manager: Guy Baskaran

Development Editor: Lisa M. Lord

Content Project Manager: Danielle Chouhan

Executive Editor: Stephen Helba

Acquisitions Editor: Nick Lombardi

Manuscript Quality Assurance: Christian Kunciw

Senior Manufacturing Coordinator: Justin Palmeiro

Compositor: Integra—Pondicherry, India

Cover Designer: Betsy Young

Text Designer: Betsy Young

For product information and technology assistance, contact us at
**Cengage Learning Customer & Sales Support, 1-800-354-9706**

For permission to use material from this text or product, submit all requests online at **cengage.com/permissions**.
Further permissions questions can be emailed to
**permissionrequest@cengage.com**

ISBN-13: 978-0-619-21763-1
ISBN-10: 0-619-21763-4

**Course Technology**
25 Thomson Place,
Boston, Massachusetts, 02210.

Disclaimer

Cengage Course Technology reserves the right to revise this publication and make changes from time to time in its content without notice.

Printed in the United States of America
4 5 6 7 8 TC 12 11 10 09 08

# Table of Contents

# Preface

This lab manual is designed to be the best tool on the market to enable you to get the hands-on practical experience you need to learn to troubleshoot and repair personal computers and operating systems. It contains more than 100 labs, each of which targets a practical problem you're likely to face in the real world when troubleshooting PCs. Every attempt has been made to write labs that allow you to use generic hardware devices. A specific hardware configuration isn't necessary to complete the labs. In learning to install, support, and troubleshoot operating systems, you learn to support Windows XP, Windows 2000 Professional, and Windows 9x and to use the command prompt. Each chapter contains labs designed to provide the structure novices need, as well as labs that challenge experienced and inquisitive students.

This book helps prepare you for the new A+ Certification exams offered through the Computer Technology Industry Association (CompTIA): A+ Essentials, 220–602, 220–603, 220–604, and 220–605 as well as the previous A+ Core Hardware examination and the Operating System Technologies examination. Because the popularity of this certification credential is quickly growing among employers, becoming certified increases your ability to gain employment, improve your salary, and enhance your career. To find more information about A+ Upgrade Certification and its sponsoring organization, CompTIA, go to the CompTIA Web site at *www.comptia.org*.

Whether your goal is to become an A+ certified technician or a PC support technician, the *Lab Manual for A+ Guide to Managing and Maintaining Your PC, Sixth Edition, Comprehensive*, along with Jean Andrews's textbooks, will take you there!

## FEATURES

To ensure a successful experience for both instructors and students, this book includes the following pedagogical features:

- **Objectives**—Every lab opens with learning objectives that set the stage for students to absorb the lab's lessons.
- **Materials Required**—This feature outlines all the materials students need to complete the lab successfully.
- **Lab Preparation**—This feature alerts instructors and lab assistants to items to check or set up before the lab begins.
- **Activity Background**—A brief discussion at the beginning of each lab provides important background information.
- **Estimated Completion Time**—To help students plan their work, each lab includes an estimate of the total amount of time required to complete it.
- **Activity**—Detailed, numbered steps walk students through the lab. These steps are divided into manageable sections, with explanatory material between each section.
- **Figures**—Where appropriate, photographs of hardware or screenshots of software are provided to increase student mastery of the lab topic.
- **Review Questions**—Questions at the end of each lab help students test their understanding of the lab material.
- **Web Site**—For updates to this book and information about other A+ and PC Repair products, go to *www.course.com/pcrepair*.

## ACKNOWLEDGMENTS

Jean would like to thank Nadine Schreiter of Lakeshore Technical College and Michael Lehrfeld of Brevard Community College, who served as technical editors of previous editions of the manual and still had an impact on this edition, and Walt Dundore of North Georgia Technical College, Scott Johns, and Jill West for their invaluable experience and help developing many of the labs.

Todd would like to give special thanks to Lisa Lord, whose encouragement and commitment to excellence guided him through the editorial process. He would also like to extend his sincere appreciation to Michelle Ruelos Cannistraci, Danielle Chouhan, and all the Thomson Course Technology staff for their instrumental roles in developing this lab manual. Most of all, he would like to thank Jean Andrews for her generosity in giving him this opportunity.

Many thanks to the peer reviewers: Gus Chang of Heald College, San Jose/Milpitas; Dennis Lewis of Colorado Technical University; Don Stroup of Ivy Tech Communication College, Fort Wayne; and Keith Conn of the Cleveland Institute of Electronics.

## CLASSROOM SETUP

Lab activities have been designed to explore many different hardware setup and troubleshooting problems while attempting to keep the requirements for specific hardware to a minimum. Most labs can be done alone, although a few ask you to work with a partner. If you prefer to work alone, simply do all the steps yourself. Other lab activities have been designed to progressively explore several operating systems so that you can install and use Windows XP Professional, Windows 2000 Professional, and Windows 9x.

Most labs take 30 to 45 minutes; a few might take a little longer. For several of the labs, your classroom should be networked and provide access to the Internet. When access to Windows setup files is required, these files can be provided on the Windows installation CD, a network drive made available to the PC, or some other type of removable storage media.

When the OS isn't of concern, the minimum hardware requirements are as follows:

- 90 MHz or better Pentium-compatible computer
- 24 MB of RAM
- 540 MB hard drive
- A PC toolkit with an antistatic ground bracelet (ESD strap)

These are the minimum hardware requirements for Windows XP Professional:

- 233 MHz or better Pentium-compatible computer (300 MHz preferred)
- 64 MB of RAM (128 MB preferred)
- 1.5 GB hard drive (2 GB preferred)
- An NTFS partition that can be the partition where Windows XP is installed
- A user account with administrative privileges

These are the minimum hardware requirements for Windows 2000 Professional:

- 133 MHz or better Pentium-compatible computer
- 64 MB of RAM
- 650 MB hard drive

◢ An NTFS partition that can be the partition where Windows 2000 is installed
◢ A user account with administrative privileges

Here are the requirements for Windows 9x:

◢ 90 MHz or better Pentium-compatible computer
◢ 24 MB of RAM
◢ 195 MB hard drive

A few labs focus on special hardware. For example, one lab requires installing a CD-ROM drive, sound card, and speakers, and another lab uses a PC camera, a sound card, microphone, and speakers. Two labs require a multimeter, one lab requires a modem and a working phone line, and one lab requires a wireless card and router.

## LAB SETUP INSTRUCTIONS

### CONFIGURATION TYPE AND OPERATING SYSTEMS

Each lab begins with a list of required materials. Before beginning a lab activity, verify that each student workgroup or individual has access to these materials. Then make sure the correct operating system is installed and in good health. Note that in some cases, installing an operating system isn't necessary. When needed, the Windows setup files can be made available on the Windows CD, a network drive, or some type of removable media storage. In some labs, device drivers are needed. Students can work more efficiently if these drivers are available before beginning the lab.

### PROTECT DATA

In several labs, data on the hard drive might get lost or corrupted. For this reason, it's important that valuable data stored on the hard drive is backed up to another medium.

### ACCESS TO THE INTERNET

Several labs require access to the Internet. If necessary, you can use one computer to search the Internet to download software or documentation and another computer for performing the lab procedures. If the lab doesn't have Internet access, you can download the required software or documentation before the lab and bring the files to lab on some sort of storage medium.

## THE TECHNICIAN'S WORK AREA

When opening a computer case, it's important to have the right tools and be properly grounded to ensure that you don't cause more damage than you repair. Take a look at the components of an ideal technician's work area:

◢ Grounding mat (with grounding wire properly grounded)
◢ Grounding wrist strap (attached to the grounding mat)
◢ Non-carpet flooring
◢ A clean work area (no clutter)
◢ A set of screwdrivers

- 1/4-inch Torx bit screwdriver
- 1/8-inch Torx bit screwdriver
- Needlenose pliers
- A PLCC (plastic leadless chip carrier)
- Pen light (flashlight)
- Several new antistatic bags (for transporting and storing hardware)

At minimum, you must have at least two key items. The first is a grounding strap. If a grounding mat isn't available, you can attach the grounding strap to the computer's chassis and, in most cases, provide sufficient grounding for handling hardware components inside the computer case. The second key item is, of course, a screwdriver. You won't be able to open most cases without some type of screwdriver.

## PROTECT YOURSELF, YOUR HARDWARE, AND YOUR SOFTWARE

When you work on a computer, harming both the computer and yourself is possible. The most common accident when attempting to fix a computer problem is erasing software or data. Experimenting without knowing what you're doing can cause damage. To prevent these sorts of accidents as well as physically dangerous ones, take a few safety precautions. The following sections describe potential sources of damage to computers and explain how to protect against them.

### POWER TO THE COMPUTER

To protect yourself and the equipment when working inside a computer, turn off the power, unplug the computer, and always use an antistatic grounding strap. Consider the monitor and the power supply to be "black boxes." Never remove the cover or put your hands inside this equipment unless you know the hazards of charged capacitors. Both the power supply and the monitor can hold a dangerous level of electricity even after they're turned off and disconnected from a power source.

## STATIC ELECTRICITY OR ESD

Electrostatic discharge (ESD), commonly known as static electricity, is an electrical charge at rest. A static charge can build up on the surface of a nongrounded conductor and on non-conductive surfaces, such as clothing or plastic. When two objects with dissimilar electrical charges touch, static electricity passes between them until the dissimilar charges are made equal. To see how this works, turn off the lights in a room, scuff your feet on the carpet, and touch another person. Occasionally you see and feel the charge in your fingers. If you can feel the charge, you discharged at least 3000 volts of static electricity. If you hear the discharge, you released at least 6000 volts. If you see the discharge, you released at least 8000 volts of ESD. A charge of less than 3000 volts can damage most electronic components. You can touch a chip on an expansion card or system board and damage the chip with ESD and never feel, hear, or see the discharge.

ESD can cause two types of damage in an electronic component: catastrophic failures and upset failures. A catastrophic failure destroys the component beyond use. An upset failure damages the component so that it doesn't perform well, even though it might still function to some degree. Upset failures are the most difficult to detect because they aren't easily observed.

## PROTECT AGAINST ESD

To protect the computer against ESD, always ground yourself before touching electronic components, including the hard drive, system board, expansion cards, processors, and memory modules. Ground yourself and the computer parts, using one or more of the following static control devices or methods:

- *Grounding strap or antistatic strap:* A grounding strap is a bracelet you wear around your wrist. The other end is attached to a grounded conductor, such as the computer case or a ground mat, or it can plug into a wall outlet. (Only the ground prong makes a connection!)
- *Grounding mats:* Grounding mats can come equipped with a cord to plug into a wall outlet to provide a grounded surface on which to work. Remember, if you lift the component off the mat, it's no longer grounded and is susceptible to ESD.
- *Static shielding bags:* New components come shipped in static shielding bags. Save the bags to store other devices that aren't currently installed in a PC.

The best way to protect against ESD is to use a grounding strap with a grounding mat. You should consider a grounding strap essential equipment when working on a computer. However, if you're in a situation where you must work without one, touch the computer case before you touch a component. When passing a chip to another person, ground yourself. Leave components inside their protective bags until you're ready to use them. Work on hard floors, not carpet, or use antistatic spray on carpets.

There's an exception to the ground-yourself rule. Inside a monitor case, the electricity stored in capacitors poses a substantial danger. When working inside a monitor, you *don't* want to be grounded, as you would provide a conduit for the voltage to discharge through your body. In this situation, be careful *not* to ground yourself.

When handling system boards and expansion cards, don't touch the chips on the boards. Don't stack boards on top of each other, which could accidentally dislodge a chip. Hold cards by the edges, but don't touch the edge connections on the card.

After you unpack a new device or software that has been wrapped in cellophane, remove the cellophane from the work area quickly. Don't allow anyone who's not properly grounded to touch components. Don't store expansion cards within one foot of a monitor because the monitor can discharge as much as 29,000 volts of ESD onto the screen.

Hold an expansion card by the edges. Don't touch any of the soldered components on a card. If you need to put an electronic device down, place it on a grounding mat or a static shielding bag. Keep components away from your hair and clothing.

## PROTECT HARD DRIVES AND DISKS

Always turn off a computer before moving it to protect the hard drive, which is always spinning when the computer is turned on (unless the drive has a sleep mode). Never jar a computer while the hard disk is running. Avoid placing a PC on the floor, where users could accidentally kick it.

Follow the usual precautions to protect CDs and floppy disks. Protect the bottom of CDs from scratches and keep them away from heat and direct sunlight. Keep floppies away from magnetic fields, heat, and extreme cold. Don't open the floppy shuttle window or touch the surface of the disk inside the housing. Treat disks with care, and they'll usually last for years.

# Introducing Hardware

**Labs included in this chapter:**

- **Lab 1.1:** Gather and Record System Information
- **Lab 1.2:** Identify Computer Parts
- **Lab 1.3:** Use Shareware to Examine a Computer, Part 1
- **Lab 1.4:** Use Shareware to Examine a Computer, Part 2
- **Lab 1.5:** Compare Costs
- **Lab 1.6:** Plan an Ideal System

# LAB 1.1 GATHER AND RECORD SYSTEM INFORMATION

## OBJECTIVES

The goal of this lab is to use a system's physical characteristics and other sources to determine how the system is configured. After completing this lab, you will be able to:

◢ Gather system information by observing a system

◢ Use available tools to access specific system information

## MATERIALS REQUIRED

This lab requires the following:

◢ Windows 2000/XP or Windows 98 operating system

◢ Individuals or a workgroup of 2 to 4 students

## LAB PREPARATION

Before the lab begins, the instructor or lab assistant needs to do the following:

◢ Verify that Windows starts with no errors.

## ACTIVITY BACKGROUND

When working with a computer system, it's a good idea to know what components are installed on the system. This lab helps you identify some of these components as you gather information by observing the system and by using system tools.

### ESTIMATED COMPLETION TIME: 15 minutes

### Activity

Observe the physical characteristics of your system and answer the following questions:

1. Does the system have any identification on it indicating manufacturer, model, or component information? If so, list this information:

   _hardware - Dell_

   _Window XP. Vison 2002. service pack 2_

2. How many CD or DVD drives does your system have?

   _ONe_

3. Describe the shape of the connection your mouse uses. How many pins does the connection have?

   _PS/2 Mouse port     6 pins_

4. How many floppy drives does your system have?

   _ONe "A" drive_

5. How many internal hard drives does your system have? Explain how you got your answer:

   _one          one hard DRive   ST160011A_

   _divide 2 logical drive C:_

   _D:_

Like other versions of Windows, users can customize Windows XP to behave and to display information to suit their tastes. Windows XP can also mimic the way previous versions of Windows presented menus and settings for users who are more comfortable with those methods. If the OS you're using in this lab is Windows XP, to help ensure that the step-by-step instructions are easy for you to follow, complete these steps to restore Windows XP defaults to your system:

1. Boot your system and log on, if necessary, and then click **Start, Control Panel** to open the Control Panel window.

2. Under the Control Panel heading at the left, click **Switch to Category View** if Classic view has been enabled. Figure 1-1 shows Control Panel in Category view.

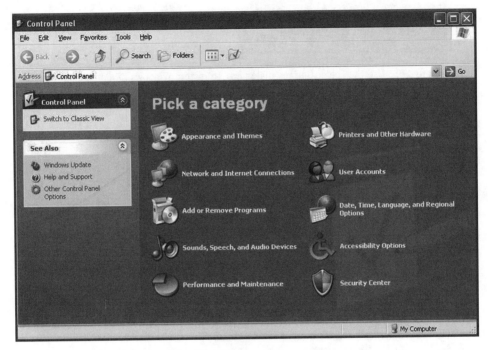

**Figure 1-1**   Windows XP Control Panel in Category view

3. With Category view enabled, click the **Appearance and Themes** category. The Appearance and Themes window opens.

4. In the Appearance and Themes window, click **Folder Options** in the Control Panel icons list to open the Folder Options dialog box.

5. In the General tab of the Folder Options dialog box, click the **Restore Defaults** button (see Figure 1-2), and then click **Apply**.

6. Click the **View** tab in the Folder Options dialog box (see Figure 1-3). Click the **Restore Defaults** button, and then click **OK** to apply the settings and close the dialog box.

7. In the Appearance and Themes window, click the **Taskbar and Start Menu** icon. The Taskbar and Start Menu dialog box opens.

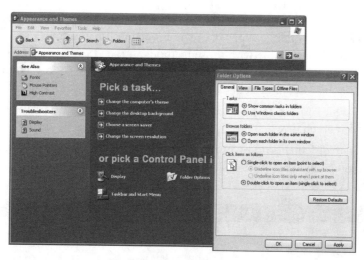

**Figure 1-2** Use the Folder Options dialog box to restore Windows XP defaults to a folder

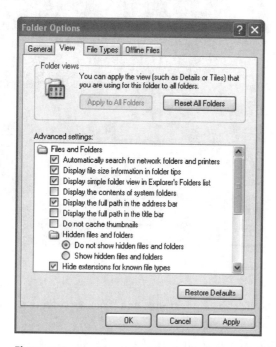

**Figure 1-3** The View tab of the Folder Options dialog box

8. In the Taskbar tab, verify that all check boxes in the Taskbar appearance section are selected except for Auto-hide the taskbar and Show Quick Launch, as shown in Figure 1-4. Click **Apply** if any changes were made.

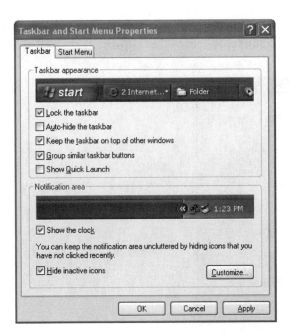

**Figure 1-4**   Use the Taskbar and Start Menu Properties dialog box to control
how the taskbar appears and functions

9. Click the **Start Menu** tab in the Taskbar and Start Menu dialog box. Verify that the Start menu option button is selected, as shown in Figure 1-5. Click **OK** to apply the settings and close the dialog box. Close the Appearance and Themes window.

**Figure 1-5**   The Start Menu tab of the Taskbar and Start Menu Properties dialog box

Regardless of the Windows OS you're using, from the Start menu, open Control Panel and click the **Performance and Maintenance** category. The Performance and Maintenance window opens.

In the Performance and Maintenance window, click the **System** icon to open the System Properties dialog box. With the General tab visible as shown in Figure 1-6, record the following:

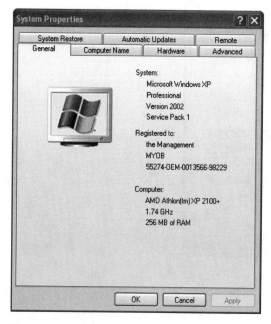

**Figure 1-6** The System Properties dialog box

1. Which OS is installed?

   *Window XP*

2. What is the version number of your operating system?

   *2002 Service pack 2*

3. Who is the system registered to?

   ~~Window~~ *NYCCT*

4. According to the System Properties dialog box, what type of CPU is your system built around?

   *Pentium 4 1.8GHz*

5. How much RAM is installed in your system?

   *128MB*

Close the System Properties dialog box and the Performance and Maintenance window.

Click **Start, My Computer** and locate the following information in the My Computer window:

1. How many floppy disk drives are listed, and which drive letters are assigned to them?

   *One    A*

2. How many other local drives are listed, and which drive letters are assigned to them?

   *2    C:  D:*

3. How many network drives are listed, and what are their names?

   *No network drive*
   ~~Network adapter~~

4. What items are listed under System Tasks at the left of the My Computer window?

*View system information*

*add or remove programs*

*change a setting*

## REVIEW QUESTIONS

1. List two other ways to get to the System Properties dialog box besides using Control Panel:

*hit F2*

① ~~My Computer~~ open — View System information at Left — System Property

② Right click computer — property — ~~system hardware~~ — device manager
*system program*

2. What's one other place, not in Windows or any documentation, where you could determine the CPU, CPU speed, and amount of RAM installed on your system?

*Hit F2 — memory — 128 MB*

*system speed*

3. What differences, if any, are there between a list of components derived from a physical inspection versus a list of components derived from My Computer and System Properties?

*physical — one hard drive*

*— 2 logical hard drive*

## LAB 1.2 IDENTIFY COMPUTER PARTS

### OBJECTIVES

The goal of this lab is to examine your computer to identify the parts inside and outside the case. After completing this lab, you will be able to:

◢ Identify computer components outside the case
◢ Identify computer components inside the case

### MATERIALS REQUIRED

This lab requires the following:

◢ A working computer
◢ A Phillips head screwdriver
◢ An antistatic ground strap
◢ Workgroup of 2 to 4 students
◢ A display of four or more computer parts to be identified by students

### LAB PREPARATION

Before the lab begins, the instructor or lab assistant needs to do the following:

◢ Provide a computer that can have the cover removed for each student workgroup.
◢ Gather up four or more computer parts for display in each student workgroup or area of the lab.

## ACTIVITY BACKGROUND

When working with a computer system, you must be able to identify the hardware components, both inside and outside the case. Components are not always labeled adequately, especially those inside the case. This lab helps you learn to recognize these components.

**ESTIMATED COMPLETION TIME: 30 minutes**

**Activity**

Observe the physical characteristics of your system and answer the following questions:

1. Is the monitor a CRT or an LCD monitor? What size monitor do you have? Measure from the upper-left corner to the lower-right corner (the diagonal) on the monitor screen. Is the measurement what you expected for the size of the monitor?

_____

2. If you're using a CRT, also measure the diagonal on an LCD monitor if possible. If you're using an LCD monitor, also measure the diagonal on a CRT. What size is the second monitor?

_____

3. How many keys are on your keyboard?

_____

4. Are there any switches on the sides or bottom of the keyboard? If so, how are these switches labeled?

_____

5. What other external components does your PC have (speakers, printer, and so forth)? Describe each component with as much detail as you can:

_____

_____

_____

6. Look at the back of your PC and list all cables and cords connected to ports and other connections. Fill in the following chart:

| Describe the port or connector the cable or cord is connected to | Purpose of the cable or cord |
|---|---|
| 1. | |
| 2. | |
| 3. | |
| 4. | |
| 5. | |
| 6. | |

7. What other ports on the PC are not being used? List them:

_____

_____

_____

_____

Next, you'll open the PC case and examine the components inside. As you work, make sure you do *not* touch anything inside the case unless you're wearing an antistatic ground strap that's clipped to the case so that any electrical charge between you and the case is dissipated.

To remove the cover from a desktop PC, follow these steps:

1. Power down the PC and unplug it. Next, unplug the monitor, printer, and any other device that has its own external power supply. Do not disconnect any cables or cords (other than the power supply cord) connected to the back of the PC case.

2. Case manufacturers use slightly different methods to open the case. Many newer cases require that you remove the faceplate on the front of the case first. Other cases require removing a side panel first, and very old cases require removing the entire sides and top as a single unit first. Study your case for the correct approach.

3. If you find screws on the rear of the case along the edges, such as those in Figure 1-7, start by removing these screws. For a desktop or tower case, locate and remove the screws on the back of the case. For a desktop case, such as the one in Figure 1-7, look for screws in each corner and one in the top. Be careful not to unscrew any screws besides these. The other screws are probably holding the power supply in place (see Figure 1-8).

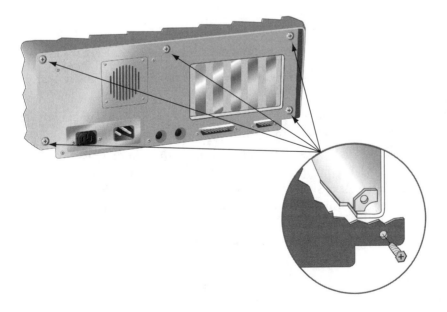

**Figure 1-7**  Locate the screws that hold the cover in place

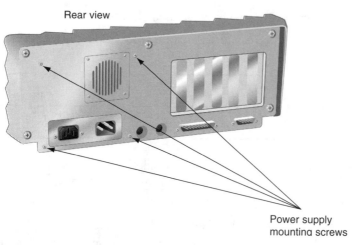

**Figure 1-8**　Power supply mounting screws

**4.** After you remove the cover screws, slide the cover forward and up to remove it from the case, as shown in Figure 1-9.

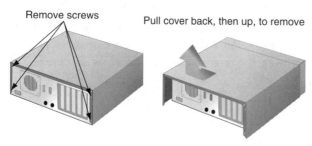

**Figure 1-9**　Removing the cover

To remove the cover from an older tower PC with case screws on the rear of the case, follow these steps:

**1.** Power down the PC and unplug it from its power outlet. Next, unplug the monitor and any other device with an external power source from the power outlet.

**2.** Some cases are a solid piece of metal and come apart in one piece; others come in pieces and the sides or top can be removed separately. Look for screws in all four corners and down the sides. For one-piece covers, remove the screws and then slide the cover back slightly before lifting it up to remove it, as shown in Figure 1-10.

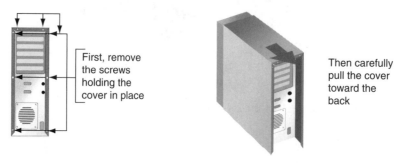

**Figure 1-10**　Removing a tower cover

For cases with panels on either side of the case held in place with screws on the back of the case, remove the screws and slide each panel toward the rear and then lift it off the case (see Figure 1-11).

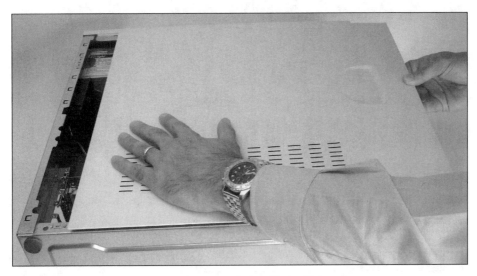

**Figure 1-11**   Slide a side panel to the rear and then lift it off the case

To remove the cover from a newer tower PC with no visible case screws, follow these steps:

1. Power down the PC and unplug it from its power outlet. Next, unplug the monitor and any other device with an external power source from the power outlet.

2. On newer cases, you must pop the front panel off the case before removing the side panels. Look for a lever on the bottom of the panel and hinges at the top. Squeeze the lever to release the front panel and lift it off the case (see Figure 1-12). Then remove any screws holding the side panel in place, as shown in Figure 1-13, and slide the side panel to the front and then off the case.

**Figure 1-12**   Newer cases require removing the front panel before removing the side panels of a computer case

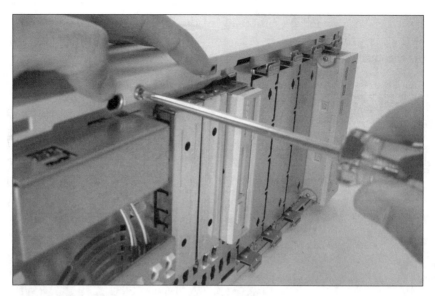

**Figure 1-13**   One screw holds the side panel in place

Some case panels don't use screws; these side panels simply pop up and out with a little prying and pulling.

With the cover removed, you're ready to look for some components. As you complete the following, refer to drawings and photos in Chapters 3, 4, and 5 of *A+ Guide to Hardware* or Chapters 4, 5, and 6 of *A+ Guide to Managing and Maintaining Your PC*, if necessary.

1. Put on your antistatic ground strap and connect the clip to the side of the computer case.

2. Identify and describe the following major components. List any other components you find inside the case. Fill in the following chart:

| Component | Description (include size, location, what it connects to, and what's connected to it in the system) |
|---|---|
| Power supply | |
| Floppy disk drive | |
| Hard drive | |
| CD-ROM drive | |
| Motherboard | |
| CPU | |
| Cooling fan (not inside the power supply) | |
| Video card | |
| Network card | |
| Sound card | |
| | |
| | |
| | |

## CHALLENGE ACTIVITY

If your instructor has prepared a display of four or more assorted computer parts, fill in the following chart:

| Identify the part | Describe how you determined your answer |
| --- | --- |
| 1. | |
| 2. | |
| 3. | |
| 4. | |
| 5. | |
| 6. | |

## REVIEW QUESTIONS

1. Describe how you decided which expansion card was the video card:

2. If your system has a CD-ROM drive, describe how you determined which drive was the CD-ROM drive:

3. Describe how you identified the type of CPU you have:

4. How did you know that you were or were not connected to a network?

5. Does your system have much room for adding new components? What type of component might be added?

6. If you were adding or upgrading a component, what would it be and where would you install it in the computer case?

# LAB 1.3 USE SHAREWARE TO EXAMINE A COMPUTER, PART 1

## OBJECTIVES

The goal of this lab is to use Sandra, Standard version, to examine your system. After completing this lab, you will be able to:

▲ Download a file from the Internet

▲ Install Sandra

▲ Use Sandra to examine your system

## MATERIALS REQUIRED

This lab requires the following:

⊿ Windows 2000/XP or Windows 98 operating system

⊿ Internet access

⊿ If using Windows 98 or Windows 2000, software such as WinZip to uncompress a zipped file

## LAB PREPARATION

Before the lab begins, the instructor or lab assistant needs to do the following:

⊿ Verify that Internet access is available.

⊿ For labs that don't have Internet access, download these files to a file server, flash drive, CD-R, or other media available to students in the lab:

 • Sandra executable file downloaded from *www.sisoftware.co.uk*

 • For Windows 98 or Windows 2000 systems, an uncompress utility, such as WinZip, downloaded from *www.winzip.com*

## ACTIVITY BACKGROUND

Good PC support people are always good investigators. This lab is designed to help you learn how to conduct an investigation using the Internet. As you'll see, the Internet offers a wealth of resources to those who take the time to search, download, and investigate the possible uses of software available there. This lab helps you learn to be such an investigator. Follow these directions to find and download a shareware utility that you can use to diagnose PC problems. If you have a classroom printer available, you'll print a report from the downloaded software about the hardware and software on your computer.

**ESTIMATED COMPLETION TIME: 30 minutes**

 Activity

 Notes

If the SiSoftware Web site is unavailable, you can use a search engine to locate the shareware.

1. Open your browser and go to **www.sisoftware.co.uk**.

2. Click the **Downloads** link.

3. Follow one of the links pointing to a location for the Sandra download.

4. Follow the instructions on the site you selected to begin the download process.

5. When the File Download dialog box opens, save the file to your PC desktop. You can then disconnect from the Internet. What is the name of the downloaded file?

Next, follow these steps to install Sandra on your PC:

1. If the file has a .zip file extension, double-click it to uncompress the Sandra zip file and extract the setup file.

2. Run the setup program by double-clicking the executable file, which has an .exe file extension. (It might be the downloaded file or the extracted file.) In the installation

wizard, use English as the language selection, accept the end user license agreement (EULA), and accept the default settings throughout. The Sandra installation creates a new item in your Programs or All Programs menu and adds an icon to your desktop.

3. When you finish the installation, Sandra will start. Read the Tip of the Day, click to clear the **Show Tips on Start-up** check box, and then click **OK** to close. If you're using Windows XP, you should see a screen similar to the one in Figure 1-14.

**Figure 1-14**   SiSoftware Sandra main window in Windows XP

The screens for Windows 98 and Windows 2000 look similar, but, as shown in Figure 1-15, the icons aren't grouped under headings.

**Figure 1-15**   SiSoftware Sandra main window in Windows 2000 or Windows 98

You can run each utility by double-clicking its icon, or you can create a composite report of the results of each selection. To learn more, complete the following:

1. Double-click the **System Summary** icon (in the Information Modules group for Windows XP). The System Summary utility starts and gathers information about your system before displaying it in a format similar to Device Manager, with devices listed by type.

2. Click the red X at the bottom of the System Summary window or press **Esc** to close the System Summary utility.

3. Double-click the **Windows Information** icon (in the Information Modules group for Windows XP) to start that utility. Scroll down and note the information types that are listed. According to this utility, which version of Windows are you using?

_____

4. What is the path to the Temporary folder on your system?

_____

5. What is your Windows installation product key?

_____

6. Click the red X at the bottom of the Windows Information window or press **Esc** to close the Windows Information utility.

7. Double-click the **Drives Information** icon (in the Information Modules group for Windows XP). The utility begins to gather information about your drives. Do not move the mouse or touch the keyboard while this procedure is in progress. How much total space does the hard drive contain? How much free space does the hard drive contain? What type of file system does the hard drive use?

_____

_____

8. Click the red X at the bottom of the Drives Information window or press **Esc** to close the Drives Information utility.

9. Double-click the **DMA Settings** icon to start that utility. Why are you unable to view the DMA Settings information?

_____

10. Close the DMA Settings utility.

You can also use Sandra to create a composite report of your system. To learn more, follow these steps:

1. From the SiSoftware Sandra menu, click **File, Create a Report Wizard**.

2. In the wizard introduction window, click **Next** (right-pointing arrow in a green circle).

3. In the Step 1 of 9 window, verify that **Make choices and generate report** is selected in the drop-down list, and click **Next** to continue.

4. In the Step 2 of 9 window, click the **Clear All** (red X over a box) button. Click to select the **Mainboard Information** and **Windows Memory Information** check boxes, and then click **Next** to continue.

5. In the Step 3 of 9 window, click the **Clear All** button, and then click **Next** to continue.

6. In the Step 4 of 9 window, click the **Clear All** button, and then click **Next** to continue.

7. In the Step 5 of 9 window, click **Next** to continue.

8. In the Step 6 of 9 window, add any comments, if you like, and then click **Next** to continue.

9. In the Step 7 of 9 window, click the **Print or Fax** option in the drop-down list, and then click **Next** to continue.

10. In the Print dialog box, click **OK** for Windows 98 or **Print** for Windows 2000 and Windows XP. Click the **Exit** button (red X) to close the wizard, and then collect your report from the printer.

11. Continue to explore each utility in Sandra, and then close it. You'll use Sandra again in later chapters, so don't uninstall it.

In this lab, you downloaded Sandra from the SiSoftware Web site, but many popular utilities are available from multiple sources on the Internet. To see for yourself, follow these steps:

1. Attempt to find Sandra at *www.zdnet.com*.

2. Is the program available through this avenue as well? Print the Web page or pages to support your answer.

---

## REVIEW QUESTIONS

1. What URL can you use to find a link to download Sandra?

2. Is Sandra capable of hardware diagnostics only?

3. Which two of the four system resources are you *not* able to view with the version of Sandra you downloaded, and why?

4. Some software is called diagnostic software and other software is called application software. Which type of software is Sandra?

---

# LAB 1.4 USE SHAREWARE TO EXAMINE A COMPUTER, PART 2

## OBJECTIVES

The goal of this lab is to use Belarc Advisor to examine your system. After completing this lab, you will be able to:

◢ Download a file from the Internet

◢ Install Belarc Advisor

◢ Use Belarc Advisor to examine your system

## MATERIALS REQUIRED

This lab requires the following:

◢ Windows 2000/XP or Windows 98 operating system

◢ Internet access

## LAB PREPARATION

Before the lab begins, the instructor or lab assistant needs to do the following:

◢ Verify that Internet access is available.

◢ For labs that don't have Internet access, download Belarc Advisor (Advisor.exe) from *www.belarc.com* and make the file available to students in the lab.

## ACTIVITY BACKGROUND

Good PC support people know that there's always more than one way to do something. In Lab 1.3, you learned to use Sandra to investigate your system. In this lab, you use another shareware utility, Belarc Advisor, to examine your system. Follow these directions to find and download this utility that you can use to diagnose PC problems. Then you print a report from the downloaded software about the hardware and software on your computer.

If your lab doesn't have Internet access, ask your instructor for the location of files downloaded previously for you to use. Write the path to those files here:

---

**ESTIMATED COMPLETION TIME: 30 minutes**

 Activity

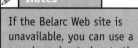
**Notes**

If the Belarc Web site is unavailable, you can use a search engine to locate the shareware.

1. Open your browser and go to **www.belarc.com**.

2. Click the **FREE DOWNLOAD** link.

3. Follow one of the links pointing to a location that offers Belarc Advisor for download.

4. Follow the instructions on the site you selected to begin the download process.

5. When the File Download dialog box opens, save the file to your PC desktop. You can then disconnect from the Internet. At the time I tested this lab, the downloaded file name was Advisor.exe, but sometimes Web sites and file names change. What is the name of your downloaded file?

---

Next, follow these steps to install Belarc Advisor on your PC:

1. Run the setup program by double-clicking the downloaded executable file, **Advisor.exe** (or the name of your downloaded file). In the installation wizard, click **Install,** and accept the EULA. The Belarc Advisor installation automatically takes a snapshot of your computer, and then creates an item in your Start menu and adds an icon to your desktop.

2. When you finish the installation, Belarc Advisor uses your default Web browser to show the results of the snapshot. If you're using Windows XP, you should see a screen similar to the one in Figure 1-16.

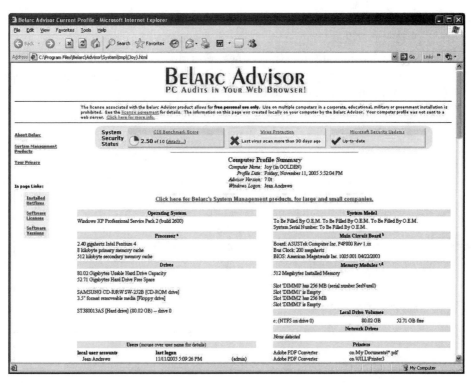

**Figure 1-16** Belarc Advisor uses your browser to display information about your system

Answer the following questions to learn what Belarc Advisor is telling you about your system:

1. What is the name of the manufacturer and model of the motherboard installed on your system?

   _____

2. What is the version of Windows you're using?

   _____

3. What is the product key for Windows?

   _____

4. What is the speed and model of the processor for the system?

   _____

5. Are there any security updates that need to be applied?

   _____

6. How much total space does the hard drive contain? How much free space does the hard drive contain? What type of file system does the hard drive use?

   _____

   _____

7. To print the Belarc results, from your browser's menu, click **File, Print**.

8. In the Print dialog box, click **OK** for Windows 98 or **Print** for Windows 2000 and Windows XP.

9. Take a few minutes to explore the report that Belarc Advisor generated. List three other items of information not mentioned already in this lab that you think might be useful when troubleshooting a computer:

_____

_____

_____

You'll use Belarc Advisor again in later chapters, so don't uninstall it.

In this lab, you downloaded Belarc Advisor from the Belarc Web site, but many popular utilities are available from multiple sources on the Internet. To see for yourself, follow these steps:

1. Attempt to find Belarc Advisor at *www.zdnet.com*.

2. Is the program available through this avenue as well? Print the Web page or pages to support your answer.

_____

## REVIEW QUESTIONS

1. What URL can you use to find a link to download Belarc Advisor?

_____

2. What tool do you use to get a printed report from Belarc Advisor?

_____

3. What type of software is Belarc Advisor?

_____

4. Compare Belarc Advisor to Sandra that you downloaded and used in Lab 1.3. Which utility do you think is the most useful, and why? Which is easier to use?

_____

_____

# *LAB 1.5 COMPARE COSTS*

## OBJECTIVES

The objective of this lab is to compare a preassembled system with the components that could be assembled to build a comparable system. After completing this lab, you will be able to:

◢ Identify the key components of a preassembled system

◢ Locate prices for components needed to assemble a comparable system

◢ Compare the cost of a preassembled system and a self-assembled system

## MATERIALS REQUIRED

This lab requires the following:

◢ Internet access and/or access to a computer publication, such as *Computer Shopper*

## LAB PREPARATION

Before the lab begins, the instructor or lab assistant needs to do the following:

◢ Verify that Internet access is available.

## ACTIVITY BACKGROUND

In this lab, you compare the cost of a brand-name system with the cost of a system having similar specifications but assembled from separate components. Brand-name manufacturers typically build their systems from parts only they market, called "proprietary" parts. Therefore, it's unlikely that you'll be able to find exact matches for brand-name components. However, you can find comparable components. For example, if a Gateway computer has a 40 GB hard drive installed, find another 40 GB hard drive for your list of parts. The idea is to find a close match for each major component so that you can compare the total cost of a brand-name system and a similar system built from parts. Use the Internet and available computer-related publications as your sources for information.

**ESTIMATED COMPLETION TIME: 45 minutes**

 **Activity**

1. Find an advertisement for a complete, preassembled system similar to the one in Figure 1-17. Some manufacturers you might want to check out are Gateway (*www.gateway.com*), Dell (*www.dell.com*), and IBM (*www.ibm.com*).

**Figure 1-17** Complete, preassembled system

2. Study the advertisement and list the following specifications:

◢ Processor/MHz _____

◢ RAM: _____

◢ OS: _____

◢ HDD capacity: _____

◢ Monitor: _____

◢ Video card: _____

◢ Sound/speakers: _____

◢ Other drives: _____

◢ Bonus items: _____

◢ Bundled software: _____

◢ Total price: _____

3. Find advertisements similar to those in Figure 1-18. Notice that the items are grouped by component type.

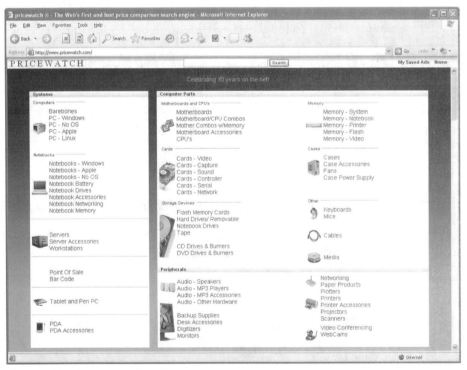

**Figure 1-18**   Components for sale

Using the following chart, list and describe the comparable components, their prices, and the source of your information. You might want to check several sources to find the best price. Remember, most mail-order or online purchases have shipping costs. If you can determine an exact shipping price for each component, include this information as part of the component's price. If you can't find the exact shipping price, include a 10% fee as part of the price for each shipped component. You might have to include tax, depending on the state-to-state taxing laws that apply. Sometimes the shipping cost is offset by not having to pay state sales tax on an item. Also, because you're early in the course, you might not know enough details about matching components inside the computer case, such as matching a processor to a motherboard. How to find correct matches is covered later in the book, but for now, a close match is all that's necessary.

| Component | Description | Source | Price |
|---|---|---|---|
| Processor/MHz | | | |
| Motherboard | | | |
| RAM | | | |
| Case and power supply | | | |
| OS | | | |
| HDD capacity | | | |
| Monitor | | | |
| Sound/speakers | | | |
| CD-ROM drive | | | |
| Other drives | | | |
| Bonus items (such as video card) | | | |
| Bundled software | | | |
| TOTAL SYSTEM PRICE | | | |

## REVIEW QUESTIONS

1. Which approach to acquiring a system seems to be less expensive?

   _____

2. What is the single most expensive component of a system built from separate components?

   _____

3. What was the estimated cost of shipping (if any) for the component-built system?

   _____

   _____

4. What are some potential pitfalls of building your own PC? Rewards?

   _____

   _____

> **Notes**
>
> As you continue with this course, you'll be better able to answer this last question based on your own experiences.

# LAB 1.6 PLAN AN IDEAL SYSTEM

## OBJECTIVES

The objective of this lab is to plan and price your own ideal system within a budget. After completing this lab, you will be able to:

▲ Describe what you want your system to be able to do

▲ Pick components that best meet your goal

▲ Stay within a budget

## MATERIALS REQUIRED

This lab requires the following:

▲ Internet access and/or access to a computer publication, such as *Computer Shopper*

## LAB PREPARATION

Before the lab begins, the instructor or lab assistant needs to do the following:

▲ Provide Internet access in the lab or announce that students need to bring computer publications, such as *Computer Shopper*, to the lab.

## ACTIVITY BACKGROUND

In the future, you might be in a position to build a system to your specifications from separate components. Within a budget of $800, what system would you put together? In this lab, you determine the answer based on your current knowledge and experience. Expect that your opinions will likely change as you continue in this course.

**ESTIMATED COMPLETION TIME: 30 minutes**

 **Activity**

1. On a separate piece of paper, make a chart similar to the one used in Lab 1.5. Use it to list the components you would like to include in your system, the cost of each component, and the source for each component. To begin, list everything you want without considering price.

2. After you have determined the total price of all the components you want to include in your ideal system, add up the prices and see whether you are within your $800 budget.

3. If you are under budget, consider including additional components or better versions of components. If you're over budget, determine what components you need to exclude or whether you need to use less expensive versions of some components. Either way, record what components you choose. Also, note how you altered your ideal system to meet your budget.

## REVIEW QUESTIONS

1. What is the goal of your system? In other words, how do you plan to use your system? Explain your choices for components.

_____

_____

_____

2. How would you change your choices if you were to use this computer in a corporate office as a business workstation?

_____

_____

_____

3. What single change would you make if you had an extra $200 in the budget?

_____

_____

4. How might you change your design if your budget was only $600?

_____

_____

 **Tip**

Keep your responses to this lab for later reference. As you learn more about PCs in this course, you can look back at these responses and see where you might change your mind based on new information you have learned.

# Introducing Operating Systems

**Labs included in this chapter:**

- **Lab 2.1:** Examine Files and Directories
- **Lab 2.2:** Convert Numbers
- **Lab 2.3:** Explore the Macintosh World
- **Lab 2.4:** Investigate Linux
- **Lab 2.5:** Compare Operating Systems
- **Lab 2.6:** Use Windows Keyboard Shortcuts

# LAB 2.1 EXAMINE FILES AND DIRECTORIES

## OBJECTIVES

The goal of this lab is to use different methods to examine files and directories. After completing this lab, you will be able to:

▲ Use the command line to view information about files and directories

▲ Use My Computer to view information about files and directories

▲ Display information about files and directories in other ways

## MATERIALS REQUIRED

This lab requires the following:

▲ Windows 2000/XP or Windows 9x operating system

## LAB PREPARATION

Before the lab begins, the instructor or lab assistant needs to do the following:

▲ Verify that Windows starts with no errors.

## ACTIVITY BACKGROUND

You can access information about a PC's file structure in several ways. From the command line, you can use the DIR command to list files and directories. In Windows, you can use Windows Explorer or My Computer to view the same information. In the following lab, you practice using the DIR command and My Computer.

**ESTIMATED COMPLETION TIME: 30 minutes**

 **Activity**

Follow these steps to access file information via the command line:

1. To open a command prompt window in Windows 2000/XP, click **Start, Run**. Type **cmd** and press **Enter**. In Windows 9x, click **Start, Run**. Type **command** and press **Enter**. The MS-DOS command prompt window opens.

2. When the command prompt window opens, type **dir /?** and press **Enter**. Information and parameters (also called "switches" or "options") for the DIR command are displayed. How many different parameters does the command have?

   _14 different /A /B /C /D /L /P /N /O_

3. In a command prompt window, the prompt indicates the current directory. Type **dir** and press **Enter**. A detailed list of files and directories in the current directory is displayed. If there are many files and directories, only the last several are visible on the screen.

4. Try these variations of the DIR command and explain how the information is displayed:

   **dir/p**

   **dir/w** — _Wide_

5. Examine the results of the DIR command. The results vary with different versions of Windows, but each listing should include the following information:

  ◢ The date and time the file was created

  ◢ The directory markers (directories do not include an extension; instead, they are indicated by a <DIR> marker tag)

  ◢ The file size in bytes

  ◢ The name of a file or directory (most files have an extension)

  ◢ A summary, including the number of files and directories in that directory, the number of bytes those files use, and the number of bytes of free space on the drive

To print this file information, you can copy the contents of the command prompt window to Windows Clipboard, open the Notepad program, paste the file information into Notepad, and then use Notepad's Print command. To try that technique now, follow these steps:

1. On the far left of the command prompt window's title bar, click the **Command Prompt** icon (for Windows 2000/XP) or the **MS-DOS Prompt** icon (for Windows 9x). A drop-down list appears.

2. On the drop-down list, point to **Edit**, and then click **Mark**. A blinking cursor then appears at the top of the command prompt window.

3. Click and drag the cursor over the information you would like to copy to the Clipboard; the information should then be highlighted. You might need to scroll the window to capture all the necessary information.

4. After you have highlighted all the information you want to copy, click the **Command Prompt** icon (for Windows 2000/XP) or the **MS-DOS Prompt** icon (for Windows 9x) on the title bar.

5. On the drop-down list, point to **Edit**, and then click **Copy**. The highlighted contents are copied to the Clipboard.

6. To open Notepad, click **Start**, point to **All Programs** (**Programs** in Windows 2000 and 9x), point to **Accessories**, and click **Notepad**.

7. Click **Edit**, **Paste** from the Notepad menu.

8. Click **File**, **Print** from the Notepad menu. Use the print options to print your document.

9. Close the command prompt window and Notepad without saving the file.

In addition to the command prompt window, you can use My Computer to examine files and directories. My Computer can display information in a variety of ways. Before you view files and directories with this tool, you need to change some settings to control how information is displayed.

To change settings in Windows 2000/XP, follow these steps:

1. To open the My Computer window in Windows 2000, double-click the **My Computer** desktop icon. In Windows XP, click **Start**, **My Computer**.

2. Click **Tools**, **Folder Options** from the menu. The Folder Options dialog box opens.

3. In the Folder Options dialog box, click the **View** tab (if necessary), click to select the **Show hidden files and folders** check box, and click to clear the **Hide file extensions for known file types** check box.

4. Click **Apply**, and then click **OK** to close the Folder Options dialog box.

In Windows 9x, follow these steps:

1. On the Windows 9x desktop, double-click the **My Computer** icon. The My Computer window opens.

2. Click **View, Folder Options** from the My Computer menu. The Folder Options dialog box opens.

3. Click the **General** tab (if necessary), click the **Custom, based on settings you choose** option button, and then click the **Settings** button.

4. In the Browse Folders as Follows section, click the **Open each folder in its own window** option button, and then click **OK**. The Custom Settings dialog box closes.

5. Click **Apply**, and then click **OK** to close the Folder Options dialog box.

Now that you have changed the way information is displayed, you're ready to use My Computer to access specific information about your system's files and directories. Complete the following in both Windows 2000/XP and Windows 9x:

1. Maximize the My Computer window, click the icon representing drive C, and you'll see details about the drive displayed in the left pane.

2. How much free space is available on drive C? What is the total size of the drive? _3.52 GB_ _4.87 GB_

3. Based on total size and free space, how much space is used on drive C? _1.55 GB_

4. Double-click the drive C icon. What information about each folder is displayed in this window: 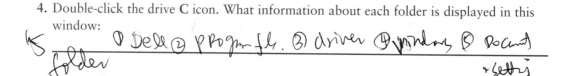 _① Dell ② Program fls. ③ driver ④ windows ⑤ Document + Setting_ _folder_

5. Windows uses different icons for different file types. Describe three different icons and the files they represent: _txt. doc p_

6. From the My Computer menu, click **View, Details**. Notice that this command displays the same information as the DIR command.

7. Close all open windows.

## REVIEW QUESTIONS

1. What command displays a list of files and directories at the command line? _div_

2. Does Windows display all system files by default? _No_

3. How can you change the way Windows displays file extensions?

4. What tool other than My Computer can you use to explore a file structure graphically?  _Explore_

5. In My Computer, what type of graphic displays information about a drive?

_____

6. How does Windows graphically distinguish between different file types?

_____

## LAB 2.2 CONVERT NUMBERS

### OBJECTIVES

The goal of this lab is to practice converting numbers between decimal, binary, and hexadecimal forms. After completing this lab, you will be able to:

◢ Convert decimal numbers (base 10) to hexadecimal and binary form

◢ Convert hexadecimal numbers (base 16) to binary and decimal form

◢ Convert binary numbers (base 2) to decimal and hexadecimal form

*2. 1*
*2. 6.*

*3. 1*

*3. 4.*

*3. 6.*

### MATERIALS REQUIRED

This lab requires the following:

◢ A pencil and paper and/or Windows Calculator

◢ Access to the online content "The Hexadecimal Number System and Memory Addressing," downloaded from *www.course.com*

◢ Windows 2000/XP or Windows 9x operating system

### LAB PREPARATION

Before the lab begins, the instructor or lab assistant needs to do the following:

◢ Announce to students that, before they come to lab, they should read the online content "The Hexadecimal Number System and Memory Addressing." They might like to bring this content to class in printed form.

### ACTIVITY BACKGROUND

Sometimes you need to know what resources are being reserved for a device. This information is often displayed on a computer in hexadecimal (or hex) numbers; this numbering system is shorthand for the binary numbers that computers actually use. Often, you'll want to convert these hex numbers into more familiar decimal numbers to get a better picture of which resources are reserved for a device.

**ESTIMATED COMPLETION TIME: 60 minutes**

 **Activity**

1. Convert the following decimal numbers to binary numbers using a calculator or the instructions in the online content "The Hexadecimal Number System and Memory Addressing." (To access Windows Calculator, click **Start**, point to **All Programs** (**Programs** in Windows 2000 and 9x), point to **Accessories**, and then click **Calculator**. If necessary, click **View**, **Scientific** from the Calculator menu to perform the conversions in these steps.)

   ◢ 14 = _____

   ◢ 77 = _____

◢ 128 = _____

◢ 223 = _____

◢ 255 = _____

2. Convert the following decimal numbers to hexadecimal notation:

◢ 13 = _____

◢ 240 = _____

◢ 255 = _____

◢ 58880 = _____

◢ 65535 = _____

3. Convert the following binary numbers to hexadecimal notation:

◢ 100 = _____

◢ 1011 = _____

◢ 111101 = _____

◢ 11111000 = _____

◢ 10110011 = _____

◢ 00000001 = _____

4. Hexadecimal numbers are often preceded with "0x." Convert the following hex numbers to binary numbers:

◢ 0x0016 = _____

◢ 0x00F8 = _____

◢ 0x00B2B = _____

◢ 0x005A = _____

◢ 0x1234 = _____

5. Convert the following hex numbers to decimal:

◢ 0x0013 = _____

◢ 0x00AB = _____

◢ 0x01CE = _____

◢ 0x812A = _____

6. Convert the following binary numbers to decimal:

◢ 1011 = _____

◢ 11011 = _____

◢ 10101010 = _____

◢ 111110100 = _____

◢ 10111011101 = _____

◢ 1111000001111 = _____

A network card, also called a network adapter, is assigned an address that identifies the card on the network. In Windows 98, the address is called the adapter address; in Windows 2000/XP, it's called the physical address. Either way, the address assigned to the network card is expressed in a series of paired hexadecimal numbers separated by dashes. In the following steps, you find out the network address for your network card and then convert the address to a binary number:

1. To open a command prompt window, click **Start**, point to **All Programs** (**Programs** in Windows 2000), point to **Accessories**, and then click **Command Prompt**. At the command prompt, type **ipconfig /all** and press **Enter**.

2. In Windows 98, click **Start**, **Run**. The Run dialog box opens. Type **winipcfg**, and then click **OK**. In the IP Configuration window, click the **More Info** button.

3. Write down the following information for your system:

   ◢ Network adapter address in hexadecimal form: _____

   ◢ Network adapter address in binary pairs: _____

4. Referring to Figure 2-1, convert the numbers in the network adapter's memory range and determine how many bytes, expressed in a decimal number, are in its memory address range.

_____

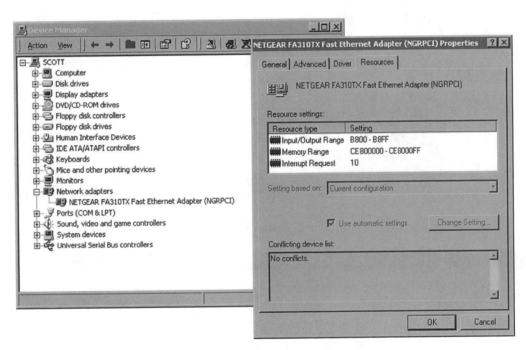

**Figure 2-1**   Memory range and input/output range expressed as hex numbers

## REVIEW QUESTIONS

1. Computers actually work with _____ numbers.

2. Computers often express numbers in _____ format, which is a base 16 numbering system.

3. Most people are more comfortable working with a(n) _____ , or base 10, numbering system.

4. In the hexadecimal system, what decimal value does the letter A represent?

_____

5. Hexadecimal numbers are often preceded by _____ so that a value containing only numerals is not mistaken for a decimal number.

# LAB 2.3 EXPLORE THE MACINTOSH WORLD

## OBJECTIVES

The goal of this lab is to familiarize you with Macintosh operating systems and the hardware they support. After completing this lab, you will be able to:

▲ Describe the various Apple operating systems, hardware, and applications

▲ Research Apple technology on the Apple Web site (*www.apple.com*)

## MATERIALS REQUIRED

This lab requires the following:

▲ Internet access

## LAB PREPARATION

Before the lab begins, the instructor or lab assistant needs to do the following:

▲ Verify that Internet access is available.

> **✎ Notes**
>
> If a Macintosh system is available, instructors might want to give a brief demonstration for students.

## ACTIVITY BACKGROUND

Macintosh operating systems are designed to be used only on Macintosh (Mac) computers; they can't be used on PCs. Many developers (including Apple, the company that created the Macintosh computer) have created Macintosh applications. The Apple Web site (*www.apple.com*) is the best source of information about Macintosh products.

In this lab, you investigate Macintosh operating systems, hardware, and applications.

**ESTIMATED COMPLETION TIME: 30 minutes**

### 🖑 Activity

1. Open your browser and go to **www.apple.com**. Explore the site, and when you're done, return to the main page. Use the links on the site to answer the following questions.

2. What version of the Mac operating system comes preinstalled on an iMac?

3. What is the cost of upgrading your operating system from OS 9 to OS X?

4. Comparing the iMac, Mac mini, and Power Mac systems available for sale on the Apple Web site, what are the speeds or frequencies of the processors in each computer?

5. How much does a 20-inch iMac cost?

6. What software comes bundled with an iMac?

7. What is a MacBook?

_____

8. How much does the most expensive MacBook cost?

_____

9. What features are included with the least expensive MacBook?

_____

10. Describe the features of an Apple Mighty Mouse:

_____

11. What is the function of an AirPort Extreme Base Station?

_____

12. What Apple computer can use the AirPort Extreme card?

_____

13. What is the purpose of QuickTime software?

_____

14. Describe what the AppleWorks software does:

_____

15. Describe the purposes of iMovie software:

_____

## REVIEW QUESTIONS

1. What is one advantage of using an Apple computer instead of a PC?

_____

_____

2. For what type of user do you think Apple applications are intended?

_____

_____

3. Why do you think it's easier for Apple to provide compatibility between hardware and the operating system than it is for Microsoft or Linux?

_____

_____

4. For what type of user is the iMac intended?

_____

_____

## *LAB 2.4 INVESTIGATE LINUX*

### OBJECTIVES

The goal of this lab is to find information about Linux. After completing this lab, you will be able to:

⊿ Research Linux on the Linux Web site (*www.linux.org*)

⊿ Compare Linux with other operating systems

⊿ Use the Linux tutorial on the Linux Web site

### MATERIALS REQUIRED

This lab requires the following:

⊿ Internet access

### LAB PREPARATION

Before the lab begins, the instructor or lab assistant needs to do the following:

⊿ Verify that Internet access is available.

### ACTIVITY BACKGROUND

UNIX is a popular OS used to control networks and support applications on the Internet. Linux is a scaled-down version of UNIX that is provided, in basic form, free of charge and includes open access to the programming code of the OS. Linux can be used as both a server platform and a desktop platform, but its greatest popularity has come in the server market. In this lab, you search the *www.linux.org* site for general information on Linux and survey the Linux tutorial.

**ESTIMATED COMPLETION TIME: 45 minutes**

 **Activity**

1. Open your browser and go to **www.linux.org**. Spend a few minutes exploring the site on your own, and then return to the main page.

2. Click the **General Info** link (on the navigation bar). Using the information on the "What is Linux" page, answer the following:

⊿ What is the current, full-featured version of Linux?

_____

⊿ Who is credited with inventing the Linux kernel?

_____

⊿ How is Linux licensed? Read the GNU General Public License. Give a brief description of the terms and conditions of this license:

_____

_____

◢ How much does Linux cost?

For an operating system to be useful, applications must be written for it. Suppose a small business is interested in using Linux on its desktop computers. Will this business be able to run common business-type applications on its Linux desktops? To find out, click the Applications link (on the navigation bar). The types of applications are listed by category. Search this page and its links to answer the following questions:

1. Will the business be able to send faxes from a Linux machine?

2. List two Web browsers suitable for Linux.

3. How many antivirus software packages are available for Linux? List at least two.

4. Searching under Office and Word Processor, list at least three word-processing applications available for Linux.

5. How many accounting applications are available for Linux? List at least two and the URLs where you found them.

Now you can continue exploring the Linux Web site. Follow these steps to compare Linux to other operating systems:

1. Click the **Documentation** link on the navigation bar.
2. Read about the Linux Documentation Project.
3. Use the information on the Linux Web site to answer the following questions:

   ◢ Give a brief description of the Linux Documentation Project:

   ◢ Who is responsible for writing documentation for the Linux operating system?

Next, follow these steps to explore the Web site's Linux tutorial:

1. Return to the home page, scroll down to display the heading Linux 101, and then click **more** at the bottom of that section.
2. Scroll down, and then click **Getting Started with Linux**. Browse through this tutorial and answer the following questions.

3. What are the distributions (flavors) of Linux and how are they categorized?

_____

_____

4. Can you install Linux on a computer that has another operating system already installed? Print the Web page supporting your answer:

_____

5. When preparing to install Linux, what is a good computer use practice?

_____

Continue exploring the Web site by completing the following:

1. Click the **Distributions** link. A link to the source code for Linux kernels is available on this page. Notice the Distribution search area. When searching for a distribution of Linux, if you don't narrow your search, you might get an overwhelming number of returns. The next steps limit your search.

2. Click **English** in the Language drop-down list.

3. Click **Mainstream/General Public** in the Category drop-down list.

4. Click **Intel compatible** in the Platform list, and then click **Go**. How many distributions do you see listed?

_____

5. Browse through the list, looking for SUSE Linux, Mandriva Linux, and Red Hat. Which distribution appears to be easiest to use? What is its intended purpose?

_____

6. Can Linux be used on other systems that don't run Intel-compatible processors? Print the Web page supporting your answer:

_____

## REVIEW QUESTIONS

1. What is the least amount of money you'll pay for Linux?

_____

2. Why might a company not want to use Linux on its desktop computers?

_____

_____

3. What is one advantage of using Linux rather than a Windows operating system on a desktop?

_____

4. Based on what you learned from the Linux Web site, how do you think companies that provide Linux make the most profit?

_____

## *LAB 2.5 COMPARE OPERATING SYSTEMS*

### OBJECTIVES

The goal of this lab is to help you learn about the history of PC operating systems and appreciate why many of today's operating systems share similar features. After completing this lab, you will be able to:

◢ Better understand the relationship between operating systems

### MATERIALS REQUIRED

This lab requires the following:

◢ Internet access

### LAB PREPARATION

Before the lab begins, the instructor or lab assistant needs to do the following:

◢ Verify that Internet access is available.

### ACTIVITY BACKGROUND

Modern operating systems, such as Windows, Linux, and Mac OS, have many similar features because they share a common history. Figure 2-2 shows some highlights of this history. The arrows indicate a direct or indirect influence from an earlier operating system.

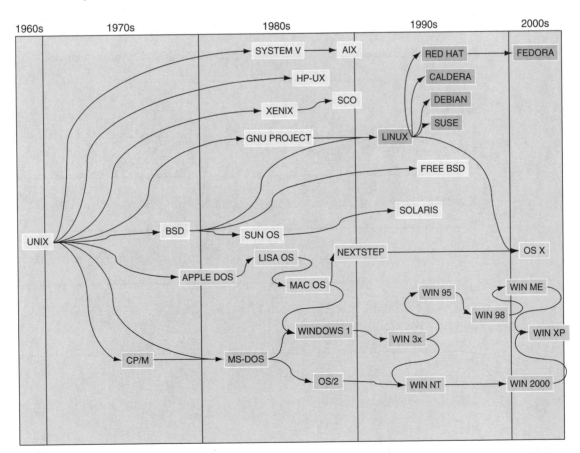

**Figure 2-2** OS timeline

**ESTIMATED COMPLETION TIME: 30 minutes**

 **Activity**

Use your favorite search engine, such as *www.google.com*, to answer the following questions:

1. Search for the "history of operating systems." List the URLs of three sites that you think do a good job of explaining this development:

2. What are two similarities and two differences between the original Mac OS and Windows?

3. How is OS/2 loosely connected to Windows NT?

4. What is the relationship of QDOS to CP/M and MS-DOS?

5. Modify the timeline by adding any other operating systems you think are important, such as BeOS or VMS.

## CHALLENGE ACTIVITY (ADDITIONAL 15 MINUTES)

1. Extend the timeline into the future by adding any new operating systems with their expected release dates.
2. What is the next operating system planned in the Windows line and when will it be released?

## REVIEW QUESTIONS

1. Based on the OS timeline in Figure 2-2, why do you think Linux and UNIX share more commands than Windows XP and UNIX?

2. Which line of operating systems has recently become more similar to UNIX?

3. Which line of operating systems split into two lines, only to merge again later?

4. Why do you think most versions of Linux and Windows use the CD command to change directories?

# LAB 2.6 USE WINDOWS KEYBOARD SHORTCUTS

## OBJECTIVES

The goal of this lab is to introduce you to some keyboard shortcuts. After completing this lab, you will be able to use the keyboard to:

- Display the Start menu
- Switch between open applications
- Launch utilities with the Windows logo key

## MATERIALS REQUIRED

This lab requires the following:

- Windows XP operating system

## LAB PREPARATION

Before the lab begins, the instructor or lab assistant needs to do the following:

- Verify that Windows starts with no errors.

## ACTIVITY BACKGROUND

You can use certain keys or key combinations (called keyboard shortcuts) to perform repetitive tasks more efficiently. These shortcuts are also useful when the mouse isn't working. In this lab, you learn to use some common keyboard shortcuts. You can find a full list of keyboard shortcuts by searching for "keyboard shortcuts" in the Windows Help and Support Center.

**ESTIMATED COMPLETION TIME: 30 minutes**

 **Activity**

The F1 key is the universal keyboard shortcut for launching Help. To learn more, follow these steps:

1. Open Paint and then minimize it.
2. Open Control Panel and then minimize it.
3. Click the desktop, and then press **F1**. Windows Help opens.
4. Close Windows Help, and restore Paint.
5. Press **F1**. Because Paint is the active window, Help for Paint opens. Close Help for Paint.
6. Restore Control Panel, and then press **F1**. Help for Control Panel opens.

You can activate many shortcuts by pressing the Windows logo key in combination with other keys. An enhanced keyboard has two Windows logo keys, usually located between the Ctrl and Alt keys on either side of the spacebar. Try the combinations listed in Table 2-1, and record the result of each key combination in the Result column. (Close each window you open before proceeding to the next key combination.)

| Key or key combination | Result |
|---|---|
| Windows logo | *Administrator* |
| Windows logo+E | *my computer* |
| Windows logo+F | *search Results* |
| Windows logo+R | *cmd.* |
| Windows logo+Break | *System property* |
| Windows logo+M | *Minimize all windows* |

**Table 2-1**   Key combinations using the Windows logo key

Suppose for some reason that your mouse isn't working and you have to print a text file. You would have to use the keyboard to find, select, open, and print the document. To learn more, follow these steps:

1. Boot the computer, wait for the Windows desktop to appear, and then unplug the mouse.

2. Press **Tab** a few times until one of the desktop icons is highlighted.

3. Use the arrow keys to highlight **My Computer**.

4. Press **Enter**. My Computer opens.

5. Press **Tab** a few times until drive **A** is highlighted.

6. Use the arrow keys again to select the **C** drive, and then press **Enter** to open it.

7. Use similar methods to find, select, and open the Notepad program (from **Start, All Programs, Accessories, Notepad**) and type "Have a Nice Day."

8. Notice in the Notepad window that one letter of each menu item becomes underlined after you press **Alt**. You can select menu options by holding down the Alt key while you press this underlined letter. For example, to open the File menu in Notepad, hold down the **Alt** key and press F. After the menu is open, you can use the arrow keys to move over the menu and select an option by pressing Enter, or you can type the underlined letter of a menu option. With the **Alt** key pressed down, press **F**. The File menu opens.

9. Press **P** to select Print. The Print dialog box opens.

10. Verify that the correct printer is selected. (To select a different printer, use the arrow keys.)

11. To send the print job to the printer, press **Tab** until the Print button is active, and then press **Enter**. (Or you can press Alt+P.)

12. Practice editing text, using the following shortcuts for cutting, copying, and pasting:

   ◢ To delete one or more characters, move your cursor to the beginning of the text you want to delete, hold down the **Shift** key, and use the arrow keys to highlight the text. (If you were using a mouse, you could hold down the left mouse button and drag the mouse until the entire block was highlighted.)

   ◢ With the text highlighted, hold down the **Ctrl** key, press **X**, and then release both keys. This action cuts the highlighted text from its original location and moves it to the Clipboard. You can then paste it in another location.

   ◢ To copy a highlighted block of characters to the Clipboard (without removing it from its original location), hold down the **Ctrl** key, press **C**, and then release both keys. A copy of the highlighted block of characters is placed in the Clipboard. You can then paste it in another location.

◢ To paste text from the Clipboard to a new location, move the cursor to the desired location, press and hold the **Ctrl** key, press **V**, and then release both keys.

## CRITICAL THINKING (ADDITIONAL 15 MINUTES)

Using the keyboard skills you have learned in this lab, perform the following steps without using the mouse and answer the questions:

1. Open Device Manager and view resources for the mouse. What status does Device Manager report about the mouse?

   _____

2. What IRQ is used by the mouse?

   _____ 12 _____

3. According to Windows Explorer, how much space is available on the hard drive?

   _____ 3.24 GB _____

## REVIEW QUESTIONS

1. What key is universally used to launch Help?

   _____ click desk Top then F1 _____

2. How many Windows logo keys are usually included on an enhanced keyboard?

   _____ 2 Keys _____

3. What shortcut combination can you use to paste a block of text?

   _____ CTL. V. _____

4. What key combination can you use to switch between open applications? (*Hint*: Check Windows Help and Support.)

   _____ CTL + tab switch to the last open Program or ALT repeating Tab _____

5. Is it possible to open the Start menu by pressing only one key?

   _____ Window logo _____

# PC Repair Fundamentals

**Labs included in this chapter:**

- **Lab 3.1:** Observe the Boot Process
- **Lab 3.2:** Take a Computer Apart and Put It Back Together
- **Lab 3.3:** Choose a System
- **Lab 3.4:** Determine System Requirements
- **Lab 3.5:** Compare What You Need with What You Can Afford
- **Lab 3.6:** Check System Compatibility
- **Lab 3.7:** Evaluate an Upgrade

# LAB 3.1 OBSERVE THE BOOT PROCESS

## OBJECTIVES

The goal of this lab is to give you the opportunity to observe the sequence of events in a PC's boot process. After completing this lab, you will be able to:

- Describe the boot process in detail
- Halt the boot process
- Diagnose problems in the boot process

*F2 - Setup*

*F8*

*Fn~ - utility*

## MATERIALS REQUIRED

This lab requires the following:

- Windows 2000/XP or Windows 9x operating system
- A blank floppy disk
- A workgroup of 2 to 4 students

## LAB PREPARATION

Before the lab begins, the instructor or lab assistant needs to do the following:

- Verify that Windows starts with no errors.
- Make sure that in CMOS setup, the boot sequence is the floppy drive first and then the hard drive.

## ACTIVITY BACKGROUND

This lab familiarizes you with the boot process and gives you some practice recognizing when the boot process halts and observing the resulting information displayed on the screen. Working in teams, you begin by observing a PC booting up and noting every step, from turning on the power to the appearance of the Windows desktop. When you're familiar with all the steps in the boot process, your team then intentionally introduces problems that cause the boot process to fail on your PC and then observes the results. Next, you introduce one problem on your PC, and your team switches PCs with another team's PC and attempts to figure out why that team's PC failed to boot.

**ESTIMATED COMPLETION TIME: 30 minutes**

 **Activity**

Boot your team's PC and then, using the information on the screen as a guide, record every step in the process. (List this information on a separate piece of paper.) For example, you're looking for RAM initialization, display of CPU speed, a list of devices that are detected, what happens when the screen turns from black to another color, and other similar events. You might have to boot the PC several times to record all the steps. Also, sometimes you can use the Pause key to pause what's on the screen so that you can read it before it flies by.

Perform the following steps to introduce a problem in the boot process of your team's PC. For each problem, boot the PC and describe the problem as a user unfamiliar with PC technology might describe it. List any error messages you see.

**3**

1. Insert a blank floppy disk into the floppy drive. Describe the problem as a user sees it, including error messages: *Blank. Remove disks or other media*

2. Unplug the keyboard. Describe the problem. Does the computer still boot into Windows? *Yes*

3. Unplug the mouse. Describe the problem. Does the computer still boot into Windows? *Yes*

4. Unplug the monitor. Describe the problem: *Check Signal Cable*

5. After a minute, plug the monitor in. Did the system boot correctly?

6. Now cause one problem in the preceding steps and switch places with another team. Do not tell the other team what problem you caused.

7. Detect, diagnose, and remedy the problem on the other team's PC.

## REVIEW QUESTIONS

1. What is the first message displayed on the screen after you turn on the power?

2. What devices are detected during the boot process?

3. Of all the problems you studied during the lab, which one halts the boot process earliest in the process?

4. Which problem results in messages about the operating system not being displayed?

5. Why do you think being familiar with all steps in the boot process is useful?

# LAB 3.2 TAKE A COMPUTER APART AND PUT IT BACK TOGETHER

## OBJECTIVES

The goal of this lab is to help you get comfortable working inside a computer case. After completing this lab, you will be able to:

▲ Take a computer apart

▲ Recognize components

▲ Reassemble the computer

## MATERIALS REQUIRED

This lab requires the following:

▲ A computer designated for disassembly

▲ A PC toolkit with an antistatic ground strap and mat

▲ A marker and masking tape

▲ Small containers, such as paper cups, to hold screws as you work

▲ A workgroup of 2 to 4 students or individual students

## LAB PREPARATION

Before the lab begins, the instructor or lab assistant needs to do the following:

▲ Verify that a computer designated for disassembly is available to each student or workgroup.

## ACTIVITY BACKGROUND

If you follow directions and take your time, there's no reason to be intimidated by working inside a computer case. This lab takes you step by step through the process of disassembling and reassembling a PC. Follow your computer lab's posted safety procedures when disassembling and reassembling a PC, and remember to always wear your antistatic ground strap. Also, never force a component to fit into its slot.

You begin this lab by removing the cover of your PC and then removing the components inside. Next, you reassemble the components and replace the cover. This lab includes steps for working with a desktop PC and a tower PC. Follow the steps that apply to your computer.

Also, in this lab, you're instructed to disassemble your PC in this order: expansion cards, interior cables and cords, power supply, case fans, motherboard, and drives. Because some systems are designed so that the disassembly order is different from this one, your instructor might change the order. For example, you might not be able to get to the power supply to remove it until drives or the motherboard are out of the way. Be sure to follow any specific directions from your instructor.

 **Notes**

In a lab environment, the instructor might consider giving a demonstration of tearing down a PC and putting it back together before students begin this lab.

As you work, when you remove a screw, place it in a paper cup or on a piece of paper so that you can keep different size screws separated. Later, when you reassemble, organizing the screws in this way makes it easier to match the right size screw to the hole.

### Activity

Follow the procedure outlined in the following steps to remove the case cover and expansion cards. (If you're working with a tower case, lay it on its side so that the motherboard is on the bottom.)

1. Remove the cover from your desktop PC.

2. To make reassembly easier, take notes or make a sketch of the current placement of boards and cables and identify each board and cable. You can mark the location of a cable on an expansion card with a marker, if you like. Note the orientation of the cable on the card. Each cable for the floppy disk drive, parallel ATA hard drive, or CD-ROM drive has a colored marking on one side of the cable called the "edge color." This color marks pin 1 of the cable. On the board, pin 1 is marked with the number 1 or 2 beside the pin or with a square soldering pad on the back side of the board, as shown in Figure 3-1. You might not be able to see this soldering pad now.

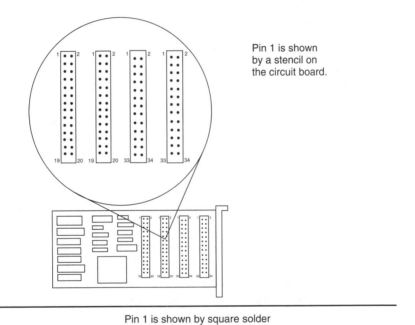

Pin 1 is shown by a stencil on the circuit board.

Pin 1 is shown by square solder pads on the reverse side of the circuit board.

**Figure 3-1**   How to find pin 1 on an expansion card

3. Remove the cables from the expansion cards. There's no need to remove the other end of the cable from its component (floppy disk drive, hard drive, or CD-ROM drive). Lay the cable over the top of the component or case.

4. Remove the screw holding the card to the back of the case. If you aren't wearing an antistatic ground strap, touch the case before you touch the card.

5. Grasp the card with both hands and remove it by lifting straight up and rocking the card from end to end (not side to side). Rocking the card from side to side might spread the slot opening and weaken the connection. When you remove the card, be sure you don't touch the edge connectors on the card to avoid causing ESD damage.

6. If the card had a cable attached, examine the card connector for the cable. Can you identify pin 1? Lay the card aside on a flat surface.

7. Remove any other expansion cards in the same way.

8. In some proprietary systems, an expansion card assembly attaches to the motherboard, with each card attached to the assembly. If your system has this arrangement, remove it now. It's probably held in place by screws or clips and may or may not have a rail guide you can use to locate the assembly in the case.

9. To remove the power supply, first remove the power cables to the motherboard, case fans, other remaining components, and the power switch, if necessary. Make notes about which cable attaches to what hardware. After the cables are removed, support the power supply with one hand, and remove the screws attaching it to the case.

10. Remove any case fans.

In some systems, it's easier to remove the drives first and then the motherboard. In other systems, it's easier to remove the motherboard first. In these instructions, to make sure you don't risk dropping a drive on the motherboard when removing the drive, you're directed to remove the motherboard first and then the drives. Your instructor, however, might prefer that you remove the drives first and then the motherboard.

1. Begin removing the motherboard by removing any power cables connected to any case or component fans. Be sure to make notes or label the cables so that you can reinstall them correctly.

2. Finish removing the motherboard by removing the screws holding the board to the stand-offs. Usually six to nine screws attach the motherboard to the case. Be careful not to gouge the board or damage components with the screwdriver. Because the screws on the motherboard are often located between components, they can be hard to reach. Be very careful not to damage the motherboard.

3. To remove drives, remove the ribbon cable if it's still attached. Many cases have a removable drive bay. The drives are attached to this bay, and the bay can be removed with all the drives attached. This arrangement gives you easier access to drive-mounting screws than from inside the case. If your case has a removable drive bay, this removal method is preferred. Otherwise, remove each drive separately. Be careful not to jar the drive as you remove it from the case.

4. If your system has a removable drive bay, the floppy drive likely came out with the removable bay. If the floppy drive is still in the system, remove the screws holding the drive in place, and slide the drive out of the case.

5. Remove any CD-ROM, DVD, or tape drives from the case. These drives are usually in the 5-inch drive bays and are normally held in place by four to eight screws. After the screws are removed, the drive slides out the front of the case.

6. Remove any other components.

Now that you have removed all the components, you're ready to reassemble the PC. Replace each component carefully. Take care to install each component firmly without overtightening the screws. Don't force components to fit. If a component won't fit easily the way it should, look for some obstruction preventing it from falling into place. Look carefully for the reason the component won't fit correctly, and make any small adjustments as necessary. The following steps outline the required procedure, which is essentially the reverse of the disassembly procedure:

1. Install the power supply and replace the screws holding it in position.

2. Install the drives in their bays and then install the motherboard, unless your instructor prefers that you install the motherboard first.

3. Connect the power cables from the power supply to the drives and the motherboard. Double-check to make sure the power supply connectors to the motherboard are connected correctly, especially the relative positions of the P8 and P9 connectors (remember the black-to-black rule) if you're dealing with an older AT power supply.

4. Place each card in its slot (it doesn't have to be the same slot, just the same bus), and replace the screw. Don't place a PCI or an ISA video card near the power supply; otherwise, electromagnetic interference (EMI) from the power supply might affect the video picture.

5. Replace the cables, being sure to align the colored edge with pin 1. (In some cases, it might work better to connect the cable to the card before you put the card in the expansion slot.)

6. Check to make sure no cables are interfering with any fan's ability to turn. A common cause of an overheated system is a fan that can't move air because a cable is preventing it from spinning.

7. When all components are installed, you should have refitted all the screws you removed earlier. If some screws are missing, it's important to turn the case upside down and *gently* shake the case to dislodge any wayward screws. Any screw lying on a board has the potential to short out that board when power is applied. Don't use a magnet to try to find missing screws in the case because you might damage data on hard drives and floppy disks left in the floppy disk drives.

8. Plug in the keyboard, monitor, and mouse.

9. In a classroom environment, have the instructor check your work before you power up.

10. Plug in the power cord to the PC and to the power outlet or surge protector. Verify that any power switches on the rear of the case are set correctly. Some cases have a power switch to close the AC voltage, and others have an on/off switch.

11. Using the power button on the front of the case, turn on the power and check that the PC is working properly before you replace the cover. Don't touch the inside of the case while the power is on.

12. If all is well, turn off the PC and replace the cover and its screws. If the PC doesn't work, don't panic. Turn off the power, and then go back and check each cable connection and each expansion card. You probably haven't seated a card solidly in the slot. After you have double-checked everything, try again.

## REVIEW QUESTIONS

1. When removing the cover, why should you take care to remove only the screws that hold the cover on?

2. How should you rock a card to remove it from its slot? Why is it important to know how to rock a card correctly?

_____

_____

3. What should you do to help you remember which components connect to which cables?

_____

4. What marking on a ribbon cable identifies pin 1?

_____

5. What component(s) defines the system's form factor?

_____

_____

6. What form factor does your PC use?

_____

7. Why would a PC technician ever have to change out a computer's motherboard?

_____

_____

## LAB 3.3 CHOOSE A SYSTEM

### OBJECTIVES

The goal of this lab is to help you determine what system you might purchase or build to meet your needs and desires. After completing this lab, you will be able to:

◢ List applications you want to run on your system

◢ Determine the type of system required for several types of application

### MATERIALS REQUIRED

This lab requires the following:

◢ A workgroup of 2 to 4 students

### ACTIVITY BACKGROUND

The goal of this chapter is to help you learn how to plan and build a new system from scratch. One of the first steps in planning and constructing your own PC is deciding what you're going to use it for and what applications you'll be running on it. After you make these decisions, you can determine what components are required to meet your needs. In this lab, you describe and discuss the kind of system you would build for particular uses. Some labs in this chapter require doing research, but in this case, all you need to do is discuss issues with your workgroup partners.

**Activity**

In the following steps, you plan four different systems. Each member of the workgroup should work separately, with each member planning four systems. Follow these steps:

1. Plan a system that will be used for gaming and Web surfing. Complete the following:

   ◢ Applications you are likely to install:

   _____

   _____

   ◢ Hardware needed:

   _____

   _____

   ◢ Most important hardware components needed for gaming and Web surfing:

   _____

   _____

2. Plan a system that will be used for programming. Complete the following:

   ◢ Applications you are likely to install:

   _____

   _____

   ◢ Hardware needed:

   _____

   _____

   ◢ Most important hardware components needed for programming:

   _____

   _____

3. Plan a system that will be used for office applications. Complete the following:

   ◢ Applications you are likely to install:

   _____

   _____

   ◢ Hardware needed:

   _____

   _____

◢ Most important hardware components needed for office applications:

_____

_____

4. Plan a system that will be used for a company file server. Complete the following:

   ◢ Applications you are likely to install:

   _____

   _____

   ◢ Hardware needed:

   _____

   _____

   ◢ Most important hardware components needed for a company file server:

   _____

   _____

5. For each type of system, discuss the differences in the systems each member of your group planned. List the major differences here:

   _____

   _____

   _____

6. As a group, agree on a set of specifications for each system. How do the specifications your group agreed on differ from your original specifications?

   _____

   _____

7. Assign one type of system to each member of the group. List the assignments for each group member. In Labs 3.4 and 3.5, each member of the group will continue planning the type of system assigned here:

   _____

   _____

## REVIEW QUESTIONS

1. What type of system was assigned to you?

   _____

   _____

2. What resources do you need to produce a detailed design for this system?

_____

_____

_____

3. Did you find the process of discussing different types of systems helpful? Why or why not?

_____

_____

4. On which type of system was there the most disagreement on requirements?

_____

5. If you had a budget crunch, where would you sacrifice on your system? Justify your reasoning:

_____

_____

## LAB 3.4 DETERMINE SYSTEM REQUIREMENTS

### OBJECTIVES

The goal of this lab is to help you determine the specific requirements for the system you plan to build. After completing this lab, you will be able to:

◢ List minimum software and hardware components required for a particular type of system

### MATERIALS REQUIRED

This lab requires the following:

◢ Internet access
◢ A workgroup of 2 to 4 students (different people than in Lab 3.3)

### LAB PREPARATION

Before the lab begins, the instructor or lab assistant needs to do the following:

◢ Verify that Windows starts with no errors.
◢ Verify that Internet access is available.
◢ Ask students to break into different groups from Lab 3.3.

### ACTIVITY BACKGROUND

In the previous lab, you were assigned a type of system to build, and you made some preliminary plans for it. In this lab, you make more specific decisions about the required software and hardware components. For now, ignore budget constraints; you address those issues in Lab 3.5.

**Activity**

1. Working from the preliminary requirements you formed in Lab 3.3, use the Internet to research system requirements for your assigned type of system. Complete the following list of requirements:

   ▲ CPU speed:

   _____

   ▲ Memory:

   _____

   ▲ Hard drive size:

   _____

   ▲ Case:

   _____

   ▲ Motherboard:

   _____

   ▲ Monitor size and resolution:

   _____

   ▲ Type of printer:

   _____

   ▲ Expansion cards:

   _____

   ▲ Other peripheral hardware (such as keyboard, mouse, PC camera, speakers, and so on):

   _____

   ▲ Drives needed (for example, hard drives, CD or DVD, tape backup, or floppy):

   _____

   ▲ Operating system:

   _____

   ▲ Applications:

   _____

   ▲ Any other requirements:

   _____

2. Use the Internet or your local computer store to learn more about each component. List the description and cost of each component. If you're doing your research on the Internet, print

the Web page describing each component. (The Web page you print should include the component's price.) If you're conducting your research at a computer store, take careful notes, and be sure to note a price for each component. At this point, you're interested in evaluating your options for each component, so collect information on more than one possibility. For example, for a motherboard, gather information for two or three different motherboards that satisfy your system requirements. Although you need to list the price for each component, don't be concerned about total cost at this point in your research. The following Internet resources might be helpful in your search, although you can use others as well:

▲ *www.cnet.com*

▲ *www.tomshardware.com*

▲ *www.motherboards.com*

▲ *www.pricewatch.com*

▲ *www.dirtcheapdrives.com*

3. After you have finished gathering system requirements, find another student from another group who planned the same type of system you did. Compare your plans and note the differences.

## REVIEW QUESTIONS

1. What sites did you use for your research besides the previously listed ones?

_____

_____

_____

2. Did you add any components to your list or remove any from it after researching the type of system you want to build? Explain:

_____

_____

_____

3. What processor manufacturer, model, and speed did you select? Why? How much would the same speed processor from another manufacturer cost?

_____

_____

_____

4. What amount of memory and hard drive size do you plan to use? How did you make your choices?

_____

_____

_____

5. What components did you decide to use in your system other than the ones listed in the lab? What purpose will they serve in the new system?

_____

_____

_____

6. List any differences between your plans and another student's plans for the same type of system:

_____

_____

_____

# LAB 3.5 COMPARE WHAT YOU NEED WITH WHAT YOU CAN AFFORD

## OBJECTIVES

The goal of this lab is to help you determine the cost of building your own PC. After completing this lab, you will be able to:

▲ Research and compare component prices

▲ Determine how to build a system within your budget

## MATERIALS REQUIRED

This lab requires the following:

▲ Internet access

▲ A workgroup of 2 to 4 students

## LAB PREPARATION

Before the lab begins, the instructor or lab assistant needs to do the following:

▲ Verify that Internet access is available.

## ACTIVITY BACKGROUND

When planning a system, it's important to consider the cost of the components you want to include. You might not be able to afford everything you'd like to have in the system, or you might have to buy less expensive versions of some components to get what you want in another area. In this lab, you develop several versions of a budget for the system you want to build. You begin without a budget—that is, by figuring out what your dream system would cost. Then you prioritize your list of components and determine ways to reduce the system's total cost.

**Activity**

1. Use the information about specific hardware components that you compiled in Lab 3.4 to fill in Table 3-1. List the price of each component in your dream system in Table 3-1. (Note that you might not use all the rows in the table.) At the bottom of the table, list the total cost for your dream system.

| Component | Manufacturer and model | Cost |
| --- | --- | --- |
| Processor | | |
| Motherboard | | |
| Memory | | |
| Case | | |
| Video card | | |
| Expansion card 1 | | |
| Expansion card 2 | | |
| Expansion card 3 | | |
| Hard drive | | |
| CD or DVD drive | | |
| Floppy drive | | |
| Other drives | | |
| Tape drive | | |
| Monitor | | |
| Keyboard | | |
| Mouse | | |
| Speakers | | |
| Printer | | |
| Operating system | | |
| Application 1 | | |
| Application 2 | | |
| Application 3 | | |
| Application 4 | | |
| Other | | |
| Other | | |
| Other | | |
| Total cost of the system | | |

**Table 3-1** Dream system

2. Review your list of components in Table 3-1 and prioritize them. In Table 3-2, list the components in order of importance. In the Notes column, make notes on how much you need each component and whether you can use a lower-cost version or eliminate it altogether. Indicate which (if any) components you're most willing to sacrifice to be able to afford a better component in another area of the system.

| Component | Priority | Notes |
|---|---|---|
| Processor | | |
| Motherboard | | |
| Memory | | |
| Case | | |
| Video card | | |
| Expansion card 1 | | |
| Expansion card 2 | | |
| Expansion card 3 | | |
| Hard drive | | |
| CD or DVD drive | | |
| Floppy drive | | |
| Other drives | | |
| Tape drive | | |
| Monitor | | |
| Keyboard | | |
| Mouse | | |
| Speakers | | |
| Printer | | |
| Operating system | | |
| Application 1 | | |
| Application 2 | | |
| Application 3 | | |
| Application 4 | | |
| Other | | |
| Other | | |
| Other | | |
| Total cost of the system | | |

**Table 3-2**   Priority of system components

3. Pare down your list to the absolute minimum for the type of system you're building: the lowest amount of memory and hard drive space, the cheapest monitor, and so on. In Table 3-3, list the lowest prices available for each component, and calculate the total cost of your bare-bones system.

| Component | Manufacturer and model | Cost |
|---|---|---|
| Processor | | |
| Motherboard | | |
| Memory | | |
| Case | | |
| Video card | | |
| Expansion card 1 | | |
| Expansion card 2 | | |
| Expansion card 3 | | |
| Hard drive | | |
| CD or DVD drive | | |
| Floppy drive | | |
| Other drives | | |
| Tape drive | | |
| Monitor | | |
| Keyboard | | |
| Mouse | | |
| Speakers | | |
| Printer | | |
| Operating system | | |
| Application 1 | | |
| Application 2 | | |
| Application 3 | | |
| Application 4 | | |
| Other | | |
| Other | | |
| Other | | |
| Total cost of the system | | |

**Table 3-3** Bare-bones system

4. In Table 3-4, list the components of a system that's a reasonable compromise between the dream system and the bare-bones system. This midrange system is the one you work with in Lab 3.6.

| Component | Manufacturer and model | Cost |
|---|---|---|
| Processor | | |
| Motherboard | | |
| Memory | | |
| Case | | |
| Video card | | |
| Expansion card 1 | | |
| Expansion card 2 | | |
| Expansion card 3 | | |
| Hard drive | | |
| CD or DVD drive | | |
| Floppy drive | | |
| Other drives | | |
| Tape drive | | |
| Monitor | | |
| Keyboard | | |
| Mouse | | |
| Speakers | | |
| Printer | | |
| Operating system | | |
| Application 1 | | |
| Application 2 | | |
| Application 3 | | |
| Application 4 | | |
| Other | | |
| Other | | |
| Other | | |
| Total cost of the system | | |

**Table 3-4**  Midrange system

5. Compare your results from Steps 1 through 4 with the results of another student planning the same type of system. Compare cost estimates and note differences in the components you both planned to include. Note how you arrived at your calculation:

_____

_____

_____

6. Repeat Step 5 with at least one student planning a different type of system.

## REVIEW QUESTIONS

1. What was the cost difference between your dream system and the bare-bones version?

_____

_____

2. On which components were you willing to compromise and why?

_____

_____

_____

3. On which components were you *not* willing to compromise and why?

_____

_____

_____

4. How would the performance of your midrange system compare to the dream system? How would the performance of the midrange system compare to the bare-bones system? How would the performance of the dream system compare to the bare-bones system?

_____

_____

_____

## *LAB 3.6 CHECK SYSTEM COMPATIBILITY*

### OBJECTIVES

The goal of this lab is to help you verify that the components in a proposed system are compatible. After completing this lab, you will be able to:

◢ Find incompatibilities between components in a proposed system

◢ Suggest an alternative system of approximately the same price

### MATERIALS REQUIRED

This lab requires the following:

◢ Internet access

◢ A workgroup of 2 to 4 students

### LAB PREPARATION

Before the lab begins, the instructor or lab assistant needs to do the following:

◢ Verify that Internet access is available.

## ACTIVITY BACKGROUND

No matter how much time you spend planning and building a PC, the system won't work correctly unless the system components are compatible. You can save yourself a lot of trouble by attempting to discover incompatibilities before you begin to build a system. In this lab, you figure out which components in your proposed system are incompatible and suggest compatible components so that the cost of building the system remains approximately the same.

**ESTIMATED COMPLETION TIME: 45 minutes**

 **Activity**

1. Alter your plan for your midrange system (from Lab 3.5) by introducing component incompatibilities. Write this altered version on a separate piece of paper or develop a new plan that incorporates incompatible components. Incompatibilities are suggested in the following list, but you can introduce a problem not listed here:

   ◢ A processor not supported by the motherboard

   ◢ Not enough space in the case for all your drives (hard drive, CD-ROM, tape drive)

   ◢ Power supply not powerful enough

   ◢ Too much RAM for the motherboard

   ◢ An incompatible mix of SCSI and IDE devices

   ◢ A type of memory not supported on the motherboard

   ◢ Five parallel ATA IDE devices on a system

   ◢ A video card that uses the wrong kind of expansion slot for the motherboard

   ◢ Expansion cards used with a motherboard that already has built-in logic

2. Calculate and record the total cost of components in the system:

   _____

   _____

   _____

3. Trade revised system plans with another student in your group. Ask the other student to find the incompatible components in your plan and suggest replacement components while keeping the price about the same. Do the same with the plan you receive, recording incompatibilities you find, the original cost of the system, replacement components, and the final cost of the altered system:

   _____

   _____

   _____

4. With the group, discuss incompatibilities found in the plans and how you fixed them. Make note of incompatibilities that were introduced but not found:

   _____

   _____

   _____

**REVIEW QUESTIONS**

1. Did you, or the other students in your group, introduce incompatibilities not suggested in Step 1? If so, list them here:

_____

_____

2. Were all the incompatibilities introduced in the plans discovered? If not, which ones were not, and why do you think they have been more difficult to find?

_____

_____

_____

3. List the incompatibility problems you found in the other student's plan and explain how you solved them:

_____

_____

_____

4. Did the students in your group have different ways of solving the same incompatibility problems? Explain:

_____

_____

5. For the plan you reviewed and revised, what was the difference in the original cost and the cost after you incorporated your solutions?

_____

_____

# LAB 3.7 EVALUATE AN UPGRADE

## OBJECTIVES

The goal of this lab is to help you determine the ease and cost of upgrading a PC. After completing this lab, you will be able to:

◢ Determine whether a system needs to be upgraded

◢ Explain why a system needs to be upgraded

◢ List the components needed to upgrade a system

## MATERIALS REQUIRED

This lab requires the following:

- ◢ A lab computer
- ◢ Documentation for computer components, if available
- ◢ Internet access

## LAB PREPARATION

Before the lab begins, the instructor or lab assistant needs to do the following:

- ◢ Verify that Windows starts with no errors.
- ◢ Verify that Internet access is available.
- ◢ Provide documentation or manuals that came with the system.

## ACTIVITY BACKGROUND

An important factor to consider when purchasing or building a PC is how easy upgrading the system will be. You might upgrade an existing system instead of replacing it with a new system. Factors that affect the ease of upgrading include the processors supported by the motherboard, the size of the case, and the number and type of ports and expansion slots on the motherboard. In this lab, you examine a system to determine whether you can make upgrades to it and then evaluate how practical the upgrades are.

**ESTIMATED COMPLETION TIME: 45 minutes**

 **Activity**

Follow these steps to determine whether your system can be upgraded:

1. In Table 3-5, list the components currently installed on your system. Useful sources of information include Device Manager, Control Panel, and the Properties dialog boxes for drives and devices.

| Device | Description |
| --- | --- |
| Motherboard (make and model) | |
| BIOS type | |
| Memory (type and size) | |
| Hard drive (type and size) | |
| Other drives installed (floppy, Zip, CD-ROM, and so on) | |
| Monitor (type and size) | |
| Printer | |
| Sound card | |
| Modem (or other Internet connection) | |
| NIC | |
| Other devices | |
| Operating system (including version number) | |
| Applications (including version number) | |

**Table 3-5** Current system components

2. Using the Internet and available documentation, select three components to upgrade. Record the following information for each component.

Component 1

▲ Replacement component:

_____

▲ Cost of the upgrade:

_____

▲ Do other components need to be upgraded for this upgrade to work? If so, what are they?

_____

Component 2

▲ Replacement component:

_____

▲ Cost of the upgrade:

_____

▲ Do other components need to be upgraded for this upgrade to work? If so, what are they?

_____

Component 3

▲ Replacement component:

_____

▲ Cost of the upgrade:

_____

▲ Do other components need to be upgraded for this upgrade to work? If so, what are they?

_____

3. Print a Web page showing the specifications and cost of each new component. What is the total cost of the upgrades?

_____

4. Suppose you had to sell the system in its current state (without the upgrades). What would be a reasonable price?

_____

5. When upgrading an existing system, the cost of the upgrade should not exceed half the value of the existing system. Will your proposed upgrade go over that limit?

_____

6. Using *www.cnet.com* (or another Web site where you can compare systems), locate a notebook computer with specifications similar to your lab PC. Compare the cost of upgrading the memory, processor, and CD-ROM drive on each system. (Substitute another component if your computer doesn't have a CD-ROM drive.) In Table 3-6, compare the cost of upgrading your lab PC with a similar upgrade for a notebook computer.

| Component | Cost of upgrading on PC | Cost of upgrading on notebook |
|-----------|------------------------|-------------------------------|
| Processor |                        |                               |
| Memory    |                        |                               |
| CD-ROM drive |                     |                               |

**Table 3-6** PC upgrade versus notebook upgrade

## REVIEW QUESTIONS

1. What components did you choose to upgrade and why?

   _____

   _____

2. Which would be cheapest to upgrade: your lab PC or a comparable notebook? Explain your answer:

   _____

   _____

3. What other resources, besides the ones you used in the lab, do you think might be helpful in planning an upgrade?

   _____

   _____

4. Among the components you selected, which upgrade was the most expensive?

   _____

   _____

5. If you were actually performing these upgrades, is there any component or any system you would *not* choose to upgrade? Explain your answer:

   _____

   _____

6. Which component is the most popular to upgrade? The easiest? The hardest?

   _____

   _____

   _____

# CHAPTER 4

# Electricity and Power Supplies

**Labs included in this chapter:**

- **Lab 4.1:** Identify Form Factors
- **Lab 4.2:** Measure the Output of Your Power Supply
- **Lab 4.3:** Replace a Power Supply
- **Lab 4.4:** Find Documentation on the Internet
- **Lab 4.5:** Choose the Right Power Supply

# LAB 4.1 IDENTIFY FORM FACTORS

## OBJECTIVES

The goal of this lab is to give you experience in identifying form factors. After completing this lab, you will be able to:

◢ Identify the form factor of the case, motherboard, and power supply

◢ Select appropriate components to match an existing form factor

## MATERIALS REQUIRED

This lab requires the following:

◢ A PC designated for this lab

◢ A PC toolkit with antistatic ground strap

◢ Internet access

## LAB PREPARATION

Before the lab begins, the instructor or lab assistant needs to do the following:

◢ Verify that Windows starts with no errors.

◢ Verify that Internet access is available.

## ACTIVITY BACKGROUND

The form factor is a set of specifications about the size, shape, and configuration of the components that make up a computer system. Sharing a common standard allows components such as the case, motherboard, and power supply to fit together and function properly. There are three common types of form factors: AT, ATX, and BTX. Each comes in several variations that determine characteristics such as size and shape. In this lab, you identify your system's form factor and research some identifying characteristics of common form factors.

**ESTIMATED COMPLETION TIME: 30 minutes**

### Activity

1. Open your browser and go to your favorite search engine, such as *www.google.com*.

2. Use the Internet to research the main differences between AT and ATX and list them here:

_____

_____

3. Now explain the main differences between ATX and BTX:

_____

_____

4. Each form factor comes in several sizes. How could you tell whether a system was Regular BTX, Micro BTX, or Pico BTX?

_____

_____

5. Form factors are also available in various shapes. What slimline form factor is similar to ATX?

_____

6. Now turn the computer off and unplug the power cord.

7. Disconnect all peripherals and remove the case cover. Remove the cover from your desktop PC.

8. Examine the case, motherboard, and power supply.

9. What is the form factor of this system?

_____

10. Close the case, reattach the peripherals, and test the system to make sure it boots without errors.

## REVIEW QUESTIONS

1. Why is it important that your case and motherboard share a compatible form factor?

_____

2. When might you want to use a slimline form factor?

_____

3. What advantages does ATX have over Micro ATX?

_____

4. Where is the CPU located on the BTX motherboard? Why?

_____

5. Is it possible to determine the form factor without opening the case?

_____

# LAB 4.2 MEASURE THE OUTPUT OF YOUR POWER SUPPLY

## OBJECTIVES

The goal of this lab is to use a multimeter to measure the voltages provided by a power supply. After completing this lab, you will be able to:

◢ Use a multimeter

◢ Measure voltage provided by a power supply

## MATERIALS REQUIRED

This lab requires the following:

◢ A computer designated for this lab

◢ A PC toolkit with antistatic ground strap

◢ A multimeter

◢ Access to the online content "Electricity and Multimeters," downloaded from *www.course.com*

◢ A workgroup of 2 to 4 students

## LAB PREPARATION

Before the lab begins, the instructor or lab assistant needs to do the following:

◢ Announce to students that before they come to lab, they should read the online content "Electricity and Multimeters." They might like to bring this content to class in printed form.

## ACTIVITY BACKGROUND

In most situations, if you suspect a problem with a power supply, you simply exchange it for a known good one. In a few instances, however, you might want to measure your power supply's output by using a multimeter.

A multimeter is an electrical tool that performs several tests. It can typically measure continuity, resistance, amperage, and voltage. It might have a digital or an analog meter that displays output. It also has two leads used to contact the component you're testing. The various models of multimeters work slightly differently. Follow the correct procedure for your specific multimeter. In this lab, you measure the electrical voltage supplied to the motherboard and floppy drive. Follow your computer lab's posted safety procedures when completing this lab.

**ESTIMATED COMPLETION TIME: 30 minutes**

 **Activity**

 **Caution**

Be sure you have your multimeter set to measure voltage, not current (amps). If the multimeter is set to measure current, you might damage the power supply, the motherboard, or both.

Using your multimeter, measure the power output to your system's motherboard and to the floppy drive, and then fill in the following charts that apply to your system. Note that the column headings "Red Lead" and "Black Lead" refer to the color of the probes.

Detailed directions for using a multimeter can be found in the online content "Electricity and Multimeters" supplied with this lab manual. Be very careful as you work inside the computer case with the power on. Don't touch any components other than those described in the steps.

The following steps outline the basic procedure for using a multimeter:

1. Remove the cover from the computer case.

2. Set the multimeter to measure voltage in a range of 20 volts, and set the AC/DC switch to DC. Insert the black probe into the meter's - jack and the red probe into the meter's + jack.

3. Turn on the multimeter, and then turn on the computer.

4. Measure each circuit by placing a red probe on the lead and a black probe on ground (see Figure 4-1).

5. Figure 4-2 shows the connections for an AT power supply. If you're using an AT power supply, refer to Table 4-1 for the purposes of these 12 leads.

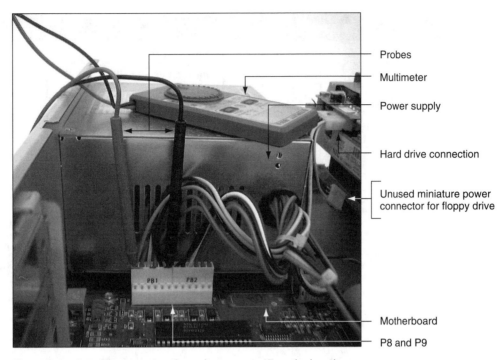

**Figure 4-1**   A multimeter measuring voltage on an AT motherboard

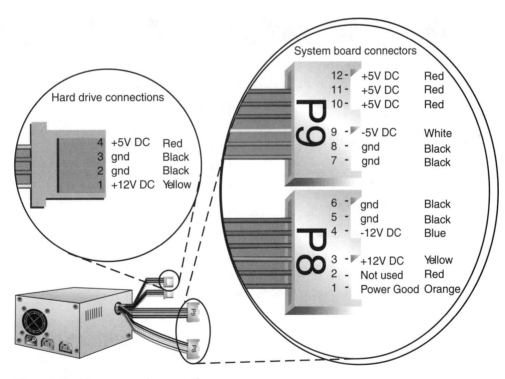

**Figure 4-2**   AT power supply connections

| Connection | Lead | Description | Acceptable range |
|---|---|---|---|
| P8 | 1 | Power good | |
| | 2 | Not used or +5 volts | +4.4 to +5.2 volts |
| | 3 | +12 volts | +10.8 to +13.2 volts |
| | 4 | -12 volts | -10.8 to -13.2 volts |
| | 5 | Black ground | |
| | 6 | Black ground | |
| P9 | 7 | Black ground | |
| | 8 | Black ground | |
| | 9 | -5 volts | -4.5 to -5.5 volts |
| | 10 | +5 volts | +4.5 to +5.5 volts |
| | 11 | +5 volts | +4.5 to +5.5 volts |
| | 12 | +5 volts | +4.5 to +5.5 volts |

**Table 4-1**    12 leads to the AT motherboard from the AT power supply

6. Complete the following chart for an AT motherboard. Write the voltage measurement for each connection in the Voltage measure column.

| Red lead | Black lead | Voltage measure |
|---|---|---|
| 3 | 5 | |
| 3 | 6 | |
| 3 | 7 | |
| 3 | 8 | |
| 4 | Ground | |
| 9 | Ground | |
| 10 | Ground | |
| 11 | Ground | |
| 12 | Ground | |

7. The 20-pin P1 power connector on an ATX motherboard is shown in Figure 4-3. Refer to Table 4-2 for the purpose of each pin.

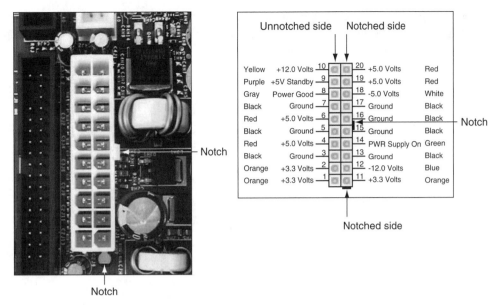

**Figure 4-3** Power connection on an ATX motherboard

| Unnotched side | | | Notched side | | |
|---|---|---|---|---|---|
| Lead | Description | Acceptable range (Volts = V) | Lead | Description | Acceptable range (Volts = V) |
| 1 | +3.3 volts | +3.1 to +3.5 V | 11 | +3.3 volts | +3.1 to +3.5 V |
| 2 | +3.3 volts | +3.1 to +3.5 V | 12 | -12 volts | -10.8 to -13.2 V |
| 3 | Black ground | | 13 | Black ground | |
| 4 | +5 volts | +4.5 to +5.5 V | 14 | Power supply on | |
| 5 | Black ground | | 15 | Black ground | |
| 6 | +5 volts | +4.5 to +5.5 V | 16 | Black ground | |
| 7 | Black ground | | 17 | Black ground | |
| 8 | Power good | | 18 | -5 volts | -4.5 to -5.5 V |
| 9 | +5 volts standby | +4.5 to +5.5 V | 19 | +5 volts | +4.5 to +5.5 V |
| 10 | +12 volts | +10.8 to +13.2 V | 20 | +5 volts | +4.5 to +5.5 V |

**Table 4-2** 20 leads to the ATX motherboard from the ATX power supply

8. Complete the following chart for an ATX motherboard:

| Red lead | Black lead | Voltage measure |
|---|---|---|
| 10 | 7 | |
| 10 | 5 | |
| 10 | 3 | |
| 10 | 17 | |
| 10 | 16 | |
| 10 | 15 | |

| Red lead | Black lead | Voltage measure |
|----------|-----------|-----------------|
| 10 | 13 | |
| 9 | Ground | |
| 6 | Ground | |
| 4 | Ground | |
| 2 | Ground | |
| 1 | Ground | |
| 20 | Ground | |
| 19 | Ground | |
| 18 | Ground | |
| 12 | Ground | |
| 11 | Ground | |

9. The BTX motherboard and power supply are designed so that the power supply monitors the range of voltages provided to the motherboard and halts the motherboard if voltages are inadequate. Therefore, measuring voltage for a BTX system isn't usually necessary. However, in a lab environment, if you have access only to a BTX system, you can fill in the same chart you did for the previous motherboards for practice. Figure 4-4 shows the 24-pin power connector for a BTX motherboard, and the purposes of the pins are listed in Table 4-3.

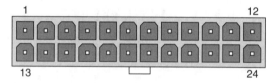

**Figure 4-4**    BTX 24-pin power connector on the motherboard

| Lead | Signal | Acceptable range (Volts = V) |
|------|--------|------------------------------|
| 1 | +3.3 volts | 3.2 to 3.5 V |
| 2 | +3.3 volts | 3.2 to 3.5 V |
| 3 | COM | |
| 4 | +5 volts | 4.75 to 5.25 V |
| 5 | COM | |
| 6 | +5 volts | 4.75 to 5.25 V |
| 7 | COM | |
| 8 | Power OK | Voltages are in acceptable range |
| 9 | +5 volts | Standby voltage always on |
| 10 | +12 volts | 11.4 to 12.6 V |
| 11 | +12 volts | 11.4 to 12.6 V |

**Table 4-3**    BTX 24-pin power connector

| Lead | Signal | Acceptable range (Volts = V) |
|------|--------|------------------------------|
| 12 | +3.3 volts | 3.2 to 3.5 V |
| 13 | +3.3 volts | 3.2 to 3.5 V |
| 14 | -12 volts | -10.8 to -13.2 V |
| 15 | COM | |
| 16 | PS ON | Power supply is on |
| 17 | COM | |
| 18 | COM | |
| 19 | COM | |
| 20 | NC | |
| 21 | +5 volts | 4.75 to 5.25 V |
| 22 | +5 volts | 4.75 to 5.25 V |
| 23 | +5 volts | 4.75 to 5.25 V |
| 24 | COM | |

**Table 4-3**  BTX 24-pin power connector (continued)

10. Complete the following chart for a BTX motherboard:

| Red lead | Black lead | Voltage measure |
|----------|-----------|-----------------|
| 1 | Ground | |
| 2 | Ground | |
| 4 | Ground | |
| 6 | Ground | |
| 9 | Ground | |
| 10 | Ground | |
| 11 | Ground | |
| 12 | Ground | |
| 13 | Ground | |
| 14 | Ground | |
| 21 | Ground | |
| 22 | Ground | |
| 23 | Ground | |

11. The power connectors for a drive power cord were shown in Figure 4-2. Complete the following chart for the floppy drive:

| Red lead | Black lead | Voltage measure |
|----------|-----------|-----------------|
| 1 | 3 | |
| 4 | 2 | |

12. Turn off the PC and replace the cover.

## REVIEW QUESTIONS

1. What is the electrical voltage from the house outlet to the power supply?

   _____

2. What voltages are supplied by the power supply on your system?

   _____

3. What model of multimeter are you using?

   _____

4. List the steps to set your multimeter to measure resistance:

   _____

   _____

   _____

5. Besides voltage and resistance, what else can your multimeter measure?

   _____

# LAB 4.3 REPLACE A POWER SUPPLY

## OBJECTIVES

The goal of this lab is to give you experience in replacing a power supply. After completing this lab, you will be able to:

▲ Identify the power supply

▲ Remove the power supply from the case

▲ Install a new power supply and new cabling

## MATERIALS REQUIRED

This lab requires the following:

▲ A PC designated for this lab

▲ A PC toolkit with antistatic ground strap

▲ A workgroup of 2 to 4 students

## LAB PREPARATION

Before the lab begins, the instructor or lab assistant needs to do the following:

▲ Verify that a computer designated for disassembly is available for each workgroup.

## ACTIVITY BACKGROUND

This lab tests your ability to remove and replace a power supply. Power supplies, as a rule, are considered field replaceable units (FRUs). To save time and avoid the danger of working inside power supplies, PC technicians don't repair power supplies; they replace them.

If you find that a power supply is faulty, replace it with a compatible power supply, and then send the original off to be reconditioned or recycled.

**ESTIMATED COMPLETION TIME: 30 minutes**

**Activity**

1. Turn the computer off and unplug the power cord.

2. Disconnect all peripherals and remove the case cover.

3. Examine the label on the power supply. What is the peak load rating of the power supply? A system requiring more power than the power supply provides can contribute to an early failure of the power supply.

   _____

4. What type of power connectors to the motherboard does the power supply provide? Possible answers are P8, P9, P1, or auxiliary power connectors, such as the four-pin auxiliary connector for the Pentium processor.

   _____

5. What is the form factor of the power supply?

   _____

6. Remove the cabling and the power supply. Usually the power supply is held in place by four screws in the back of the case. Some proprietary systems might use other methods of securing the power supply.

7. Examine the power supply designated by your instructor, or swap your power supply with another workgroup.

8. What is the form factor of this new power supply?

   _____

9. What is the power rating of this new power supply?

   _____

10. Will this new power supply satisfy the needs of your system?

    _____

11. Install the new power supply. *Ask your instructor to check your work before you close the case.* This check is crucial because some older power supplies must be connected correctly so that they aren't damaged when they're turned on.

12. Close the case, reattach the peripherals, and test the system.

## REVIEW QUESTIONS

1. How many connectors linked your original power supply to the motherboard?

   _____

2. How many watts of peak power could the original power supply provide?

   _____

3. Why is it important to be able to calculate the peak power required for all components? (You learn how to do this in Lab 4.5.)

_____

_____

4. What are two reasons that PC technicians don't usually repair a power supply?

_____

_____

5. What term is used to refer to components that are commonly replaced but not repaired?

_____

6. What is the most efficient way to determine whether your power supply is bad?

_____

## LAB 4.4 FIND DOCUMENTATION ON THE INTERNET

### OBJECTIVES

The goal of this lab is to show you how to locate documentation on the Internet so that you can determine how much power a component uses. After completing this lab, you will be able to:

◢ Find the manufacturer and model of a component

◢ Search for a product's documentation or manual

◢ Download and view a product manual

### MATERIALS REQUIRED

This lab requires the following:

◢ A computer designated for disassembly

◢ Internet access

◢ Adobe Acrobat Reader

◢ A PC toolkit with antistatic ground strap

◢ A workgroup of 2 or 3 students or individual students

### LAB PREPARATION

Before the lab begins, the instructor or lab assistant needs to do the following:

◢ Verify that a computer designated for disassembly is available for each student or workgroup.

◢ Verify that Internet access is available.

### ACTIVITY BACKGROUND

Often the power specifications for a component aren't labeled on the component itself but are included in the documentation. When working with PCs, it's common to encounter a component for which you have no documentation on hand. In this lab, you learn to find a component's make and model and, if possible, find online documentation for it.

**ESTIMATED COMPLETION TIME: 30 minutes**

 **Activity**

1. Open the PC's case and locate the component your instructor assigned to you (or select a component randomly). If you're in a workgroup, each person should be assigned a different component.

2. Examine the component until you find a sticker or stenciled label identifying its manufacturer and model number.

3. Take your notes to a computer that has Internet access.

> **Notes**
>
> The manufacturer and model aren't marked clearly on every component. If you're having trouble finding this information on a component, such as a video card, try researching based on the component's chipset. The information identifying the chip is usually stenciled on the chip. For communication devices, such as a modem or network card, look for an FCC number printed on the card and use it for your search. If you need to find out how much power an unlabeled component uses, sometimes it's helpful to consult the documentation for similar components.

4. If you already know the manufacturer's URL, go to that site and try to find documentation in these locations:

   ◢ The Support section of the site, as shown in Figure 4-5

   ◢ The Downloads section

   ◢ The Customer Service section

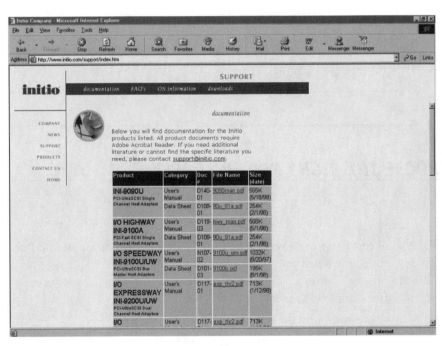

**Figure 4-5** Manuals are available for download from the Support section of a manufacturer's Web site

If you're not sure of the manufacturer's URL, try searching for the manufacturer or model number with a good search engine. In fact, searching by model number can often get you to the information in the fewest steps. For example, if SD11 is imprinted on your motherboard, searching on "SD11" can take you right to the documentation you need. Keep in mind that most documentation is in PDF format, which means you might need Adobe Acrobat Reader or a browser plug-in to view the documentation.

5. Print or save the documentation, and file it as a reference for when you need information about that component.

6. What CPU does your system use?

_____

7. Go to the manufacturer's Web site, and find and print the Web page showing the power consumption of your CPU expressed in watts.

## REVIEW QUESTIONS

1. How is a component commonly marked for identification?

_____

_____

2. In what sections of a Web site are manuals commonly found?

_____

3. In what format are manuals usually provided?

_____

4. What software do you need to view a PDF document?

_____

5. Why would a PC repair technician need to know the power consumption of a peripheral component?

_____

_____

# LAB 4.5 CHOOSE THE RIGHT POWER SUPPLY

## OBJECTIVES

The goal of this lab is to show you how to locate documentation on the Internet so that you can determine how much power a system as a whole uses. You can use this information to decide the wattage rating of the power supply you need to purchase for a new or upgraded system. After completing this lab, you will be able to:

▲ Calculate the total wattage requirements for a system

▲ Choose the correct type and rating of a power supply

## MATERIALS REQUIRED

This lab requires the following:

▲ A computer designated for disassembly

▲ _Optional_: Internet access

▲ A PC toolkit with antistatic ground strap

▲ A workgroup of 2 or 3 students or individual students

## LAB PREPARATION

Before the lab begins, the instructor or lab assistant needs to do the following:

▲ Verify that a computer designated for disassembly is available for each student or workgroup.

▲ *Optional*: Verify that Internet access is available.

## ACTIVITY BACKGROUND

When selecting a power supply for a computer system, you must take many factors into account. It's important to look at the system's components as a whole and how the system will be used. You might be tempted to simply purchase a power supply that has a very high wattage rating, but this choice isn't always the most economical. The typical efficiency rating of a power supply is 60% to 70%. Usually, this rating means 30% to 40% of the power is blowing out of the case as wasted heat. You want to keep waste to a minimum. On the other hand, if you intend to upgrade your system, buying an overrated power supply might be wise.

Running a system with an inadequate power supply can cause the power supply to wear out faster than normal. Also, an inadequate power supply can cause a system to reboot at odd times and exhibit other types of intermittent errors. It pays to install a correctly rated power supply for a system.

**ESTIMATED COMPLETION TIME: 45 minutes**

 **Activity**

1. The following chart shows the estimated power requirements for components inside a computer case. These estimates come from the Web site PC Power and Cooling, Inc. at *www.pcpowercooling.com/technology/power_usage*. Open the PC's case. Locate each component listed in the chart, and record how many components are present. Note that some entries will be zero.

| Component | Wattage requirement | How many present | Total wattage |
|---|---|---|---|
| AGP video card | 30 W–50 W | | |
| PCI Express video card | 50 W–100 W | | |
| Average PCI cards | 10 W | | |
| DVD or CD drives | 20 W–40 W | | |
| Hard drives | 10 W–30 W | | |
| Case fans and CPU fans | 3 W (each) | | |
| Motherboard | 50 W–100 W | 1 | |
| RAM modules | 8 W per 128 MB | | |
| Pentium 3 processor | 30 W | | |
| Pentium 4 processor | 70 W–100 W | | |
| AMD Athlon processor | 70 W–100 W | | |
| Total wattage: | | | |

2. To fill in the Total wattage column, first check the manufacturer's Web site for each component to find the exact wattage amounts. If this information isn't available, use the estimate provided or the midpoint of the estimate. Add the wattage for all components to come up with the total wattage. Record the system's total wattage in the last row of the chart.

3. Multiply the total wattage by 1.5. This multiplier takes into account the overhead the system and a power supply need so that the system can run at about 30% to 70% of its maximum capacity. What is your calculated total wattage, taking into account the required overhead?

4. Now look at the power supply, and make sure it has the number and type of connectors needed for your system. Figure 4-6 can help you identify connectors. Many power supplies don't provide the new serial ATA (SATA) connector shown in Figure 4-7. However, you can use an adapter power cord like the one in the figure to accommodate SATA hard drives.

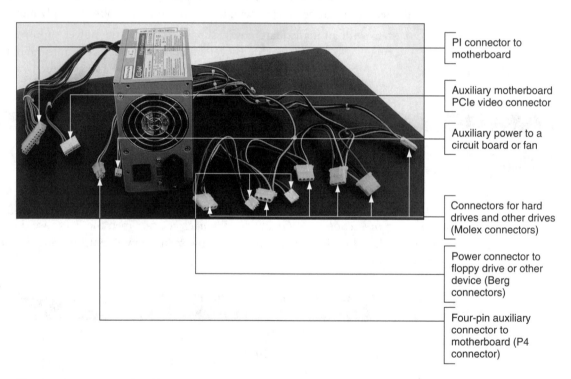

PI connector to motherboard

Auxiliary motherboard PCIe video connector

Auxiliary power to a circuit board or fan

Connectors for hard drives and other drives (Molex connectors)

Power connector to floppy drive or other device (Berg connectors)

Four-pin auxiliary connector to motherboard (P4 connector)

**Figure 4-6** Power supply with connectors labeled

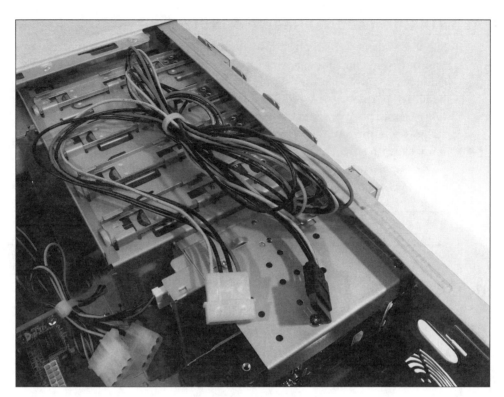

**Figure 4-7** Adapter power cord can be used for an SATA hard drive

5. Fill in the following chart to show the available power connectors and how many are needed for your system:

| Connector | Current quantity | Quantity needed |
| --- | --- | --- |
| EIDE drive connectors (Molex) | | |
| Floppy drive connectors (Berg) | | |
| SATA connectors | | |
| ATX connector (20 or 24 pins) | | |
| Auxiliary power connector (P4) | | |
| PCIe connector | | |

6. Look on the power supply label for the peak load rating in watts. What is this value?

_____

7. Based on what you have learned in this lab, is the power supply adequate for the job? Why or why not?

_____

_____

## CRITICAL THINKING (ADDITIONAL 30 MINUTES)

Suppose your power supply stops working, and you must buy a replacement. Search the Internet for a comparable power supply. The cost of power supplies varies widely. For example, a 400-watt power supply can cost from $15 to $75. The difference in quality can be judged partly by the weight of the power supply because, in general, the heavier it is, the more transistors it has and the more heavy-duty the transistors are, which make for a better power supply. Another factor to consider is noise level; quiet power supplies can be more expensive than noisy ones. Print two Web pages showing a high-end and a low-end power supply that would meet your system's needs. Which power supply would you recommend purchasing for your system, and why?

_____

_____

## REVIEW QUESTIONS

1. The estimated wattages for individual components were provided in the lab. How can you find the actual wattage for each component?

_____

2. What is the typical efficiency rating for a power supply?

_____

3. Are there any connectors your system needs that the power supply doesn't have? If so, what are they?

_____

4. Are there any connectors provided by the power supply that your system isn't using? If so, what are they?

_____

5. Why is it important to buy a power supply that's close to the requirements for your system instead of buying a higher wattage power supply?

_____

_____

# Processors and Chipsets

**Labs included in this chapter:**

- **Lab 5.1:** Remove and Replace a CPU
- **Lab 5.2:** Install Chipset Drivers
- **Lab 5.3:** Benchmark and Burn-in a CPU
- **Lab 5.4:** Compare CPU Benchmarks
- **Lab 5.5:** Choose a CPU Cooling Solution

## *LAB 5.1 REMOVE AND REPLACE A CPU*

### OBJECTIVES

The goal of this lab is to help you learn the correct procedure for removing and reinstalling a CPU. After completing this lab, you will be able to:

- Remove the CPU from your system
- Install a CPU into your system

### MATERIALS REQUIRED

This lab requires the following:

- Flathead screwdriver
- An antistatic ground strap
- Masking tape and marker or other method of labeling parts
- Another computer with an active Internet connection
- Alcohol wipe to remove thermal compound from the CPU

### LAB PREPARATION

Before the lab begins, the instructor or lab assistant needs to do the following:

- Verify that Windows starts with no errors.
- Verify that Internet access is available.

### ACTIVITY BACKGROUND

Removing and installing a CPU isn't difficult after you have done it a time or two. However, in today's systems, it's fairly rare for the CPU to be the source of a problem. Instead, a CPU replacement is usually done to increase the system's operating speed. In this lab, you remove the CPU and cooling unit and then replace both. Many times, when disassembling or assembling parts to a system, you won't have step-by-step directions but must discover how to do so. Removing the heat sink for the CPU is one of these tasks. Because of the overwhelming number of models on the market, you might need to refer to the manufacturer's documentation on how to remove the unit.

When you're considering upgrading the CPU in a system, be aware that if you upgrade the CPU, you might not realize the new processor's full potential if all the other components are obsolete.

**An important note on electrostatic discharge (ESD):** The CPU is an intricate and complicated array of wires and transistors. When you feel a static shock, you're feeling somewhere in the neighborhood of 3000 volts or more. The CPU can be damaged by a shock of 10 to 1000 volts, a discharge you would never feel. It's important to wear your ground strap while handling the CPU and memory, or you could easily damage components and never know that you have done so.

**ESTIMATED COMPLETION TIME: 45 minutes**

**Activity**

Because the CPU is a delicate component and is easily damaged, watch your instructor demonstrate how to remove and replace one before you attempt to do so. Answer the following questions about the demonstration:

1. What CPU did the instructor remove and replace?

   _Pentium I4_

2. What type of heat sink or cooler was attached to the CPU?

   _ThM P/N 74729_

3. What precautions did the instructor take to protect the CPU against ESD?

   _You touch computer to detect dk charge ESD_

4. How did the instructor protect the CPU while it was out of its socket?

   _You have special Estove plastic bag to protect from ESD_

Do the following to remove the CPU from your system:

1. Power down the computer.

2. Unplug any cords or cables connected to it.

3. Remove the case cover.

4. Examine the inside of the case and decide what you need to remove so that you have easy access to the CPU. Next, remove and carefully label any wires or other parts that need to be removed to expose the CPU. With some system cases, the power supply needs to be removed to be able to proceed.

5. Disconnect the power cord from the heat sink and fan (HSF) to the motherboard.

6. Depending on the CPU that's installed, there are different methods for removing and installing an HSF unit. Some units can be removed by hand simply by opening the levers that attach them to the socket. Other units require using the eraser end of a pencil to carefully dislodge the unit from the retaining mechanism hooks. Typically, the HSF is latched on both sides. After the pressure is removed from the main latch, it unlatches easily from the opposite side. Rather than use a screwdriver or other metal object to unlatch a stubborn latch, the preferred method is to use the eraser end of a pencil. If you slip while releasing the latch mechanism and the motherboard is damaged, it might be beyond repair. Also, some heat sinks are permanently glued to the processor and aren't intended to be removed. In this case, leave the heat sink attached. Decide how to proceed and, if appropriate, remove the heat sink and fan unit carefully.

7. After you have removed the HSF unit, you can proceed to actually removing the CPU. Handling the CPU must be done with your full attention. The tiny pins on the bottom of socket chips can be bent easily and need to be handled with care. Typically, CPUs and motherboards are shipped with antistatic foam that's an ideal surface to set CPU pins into for protection. If you don't have this shipping container, when you remove the CPU, lay it bottom-side up so that the pins aren't sitting on your work surface. Find the CPU shipping container or plan for a way to store the CPU safely.

8. You'll see a metal bar right next to the socket of the base of the CPU. This metal bar is the lever for the zero insertion force (ZIF) socket. Pull the lever out slightly and then up 90 degrees to release the pins on the underside of the CPU. In Figure 5-1, you can see the lever about to be released from an empty LGA775 socket.

**Figure 5-1**   Open the socket lever

9. Carefully grasp the sides of the CPU and pull up gently to remove it from the socket.

10. Using an alcohol wipe, carefully remove any thermal grease (also called thermal compound) that's smeared on the top of the CPU. You can now safely store the CPU.

Now you're ready to install the new CPU or, for this lab, replace the CPU. If you're actually upgrading to a new CPU, you need to make several checks before installing the new CPU into a motherboard. You need to verify that the socket type, clock speed, and multiplier match the new CPU.

In this lab, you're replacing the existing CPU; however, go through the following steps to practice as though you were installing a new upgraded CPU:

1. Remember that the CPU is a delicate piece of equipment. The pins on the processor can be bent easily, and if the heat sink isn't connected properly, you run the risk of allowing the CPU to overheat. Inspect the new CPU to verify that it has no bent pins. If you suspect the CPU has been damaged or if the pins are bent, you might need to replace the CPU.

2. Visually inspect the socket on the motherboard for any indication as to what type of socket it is. Usually it's clearly marked as to the type. Double-check that the CPU was manufactured for the type of socket on the motherboard. What is the CPU socket this motherboard is using?

_____

3. Using the manual for the CPU, determine the correct front-side bus (FSB) speed, multiplier, and voltage for the CPU. If you don't have the manual, visit the manufacturer's Web site. Although some motherboards configure this information automatically, as a technician you need to be able to determine that it was done correctly. Your CPU is

most likely manufactured by Intel (*www.intel.com*) or AMD (*www.amd.com*). Go to the manufacturer's Web site and fill in these blanks:

◢ FSB speed:

_____

◢ Multiplier:

_____

◢ Voltage:

_____

4. You might need to set the FSB speed, multiplier, and voltage on the motherboard. Again, read the manufacturer's documentation if you have it. If you don't have the documentation, visit the manufacturer's Web site and download it. Some motherboards require you to set this information by using DIP switches or jumpers, but others allow you to do so in CMOS setup. Still others detect the CPU and configure everything for you automatically. How does this motherboard recognize and configure the CPU?

_____

_____

5. Before you install the CPU in the socket, practice raising and lowering the socket lever so that you can feel how much force is necessary to close the lever.

6. Now you're ready to install the CPU. Verify that the power cable has been removed from the machine. Unlatch the ZIF lever and bring it to the up position. It should be pointing directly upward. The pins on the CPU are keyed to line up with the grid array on the socket. Gently align the CPU with the socket (see Figure 5-2) and allow it to fall into place.

**Figure 5-2** Align the CPU over the socket

7. Carefully replace the socket lever so that force is applied to the top of the CPU and the CPU is installed securely in the socket. You need to place a little more pressure on the lever than you did when no CPU was present, but don't force it! If you have to force it, most likely the CPU isn't oriented in the socket correctly.

8. Now you're ready to install the heat sink. First, examine the underside of the heat sink for any foreign matter. It's common for a new heat sink to come with a thermal pad that's covered by a protective film of plastic. If this plastic isn't removed, you run the risk of damaging your CPU. If there's no thermal pad, put on latex gloves and gently apply a thin layer of thermal grease to the portion of the heat sink that will come into contact with the CPU. Be careful not to apply thermal grease so that it later comes in contact with the edges of the processor or the socket. You don't want grease to get down into the CPU socket. Figure 5-3 shows just about the right amount of thermal grease applied.

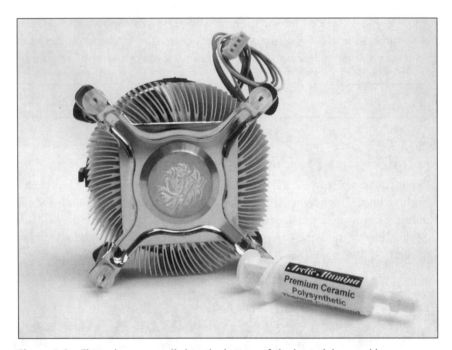

**Figure 5-3** Thermal grease applied to the bottom of the heat sink assembly

9. Carefully align the bottom of the heat sink with the socket and attach the heat sink. Plug the heat sink fan's power cord into the motherboard.

10. Have your instructor inspect your work to make sure the heat sink is attached correctly. (Booting up a system with an incorrectly attached heat sink can cause damage to the processor because it will overheat.)

11. Boot your machine and test for errors.

## REVIEW QUESTIONS

1. Why shouldn't you use a screwdriver to remove a heat sink?

_____

_____

2. What is the minimum voltage of an electrostatic discharge (ESD) that you can feel?

*10 volts*

3. What is the voltage range in which ESD can affect components?

*10 — 1000 volts*

4. Why is it important to double-check the bottom of the heat sink before attaching it to the CPU socket?

*had to be compound. otherwise no work.*

# LAB 5.2 INSTALL CHIPSET DRIVERS

## OBJECTIVES

The goal of this lab is to learn to install the correct chipset drivers for your motherboard. After completing this lab, you will be able to:

◢ Locate the chipset drivers for your motherboard

◢ Install the chipset drivers

## MATERIALS REQUIRED

This lab requires the following:

◢ Internet access

◢ A flash drive

## LAB PREPARATION

Before the lab begins, the instructor or lab assistant needs to do the following:

◢ Verify that Internet access is available.

## ACTIVITY BACKGROUND

Most of the time, when you install the operating system, the chipset drivers are installed automatically. However, if your motherboard is very new, drivers for your chipset might not be included with the operating system you have chosen. Also, you should know how to do install these drivers because sometimes doing so can fix problems on a system. Typically, chipset drivers for your motherboard come on a CD with the purchase of that motherboard. However, finding the original CD that came with the motherboard can be difficult. This lab assumes that the original CD for the motherboard is unavailable. If it's available, however, insert that CD into the CD-ROM drive and use the drivers on the CD.

If the motherboard becomes unstable, one thing you can do is update the chipset drivers. However, if the system is giving you problems, most likely it can't connect to a network to download drivers directly. Therefore, it's a good idea to know how to download drivers to one computer to use them on another computer. In this lab, you download the drivers and copy them to a flash drive (also called a USB thumb drive or jump drive) or burn them to a CD on one computer to be used on another computer.

**Activity**

1. First, you must identify your motherboard. To do that, open the computer case and look on the motherboard for the stenciled or silkscreened label printed somewhere on the board, most likely in the middle. If you need help finding this label, check out the first few steps of Lab 6.3 and Figure 6-2. What is the brand and model of your motherboard?

_____

2. The next step is to find out what chipset this motherboard uses. You can search the documentation that came with the motherboard, or you can find the information on the motherboard manufacturer's Web site. Table 5-1 lists the URLs for major motherboard manufacturers.

   ▲ What is the motherboard manufacturer's Web site?

   _____

   ▲ What chipset does this motherboard use?

   _____

| Manufacturer | URL |
| --- | --- |
| Motherboards.com | www.motherboards.com |
| American Megatrends, Inc. | www.megatrends.com |
| ASUS | www.asus.com |
| Dell | www.dell.com |
| Diamond Multimedia | www.diamondmm.com |
| First International Computer, Inc. | www.fica.com |
| Gateway | www.gateway.com |
| Giga-Byte Technology Co., Ltd. | www.giga-byte.com |
| IBM | www.ibm.com |
| Intel Corporation | www.intel.com |
| Supermicro Computer, Inc. | www.supermicro.com |
| Tyan Computer Corporation | www.tyan.com |

**Table 5-1**  URLs for major motherboard manufacturers

3. Now you need to find the chipset drivers for this motherboard on the Internet. First, look for the drivers on the motherboard manufacturer's Web site. If you can't find the drivers there, most chipsets are made by Intel, NVidia, VIA, or SIS. Try going to the chipset manufacturer's Web site:

   ▲ _www.intel.com_

   ▲ _www.nvidia.com_

   ▲ _www.via.com.tw_

   ▲ _www.sis.com_

4. Using the Service and Support or Downloads section on the Web site, download the chipset drivers. Save this file to the desktop of the computer you're not repairing.

5. Copy the drivers to a USB thumb drive, and transport the driver to the computer you're working on. Run the installation package you downloaded to install the driver.

## REVIEW QUESTIONS

1. Why would you need to install chipset drivers?

_____

_____

2. If the motherboard manufacturer doesn't have the chipset drivers available on its Web site, where else can you download the drivers?

_____

_____

3. What is the purpose of copying drivers to a thumb drive?

_____

_____

# LAB 5.3 BENCHMARK AND BURN-IN A CPU

## OBJECTIVES

The goal of this lab is to learn how to compare your CPU's performance in relation to other processors, to make sure the CPU is stable, and to ensure that the heat sink and fan are working correctly. After completing this lab, you will be able to:

- Benchmark a CPU
- Burn-in a CPU
- Monitor CPU temperature

## MATERIALS REQUIRED

This lab requires the following:

- An active Internet connection
- SiSoftware Sandra (installed in Lab 1.3)
- A Web browser
- A computer running Windows 2000/XP or Windows 9x

## LAB PREPARATION

Before the lab begins, the instructor or lab assistant needs to do the following:

- Verify that Windows starts with no errors and the Internet connection is working.
- Verify that SiSoftware Sandra is installed (see Lab 1.3).

## ACTIVITY BACKGROUND

Although today's CPUs are very reliable and fast, after completing a system build, it's a good idea to test the CPU and be sure everything is working correctly. A good technician always tests a system for stability before sending it out to the owner. Although a system might boot without any errors, an unstable machine usually shows problems when a load has been placed on the system. Any time you're running a stress test, it's crucial to monitor the temperature of the CPU so that you don't damage it if there's a problem. SiSoftware Sandra (installed in Lab 1.3) allows both burn-in testing and temperature monitoring.

> **ESTIMATED COMPLETION TIME: 60 minutes to 24 hours**

 **Activity**

It's best to devote 24 hours to burning in a CPU for verification that it's truly stable. In a lab environment, however, this amount of time might not always be practical. Therefore, this lab allows for one hour of testing. Follow these steps:

1. First, you'll run a short test to make sure the CPU is not overheating. Start SiSoftware Sandra. Under Wizard Modules, click the **Burn-in Wizard** link to run this module. On the opening screen, click the **forward arrow**.

2. Under the Benchmarking Modules menu, click to clear all check boxes except **CPU Arithmetic Benchmark** and **CPU Multi-Media Benchmark.** Click the **forward arrow**.

3. On the Count Down page, leave all the options at their default settings, and then click the **forward arrow.** How many times will the test run?

_____

4. On the Processor page, leave the Minimum Utilization setting at 100%, and then click the **forward arrow.**

5. On the Maximum Temperature page, enter the maximum temperature that the CPU manufacturer recommends for the processor you're using. If you don't know this temperature, leave the entry blank. Click the **forward arrow.**

6. On the Minimum Fan Speed page, leave all entries blank, and then click the **forward arrow.**

7. On the Burn, Baby, Burn! page, click the check mark to begin the burn-in test. Figure 5-4 shows the burn test in progress.

8. When the test has finished, verify that the CPU's temperature has stayed within the correct range. Are there any unusual results from this test?

_____

_____

9. If time permits, run SiSoftware Sandra again, but on the Count Down page, click to enable the **Run Continuously (Background Use)** check box. This time, when the program runs, it won't stop running until you tell it to. This way, you can allow the program to run overnight, and then come back the next day to check for errors. If there are no errors, you can assume that the system is stable.

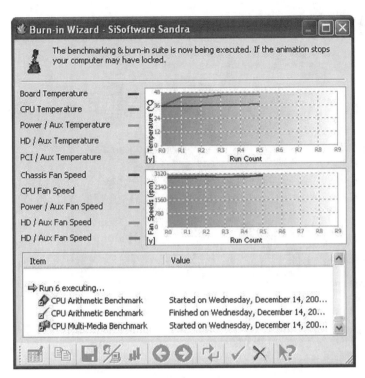

**Figure 5-4** SiSoftware Sandra Burn-in Wizard showing a burn test in progress

After you're sure the system is stable, you can see how the system compares to other systems with similar configurations. Follow these steps:

1. Open SiSoftware Sandra. Under Wizard Modules, click **Combined Performance Index Wizard** to run this module.

2. Click the green check mark to start the benchmark. The system will appear to hang while the test is running. To show you that the test is still running, an animated computer at the top-right corner continues to move.

3. When the test is complete, your computer is then compared to other systems using the coverage matrix. The red color in the graphic represents your system, and the blue color represents the reference system. Figure 5-5 shows the results for one computer. Looking at this figure, you can deduce that this computer is strong on memory performance but weakest on network performance. Based on the results of your test, which area is strongest and which area is weakest on your system?

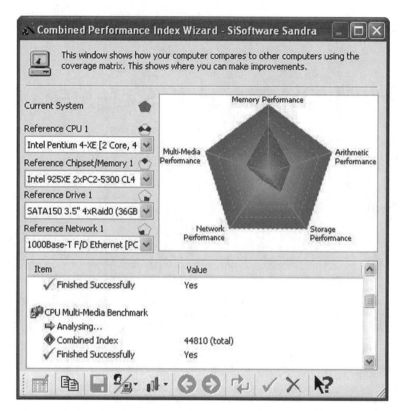

**Figure 5-5** Results of the Combined Performance Index Wizard in SiSoftware Sandra

## CHALLENGE ACTIVITY (ADDITIONAL 30 MINUTES)

Sometimes updating chipset drivers on a motherboard can improve a system's overall performance. After you have used the Combined Performance Index Wizard to test performance, follow the directions in Lab 5.2 to download and install updated chipset drivers. Then retest the performance and note any improvements.

## REVIEW QUESTIONS

1. Why do you place the system under a load to test for errors?

_____

_____

2. If the performance of your CPU is much lower than that of the reference comparables, how can you improve your CPU's performance?

_____

_____

3. Using the Burn-in Wizard, if you decide to run the test 10 times, can you know for certain how long it will take? Why or why not?

_____

_____

5

4. When using the Burn-in Wizard, if the animation hangs while the test is being performed, what does it probably mean?

_____

_____

# LAB 5.4 COMPARE CPU BENCHMARKS

## OBJECTIVES

The goal of this lab is to allow you to compare different CPU choices and determine which is best for a given budget. After completing this lab, you will be able to:

▲ Find CPU benchmarks

▲ Compare CPU benchmarks

▲ Compare CPU performance and price

## MATERIALS REQUIRED

This lab requires the following:

▲ An active Internet connection

▲ A Web browser

## LAB PREPARATION

Before the lab begins, the instructor or lab assistant needs to do the following:

▲ Verify that Windows starts with no errors and the Internet connection is working.

▲ Verify each Web site to see whether the content has changed.

## ACTIVITY BACKGROUND

When purchasing or building a computer system, you need to make many choices. The CPU is one of the most critical components in your system and has a major impact on the machine's overall performance. The CPU you select must match the motherboard you plan to use. If you have already selected the motherboard or you're buying a CPU to install in an existing motherboard, you're limited in selecting a CPU that matches the motherboard. A motherboard has a socket the CPU must fit into and supports only certain ranges of CPU speed and features. However, if you haven't yet selected a motherboard, you can select the CPU first and then choose a motherboard that supports this CPU. In this lab, you begin your purchasing decisions by first selecting the CPU.

It's important to be able to choose the fastest processor your budget allows without having to give up other features. CPU manufacturers used to label their products with the chip speed, so it was easy to compare a 400 MHz AMD with a 400 MHz Intel, for example. However, as the technologies used by competing manufacturers changed, the public relations (PR) system emerged. The AMD 1800+ was clocked at 1533 MHz, but benchmarks showed it to be a comparable product to Intel's 1800 MHz chip, hence the name 1800+. Today's market is full of many different naming conventions, with names such as Pentium, Athlon, Xeon, Opteron, Celeron, and Duron. To be able to make an informed decision on which CPU to purchase, you must be able to compare CPU benchmarks.

**ESTIMATED COMPLETION TIME: 30 minutes**

## Activity

Given a budget of $300 for a CPU, you'll compare different choices and decide on the best choice for a given situation. The first step is to see which CPUs fall into this specified price range. Follow these steps:

1. Use your Web browser to navigate to **www.pricewatch.com**. Under the heading Computer Parts, click **CPUs**. To make a valid comparison, you must look at several models. From this list of CPUs, make note of which four are closest to $300 without going over that limit:

_____

_____

2. Now click the name of each CPU you have selected. In the following chart, make note of the socket type and speed (in GHz or MHz) of each. For example, in the entry "Intel Pentium P4 660 3.6 GHz 1 MB Processor 800 MHz FSB Cache Socket LGA775 3600 MHz with 1 year warranty," the speed is 3.6 GHz and the socket type is LGA775.

| CPU | Speed | Socket | Price |
|-----|-------|--------|-------|
|     |       |        |       |
|     |       |        |       |
|     |       |        |       |
|     |       |        |       |

When choosing a benchmark for a CPU, it's important to consider the system's primary use. Different CPUs have different strengths and weaknesses, and there are several tests you can choose from to look at performance.

3. Go to Tom's Hardware Guide (THG) Web site at **www.tomshardware.com**. On the right side of the page, under the heading CPU Charts, click **Interactive CPU Charts**.

4. Examine the resulting page. When the chart is displayed, it lists CPUs from top to bottom, with the best performing models at the top of the page for the given benchmark test. Intel CPUs are listed in blue, and AMD CPUs are listed in green. The models chosen in the drop-down lists are in red. If you click a CPU in the list, an information box about the CPU is displayed.

5. From the drop-down lists, under the heading "Choose first model," click the first CPU on your list. Under the heading "Choose second model," click the second one on your list. Now you're ready to see how these two models compare in performance.

6. Assuming you're building a computer for gaming purposes, the tests that are going to interest you most are the game-related tests. This will give you the best possible comparison for how you'll be using the system. In the Choose benchmark drop-down list, click **Doom III**, and then click **Go**. Wait until the screen refreshes, which might take a few minutes.

7. The chart changes to reflect the scores for the benchmark test you selected. Note the red benchmarks in the chart. They should now be the ones for the first and second CPUs you chose earlier. What are the scores for these CPUs?

   ◢ CPU 1: _____

   ◢ CPU 2: _____

8. Look at the price for CPU 1 from the previous chart, and then look at the price for CPU 2. Based on the performance in this test, which one is a better buy?

   _____

9. You should make this type of comparison for each processor you're considering. Also, it's important to choose a benchmark that's closest to the actual type of work you'll be performing on the system. Using what you've learned in the preceding steps, make comparisons for the Doom III and Quake III benchmarks for the four CPUs you're considering. Complete the following chart with the information from the comparison charts and the two benchmark tests:

| CPU | Doom III benchmark | Quake III benchmark | Price |
|-----|--------------------|--------------------|-------|
|     |                    |                    |       |
|     |                    |                    |       |
|     |                    |                    |       |
|     |                    |                    |       |

After you have compared the CPUs based on performance and price, you should be able to choose a winner. Sometimes you must make trade-offs to stay within your budget range. Unfortunately, making trade-offs isn't an exact science and is a source of major debate among enthusiasts.

## CHALLENGE ACTIVITY (ADDITIONAL 20 MINUTES)

In this lab, you used Tom's Hardware Guide (THG) Web site (*www.tomshardware.com*), a long-standing and reliable Web site, to find reviews and comparisons of computer components. However, many other similar sites exist on the Web. Using a good search engine, locate three more Web sites that offer technical reviews of computer parts. Complete the following chart:

| Web site | Products reviewed |
|----------|-------------------|
|          |                   |
|          |                   |
|          |                   |

## REVIEW QUESTIONS

1. How would the results change if you were using the computer system for encoding DivX 5.2 home movies instead of for gaming? (Note that DivX 5.2 is the benchmark initially displayed in the chart.)

_____

_____

2. Why shouldn't a technician simply put the lowest price CPU into a machine to save costs?

_____

_____

3. What is the purpose of choosing four models of CPUs for comparison?

_____

_____

4. It seems that for the best performance, you could simply look at the chart and choose the fastest model in each category. Why isn't this method a good way to choose a CPU?

_____

_____

_____

5. How would you predict that the benchmark test results would change if you were given only a $100 budget to work with?

_____

_____

# LAB 5.5 CHOOSE A CPU COOLING SOLUTION

## OBJECTIVES

Years ago, you could run your 25 MHz computer all day long without a heat sink. Not so today. Because users continue to demand more speed from their CPUs and many hobbyists overclock their CPUs, their systems must constantly battle high temperatures. The most common solution for cooling a CPU is an air-cooled solution: a heat sink and fan (HSF). Although water cooling is effective and extremely quiet, it's still not a mature enough technology to be considered safe for a system's internals. The heat sink is a metal unit that conducts heat away from the CPU and dissipates that heat into the air, typically with a fan forcing air over the top. Some fans are variable-speed fans that adjust their speeds according to the CPU's temperature. Varying the fan speed must be supported by the motherboard chipset.

If you purchase a retail CPU, odds are the HSF will be included. However, most system builders choose to purchase an original equipment manufacturer (OEM) CPU to save money, so they must purchase the HSF separately. Another reason to purchase the HSF separately is that the HSF that comes with the CPU isn't adequate if the builder intends to overclock the CPU. After completing this lab, you will be able to:

◢ Choose a heat sink and fan

## MATERIALS REQUIRED

This lab requires the following:

◢ An active Internet connection

## LAB PREPARATION

Before the lab begins, the instructor or lab assistant needs to do the following:

◢ Verify that Windows starts with no errors and the Internet connection is working.

## ACTIVITY BACKGROUND

There are several things to look for when choosing an HSF. First and foremost, the unit must fit the CPU and socket you're using. Next, the unit must provide adequate cooling at an acceptable noise level. Finally, the preferred unit should be easy to mount. In a perfect world, you would be able to test all these cooling units and make an educated decision based on performance, but it's not practical in a lab environment. The most common model of CPU that's purchased OEM is the AMD Athlon series; therefore, you'll look at the tests Tom's Hardware has run on 55 coolers and make a decision based on those results. AMD's weight limit for the HSF is 300 grams, which is a good idea because an HSF that's too heavy can damage the CPU, CPU socket, or motherboard components.

**ESTIMATED COMPLETION TIME: 45 minutes**

 **Activity**

It's essential to choose an HSF made specifically for the processor you're using. Just because a unit fits doesn't mean it will cool the CPU sufficiently. Follow these steps:

1. Go to the Tom's Hardware Guide (THG) Web site at **www.tomshardware.com**, where you need to search the site for articles about coolers. To do that, in the SITE SEARCH box on the right side of the home page, click **Tom's Hardware** in the drop-down list and type **Coolers** in the text box. Click **Search** to search the site for articles about coolers.

2. Look for the article "Cool Stuff: How THG Tests Coolers." After reading it, answer these questions:

   ◢ How did THG measure the performance level of coolers?

   _____

   _____

   ◢ How did THG test the noise level of coolers?

   _____

   _____

◢ Why is it important to know the weight of a cooler when comparing coolers?

_____

_____

◢ What type of guarantee should you look for when comparing coolers?

_____

_____

◢ What are some factors to consider about the ease of installation and size of coolers?

_____

_____

_____

3. Now look for the article "A Cool Bunch: How To Put a Lid on the Die Temperature of Your Athlon." After reading it, answer these questions:

◢ Click page 59 of the article and look at the performance ratings of the heat sinks that were tested. What are the top three units in keeping the lowest temperature?

_____

_____

_____

◢ Click page 58 of the article. What are the top three units in terms of noise? They will be the units with the lowest decibel (dB(A)) rating.

_____

_____

_____

◢ Click page 60 of the article. One cooler listed on this page is the Alpha PAL8045, which has a good blend of performance and noise level. What is its weight in grams?

_____

## CHALLENGE ACTIVITY (ADDITIONAL 20 MINUTES)

Based on what you've learned in this lab, do the following to select a cooler for an AMD processor you plan to use in a computer for gaming:

1. Using the AMD Web site (*www.amd.com*), select a processor for gaming, and then answer these questions:

◢ Which processor did you select?

_____

◢ Describe the processor:

_____

_____

◢ Why did you select this processor?

_____

_____

2. Using other Web sites that sell or manufacturer coolers, select the best cooler for the processor. Answer these questions:

◢ What is the cooler manufacturer and model?

_____

_____

◢ Why did you select this cooler?

_____

_____

_____

## REVIEW QUESTIONS

1. List five factors mentioned in this lab that you should consider when selecting a cooler:

_____

_____

2. If you were in an office building and needed a very quiet system, which of the coolers tested would be a good choice?

_____

_____

3. If you have a CPU that gets very hot and will be used in a noisy industrial building, what effect would these conditions have on your choice of coolers? Would you choose a different cooler than the one you selected in Question 2? Which cooler would you choose?

_____

_____

4. When you purchase a boxed CPU with a cooler, the cooler is usually one with a blend of cooling performance and low noise level. Which of the units that you see in the charts would be a good unit for the manufacturer to include?

_____

_____

5. Can you see any reason that AMD wouldn't recommend the Alpha PAL8045 cooler?

_____

# CHAPTER 6

# Motherboards

**Labs included in this chapter:**

- **Lab 6.1:** Examine and Adjust CMOS Settings
- **Lab 6.2:** Use a Hardware Information Utility
- **Lab 6.3:** Identify a Motherboard and Find Documentation on the Internet
- **Lab 6.4:** Identify Motherboard Components and Form Factors
- **Lab 6.5:** Remove and Replace a Motherboard
- **Lab 6.6:** Flash BIOS

# LAB 6.1 EXAMINE AND ADJUST CMOS SETTINGS

## OBJECTIVES

The goal of this lab is to help you explore and modify CMOS settings. After completing this lab, you will be able to:

◢ Enter the CMOS setup utility

◢ Navigate the CMOS setup utility

◢ Examine some setup options

◢ Save changes to setup options

## MATERIALS REQUIRED

This lab requires the following:

◢ A computer designated for this lab

◢ SiSoftware Sandra, installed in Lab 1.3

## LAB PREPARATION

Before the lab begins, the instructor or lab assistant needs to do the following:

◢ Verify that Windows starts with no errors.

◢ Verify that SiSoftware Sandra has been installed (see Lab 1.3).

## ACTIVITY BACKGROUND

When a system is powered up, the startup process is managed by a set of instructions called the BIOS. The BIOS, in turn, relies on a set of configuration information stored in CMOS that's refreshed continuously by battery power when the system is off. You can access and modify CMOS setup information via the CMOS setup utility in the BIOS. In this lab, you examine the CMOS setup utility, make some changes, and observe the effects of your changes.

Setup utilities vary slightly in appearance and function, depending on the manufacturer and version. The steps in this lab are based on the CMOS setup program for Award BIOS, which is a common BIOS. You might have to perform different steps to access and use the CMOS utility on your computer.

For most computers today, you seldom need to make changes in CMOS setup except to set the date and time for a new system or perhaps to change the boot sequence. The exception is if you're attempting to overclock a system, which is done by changing the default frequencies of the processor and/or motherboard. Overclocking isn't a recommended best practice, however, because of problems with overheating and possibly causing the system to become unstable.

**ESTIMATED COMPLETION TIME: 30 minutes**

 **Activity**

Before you access the BIOS on your computer, you need to record the exact date and time indicated by your computer's internal clock. (You use this information later to confirm that you have indeed changed some CMOS settings.) After you record the date and time, you use the Sandra utility (installed in Lab 1.3) to determine which version of BIOS is installed on your computer. Follow these steps:

1. In Windows, double-click the clock on the taskbar, and record the time and date:

 

2. Close the Date and Time Properties dialog box.

3. Start Sandra, and then double-click the **CPU & BIOS Information** icon (under the Information Modules heading in Windows XP).

4. Click **System BIOS** in the Device drop-down list.

5. Record the manufacturer and version information for your BIOS:

 

6. Close Sandra.

Now that you know what BIOS your computer runs, you can determine how to enter the setup utility. In general, to start the setup utility, you need to press a key or key combination as the computer is booting. Some CMOS utilities are password protected with a supervisor password and a user password (also called a power-on password). The supervisor password allows full access to CMOS setup, and the user password allows you to view CMOS setup screens, but you won't be able to change any settings or sometimes you can change only certain settings. In addition, if the user password is also set to be a power-on password and you don't know this password, you won't be able to boot the system. When you attempt to access CMOS setup, if password protection has been enabled, you're asked for a password, and you must enter a valid password to continue.

**Notes**

CMOS setup supervisor, user, and power-on passwords are different from the Windows password required to log on to Windows. Also, if you're responsible for a computer and have forgotten the supervisor password, you can remove a jumper on the motherboard to return all CMOS settings to their default values, which erases any CMOS passwords. Lab 6.5 covers how to find this jumper.

To learn more about entering the setup utility on your computer, follow these steps:

1. Using the information you recorded previously in Step 5, consult Table 6-1 to find out how to enter your system's setup utility. (Alternatively, when you first turn on your PC, look for a message on your screen, which might read something like "Press F2 to access setup.")

| BIOS | Method for entering CMOS setup utility |
| --- | --- |
| AMI BIOS | Boot the computer, and then press the Delete key. |
| Award BIOS | Boot the computer, and then press the Delete key. |
| Older Phoenix BIOS | Boot the computer, and then press the Ctrl+Alt+Esc or Ctrl+Alt+S key combination. |
| Newer Phoenix BIOS | Boot the computer, and then press the F2 or F1 key. |
| Dell Computers with Phoenix BIOS | Boot the computer, and then press the Ctrl+Alt+Enter key combination. |
| Some older Compaq computers, such as Deskpro 286 or 386 | Place the diagnostics disk in the drive, reboot the system, and choose Computer Setup from the menu. |
| Some newer Compaq computers, such as Prolinea, Deskpro, DeskproXL, Deskpro LE, or Presario | Boot the computer, wait for two beeps, and when the cursor is in the upper-right corner of the screen, press the F10 key. |
| All other older computers | Use the setup program on the floppy disk that came with the PC. If the floppy disk is lost, contact the motherboard manufacturer to get a replacement. |

**Table 6-1**   Methods for entering CMOS setup utilities by BIOS

> **Notes**
>
> For Compaq computers, the CMOS setup program is stored on the hard drive in a small, non-DOS partition of about 3 MB. If this partition becomes corrupted or the computer is an older model, you must run setup from a diagnostic disk. If you can't run setup by pressing F10 at startup, a damaged partition or virus is likely taking up space in conventional memory.

Now you're ready to enter the CMOS setup utility included in your BIOS. Follow these steps:

1. If a floppy disk is necessary to enter the CMOS setup utility, insert it now.

2. Restart the computer.

3. When the system restarts, enter the setup utility using the correct method for your computer.

4. Notice that the CMOS utility groups settings by function. For example, all the power management features are grouped together in a Power Management section.

5. The main screen usually has a Help section that describes how to make selections and exit the utility. Typically, you can use the arrow keys or Tab key to highlight options. After you have highlighted your selection, usually you need to press Enter, Page Down, or the spacebar. The main screen might display a short summary of the highlighted category. Look for and select a category called something like **Standard CMOS Setup**.

6. In the Standard CMOS Setup screen, you should see some or all of the following settings. List the current setting for each of the following:

   ◢ Date: _____

   ◢ Time: _____

   ◢ For IDE hard drives, a table listing drive size, mode of operation, and cylinder, head, and sector information: _____

   ◢ Floppy drive setup information, including drive letter and type: _____

   ◢ Halt on error setup (the type of error that halts the boot process): _____

   ◢ Memory summary (summary of system memory divisions): _____

   ◢ Boot sequence (drives the BIOS searches for an OS): _____

7. Exit the Standard CMOS setup screen and return to the main page. Select a section called something like **Chipset Features Setup**.

8. Record settings for the following as well as any other settings in this section:

   ◢ RAM setup options: _____
   _____

◢ AGP setup options:

_____

_____

◢ CPU-specific setup options:

*Cpu speed*

_____

◢ Settings for serial and parallel ports:

*Serial port 1, 2*

*Parallel port. 278h.*

◢ Provisions for enabling and disabling onboard drive controllers and other embedded devices:

*Speaker.*

_____

_____

_____

9. Exit to the CMOS setup main screen. Explore the menus and submenus of the CMOS setup utility and answer these questions:

> **Notes**
>
> Most of the CMOS settings never need changing, so understanding every setting isn't necessary.

◢ Does CMOS setup offer the option to set a supervisor password? If so, what's the name of the screen where the password is set?

*Yes*          *not enabled.*

_____

◢ Does CMOS setup offer the option to set a user password? Is so, what options can affect the way users can access and use CMOS setup?

*no*

_____

_____

10. Exit to the CMOS setup main screen. You might see options for loading CMOS defaults (which restore factory settings and can be helpful in troubleshooting) as well as options for exiting with or without saving changes. There might be an option to set user and supervisor passwords as well as a utility to detect IDE hard disk drives automatically.

Now that you're familiar with the way the CMOS setup utility works, you can change the date and time settings. Then you reboot the computer, confirm that the changes are reflected in the operating system, and return the CMOS date and time to the correct settings. Follow these steps:

1. Return to the Standard CMOS setup screen.

2. Highlight the time field(s) and set the time ahead one hour.

3. Move to the date field(s) and set the date ahead one year.

4. Return to the main CMOS setup screen, and click an option named something like **Save Settings and Exit**. If prompted, verify that you want to save the settings.

5. Wait while the system reboots. Allow Windows to load.

6. At the desktop, check the time and date. Are your CMOS setup changes reflected in Windows?

   _____

7. Reboot the computer, return to CMOS setup, and set the correct time and date.

8. Verify again that the changes are reflected in Windows.

## CRITICAL THINKING (ADDITIONAL 30 MINUTES)

Form workgroups of two to four people, and do the following to practice troubleshooting problems with CMOS:

1. Propose a change you could make to CMOS setup that would prevent a computer from booting successfully. What change did you propose?

   _____

2. Have your instructor approve the change because some changes might cause information written to the hard drive to be lost, making it difficult to recover from the problem without reloading the hard drive. Did your instructor approve the change?

   _____

3. Now go to another team's computer and make the change to CMOS setup while the other team makes a change to your system.

4. Return to your computer and troubleshoot the problem. Describe the problem as a user would:

   _____

   _____

5. What steps did you go through to discover the source of the problem and fix it?

   _____

   _____

6. If you were to encounter this same problem in the future, what might you do differently to troubleshoot it?

   _____

   _____

## REVIEW QUESTIONS

1. Do all systems use the same method to enter CMOS setup? Can you enter CMOS setup after the system has booted?

   _____

2. How are settings usually grouped in the CMOS setup utility?

   _____

3. In what section do you usually find time and date setup in the CMOS setup utility?

   _____

   _____

4. What types of options are shown on the CMOS setup main screen?

   _____

5. What happens automatically after you exit CMOS setup?

   _____

6. What tool in Sandra can you use to find information on your version of BIOS?

   _____

   _____

7. Why does a computer need CMOS?

   _____

   _____

8. When troubleshooting a computer, when might you have to enter CMOS setup? List at least three reasons:

   _____

   _____

   _____

# LAB 6.2 USE A HARDWARE INFORMATION UTILITY

## OBJECTIVES

The goal of this lab is to help you learn how to use a hardware information utility. After completing this lab, you will be able to:

⊿ Download and install the HWiNFO32 utility by Martin Malik

⊿ Use the HWiNFO32 utility to examine your system

## MATERIALS REQUIRED

This lab requires the following:

◢ A computer designated for this lab

◢ Windows 2000/XP or Windows 9x operating system

◢ Internet access for file downloading only

## LAB PREPARATION

Before lab begins, the instructor or lab assistant needs to do the following:

◢ Verify that Windows starts with no errors.

◢ Verify that Internet access is available.

◢ For labs that don't have Internet access, download these files to a file server or other storage media available to students in the lab:

  ◢ Latest version of HWiNFO32 downloaded from *www.hwinfo.com*. At the time this lab was tested, the latest version is Version 1.59, and the file name is Hw32_159.exe. However, the version number and file name might have changed.

  ◢ Latest version of HWiNFO downloaded from *www.hwinfo.com*. At the time this lab was tested, the file name was Hwinf497.zip.

  ◢ For Windows 98 or Windows 2000 systems, download an uncompress utility, such as WinZip from *www.winzip.com*.

## ACTIVITY BACKGROUND

A hardware information utility can be useful when you want to identify a hardware component in a system without having to open the computer case. Also, a hardware information utility can help you identify features of a motherboard, video card, or processor installed in a system and establish benchmarks for these components. In this lab, you learn to use HWiNFO32 written by Martin Malik from Slovakia. The utility comes in a Windows version and a DOS version. You can use the Windows version on any Windows 2000/XP or Windows 9x computer, and you can install the DOS version on floppy disks so that the utility is available on any computer you're troubleshooting.

In this lab, you download a shareware Windows version of HWiNFO32 from the Internet and then learn how to use it. Web sites sometimes change, so as you follow the instructions in this lab, you might have to adjust for changes to the *www.hwinfo.com* site. If your lab doesn't have Internet access, ask your instructor for the location of the file downloaded previously for your use. Write the path to that file here:

_____

**ESTIMATED COMPLETION TIME: 30 minutes**

 **Activity**

1. Go to the HWiNFO32 Web site at **www.hwinfo.com**. Click **Download**. In the submenu under Download, click **HWiNFO32**. Click one of the download locations, and the File Download dialog box opens. Click **Save**. Select a folder on your computer to save the file, and click **Save**. What is the path and name of the downloaded file?

_____

2. Close your browser, open Windows Explorer, and then double-click the file name to install HWiNFO32 for Windows. If the Security Warning dialog box opens, click **Run** to start setup. Follow the directions on the screen to install the software.

3. After the software is installed, the HWiNFO32 Help window opens. Research this help program to answer the following questions about the utility:

   ◢ Why does the utility's installation program install a driver running in kernel mode?

   _____

   _____

   ◢ The utility was written for Windows 2000/XP but should also work in Windows 9x. What warning is given about running the utility in Windows 9x?

   _____

   ◢ Why is it necessary for the utility to be updated often?

   _____

4. Close the HWiNFO32 Help window.

5. To run the utility, click **Start**, point to **All Programs** (**Programs** for Windows 9x), point to **HWiNFO32**, and click **HWiNFO32 Program**. When a dialog box opens, click **Continue** to close it. The utility examines your system, and then the HWiNFO32 window shown in Figure 6-1 opens.

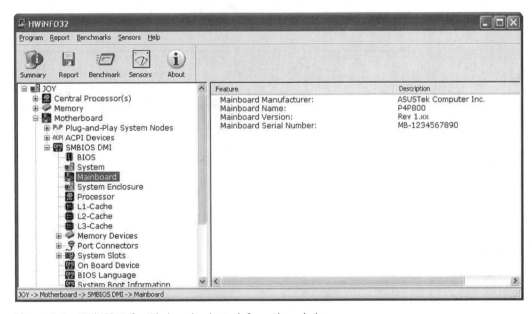

**Figure 6-1**  HWiNFO32 for Windows hardware information window

Many times you aren't given step-by-step directions when using utility software but must learn how to use it by exploring menus and using the software's help functions. The following steps give you practice in doing that:

1. Use the HWiNFO32 utility to find the following information about your system:

   ◢ Mainboard manufacturer:

   _____

◢ Mainboard name:

_____

◢ Mainboard serial number:

_____

◢ BIOS vendor:

_____

◢ BIOS version:

_____

◢ BIOS release date:

_____

◢ Processor manufacturer:

_____

◢ Processor version:

_____

◢ Current and maximum clock speed of the processor:

_____

◢ Processor socket:

_____

◢ Amount of L1 cache:

_____

◢ Amount of L2 cache:

_____

◢ Amount of L3 cache:

_____

◢ Slot type of the video bus, as reported by the video card:

_____

◢ Slot type of the video bus, as reported by the motherboard:

_____

◢ Amount of video RAM:

_____

2. To identify your motherboard's chipset, look for information under Memory Controller Hub and I/O Controller Hub. Based on this information, what chipset is your motherboard using?

_____

3. Exit the program.

## CHALLENGE ACTIVITY (ADDITIONAL 30 MINUTES)

Martin Malik also offers a DOS-based utility for finding information about hardware. If you download and install this DOS version of HWiNFO on a Windows bootable disk, you can boot a system with this disk and run the utility without using Windows. This option can be useful when Windows isn't working or you don't want to take the time to install the utility's 32-bit version in Windows. Also, if you're servicing a customer's computer, you can use the DOS-based utility on a Windows startup disk to get information about the system quickly without installing software on a customer's computer.

Create a bootable floppy disk. Download the DOS version of HWiNFO from the *www.hwinfo.com* Web site and copy it to the disk. Boot from the disk and start the utility on any Windows 2000/XP or Windows 9x computer. Answer the following questions:

1. What is the name of the downloaded compressed file for HWiNFO for DOS?

   _____

2. List the steps you took to download the utility and install it on a bootable floppy disk:

   _____

   _____

   _____

   _____

3. Describe how the software works using this method:

   _____

   _____

## REVIEW QUESTIONS

1. Why does a Windows driver need to run in kernel mode?

   _____

2. In your system, did the type of video slot reported by the video card differ from the type of video slot reported by the motherboard? If so, how can you explain this difference?

   _____

3. Using Windows XP, list the steps to create a bootable floppy disk:

   _____

   _____

   _____

4. Can you use a bootable floppy disk created in Windows XP to boot a Windows 2000 computer? A Windows 98 computer?

   _____

5. What is an advantage of using the DOS version instead of the Windows version of the HWiNFO utility?

_____

6. List three reasons you might use HWiNFO or HWiNFO32 when troubleshooting or upgrading a PC:

_____

_____

_____

# LAB 6.3 IDENTIFY A MOTHERBOARD AND FIND DOCUMENTATION ON THE INTERNET

## OBJECTIVES

The goal of this lab is to learn to identify a motherboard and find online documentation for it. After completing this lab, you will be able to:

▲ Identify a motherboard by examining it physically

▲ Determine a motherboard's manufacturer and model

▲ Search the Internet for motherboard documentation

## MATERIALS REQUIRED

This lab requires the following:

▲ A computer designated for disassembly

▲ SiSoftware Sandra (installed in Lab 1.3)

▲ Internet access

▲ Adobe Acrobat Reader

▲ A PC toolkit with antistatic ground strap

## LAB PREPARATION

Before the lab begins, the instructor or lab assistant needs to do the following:

▲ Verify that Windows starts with no errors.

▲ Verify that Internet access is available.

▲ Verify that SiSoftware Sandra and Adobe Acrobat Reader are installed.

## ACTIVITY BACKGROUND

Often a PC technician is asked to repair a PC, but the documentation is lost or not available. Fortunately, you can usually find documentation for a device online, as long as you have the device's manufacturer name and model number. In this lab, you learn how to find the manufacturer's name and model number on a motherboard, and then locate documentation for that device on the Internet.

**ESTIMATED COMPLETION TIME: 30 minutes**

**Activity**

1. Boot your PC and use SiSoftware Sandra (installed in Lab 1.3) to find out which type of CPU is installed on your computer. Record that information:

2. Following safety precautions, including using an antistatic ground strap, remove the PC's case cover, and then remove any components obscuring your view of the motherboard. In some cases, you might have to remove the motherboard itself, but usually this step isn't necessary.

3. Look for a stenciled or silkscreened label printed on the circuit board that indicates the manufacturer and model. Note that other components sometimes have labels printed on a sticker affixed to the component. On a motherboard, the label is usually printed directly on the circuit board. Common motherboard manufacturers include Abit, Asus, and Intel.

Also, note that the manufacturer name is usually printed in much larger type than the model number. Model numbers often include both letters and numbers, and many indicate a version number as well. Figure 6-2 shows an example of a motherboard label.

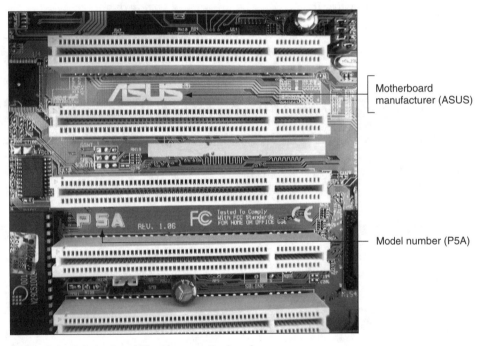

**Figure 6-2**   Label printed directly on motherboard

4. Record the information on the motherboard label:

5. Take your information to a PC with Internet access and open a browser.

6. If you know the manufacturer's URL, go directly to the Web site. (Table 6-2 lists the URLs for some motherboard manufacturers.) If you don't know the manufacturer's URL, search for the manufacturer or model

**Notes**

For a listing of Web sites about motherboards, including motherboard manufacturers, diagnostics, and product comparisons and reviews, see *www.motherboards.org*.

with your favorite search engine, as shown in Figure 6-3. In the search results, click a link associated with the manufacturer. If this link doesn't take you directly to the documentation, it usually gets you within two or three links. Continue until you find the manufacturer's Web site.

| Manufacturer | URL |
|---|---|
| American Megatrends, Inc. | www.megatrends.com |
| ASUS | www.asus.com |
| Dell | www.dell.com |
| Diamond Multimedia | www.diamondmm.com |
| First International Computer, Inc. | www.fica.com |
| Gateway | www.gateway.com |
| Giga-Byte Technology Co., Ltd. | www.giga-byte.com |
| IBM | www.ibm.com |
| Intel Corporation | www.intel.com |
| Supermicro Computer, Inc. | www.supermicro.com |
| Tyan Computer Corporation | www.tyan.com |

**Table 6-2**   URLs for major motherboard manufacturers

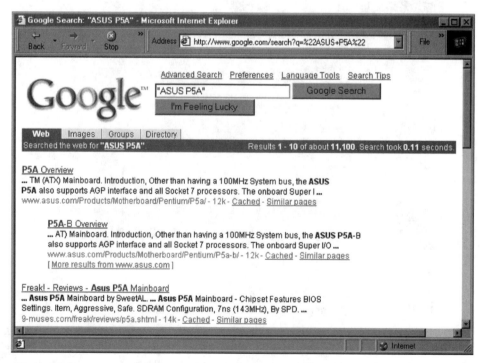

**Figure 6-3**   Search results using manufacturer name and model number

7. When you have found the site of your motherboard's manufacturer, look for a link to service or support. Click this link, and, if necessary, select a product category and model number. Sometimes knowing the type of CPU the board supports can be useful in finding the right board.

8. Continue working your way through the site until you find the motherboard d▨ tation. The documentation might include a variety of documents covering techni▨ specifications and installation instructions. Often the documentation includes a bas▨ manual, which is usually a combination of technical and installation specifications.

9. When you find the documentation, you might also find a link to updated drivers. If you see such a link, click it and note the release date of these drivers. If they are newer than the current drivers, it's often advisable to update the drivers as well. If possible, record the release dates for updated drivers:

   _____

10. Return to the main documentation page, and, if it's available, select the manual. If it's not available, select the installation instructions.

11. The manual is probably in PDF format, so you need to have Adobe Acrobat Reader installed. If you have the browser plug-in, you can open the document from the source location, or you can download the manual to your computer and then open it. Using your preferred method, open the document and print the motherboard documentation. Save this documentation for use in Lab 6.5.

## REVIEW QUESTIONS

1. How is the label usually applied to a motherboard? How is it most often applied to other components?

   _____

2. On the label of a motherboard or other component, how can the manufacturer often be differentiated from the model number?

   _____

3. What type of link on a manufacturer's Web site usually leads you to manuals and other documentation?

   _____

4. What other information about your motherboard might you want to examine on the manufacturer's Web site?

   _____

5. In what format is documentation most often available for download?

   _____

6. What information besides motherboard documentation, such as BIOS updates and drivers, can be found at the manufacturer's Web site?

   _____

## MOTHERBOARD COMPONENTS AND FORM FACTORS

his lab is to help you learn to identify motherboard form factors and compo-
ompleting this lab, you will be able to:

otherboard's CPU type

nectors

Identity the form factor based on component type and placement

## MATERIALS REQUIRED

Instructors are encouraged to supply a variety of motherboards, some common and others
not so common. At the very least, this lab requires the following:

▲ Three different motherboards

 **Notes**

> If three motherboards aren't available, look on the Web sites of the motherboard manufacturers listed in
> Lab 6.3 for three boards.

## LAB PREPARATION

Before the lab begins, the instructor or lab assistant needs to do the following:

▲ Gather an assortment of motherboards, with at least one AT, ATX, and BTX board, if possible.

## ACTIVITY BACKGROUND

As a PC technician, you should be able to look at a motherboard and determine what type
of CPU, RAM, and form factor you're working with. You should also be able to recognize
any unusual components the board might have. In this lab, you examine different motherboards and note some important information about them.

**ESTIMATED COMPLETION TIME: 30 minutes**

 **Activity**

Fill in the following chart for your assigned motherboards. If you have more than three
motherboards, use additional paper. When the entry in the Item column is a question such
as "AGP slot?", write a yes or no answer.

| Item | Motherboard 1 | Motherboard 2 | Motherboard 3 |
|------|---------------|---------------|---------------|
| Manufacturer/model | Dell | | |
| BIOS manufacturer | Dell | | |
| CPU type | Pentium III | | |
| Chipset | Pentium | | |
| RAM type/pins | | | |
| How many PCI slots? | 5 | | |
| How many ISA slots? | 4 | | |
| AGP slot? | 0 | | |

| Item | Motherboard 1 | Motherboard 2 | Motherboard 3 |
|---|---|---|---|
| How many PCI Express slots? | 0 | | |
| Parallel ATA connectors? | 2 | | |
| Serial ATA (SATA) connectors? | 0 | | |
| SCSI controller? | | | |
| Embedded audio, video, and so on | 1 - 1 | | |
| Jumperless? | no | | |
| Form factor | ATX | | |
| Describe any unusual components | | | |

## REVIEW QUESTIONS

1. How can you determine whether a motherboard is an AT or ATX board based on the CPU's location in relation to the expansion slots?

_____

_____

2. How can you determine whether a motherboard is an ATX or a BTX board?

_____

_____

3. Of the motherboards you examined, which do you think is the oldest? Why?

_____

_____

_____

4. Which motherboard best supports old and new technology? Why?

_____

_____

_____

5. Which motherboard seems to provide the best possibility for expansion? Why?

_____

_____

_____

6. Which motherboard is most likely the easiest to configure? Why?

_____

7. Which motherboard do you think is the most expensive? Why?

_____

8. What are some considerations a motherboard manufacturer has to contend with when designing a motherboard? (For example, consider room for large CPUs and cooling fans, where the power supply is located in relationship to the power connector, new technologies, and so forth.)

_____

_____

# LAB 6.5 REMOVE AND REPLACE A MOTHERBOARD

## OBJECTIVES

The goal of this lab is to familiarize you with the process of replacing an old or faulty motherboard. After completing this lab, you will be able to:

◢ Use SiSoftware Sandra to determine your CPU's specifications

◢ Remove a motherboard

◢ Configure a new motherboard according to its documentation

◢ Install a replacement motherboard

## MATERIALS REQUIRED

This lab requires the following:

◢ A computer designated for this lab

◢ SiSoftware Sandra (installed in Lab 1.3)

◢ A workgroup of 2 to 4 students

◢ A PC toolkit with antistatic ground strap

## LAB PREPARATION

Before the lab begins, the instructor or lab assistant needs to do the following:

◢ Verify that Windows starts with no errors.

◢ Verify that SiSoftware Sandra has been installed.

## ACTIVITY BACKGROUND

In this lab, you exchange a motherboard with another team to simulate the process of replacing a faulty motherboard. When you install the new motherboard, you must configure it for your system by adjusting jumper and CMOS settings according to the documentation you printed in Lab 6.3. Then you install the replacement motherboard.

**ESTIMATED COMPLETION TIME: 45 minutes**

**Activity**

In this lab, follow safety precautions while you remove the motherboard. Be sure to use an antistatic ground strap.

1. Launch Sandra (installed in Lab 1.3) and use the **CPU & BIOS Information** utility to examine the CPU in your system. Record the information listed in the Processor section:

   _____

   _____

   _____

2. Power the system down, unplug everything, and remove the case cover. Then remove the cabling and expansion cards from the motherboard. Take all necessary precautions (including using an antistatic ground strap), and make a sketch of cabling and component placement.

3. Six screws usually attach the motherboard to the case via spacers or stand-offs. The spacers prevent the printed circuitry from shorting out on the metal case and provide space for air circulation. Also, it's important that the motherboard be securely attached to the case with enough spacers and screws so that the board won't crack when expansion cards are being inserted. Remove the screws attaching the motherboard, and set them aside in a cup, bag, or bowl so that you don't lose them.

**Tip**

In this lab, it's not necessary to remove the spacers from holes in the computer case. However, sometimes you might have to move a spacer from one hole to another, such as when you're replacing a motherboard and the new board lines up over different holes in the computer case. To remove a plastic spacer held in place with barbs, use needlenose pliers to pinch the spacer and slide it out of the hole. To install it in a new hole, push the spacer into the hole until it pops in place. For metal spacers, carefully squeeze the spacer with pliers and remove it from the bracket holding it to the computer case.

4. Carefully lift the motherboard out of the case. You might have to tilt the board to clear the drive bays and power supply. In some cases, you might have to remove the drives to get the motherboard out.

5. Exchange the motherboard and motherboard documentation with that of another team. You might also exchange the CPU and memory, depending on whether your current CPU and memory modules are compatible with the new motherboard. Follow directions from your instructor on what to exchange. Be sure you have the new motherboard's documentation, which you should have found on the Internet in Lab 6.3.

Your instructor might ask you to remove jumpers and reset DIP switches on your motherboard before passing it to the other team. These modifications will make the other team's configuration more challenging. As an alternative, your instructor might have a display motherboard somewhere in the lab that uses jumpers and DIP switches for part of its configuration.

1. With the new motherboard in front of you, consult its documentation and find any jumpers that must be configured to match the system. Older boards use jumpers to adjust clock multipliers and memory speeds and to clear CMOS settings. Unless otherwise instructed, _do not_ remove the jumper to clear CMOS settings. Note that newer boards are often "jumperless," with all configuration settings made in CMOS setup. The only jumper these boards have is the one to clear CMOS settings. Remove and replace the jumpers in the configuration specified to match your processor information.

2. Install the motherboard, cabling, expansion cards, and any other components you removed.

3. Have your instructor check your work before you turn on the power.

4. Boot the system and enter the CMOS setup utility. For jumperless motherboards, make any adjustments specified in the motherboard's documentation.

5. Save your settings and exit CMOS setup.

6. Reboot the system and verify that the system is functioning correctly. Describe any error messages:

_____

7. What steps do you plan to take to troubleshoot this error?

_____

## CRITICAL THINKING (ADDITIONAL 30 MINUTES)

To learn more about motherboards, do the following:

1. After the PC is working, ask your instructor to configure a power-on password on your computer.

2. Without knowing the password, boot the computer.

3. List the steps required to boot the computer without the power-on password:

_____

_____

_____

## REVIEW QUESTIONS

1. How many screws usually attach the motherboard to the computer case?

_____

2. What is the purpose of spacers?

_____

3. A jumperless motherboard is likely to have one jumper. Which jumper is it?

_____

4. Where can you access configuration settings for a jumperless motherboard?

_____

# LAB 6.6 FLASH BIOS

## OBJECTIVES

The goal of this lab is to help you examine the process of flashing BIOS. After completing this lab, you will be able to:

◢ Gather motherboard information

◢ Gather BIOS string information

◢ Research correct BIOS update information

◢ Record current BIOS settings

◢ Flash your BIOS, if permitted by your instructor

## MATERIALS REQUIRED

This lab requires the following:

◢ Windows 2000/XP or Windows 9x operating system

◢ Motherboard documentation or SiSoftware Sandra, installed in Lab 1.3

◢ Internet access

◢ A blank floppy disk

## LAB PREPARATION

Before the lab begins, the instructor or lab assistant needs to do the following:

◢ Verify that Windows starts with no errors.

◢ Verify that Internet access is available.

## ACTIVITY BACKGROUND

The BIOS on a motherboard controls many of the system's basic input/output (I/O) functions. You can update the BIOS programming by downloading the latest update from the BIOS or motherboard manufacturer's Web site and then following specific procedures to update (or "flash") the BIOS. Flashing a computer's BIOS is necessary when troubleshooting an unstable motherboard. You might also need to flash a computer's BIOS to provide support for new hardware (such as a processor, hard drive, or CD-ROM drive) or an operating system you're about to install. For example, before upgrading your operating system to Windows 2000/XP Professional, you could update your BIOS to add support for ACPI power management. In this lab, you gather information about your system, including what BIOS you're using and how to flash it. If your instructor permits, you also flash your BIOS.

**ESTIMATED COMPLETION TIME: 30 minutes**

 **Activity**

Before making hardware, software, or BIOS changes to a system, it's important to know your starting point so that if problems occur, you know whether the problems already existed or you created them by what you did to the system. Do the following:

1. Verify that your computer can boot successfully to a Windows desktop with no errors.

2. Does the PC boot without errors?

When flashing the BIOS, using the correct BIOS update is critical. Using the wrong BIOS update can render your system inoperable. Follow these steps to gather information on the motherboard chipset and BIOS:

1. Use motherboard documentation or Sandra to find and record the following:

   ◢ Motherboard manufacturer:

   _____

   ◢ Motherboard model number and version/revision:

   _____

   ◢ Chipset manufacturer:

   _____

   ◢ Chipset model number and version/revision:

   _____

2. Next, you need to record the BIOS string and manufacturer information displayed during the boot process. To make it possible to record this information, for an older PC, turn off the PC, unplug your keyboard, and then turn on the PC. In most cases, the first screen contains video BIOS information from the video card and is identified by "VGA BIOS" or "Video BIOS." Ignore this screen and wait for the next screen, which indicates the start of POST. At this point, because you unplugged the keyboard, POST stops and reports the error about a missing keyboard. This freezes the screen so that you can read the BIOS information. For a newer PC, turn off the PC and then turn it on again while pressing the Pause/Break key, which causes POST to halt.

3. Usually, you can find the BIOS manufacturer and version at the top left of the POST screen. You might also see a release date, which is useful in determining whether newer versions of the BIOS are available. The motherboard identification string is usually located at the bottom left and often contains dozens of characters. Make sure you verify that this string is correct so that you get the correct BIOS update. Record your information on the following lines:

   ◢ BIOS manufacturer and version:

   _____

   ◢ BIOS release date, if provided:

   _____

   ◢ Motherboard identification string:

   _____

If you have a name-brand PC that doesn't identify BIOS information during the boot process, you should be able to locate BIOS information on the manufacturer's Web site by computer model number and serial number. Also, some newer computers don't halt the boot process if the keyboard is missing. Alternatively, you can go to CMOS setup and look for the BIOS identifying information on the CMOS main menu screen.

Using the information you gathered, you can search the Web to determine what files you need to update your BIOS:

1. First, search the motherboard manufacturer's Web site and then the BIOS manufacturer's Web site in the Support section for information on updating your BIOS.

Alternatively, search by motherboard model number or BIOS version number. Download the files to update your BIOS or, if your computer is running the latest version of the BIOS, download the files to refresh your existing BIOS. Answer the following questions:

◢ Did you download files to update or refresh your BIOS?

_____

◢ Which manufacturer provided the BIOS: the BIOS manufacturer or motherboard manufacturer?

_____

◢ What is the name of the file you downloaded?

_____

◢ What is the release date of the latest version?

_____

2. Search the manufacturer's Web site for the steps to flash your BIOS. Print this procedure so that you can use it during the upgrade. Does the procedure call for an additional BIOS utility or flash utility? If so, download this utility as well. Research flash utilities on *www.wimsbios.com*. Wim's BIOS is an excellent Web site for researching BIOS information in general. Print information on what BIOS utilities are available.

3. The next step is to record any changes you have made previously to CMOS settings. Generally, when BIOS is updated, settings are returned to their default state, so you probably need to return the settings to their present state after you have flashed BIOS. In addition, you might need to manually input settings for all hard drives (or allow these settings to be detected automatically). Record any settings you know you changed, any hard drive settings that might have to be reconfigured after you update the BIOS, and any additional settings specified by your instructor:

◢ Hard drive information:

_____

_____

◢ Settings you have changed:

_____

_____

◢ Settings specified by your instructor:

_____

_____

4. At this point, if your update procedure requires using a bootable floppy disk, verify that the boot order allows you to boot from drive A before drive C.

5. Prepare to update your BIOS. Uncompress any files, double-check procedures, read any Readme.txt files included in the upgrade files (which often contain last-minute adjustments to the procedure), and create the upgrade boot disk, if necessary.

6. If your instructor permits, follow the BIOS update procedure to flash your BIOS. During the procedure, if you're given the opportunity to save your old BIOS, do so. This information makes it possible to return to the previous BIOS version if you encounter problems with the new BIOS.

7. Reboot, verify CMOS settings, and verify that the computer boots to a Windows desktop successfully.

## REVIEW QUESTIONS

1. At what point in the boot process is BIOS information displayed?

   _____

2. How can you freeze the screen during POST so that you can read the BIOS information?

   _____

   _____

3. Why is it so important to record BIOS and motherboard information correctly?

   _____

   _____

4. What files might contain last-minute adjustments to the upgrade procedures?

   _____

5. In what state are CMOS settings usually placed after a BIOS update?

   _____

6. If given the opportunity during the update, what should you always do and why?

   _____

   _____

# Upgrading Memory

**Labs included in this chapter:**

## *LAB 7.1 RESEARCH RAM ON THE INTERNET*

### OBJECTIVES

The goal of this lab is to help you learn how to find important information about RAM that you need when upgrading memory. After completing this lab, you will be able to:

▲ Find documentation on your system's motherboard

▲ Read documentation for your system's RAM specifications

▲ Search the Internet for RAM prices and availability

### MATERIALS REQUIRED

This lab requires the following:

▲ Windows 2000/XP or Windows 98 operating system

▲ Internet access

▲ *Optional*: A workgroup of 2 to 4 students

### LAB PREPARATION

Before the lab begins, the instructor or lab assistant needs to do the following:

▲ Verify that Internet access is available.

### ACTIVITY BACKGROUND

In the past, RAM was literally worth more than its weight in gold. When building a system, most people made do with the minimum amount of RAM needed for adequate performance. These days, RAM is more inexpensive, which means you can probably buy all the RAM you need to make your system perform at top speed. Graphics-editing software, in particular, benefits from additional RAM. In this lab, you research how to optimize RAM on a graphics workstation with a memory upgrade budget of $150.

---

**ESTIMATED COMPLETION TIME: 30 minutes**

**Activity**

1. Use My Computer to determine the amount of RAM currently installed. Record the amount of RAM here:

   *1.28 MB*

2. Using skills you learned in Lab 6.3, determine your motherboard's manufacturer and model. (If you don't have the motherboard documentation available, search for it on the Web and print it.)

Use the documentation for your motherboard to answer these questions:

1. What type (or types) of memory does your motherboard support? Be sure to include the speed as well as the category (such as SDRAM or DDR2):

2. How many slots for memory modules are included on your motherboard?

_____

3. How many memory slots on your motherboard are used, and how much RAM is installed in each slot?

_____

_____

4. What is the maximum amount of memory your motherboard supports?

_____

5. What size and how many memory modules would be needed to upgrade your system to the maximum amount of supported memory?

_____

Now that you have the necessary information about your system's memory, go to a local computer store that sells memory, or go to _http://pricewatch.com_ or a similar Web site, and answer the following questions:

1. What is the price of the memory modules required to configure your system for maximum memory?

_____

2. Does your budget allow you to install the maximum supported amount of RAM?

_____

3. Can you use the existing memory modules to upgrade to the maximum amount of supported memory?

_____

4. What is the most additional memory you could install and still stay within your budget? (Assume you'll use the existing memory modules.)

_____

Explore other types of memory on _http://pricewatch.com_ or another similar Web site, and answer the following questions:

1. On average, what is the least expensive type of memory per MB you can find? What is its price?

_____

_____

2. On average, what is the most expensive type of memory per MB you can find? What is its price?

_____

3. Is SO-DIMM memory for a notebook computer more or less expensive than an equivalent amount of DDR2 memory for a desktop PC? Give specific information to support your answer:

_____

_____

## REVIEW QUESTIONS

1. Why might you want to upgrade RAM on a system?

   _____

   _____

2. How many pins are on the different types of DIMMs?

   _____

3. Which is more expensive: DDR-DIMM or RIMM?

   _____

4. What is a disadvantage of using two 64 MB modules instead of a single 128 MB module in a system with three slots for memory modules?

   _____

   _____

5. What are two disadvantages of using only one 256 MB module rather than two 128 MB modules?

   _____

   _____

   _____

# LAB 7.2 EXPLORE THE KINGSTON WEB SITE

## OBJECTIVES

The goal of this lab is to use the Kingston Web site to learn about RAM. After completing this lab, you will be able to:

◢ Identify types of RAM

◢ Determine appropriate memory types for a system

## MATERIALS REQUIRED

This lab requires the following:

◢ Internet access

## LAB PREPARATION

Before the lab begins, the instructor or lab assistant needs to do the following:

⊿ Verify that Internet access is available.

## ACTIVITY BACKGROUND

RAM comes in a variety of shapes, sizes, and speeds. Not every type of RAM works with every system. In this lab, you use the Kingston Technology (a major RAM manufacturer) Web site to learn about RAM and see how to make sure you have the right memory module to upgrade your system.

**ESTIMATED COMPLETION TIME: 30 minutes**

### Activity

Do the following to begin learning about system memory:

1. Open your browser and go to **www.kingston.com**.

2. Notice that you can use the site's Memory Search section to search for memory based on the type of system you have. What other three ways can you search for memory?

_____

_____

_____

When you search the site based on your system, the results include a list of compatible memory types with prices, maximum memory your system supports, processors supported, and number of expansion slots on your system for memory modules. Do the following to find information about a memory upgrade for a motherboard:

1. Select one of the motherboards from the table in Lab 6.4. Which motherboard did you select?

_____

2. Perform a memory search on the Kingston site for information on this motherboard. Answer the following questions:

⊿ What types of memory modules can this board can use?

_____

_____

_____

⊿ What types of processors does the board support?

_____

_____

_____

◢ How many memory slots are on the board?

_____

◢ What is the maximum amount of memory the board supports?

_____

Now continue exploring the Kingston site by following these steps:

1. Return to the Kingston home page.
2. Click the **Memory Tools** link. A drop-down list displays several tools, one being the Memory Assessor. With this tool, you specify which OS you're researching, and Kingston displays a recommended amount of physical RAM based on usage criteria.
3. Using these tools, and perhaps other areas of the site, answer the following questions:

   ◢ In general, do operating systems for desktops and workstations require more or less memory than operating systems for servers?

   _____

   _____

   ◢ How wide is the data path on a 168-pin DIMM?

   _____

   ◢ DDR is an extension of what older memory technology?

   _____

   _____

   ◢ What does the SO in SO-DIMM represent?

   _____

   ◢ What is an advantage of loading applications entirely into RAM rather than loading part of an application into virtual memory (a page file)?

   _____

   _____

   _____

   ◢ What is another term for a page file, and why are page files used?

   _____

   _____

   ◢ How many bits of information does a single cell of a memory chip on a 256 MB PC2700 DDR module hold?

   _____

◢ Why would you have problems with a system in which you installed three known good RIMMs?

_____

_____

_____

◢ One memory technology uses only a 16-bit path. What acronym is used for this type of memory?

_____

◢ What type of material is used to make a memory "chip"?

_____

_____

◢ What function(s) does the aluminum plate on a RIMM serve?

_____

_____

◢ Why might you not mind using slower memory (in MHz) if faster memory is available for a marginal price difference?

_____

_____

◢ What is the system's bank schema, and why is it important when installing RAM?

_____

_____

◢ What is a memory performance measurement in which the lower the number, the better the performance?

_____

◢ What memory technology achieves better performance by using both the rising and falling sides of the clock cycle?

_____

_____

◢ List five considerations when upgrading memory:

_____

_____

_____

_____

_____

◢ If a motherboard can support SDRAM or EDO, which would result in better performance?

_____

◢ What memory technology uses a heat spreader?

_____

◢ What types of memory do notebook computers typically use?

_____

◢ Name two characteristics of a system using RAMBUS licensed memory:

_____

_____

## REVIEW QUESTIONS

1. Is a DIMM or RIMM more expensive, given that both hold the same amount of memory? Why do you think this is the case?

_____

_____

2. Summarize why adding RAM offers a performance advantage:

_____

_____

3. Which tool on the Kingston Web site could you use to find Kingston modules for your system if you know the model number of your system's motherboard?

_____

4. If you were planning to buy a new system, would you choose a motherboard that uses DIMMs or RIMMs? Why?

_____

_____

## LAB 7.3 UPGRADE RAM

### OBJECTIVES

The goal of this lab is to learn how to plan a memory upgrade and then perform the upgrade. After completing this lab, you will be able to:

▲ Estimate how much free memory your system has available during typical and stressed use

▲ Determine how much and what kind of memory is needed for an upgrade

▲ Upgrade RAM in your system

### MATERIALS REQUIRED

This lab requires the following:

▲ Windows 2000/XP or Windows 9x operating system

▲ SiSoftware Sandra, installed in Lab 1.3

▲ Internet access

▲ A PC designated for disassembly

▲ A PC toolkit and antistatic ground strap

▲ Additional memory module compatible with your system

### LAB PREPARATION

Before the lab begins, the instructor or lab assistant needs to do the following:

▲ Verify that a computer designated for disassembly and a compatible memory module are available to each student or workgroup.

▲ Verify that Internet access is available.

### ACTIVITY BACKGROUND

In this lab, you examine your system, gather information on its memory subsystem, and establish a memory usage baseline. Using this information, you then determine through further research whether the system can support a RAM upgrade required to run a computer-aided design (CAD) application. Finally, you install an additional memory module, examine your system again, and compare it against the baseline.

**ESTIMATED COMPLETION TIME: 45 minutes**

 **Activity**

1. Start SiSoftware Sandra, and use it to answer the following questions about your system:

    ▲ What OS are you running?

    _____

    ▲ What type of processor is your system using?

    _____

    ▲ What is your motherboard's manufacturer and model?

    _____

◢ How many MB of RAM are currently installed?

_____

◢ What type of memory modules are installed? Be as specific as you can:

_____

◢ At what speed does the memory bus operate?

_____

To establish a memory usage baseline, follow these steps:

1. Leaving Sandra open, launch one instance each of Windows Explorer, Paint, and Internet Explorer.
2. Use the Windows Memory Information tool in Sandra and record the amount of free physical memory. This is your memory baseline. How much memory is free?

_____

3. Open six more instances of Internet Explorer, browsing to a different site on each instance. Try to view a movie trailer or video, because this activity is memory intensive compared with displaying a static Web page.
4. Refresh the information in the Windows Memory Information tool by clicking the blue arrow. Record the free physical memory. How much memory is free now?

_____

The change is the result of the demands of running and displaying six additional Web pages.

Suppose your employer's Engineering Department is interested in deploying a CAD program that requires 1 GB of RAM more than what's currently in your system. Use your investigating skills to gather information on supporting the additional required RAM:

1. Can you upgrade your system's RAM without removing any of the current memory modules?

_____

2. What would be the least expensive upgrade to meet the new requirements?

_____

3. How would your answers to Questions 1 and 2 change if the CAD program required an additional 4 GB of RAM?

_____

_____

_____

_____

Next, you simulate making the upgrade by following these steps:

1. Shut down your system and remove all exterior cabling.
2. Be sure you're wearing your antistatic ground strap. Open the system case and locate the slots for memory modules.

3. Remove any data cabling and other devices preventing you from getting at the slots. Answer the following questions:

⊿ How many modules are currently installed?

⊿ Are there any empty slots in which to install an additional module?

4. Notice that the slots have a retaining mechanism at each end to secure the modules in the slot. Typically, these mechanisms are plastic levers that you spread outward to unseat and remove modules. Modules are inserted and removed straight up and down. Spread the plastic levers apart before inserting or removing the memory modules.

5. Examine an empty slot and note the raised ridges that line up with notches on the memory module's pin edge. Because modules are designed to be inserted in only one orientation, these ridges prevent them from being inserted incorrectly.

6. With the module oriented correctly, insert the module and gently but firmly push it in.

7. Reassemble your system.

Although purchasing a bad memory module is extremely rare, it's a good idea to give the system every opportunity to detect faulty memory. BIOS tests physical memory each time the system is booted. If a module is drastically flawed, usually the system won't boot. Instead, it issues a beep code indicating memory problems. Assuming that the module is in fairly good shape and the video has initialized, the system BIOS's POST routine typically displays a memory count in bytes as it tests memory.

Most POST routines run through the test three times before proceeding. You can skip this redundant testing by enabling a Quick POST in CMOS setup. Quick POST is great for cutting down bootup time during normal use, but when installing new RAM, it's best to give the system every opportunity to detect a problem. Therefore, you should disable Quick POST until you're confident the module has no obvious problem. With this in mind, follow these steps to verify that the system recognizes the upgrade:

1. Boot the system and enter CMOS setup.

> **Notes**
>
> The first time you boot after a memory upgrade, the BIOS might display a memory mismatch error to let you know the memory has been changed.

2. Verify that Quick POST is disabled, and specify that you have installed additional memory, if necessary. (Telling CMOS about new memory isn't necessary unless you have a very old motherboard.)

3. Save your settings and reboot. Record whether the additional memory was recognized and how many times it was tested:

4. Being careful to duplicate the steps, perform the same baseline tests that you did earlier in this lab. Record the results here:

⊿ Amount of free memory with Sandra, Windows Explorer, Paint, and Internet Explorer open:

⊿ Amount of free memory with the system heavily used:

5. When you have finished, remove the additional memory and return the system to its previous configuration.

## REVIEW QUESTIONS

1. What is the minimum and recommended memory requirement for the OS your system is running?

_____

_____

2. What are at least two ways you can determine how much RAM is installed?

_____

_____

3. Which Sandra module(s) can be used to display information about system memory?

_____

_____

4. What feature is used on memory slots and modules to prevent modules from being inserted incorrectly?

_____

_____

5. In what situation might you want to disable Quick POST, and why?

_____

_____

# LAB 7.4 TROUBLESHOOT MEMORY PROBLEMS

## OBJECTIVES

The goal of this lab is to give you hands-on experience in troubleshooting memory problems. After completing this lab, you will be able to:

▲ Identify some symptoms that indicate memory problems

▲ Identify a faulty module

▲ Use DocMemory to test installed RAM

## MATERIALS REQUIRED

This lab requires the following:

▲ Internet access (to download files)

▲ Windows 2000/XP or Windows 9x operating system

▲ SiSoftware Sandra, installed in Lab 1.3

▲ A printer

▲ A blank floppy disk

⊿ Adobe Acrobat Reader

⊿ A PC designated for disassembly

⊿ A PC toolkit and antistatic ground strap

## LAB PREPARATION

Before the lab begins, the instructor or lab assistant needs to do the following:

⊿ Verify that a computer designated for disassembly and a printer are available to each student or workgroup.

⊿ Verify that Internet access is available. For labs that don't have Internet access, download these files from *www.docmemory.com* to a file server or other storage media available to students in the lab: DocMem1_45a.exe, Docguide.pdf, and Docmem2_2b.zip.

⊿ Go to the *www.docmemory.com* Web site and register at the site with an e-mail address and password. Students use this information later on the Members Login page.

## ACTIVITY BACKGROUND

The symptoms of faulty RAM are many and varied. Faulty memory can cause a complete failure to boot, fatal exception errors while working with an application, or catastrophic data loss. However, sometimes faulty memory is noticeable only as annoying interruptions while you're working. RAM that's outright dead is fairly easy to identify. If the dead module is the only module installed, the system won't boot. If it's one of several modules, you'll notice that the system reports less memory than you expected.

However, it's not common for a module to fail absolutely. More often, a module develops intermittent problems that cause data corruption, applications hanging at unexpected times, or Windows 2000/XP hanging and displaying the Blue Screen of Death. In this lab, you learn how to detect and isolate faulty memory modules to prevent these problems.

**ESTIMATED COMPLETION TIME: 60 minutes**

### Activity

Reliable memory function is essential to system operation. Therefore, when the system is booted, if memory isn't detected or has major problems, the startup BIOS begins emitting a beep code to define a general or particular memory problem. If startup BIOS finds memory to be adequate, during POST startup, BIOS does a thorough test of physical memory, which is usually repeated three times before the system summary is displayed and booting continues. Then while Windows is loading, it tests memory again.

These tests are all well and good at startup, but often partially corrupted modules don't show a problem until they're running at certain temperatures. Because these faults show up only at certain times and temperatures, they are referred to as "thermal intermittents." Although these problems are difficult to nail down and document, they are actually fairly easy to remedy if the fault is on the memory module instead of the motherboard.

DocMemory is a utility that allows you to use a quick test or a burn-in test that runs until an error is encountered or there's human intervention. This burn-in test is particularly useful in discovering a thermal intermittent fault.

In the following steps, you use DocMemory to test installed RAM. The installation process for DocMemory creates a bootable disk. First, you create a boot disk with the DocMemory software on it, and then use the boot disk to boot a PC and test memory on that PC. Follow these steps:

1. Open your browser, and go to **www.docmemory.com**. Click the **Download Docmemory SPD Reader Software** link. On the next page, you must enter an e-mail address and password. Ask your instructor for that information and enter it. Click **Submit**.

   ◢ E-mail: _____

   ◢ Password: _____

2. On the next page, shown in Figure 7-1, click the **DocMemory User Guide** link at the bottom and print the user guide for later use. Click your browser's **Back** button to return to the previous page.

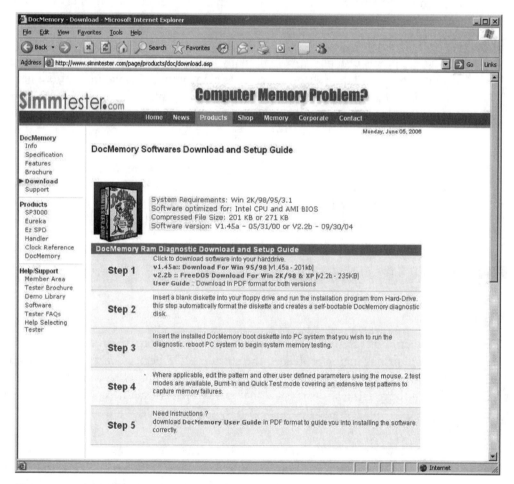

**Figure 7-1**　The DocMemory Softwares Download and Setup Guide page

3. To download the software, for a Windows 9x system, click **Download For Win 95/98**. For a Windows 2000/XP system, click **FreeDOS Download For Win 2K/98 & XP**. Save the file to a location on your hard drive. What's the location of the downloaded file?

   _____

4. In Windows 2000/XP, double-click the downloaded file to extract the compressed files. Save the uncompressed files to a folder on your hard drive named **C:\Test**. Open a command

prompt window, type the command **CD C:\test**, and press **Enter**. The prompt becomes C:\test> (see Figure 7-2). Type **Install** and press **Enter** to begin the installation process.

**Figure 7-2** Prepare a boot disk with the DocMemory software installed

5. In Windows 9x, double-click the downloaded file DocMem1_45a.exe to run it. DocMemory then opens in a command prompt window. Use the arrow keys and Enter key or the mouse to select **Make Boot Disk**.

6. Regardless of the OS you're using, a license agreement appears next. Scroll down and accept the license agreement. Next, a prompt is displayed asking you to insert a blank formatted disk. Insert the disk and press **Enter**.

7. The installation process begins. When the installation is finished, a message is displayed indicating that the process is complete. Close any open windows.

8. The disk is now ready to be used on any computer. For the purpose of this lab, leave the disk in the system and reboot.

9. The system boots into the DocMemory utility. Purchase information is displayed and then the Select Type of Test dialog box opens with options for Burn-in Test, Quick Test, or Cancel. To test for a thermal intermittent, the Burn-in Test option is the best choice. However, in the interest of time, click **Quick Test** for this lab.

10. The test begins and the status is displayed at the upper-left side. Your processor and RAM are identified at the upper-right side, and the bottom of the screen displays pass/fail results. This portion of the lab varies in time because of differences in systems' amount of RAM and processor speeds.

11. While waiting for the test to finish, consult the documentation and answer the following questions:

▲ What two things happen when a fault is detected?

_____

_____

▲ What two areas can DocMemory test?

_____

_____

▲ What type of fault is the Walk Data "0" & "1" test designed to uncover?

_____

_____

**12.** When the test ends or errors are found, record the results here:

_____

_____

_____

Follow these steps to observe the effects of a faulty memory module and interpret beep codes:

**1.** Use Sandra to determine the BIOS manufacturer for your system, and record it here:

_____

**2.** Search documentation or the Internet for a list of beep codes for that manufacturer.

**3.** Shut down the system and remove all external cabling.

**4.** Put on your antistatic ground strap, open the case, remove all memory modules, and set them aside in an antistatic bag.

**5.** Reassemble the system, leaving out the memory.

**6.** Power up the system and describe the outcome, including any beep codes:

_____

_____

_____

**7.** If you heard beep codes, using the information you found in Step 2, interpret their meaning:

_____

_____

**8.** Shut down the system, disassemble it, install the RAM, and reassemble.

**9.** Boot the system to verify that the system is functional.

Using the documentation for DocMemory, summarize the process of using a known good memory module to provide strong evidence that a memory module is faulty:

_____

_____

_____

_____

## REVIEW QUESTIONS

**1.** What are some common symptoms of a thermal intermittent?

_____

_____

2. How many times does POST usually test memory?

_____

3. Why must the DocMemory software run from a boot disk?

_____

_____

4. Describe the symptoms caused by a dead memory module:

_____

_____

_____

5. Which DocMemory test would be ideal for diagnosing a thermal intermittent?

_____

# LAB 7.5 USE HIMEM.SYS IN WINDOWS 98

## OBJECTIVES

The goal of this lab is to help you investigate ways memory can be used by observing the effects of Himem.sys. After completing this lab, you will be able to:

- Configure Himem.sys
- Configure Msdos.sys to stay in text mode throughout the boot
- Observe the effects Himem.sys has on the system

## MATERIALS REQUIRED

This lab requires the following:

- Windows 98 operating system
- Two blank floppy disks
- Windows 98 setup CD or setup files

## LAB PREPARATION

Before the lab begins, the instructor or lab assistant needs to do the following:

- Verify that the Windows 98 computer starts with no errors.
- Provide each student with access to the Windows 98 setup files, if needed.

## ACTIVITY BACKGROUND

If you often need to run programs in MS-DOS mode, setting up Config.sys and Autoexec.bat is important because these files help set environmental variables in MS-DOS mode. Himem.sys is necessary to use many DOS utilities. Another key function of Himem.sys is that it tests RAM independently during booting. By observing the effects of changing how the system uses Himem.sys, you can get an idea of its various functions. In this lab, you configure and observe Himem.sys.

**ESTIMATED COMPLETION TIME: 30 minutes**

 **Activity**

To configure your system to remain in text mode throughout bootup, complete the following steps:

1. In Windows Explorer, right-click **Msdos.sys** in the root directory of the system partition. Click **Properties** from the shortcut menu to open the Msdos.sys Properties dialog box.

2. In the Attributes section, click to clear the check box indicating that the file is read-only. Click **OK** to apply your change and close the dialog box.

3. Again, right-click **Msdos.sys**, this time clicking **Open with** from the shortcut menu to open the Open with dialog box.

4. In the Choose the program you want to use drop-down list, click **Notepad**. If necessary, click to clear the **Always use this program to open this type of file** check box, and then click **OK**. Notepad opens and displays the entries in Msdos.sys.

5. Under the [Options] heading, add the line **Logo=0**. (Be sure to type a zero, not an uppercase "O.") Using the File menu, save the changes and close Notepad.

6. Reboot the computer and record any messages you see about Himem.sys. Notice that the Windows logo screen never appears during startup. This allows you to observe the entire text-based boot sequence, which can be useful in observing and diagnosing boot problems.

_____

_____

_____

In DOS and Windows 3.x, Himem.sys was always loaded by using a Device= command line in Config.sys. Windows 9x loads Himem.sys automatically, even if a Config.sys file isn't present. However, you can use Config.sys in Windows 9x to load Himem.sys and configure how Himem.sys loads. To do this, you create a Config.sys file and add the Himem.sys command line with the appropriate switches. To configure Himem.sys and watch it load, follow these steps:

1. In the root of the system partition, right-click **Config.sys**. Click **Open with** from the shortcut menu to open the Open with dialog box.

2. In the Choose the program you want to use drop-down list, click **NOTEPAD**. If necessary, click to clear the **Always use this program to open this type of file** check box, and click **OK**. Notepad opens, displaying the entries in Config.sys.

3. In Config.sys, add the line **Device=C:\Windows\himem.sys**. Using the File menu, save your changes and close Notepad.

4. Reboot the computer, recording any messages you see concerning Himem.sys.

_____

_____

_____

5. Following Steps 1 through 4, add the **/V** switch (be sure to type an uppercase "V") to the Device= line. The resulting line should be Device=C:\Windows\Himem.sys /V, with a space before the switch. "V" stands for verbose or descriptive, meaning text is displayed to keep you informed of the command's progress. Reboot the system (if necessary, more than once), and answer the following questions:

   ◢ How much high memory did Himem.sys report available?

   _____

   ◢ What version of Himem.sys is loaded?

   _____

6. Following the previous process to edit Config.sys, add the **/TestMem:ON** switch. Reboot and record any changes:

   _____

   _____

   _____

Next, you create a Windows 98 startup disk by using the Add/Remove Programs applet in Control Panel. Then you use Scandisk on the startup disk to scan your hard drive for errors, which is a first step in demonstrating why loading Himem.sys from Config.sys is important. Follow these steps:

1. From Control Panel, open the Add/Remove Programs applet.

2. When the applet opens, click the **Startup disk** tab.

3. Click the **Create Disk** button and, if prompted, enter the location of the Windows setup files.

4. Insert the floppy disk when prompted, and click **OK** to continue and create a startup disk.

5. When the startup disk has been created, examine its contents in Windows Explorer. Does the startup disk contain both Config.sys and Himem.sys? Open the Config.sys file and write the command line that loads Himem.sys:

   _____

6. With the startup disk in the floppy drive, reboot the computer.

7. When prompted, select the option to start the computer without CD-ROM support.

8. When you arrive at the command prompt, type **Scandisk C:** and press **Enter** to scan the hard drive for errors.

9. Observe while Scandisk performs a data scan on drive C. When prompted, don't perform a surface scan. Press **X** to return to the command prompt.

10. Remove the startup disk and reboot the system.

Next, follow these steps to create a bootable disk, copy the Scandisk utility to it, and then attempt to use Scandisk without having Himem.sys loaded:

1. In Windows Explorer, insert the second blank floppy disk, and right-click the $3\frac{1}{2}$ **Floppy (A:)** drive.

2. Click **Format** in the shortcut menu to open the Format dialog box.

3. Click both **Quick (erase)** and **Copy system files,** and then click the **Start** button.

4. When the summary appears, click **Close** and then click **Close** again to exit. You have created a bootable disk. Using Windows Explorer, examine the disk and list the files on the disk:

_____

_____

_____

5. Now copy **Scandisk.exe** from the C:\Windows\Command folder to the bootable disk.

6. Reboot the system with the bootable disk in the drive. At the command prompt, type **Scandisk C:** and press **Enter** to attempt to scan the hard drive again for errors. Describe what happens:

_____

_____

_____

7. What two files must be put on the bootable disk for Scandisk to work?

_____

## REVIEW QUESTIONS

1. Other than providing access to memory, what valuable function does Himem.sys include?

_____

2. What system file is modified to make text messages during startup easier to view?

_____

3. In a command line, when more than one switch is used, what should come before each switch?

_____

4. Based on the knowledge you have gained in this lab, name three configuration files that can be used to alter the way an OS loads:

_____

5. Name one MS-DOS utility that requires Himem.sys to be loaded for the utility to run. What does Himem.sys do for this utility?

_____

_____

# CHAPTER 8

# Hard Drives

**Labs included in this chapter:**

- **Lab 8.1:** Format a Floppy Disk

- **Lab 8.2:** Test Hard Drive Performance Using Sandra

- **Lab 8.3:** Use Disk Management

- **Lab 8.4:** Use Hard Drive Utilities

- **Lab 8.5:** Troubleshoot Hard Drives

 - **Lab 8.6:** Critical Thinking: Use Debug to Examine Disk Information

 - **Lab 8.7:** Critical Thinking: Sabotage and Repair a Hard Drive Subsystem

# LAB 8.1 FORMAT A FLOPPY DISK

## OBJECTIVES

The goal of this lab is to help you use formatting options available from the command prompt and in Windows Explorer. After completing this lab, you will be able to:

◢ Use command-line switches for different formatting options

◢ Format a floppy disk using Windows Explorer

## MATERIALS REQUIRED

This lab requires the following:

◢ Windows 2000/XP or Windows 9x operating system

◢ A blank unformatted floppy disk

## LAB PREPARATION

Before the lab begins, the instructor or lab assistant needs to do the following:

◢ Verify that Windows starts with no errors.

## ACTIVITY BACKGROUND

Floppy disks must be formatted before you can use them. These days, floppy disks usually come preformatted from the factory, but you might need to reformat a used disk. The formatting process defines track and sector spacing so that data can be written to a known location. Formatting also creates the file allocation table (FAT), which lists the locations of files on the disk. You can format a disk in Windows Explorer or from the command line. When formatting disks from the command line, you can use switches to decide exactly how to format the disk. These switches enable you to cut some corners to speed the formatting process or to streamline the process of making a bootable disk. In this lab, you format a floppy disk in several different ways.

**ESTIMATED COMPLETION TIME: 45 minutes**

 **Activity**

To practice formatting a floppy disk in Windows Explorer, follow these steps:

1. Open Windows Explorer.

2. With the floppy disk inserted in drive A, right-click **3½ Floppy (A:)**, and then click **Format** in the shortcut menu. The Format dialog box opens.

3. Observe the layout of the Format dialog box, and describe the available options:

_____

It's also a good idea to know how to format disks from the command line in case the GUI isn't available or you want to use switches to speed the formatting process. Follow the procedure for the operating system you're using to practice formatting a floppy disk from the command prompt.

In Windows XP, follow these steps:

1. Insert a blank unformatted floppy disk into drive A, if necessary.

2. Open a command prompt window. Use the **Dir** command to examine drive A. Describe what you see on the screen:

_____

_____

3. The system can't provide information about the disk's contents because the disk hasn't been formatted yet. Type **format /?** and press **Enter**. This command displays a list of nine switches you can use to modify the Format command. What is the correct syntax for a Format command to format a 1.44 MB floppy disk?

_____

4. To format the disk, type **format A:** and press **Enter**. Time how long it takes for the formatting to reach 100%.

5. When prompted, press **Enter**. The formatting process begins. Throughout the process, you see a message indicating the percent completed.

6. When the formatting reaches 100%, the system gives you the opportunity to name the volume. Name the volume **FTEST**, and then press **Enter**.

7. Next, the system displays the formatting summary and prompts you to format another. Type **n** and press **Enter**.

8. Use the **Dir** command to examine drive A. Now the system can give you information about the floppy disk because it has been formatted.

9. A quick format doesn't write track and sector markings on the disk and is a fast way to reformat a previously formatted disk. To do a quick format, type **format A: /q** and press **Enter**. Continue through the formatting procedure. Compare the time it took to do a quick format to the time required for a full format:

_____

10. Again, use the **Dir** command to examine drive A. Is there a difference between the outcome of the quick format and the full format?

_____

In Windows 2000, follow these steps:

1. Insert a blank unformatted floppy disk into drive A, if nceessary.

2. Open a command prompt window. Use the **Dir** command to examine drive A. Describe what you see on the screen:

_____

_____

3. The system can't provide information about the disk's contents because the disk hasn't been formatted yet. Type **format /?** and press **Enter**. This command displays a list of 12 switches you can use to modify the Format command. What is the correct syntax for a Format command to format only one side of a disk?

_____

4. To format the disk, type **format A:** and press **Enter**. Time how long it takes for the formatting to reach 100%.

5. When prompted, press **Enter**. The formatting process begins. Throughout the process, you see a message indicating the percent completed.

6. When the formatting reaches 100%, the system gives you the opportunity to name the volume. Name the volume **FTEST**, and then press **Enter**.

7. Next, the system displays the formatting summary and prompts you to format another. Type **n** and press **Enter**.

8. Use the **Dir** command to examine drive A. Now the system can give you information about the floppy disk because it has been formatted.

9. A quick format doesn't write track and sector markings on the disk and is a fast way to reformat a previously formatted disk. To do a quick format, type **format A: /q** and press **Enter**. Continue through the formatting procedure. Compare the time it took to do a quick format to the time required for a full format:

_____

10. Again, use the **Dir** command to examine drive A. Is there a difference between the outcome of the quick format and the full format?

_____

In Windows 98, follow these steps:

1. Insert a blank unformatted floppy disk into drive A, if necessary.

2. Open a command prompt window. Use the **Dir** command to examine drive A. Describe what you see on the screen:

_____

_____

3. The system can't provide information about the disk's contents because the disk hasn't been formatted yet. Type **format /?** and press **Enter**. This command displays a list of 11 switches you can use to modify the Format command. What is the correct syntax for a Format command to test clusters on the disk in drive A that are currently marked as bad?

_____

4. To format the disk, type **format A:** and press **Enter**. Time how long it takes for the formatting to reach 100%.

5. When prompted, press **Enter**. The formatting process begins. Throughout the process, you see a message indicating the percent completed.

6. When the formatting reaches 100%, the system gives you the opportunity to name the volume. Name the volume **FTEST**, and then press **Enter**.

7. Next, the system displays the formatting summary and prompts you to format another. Type **n** and press **Enter**.

8. Use the **Dir** command to examine drive A. Now the system can give you information about the floppy disk because it has been formatted.

9. A quick format doesn't write track and sector markings on the disk and is a fast way to reformat a previously formatted disk. To do a quick format, type **format A: /q** and

press **Enter**. Compare the time it took to do a quick format to the time required for a full format:

_____

10. Again, use the **Dir** command to examine drive A. Is there a difference between the outcome of the quick format and the full format?

_____

Suppose you want to make a bootable floppy disk so that you could add utilities and use the disk for troubleshooting. You can use more than one switch at a time with most commands. To demonstrate this fact with the Format command, complete the steps for the operating system you're using.

In Windows XP, follow these steps:

1. Type **format A: /q /s** and press **Enter**. This command instructs the system to do a quick format and then copy the system files required to make the disk bootable.

2. What error message did you receive about creating a Windows XP bootable floppy disk?

_____

_____

3. Describe the formatting process:

_____

_____

4. How many bytes of free space are now included on the disk? What command did you use to get your answer?

_____

5. Close the command prompt window.

In Windows 2000, follow these steps:

1. Type **format A: /q /s** and press **Enter**. This command instructs the system to do a quick format and then copy the system files required to make the disk bootable.

2. What error message did you receive? Suppose you have a copy of a bootable floppy disk. What command could you use to create another bootable floppy disk using the one you already have?

_____

3. Describe the format process:

_____

_____

4. What command did you use to find out how many bytes of free space are included on a disk?

_____

5. Close the command prompt window.

In Windows 98, follow these steps:

1. Type **format A: /q /s** and press **Enter**. This command instructs the system to do a quick format and then copy the system files required to make the disk bootable.

2. Describe the format process:

   _____

   _____

   _____

   _____

3. How many bytes of free space are now included on the disk? What command did you use to get your answer?

   _____

4. Close the command prompt window.

## REVIEW QUESTIONS

1. Suppose you formatted a floppy disk on a Windows 98 system. Would you then be able to reformat the same disk by using the /q switch on another Windows 98 system? Why or why not?

   _____

2. Suppose you want to format a disk in drive B, making it a bootable disk. What command do you use in Windows 98?

   _____

3. In general, what difference did you see in a disk's directory listing after formatting the disk with the /s switch?

   _____

4. Why might it be less important for Windows 2000/XP to provide a switch for creating a bootable floppy disk?

   _____

   _____

5. What's the difference between a Windows 98 startup disk and a boot disk created with the Format A: /s command?

   _____

   _____

# LAB 8.2 TEST HARD DRIVE PERFORMANCE USING SANDRA

*DC57o*

## OBJECTIVES

The goal of this lab is to help you use Sandra to compare the performance of your system's drives against similar drives. After completing this lab, you will be able to:

◢ Use Sandra to test your drives' performance

◢ Use Sandra to compare your system's drives with similar drives

## MATERIALS REQUIRED

This lab requires the following:

◢ Windows XP/2000 or Windows 9x operating system

◢ SiSoftware Sandra, installed in Lab 1.3

## LAB PREPARATION

Before the lab begins, the instructor or lab assistant needs to do the following:

◢ Verify that Windows starts with no errors.

## ACTIVITY BACKGROUND

You can use Sandra to run a routine of several tests on your drive, report the results, and compare your drive to a selection of comparable drives. This lab gives you an indication of how your drive is performing and whether another product is available that better meets your performance needs. Some tasks, such as video editing, are demanding on the drive where files are stored; a faster drive can increase productivity. When making an upgrade decision, it's helpful to compare results reported by Sandra to information on other hard drives. In this lab, you use Sandra to test your drive.

---

**ESTIMATED COMPLETION TIME: 30 minutes**

---

 **Activity**

Follow these steps to test your drive:

1. Start Sandra.

2. Double-click the **Drives Benchmark** icon to open the Drives Benchmark window. (If you don't see the Drives Benchmark icon, you installed the wrong version of Sandra. You should be using the Standard version.)

3. Click the **Select Drive** list arrow, and then click the letter of the drive you're testing. What message is displayed after you select drive C?

   _____ *show performace* _____

4. Wait until Sandra has finished testing your drive before moving your mouse or doing anything else with the system. After the test is finished, a summary is displayed. Use the summary to answer the following questions:

   ◢ In the Current Drive field, what drive index is reported?

*Capacity vs price.* *performance vs price.* *component, Detailed Result*

◢ What drives were compared to the current drive?

*Reference Drive* [handwritten]

5. Click the drop-down menu of one of the compared drives to view it. Note that you can compare your drive against several drives.

6. One by one, select each drive, and note its performance ratings. List drives with a lower performance rating than the current drive:

*SanDisk Cruzer 8GB (USB2)* [handwritten]
*worst* [handwritten]

*1.0Krpm* [handwritten margin]
*300* [handwritten margin]
*7200 Krpm* [handwritten margin]

7. List the size and rpm of the two drives with the lowest performance:

*(Second worst) Transcend CompAck Flash 266×2GB (USB2)* [handwritten]
*(worst)* [handwritten]

8. Use the bottom field of the Drives Benchmark window to fill in the following chart. (Scroll down as necessary to display the information you need.)

| Category | Value |
|---|---|
| Drive class | |
| Total space | |
| Sequential read | |
| Random read | |
| Buffered write | |
| Sequential write | |
| Random write | |
| Average access time | |

## REVIEW QUESTIONS

1. Why might you want to test your drive with Sandra?

2. Based on the drive ratings information you got from Sandra, does a drive perform better if it spins faster or slower?

*① better* [handwritten]

3. Based on the drive ratings information you got from Sandra, does a drive perform better if it reads data randomly or sequentially?

*18.40* [handwritten]

4. Why shouldn't you use the system when Sandra is testing a drive?

_Sandra took all resource._

# LAB 8.3 USE DISK MANAGEMENT

## OBJECTIVES

The goal of this lab is to help you use Disk Management to work with local hard drives. After completing this lab, you will be able to:

◢ Create a partition from unused disk space

◢ Specify a file system

◢ Format a partition

◢ Delete a partition

## MATERIALS REQUIRED

This lab requires the following:

◢ Windows 2000/XP Professional operating system

◢ A printer

◢ Windows 2000/XP Professional installation CD or installation files

◢ Unallocated disk space

## LAB PREPARATION

Before the lab begins, the instructor or lab assistant needs to do the following:

◢ Verify that Windows starts with no errors.

◢ Provide each student with access to the Windows 2000/XP Professional installation files, if needed.

◢ Verify that there's unallocated space on the hard drive.

## ACTIVITY BACKGROUND

Disk Management is a Microsoft Management Console (MMC) snap-in and an administrative tool installed in the Computer Management console by default. To start Disk Management, you need to start Computer Management first. Unlike Fdisk, Disk Management allows you to partition and format disk space from within Windows. In this lab, you create and delete two different partitions using unallocated disk space.

**ESTIMATED COMPLETION TIME: 30 minutes**

### Activity

To work with your local hard drive using Disk Management, follow these steps:

1. Log on with an administrator account. In Windows XP, open Control Panel, click **Performance and Maintenance**, and then click **Administrative Tools**. In Windows 2000,

open Control Panel and double-click the **Administrative Tools** icon. The Administrative Tools window opens.

2. Double-click **Computer Management**. The Computer Management snap-in opens in an MMC. In the left pane, click **Disk Management**. The Disk Management interface opens in the right pane (see Figure 8-1).

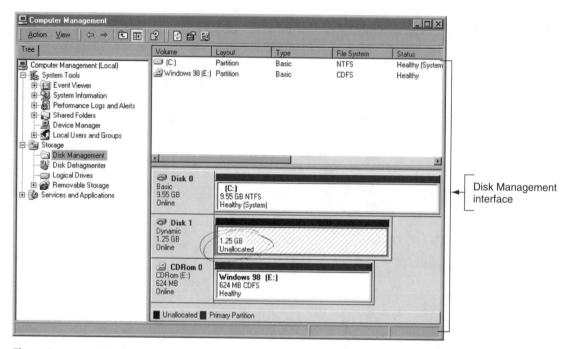

**Figure 8-1**    Use Disk Management to manage hard drives

3. Use the information at the top of the right pane to complete the following chart:

| Volume | Layout | Type | File System | Status | Capacity |
|--------|--------|------|-------------|--------|----------|
|        |        |      |             |        |          |
|        |        |      |             |        |          |
|        |        |      |             |        |          |

4. Information about each physical drive is displayed in the bottom section of the right pane. In addition, a graphic shows each drive's space distribution. Note that drives are labeled with numbers (0, 1, and so forth) and logical drives or volumes are labeled with letters (C, D, E, and so forth). If a hard drive has just been installed and not yet partitioned, the graphic shows all unallocated (unpartitioned) space, as in Figure 8-1. What drive letters are used on your system?

_C - D. DRIVE_

5. Right-click a blank area of the C drive space in the Disk Management interface. A shortcut menu opens with the following options:

◢ *Open*—Displays the drive's contents in a window similar to My Computer.

◢ *Explore*—Displays the drive's contents in a window similar to Windows Explorer.

    ◢ *Mark Active Partition*—Marks the current partition as the partition from which Windows is loaded.

    ◢ *Change Drive Letter and Path*—Allows you to select a new letter for the drive. For instance, you can change the drive letter from C to F.

    ◢ *Format*—Allows you to format a partition and make partition-related choices, including specifying the file system and sector size. *Note*: Windows XP protects itself by disabling Format on the (System) partition.

    ◢ *Delete Partition*—Allows you to delete an entire partition and all its contents.

    ◢ *Properties*—Displays information about the partition, such as how it's formatted.

    ◢ *Help*—Provides information about Disk Management.

6. Right-click the unpartitioned area of the disk drive, which is labeled Unallocated. List the differences between the options in this shortcut menu and the menu you examined in Step 5:

_____

_____

In the next set of steps, you create a new partition from unpartitioned space. Note that the partition you're creating should use only *currently unpartitioned* space. Follow these steps:

1. Using *only unpartitioned space*, create and format a new partition using the FAT32 file system and drive letter S. List the steps to perform this task:

_____

_____

_____

_____

2. Print a screen shot of the Disk Management window showing the FAT32 drive S.

3. Delete the partition you just created. List the steps to perform this task:

_____

_____

4. Using *only unpartitioned space*, create and format a new NTFS partition using the drive letter H. List the steps to perform this task:

_____

_____

_____

5. Print a screen shot of the Disk Management window showing the NTFS drive H.

6. Close the Computer Management window.

## CRITICAL THINKING: MANAGING PARTITIONS FROM THE RECOVERY CONSOLE (ADDITIONAL 60 MINUTES)

Do the following to practice managing partitions from the Recovery Console:

1. Open the Windows 2000/XP Recovery Console. List the steps to perform this task:

_____

_____

_____

2. Open Help and display information about the Diskpart command, including possible command-line options. List the steps to perform this task:

_____

_____

_____

3. Delete the NTFS partition you created earlier using Disk Management. List the steps to perform this task:

_____

_____

_____

4. Create and format a new NTFS partition, using the drive letter R. List the steps to perform this task:

_____

_____

_____

5. Delete the newly created partition. List the steps to perform this task:

_____

_____

_____

## REVIEW QUESTIONS

1. Name an advantage that Disk Management has over Fdisk:

_____

2. What happens to all the information in a partition if you delete the partition?

_____

_____

3. What feature opens if you choose Explore from a shortcut menu in Disk Management?

_____

4. Is it possible to create two partitions, using different file systems, from one area of unallocated disk space? Explain:

_____

_____

_____

5. List the steps for removing two empty partitions and creating one single NTFS partition assigned the drive letter T:

_____

_____

_____

_____

_____

_____

_____

_____

_____

## LAB 8.4 USE HARD DRIVE UTILITIES

### OBJECTIVES

The goal of this lab is to give you an opportunity to work with utilities from hard drive manufacturers that examine and diagnose hard drive problems. After completing this lab, you will be able to:

◢ Identify your hard drive manufacturer

◢ Evaluate utilities that hard drive manufacturers provide for their drives

◢ Test for hard drive problems

### MATERIALS REQUIRED

This lab requires the following:

◢ Windows 2000/XP or Windows 9x operating system

◢ Internet access

◢ A printer

◢ A blank floppy disk or burnable CD

## LAB PREPARATION

Before the lab begins, the instructor or lab assistant needs to do the following:

◢ Verify that Windows starts with no errors.

◢ Verify that Internet access is available.

## ACTIVITY BACKGROUND

Hard drive problems can manifest themselves in different ways. The drive might exhibit immediate and total failure so that it doesn't operate at all. If the failure is caused by a problem with the platters, you might not be able to boot at all if the area where system files are stored is affected. If system files aren't affected, you might be able to boot and work normally but could have file loss or file corruption. Then again, you might never realize you have a hard drive problem if your hard drive has bad sectors because data might not be saved to that particular physical area of the disk. More often, however, when a disk begins to fail, you notice errors. One tool you can use to diagnose hard drive problems is diagnostic software that your hard drive manufacturer supplies. In this lab, you identify your drive manufacturer and use its software to examine your drive.

**ESTIMATED COMPLETION TIME: 60 minutes**

 **Activity**

When you need to use a hard drive diagnostic utility, first you must identify your hard drive's manufacturer. To do that, you use a utility for that purpose from Seagate. Follow these steps to identify your drive:

1. Open your browser, and go to **www.seagate.com/support/seatools/index.html**.

2. Look for the section under SeaTools Online, and follow the links to learn more about and run the SeaTools Online Data Safe Drive Self Test. Click the **English** link to run the software in English. A new window opens, displaying the SeaTools Online testing options.

3. In the new window, click the **Drive Self Test** link to do a quick test of your drive. You might receive a warning about trusting content from Seagate or Ontrack. If you see this prompt, click **Yes** to receive the content. If your browser displays a message in the address bar asking permission to install an ActiveX control, click the address bar to continue. By doing this, you're allowing a small program to be downloaded to your PC and run to identify your drive. Follow instructions to download and run the program.

4. A window now lists your drive information. Record the drive information on the following lines as it's displayed. If you have more than one hard drive, all the drives in your system are listed. Included in the list is the hard drive manufacturer. You use the drive manufacturer information later in this lab. (Note that if the drive name begins with ST, the drive is made by Seagate.)

_____

_____

5. To select the drive to test, click the check box to the left of your drive information, and then click **Next**. A list of tests is displayed in the next window.

6. Click the **Run Short Drive Self Test**, and then click **Next**. The test begins in the same window. The test might take a few minutes. When it's done, record the results:

_____

_____

_____

_____

_____

7. When you have recorded your results, close the window. A message box informs you that you might not want to navigate away from the site. Click **OK** to close it and continue the lab.

Next, you find out about hard drive utilities supplied by several hard drive manufacturers.

Maxtor offers PowerMax to support its hard drives. Do the following to find out about this software:

1. In your Web browser, go to **www.maxtor.com**. Click the **Software Downloads** link and then the **Top Downloads** link. Answer the following questions:

   ◢ What is the purpose of the MaxBlast software?

   _____

   ◢ When might you want to use the MaxBlast software?

   _____

2. Now click the **PowerMax** link. Examine the information on the page and answer these questions:

   ◢ What types of problems does the software identify?

   _____

   _____

   ◢ How do you run the PowerMax utility?

   _____

   _____

   ◢ List the three main steps to prepare to run the utility:

   _____

   _____

   _____

3. If you have a Maxtor drive, click the link to download PowerMax and follow the directions onscreen to save it in its own folder. What is the file name and path to the file?

   _____

The IBM line of hard drives was purchased by Hitachi, which provides Drive Fitness Test for its hard drives. Do the following to find out about this software:

1. In your Web browser, go to **www.hitachigst.com**. Click **Support**, and then click **Downloads**. The software can be run from a bootable floppy disk or CD.

2. Search the information about the product, and answer the following questions:

   ◢ What types of drives are supported and what three types are expressly not supported?

   _____

   _____

   ◢ What types of analysis does the software perform?

   _____

   _____

   ◢ If you have Linux installed on your system, how can you still create a bootable floppy disk to use the utility?

   _____

   _____

3. If you have an IBM or Hitachi drive, click the link to download the Drive Fitness Test utility and save it in its own folder. What is the file name and path to the file?

   _____

Western Digital provides Data Lifeguard. Do the following to find out about this software:

1. In your Web browser, go to **http://support.wdc.com/download**, and click the link in the Data Lifeguard Tools section to download Data Lifeguard Diagnostic for Windows.

2. Examine the information and answer these questions:

   ◢ What versions of Windows can use this software?

   _____

   ◢ What is the purpose of the Write-Zeroes-To-Drive feature of the software? When would you want to use this feature?

   _____

   _____

3. If you have a Western Digital drive, click the link to download the utility and save it to its own folder. What is the file name and path to the file?

   _____

Seagate offers Data Lifeguard. Do the following to find out about this software:

1. In your Web browser, go to **www.seagate.com/support/seatools/index.html**, and click the **Learn More** link for SeaTools Desktop.

2. Examine the information and answer these questions:

   ◢ What percentage of drives returned to Seagate are found to be healthy?

   _____

◢ The utility you download runs in Windows only one time. What is the purpose of this one-time run?

_____

3. If you have a Seagate drive, click the link to download this utility and save the file to its own folder. What is the file name and path to the file?

_____

Next, follow these steps to use a manufacturer's utility to test your drive:

1. If your drive is from one of the previous manufacturers, follow the instructions on your drive manufacturer's Web site to create a bootable floppy disk and use it to perform the test for your hard drive.

2. Summarize the process and results:

_____

_____

_____

_____

If your hard drive isn't made by one of the previous manufacturers, go to your manufacturer's Web site and search for diagnostic software. What software did you find?

_____

## REVIEW QUESTIONS

1. What are some symptoms of hard drive problems listed on the hard drive manufacturers' Web sites? List three in order of seriousness:

_____

_____

_____

2. Which hard drive manufacturer's Web site was the most informative and easiest to use? Why?

_____

_____

_____

3. Which utility from a hard drive manufacturer seemed to be the most powerful? Why?

_____

_____

_____

4. What was the most common method used to run the utilities?

_____

5. Why is it useful to run the utility from a bootable floppy disk or CD rather than from Windows?

_____

6. What operating system is used on the bootable floppy disk or CD?

_____

7. How do you determine that your system is set to boot from a floppy disk or CD?

_____

# LAB 8.5 TROUBLESHOOT HARD DRIVES

## OBJECTIVES

The goal of this lab is to help you troubleshoot common hard drive problems. After completing this lab, you will be able to:

- Simulate common hard drive problems
- Diagnose and repair common hard drive problems
- Document the process

## MATERIALS REQUIRED

This lab requires the following:

- A computer with a hard drive subsystem that you can sabotage
- A bootable disk
- A PC toolkit with antistatic ground strap
- A workgroup of 2 to 4 students

## LAB PREPARATION

Before the lab begins, the instructor or lab assistant needs to do the following:

- Verify that Windows starts with no errors.
- Verify that a computer with a hard drive that can be sabotaged is available for each student or workgroup.

## ACTIVITY BACKGROUND

This lab gives you practice diagnosing and remedying common hard drive problems.

**ESTIMATED COMPLETION TIME: 45 minutes**

 **Activity**

1. Verify that your hard drive is working by using a command prompt window or Windows Explorer to display files on the drive.
2. Switch computers with another team.

3. Sabotage the other team's computer by doing one of the following:

   ◢ Remove or incorrectly configure the drive jumpers.

   ◢ Remove the power connector from the drive.

   ◢ Switch data cables to place devices on incorrect IDE channels.

   ◢ Disable IDE controllers in CMOS setup.

   ◢ If allowed by your instructor, delete partitions on the hard drive.

4. Return to your computer and examine it for any symptoms of a problem.

5. On a separate piece of paper, answer the following questions about the problem's symptoms:

   ◢ What symptoms would a user notice? (Describe the symptoms as a user might describe them.)

   ◢ Does the system boot from the hard drive?

   ◢ Does POST display the hard drive?

   ◢ Can you boot from a floppy disk and change to the drive in question?

   ◢ Does the CMOS HDD Autodetect option detect the hard drive?

6. On a separate piece of paper, before you actually begin your investigation, state your initial diagnosis.

7. Diagnose and repair the problem.

8. On a separate piece of paper, list the steps to confirm your diagnosis and solve the problem.

9. Answer the following questions about your final conclusions:

   ◢ What was the problem?

   _____

   ◢ What did you do to correct the problem?

   _____

   _____

   _____

   ◢ Was your preliminary diagnosis correct?

   _____

10. Repeat Steps 1 through 9, choosing actions at random from the list in Step 3, until your team has performed all the actions. Be sure to write down the relevant information (as instructed in the steps) for each problem.

## REVIEW QUESTIONS

1. What was the first indication that the power was disconnected from your drive?

   _____

   _____

2. In what incorrect drive configuration would you be able to access files on the hard drive by booting from the floppy drive?

   _____

   _____

3. What incorrect configurations have similar symptoms?

_____

_____

4. What problem resulted in no drives being detected except for the floppy drive?

_____

_____

5. List the steps to use a drive whose partitions have been deleted:

_____

_____

_____

_____

_____

_____

# LAB 8.6 CRITICAL THINKING: USE DEBUG TO EXAMINE DISK INFORMATION

## OBJECTIVES

The goal of this lab is to help you use the Debug utility to examine the beginning of a floppy drive. After completing this lab, you will be able to:

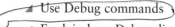

▲ Use Debug commands

▲ Explain how Debug displays information

▲ Examine the boot record on a floppy disk

## MATERIALS REQUIRED

This lab requires the following:

▲ Windows XP operating system

▲ A blank floppy disk

## LAB PREPARATION

Before the lab begins, the instructor or lab assistant needs to do the following:

▲ Verify that Windows starts with no errors.

## ACTIVITY BACKGROUND

In this lab, you use the Debug tool to examine the boot record of a startup floppy disk. The file system on a floppy disk is similar to that of a hard drive, so the concepts you learn here about floppy disks can be applied to hard drives.

Using Debug, you can view the contents of a disk or memory location. This information helps you gain the strong technical insight you need to take advantage of more user-friendly data recovery software and to be confident that you understand how these products work. The better you understand how data is constructed on the disk and exactly what problems can happen, the better your chances of recovering lost or damaged data.

**ESTIMATED COMPLETION TIME: 45 minutes**

### Activity

Follow these steps to examine the boot record of a startup disk:

1. Boot your PC into Windows and then insert a blank floppy disk.

2. Click **Start, My Computer.** In the My Computer window, right-click the $3\frac{1}{2}$ **Floppy (A:)** icon, and click **Format** in the shortcut menu. Click **Create an MS-DOS startup disk,** and then click **Start.** In the warning message box that opens, click **OK.** After the formatting is completed, you'll have a bootable startup disk. Click **OK** to close the completion message box, and then close the Format dialog box.

3. Click **Start, Run.** Type **cmd** and click **OK** to open a command prompt window. At the command prompt, type **debug** and press **Enter.** The Debug utility starts, and the prompt changes to a dash (–).

The Debug utility can be used to examine and change the contents of a location in memory. Although Debug can't edit storage devices directly, it can also be used to view data on a storage device, such as a floppy disk or hard drive, by copying the data into memory first. To examine the startup disk you just created, first you have to copy some of its contents into memory. Follow these steps:

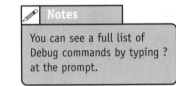

Notes

You can see a full list of Debug commands by typing ? at the prompt.

1. To view information, you're going to use the D command (which stands for "dump"). Type **D** and press **Enter.**

2. Observe the output of the D command, which shows the contents of memory beginning with a memory address (see Figure 8-2). Note that this command displays memory 128 bytes at a time. The information is in lines of 16 bytes each, with the start address at the left side, the hex value of each byte in the middle, and the ASCII interpretation (if any) of each byte at the right side.

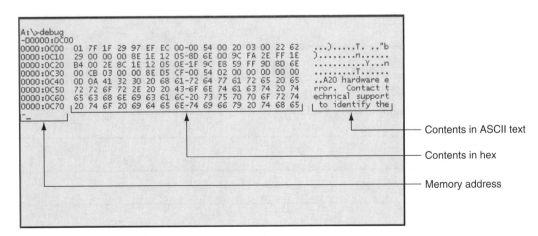

**Figure 8-2** Results of the Debug D command showing the contents of 128 bytes of memory

3. Each time you dump memory, the pointer in memory moves to the next group of 128 bytes. By using successive dump commands, you can move through memory consecutively, dumping 128 bytes of memory to the screen with each command. To view the next 128 bytes, simply type **D** and press **Enter** again.

4. If the contents of memory aren't ASCII text, the attempt to display the ASCII interpretation looks like gibberish in that section. Continue to scan each 128-byte section until you find a section of data that's readable in ASCII. This shouldn't take more than a few minutes. What does the code at these memory addresses refer to?

_____

_____

5. The next step is to copy, or load, the boot record from the floppy disk into memory. Type **L0 0 0 1** and press **Enter**. You should hear the floppy drive run. Answer these questions to decipher the command:

   ◢ What does "L" stand for?

   _____

   ◢ What does the first 0 indicate?

   _____

   ◢ What does the second 0 indicate?

   _____

   ◢ What does the third 0 indicate?

   _____

   ◢ What does the 1 indicate?

   _____

6. The information from this sector of the floppy disk is now loaded in system memory. To view this information, type **D0** and press **Enter**. Can you see any indication of which file system is used to format the floppy disk? Explain:

_____

_____

7. Figure 8-3 shows the result of this dump command for a startup disk formatted with DOS. Compare it to your dump. What differences do you see? Table 8-1 lists the items in a boot record to help you with your comparisons.

_____

_____

_____

_____

8. To exit Debug, type **Q** and press **Enter**. You return to the command prompt.

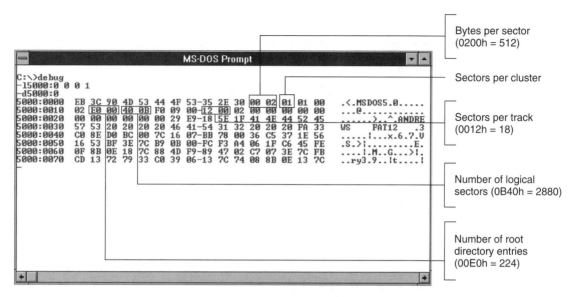

**Figure 8-3** The first 128 bytes of the boot record of a floppy disk formatted with DOS

| Description | Number of bytes |
|---|---|
| Machine code | 11 |
| Bytes per sector | 2 |
| Sectors per cluster | 1 |
| Reserved | 2 |
| Number of FATs | 1 |
| Number of root directory entries | 2 |
| Number of logical sectors | 2 |
| Medium descriptor byte | 1 |
| Sectors per FAT | 2 |
| Sectors per track | 2 |
| Heads | 2 |
| Number of hidden sectors | 2 |
| Total sectors in logical volume | 4 |
| Physical drive number | 1 |
| Reserved | 1 |
| Extended boot signature record | 1 |
| 32-bit binary volume ID | 4 |
| Volume label | 11 |
| Type of file system (FAT12, FAT16, or FAT32) | 8 |
| Program to load operating system (bootstrap loader) | Remainder of the sector |

**Table 8-1** Layout of the boot record of a floppy disk or hard drive

## REVIEW QUESTIONS

1. Why do storage devices have to be copied into memory before their contents can be viewed in Debug?

_____

_____

2. What Debug command dumps data at the beginning of the memory address space?

_____

3. What command loads two sectors from the C drive, starting at the sixth sector?

_____

_____

4. Debug displays data _128_ bytes at a time.

5. Why do you think it's important to be careful when tinkering with the Debug utility?

_____

_____

# LAB 8.7 CRITICAL THINKING: SABOTAGE AND REPAIR A HARD DRIVE SUBSYSTEM

## OBJECTIVES

The goal of this lab is to learn to troubleshoot a hard drive by repairing a sabotaged system.

## MATERIALS REQUIRED

This lab requires the following:

▲ A PC designated for sabotage (containing no important data)

▲ A workgroup of 2 to 4 students

## LAB PREPARATION

Before the lab begins, the instructor or lab assistant needs to do the following:

▲ Verify that Windows starts with no errors.

▲ Verify that a PC that can be sabotaged is available for each student or workgroup.

## ACTIVITY BACKGROUND

You have learned about several tools and methods for troubleshooting and recovering from a hard drive failure. This lab gives you the opportunity to use these skills in a troubleshooting situation. Your group will work with another group to sabotage a system, and then you recover your own sabotaged system.

*[handwritten at top: n of cyln = n of Tract.]*

**ESTIMATED COMPLETION TIME: 45 minutes**

**Activity**

*[handwritten left margin: HD, φ φ, 360K, 1.2 mB, 3½ in, 720K, 1.44MB, 2.88MB, 2×IDE-PATA, 2 HDD/Controller, MA/SL]*

1. If your system's hard drive contains important data, back it up to another medium. Is there anything else you would like to back up before another group sabotages the system?

2. Trade systems with another group and sabotage the other group's system while that group sabotages your system. Do one thing that will cause the hard drive to fail to work or return errors after the boot. Use any of the problems suggested in Lab 8.5, or you can introduce a new problem. (Do *not* alter the operating system files.) What did you do to sabotage the other group's system?

*[handwritten: blue screen, freeze screen, bad Memory]*

3. Return to your system and troubleshoot it.

4. Describe the problem as a user would describe it to you if you were working at a help desk:

5. What is your first guess as to the source of the problem?

*[handwritten left margin: SATA, 1 HDD/controller, SCSI, 7/15, disk mngmt]*

6. List the steps you took in the troubleshooting process:

*[handwritten: Statu, Both, Cache, Ecc, non-Ecc, Parity, Dynamic, Sim us, 30 pin, 72 pin, SDRam (Sync), DDR, DDR2]*

*[handwritten: ♦Sector, 512 bits]*

7. What did you do that finally solved the problem and returned the system to good working order?

*[handwritten: format, FDD, create tracts & sectors]*

*[handwritten bottom: HDD, Low - factory Sector Tractor, High - boot Sector, Create Partition assign Letter to Harddrive, NTFS, ② FAT, keep tract file, 20 GB, C: 20 GB, 10 GB, Format C, 2 (3) logical]*

## REVIEW QUESTIONS

1. Now that you have been through this troubleshooting experience, what would you do differently the next time the same symptoms are exhibited?

   _____

2. What operating system utilities did you use or could you have used to solve the problem?

   _____

3. Is there any third-party software that might have been useful in solving this problem?

   _____

4. In a real-life situation, what might happen that would cause this problem to occur? List three things:

   _____

   _____

   _____

# CHAPTER 9

# Installing and Supporting I/O Devices

**Labs included in this chapter:**

- **Lab 9.1:** Gather Information on Your System
- **Lab 9.2:** Identify Hardware Conflicts Using Device Manager
- **Lab 9.3:** Simulate Serial Port Communications
- **Lab 9.4:** Diagnose Simple Hardware Problems
- **Lab 9.5:** Use a Multimeter to Inspect Cables
- **Lab 9.6:** Critical Thinking: Sabotage and Repair a System

# LAB 9.1 GATHER INFORMATION ON YOUR SYSTEM

## OBJECTIVES

The goal of this lab is to teach you how to use Sandra, Control Panel, and other sources to compile information on your system specifications. After completing this lab, you will be able to:

◢ Use various Sandra modules to get information about your system

◢ Use Control Panel applets to get information about your system

◢ Compile a documentation notebook

## MATERIALS REQUIRED

This lab requires the following:

◢ Windows 2000/XP or Windows 9x operating system

◢ Documentation you collected about your computer in Lab 4.4

◢ SiSoftware Sandra, installed in Lab 1.3

## LAB PREPARATION

Before the lab begins, the instructor or lab assistant needs to do the following:

◢ Verify that Windows starts with no errors.

◢ Verify that Sandra is installed or available.

## ACTIVITY BACKGROUND

As you continue to work with different kinds of computers, you'll find it extremely useful to maintain a report listing the components installed on each computer. This report is especially important if you're responsible for many computers. In this lab, you create such a report. (Note that you need to refer to this document in future labs.) You can also use Sandra in this lab, which you installed in Lab 1.3.

> **ESTIMATED COMPLETION TIME: 45 minutes**

 **Activity**

Fill in Tables 9-1 through 9-3, which will become part of the total documentation you keep about your PC. When necessary, refer to the documentation about your computer that you collected in Lab 4.4 or use the Sandra software. After you have finished the tables, make copies of them and place them in your computer's documentation notebook. If you aren't sure which menus and applets to use in Sandra, experiment to find the information you need. Some information can be found in more than one place.

| Location of computer | |
|---|---|
| Owner | |
| Date purchased | |
| Date warranty expires | |
| Size and speed of CPU | |
| Type of motherboard | |
| Amount of RAM | |
| Type of monitor | |
| Type of video card | |
| Hard drive type and size | |
| Size of disk drive A | |
| Size of disk drive B (if present) | |

**Table 9-1** Computer fact sheet

| Software install name | Version | Installed by | Date |
|---|---|---|---|
| | | | |
| | | | |
| | | | |
| | | | |
| | | | |

**Table 9-2** Software installed

| Name of device | IRQ | I/O address | DMA channel device | Driver file name |
|---|---|---|---|---|
| Serial port 1 | | | | |
| Serial port 2 | | | | |
| Parallel port | | | | |
| Mouse | | | | |
| Modem | | | | |
| CD-ROM drive | | | | |
| Display adapter | | | | |
| Network card | | | | |

**Table 9-3** Other devices

Create a documentation notebook or binder for your computer that includes copies of these tables as well as any other documentation you have collected about your computer. Save space for troubleshooting steps you learn in future labs. You'll need this notebook in future labs.

## REVIEW QUESTIONS

1. How did you determine the CPU type?

_Pentium 4 CPU._

2. How did you determine the driver your display adapter uses?

*Intel.*
*Talmmtsddl*

*C:\Windows \system32\ drivers\302 sys*
*Intel 6.13.1.3162 PRver version*

3. List two ways to determine the amount of RAM installed on a system:

*device manager*
*system property      > 56MB*

4. Why is it important for PC technicians to keep documentation on computers they are responsible for?

*let everybody know what you change*
*to follow up in the future*

# LAB 9.2 IDENTIFY HARDWARE CONFLICTS USING DEVICE MANAGER

## OBJECTIVES

The goal of this lab is to help you learn to use Device Manager to identify hardware conflicts. After completing this lab, you will be able to:

⊿ Use Device Manager to investigate your system specifications

⊿ Detect hardware conflicts using Device Manager

⊿ Use Device Manager properties to determine which resources are causing a conflict

## MATERIALS REQUIRED

This lab requires the following:

⊿ Windows 2000/XP or Windows 9x operating system

⊿ A PC with no hardware resource conflicts

⊿ A hardware device, such as a sound card, you can install to create a hardware resource conflict

⊿ Windows installation CD or installation files

## LAB PREPARATION

Before the lab begins, the instructor or lab assistant needs to do the following:

⊿ Verify that Windows starts with no errors.

⊿ Verify that the system is free of resource conflicts.

⊿ Provide a device that can be used to create a resource conflict.

⊿ Provide each student with access to the the Windows installation files, if needed.

## ACTIVITY BACKGROUND

Device Manager is an excellent tool for finding information about hardware specifications. You can also use it to diagnose problems with hardware devices, including those caused by two or more devices attempting to use the same system resources (a situation called a hardware resource conflict). Among other things, Device Manager can identify faulty or disabled devices, conflicting devices, and resources currently in use. This lab teaches you how to use Device Manager to find this information. You start by examining your system and verifying that no hardware resource conflicts currently exist on your system. Then you install a device that creates a resource conflict and observe the effects.

**ESTIMATED COMPLETION TIME: 30 minutes**

### Activity

You can use Device Manager to print a report about your system. Printing one when your system is working correctly is a good idea because you can use that report later as a baseline comparison when troubleshooting conflicts or other problems.

1. Open Device Manager, and click **Action**, **Print** from the menu. In the Report type section, click the **All devices and system summary** option button. If you're using a lab PC that doesn't have access to a printer, you can save the report to a floppy disk and go to another computer to print it.

2. Answer the following:

   ◢ How many pages are in the report?

   _____

   ◢ In one or two sentences, describe the type of information included on the report:

   _____

   _____

   ◢ List two items in the report that aren't displayed in Device Manager windows:

   _____

   _____

3. Put the Device Manager report in your documentation notebook (which you created in Lab 9.1).

Next, you use Device Manager to verify that there are no hardware conflicts:

1. Using Device Manager, check for conflicts among devices. Conflicts are indicated by a yellow triangle with an exclamation point. (Note that if a device has been disabled and isn't working at all, a red circle with a slash appears over the yellow triangle and exclamation point.)

2. Shut down the system, and install the component and its drivers that your instructor supplied. This component should conflict with another component already installed on the system. If you don't have a device that causes a conflict, remove a nonessential device, such as a modem card or sound card, which at least causes Device Manager to report an error.

3. Reboot and install drivers if prompted. You might be asked to provide access to Windows setup files. Did you see a message indicating a conflict or other error? If so, record it here:

   _____

   _____

4. Open Device Manager. Does Device Manager report any conflicting devices? Describe the problem as Device Manager reports it, listing all devices causing conflicts:

_____

_____

5. For each device reporting a conflict, open the device's Properties dialog box by right-clicking the device and clicking **Properties** in the shortcut menu. What messages do you see in the Device status section?

_____

_____

6. Next, click the **Resource** tab in the Properties dialog box. What message do you see in the Conflicting device list section?

_____

7. Examine the information in the Resource type and Settings columns. What resources is the device using?

① DMA      ④ Memory

② IO

③ IRQ

8. Does it seem that you might be able to change settings for this device?

_____

9. Close the device's Properties dialog box, but leave Device Manager open if you're doing the Critical Thinking Activity.

## CRITICAL THINKING (ADDITIONAL 15 MINUTES)

While the two devices are in conflict, use Device Manager to print a report on your system. Remember that if your PC isn't connected to a printer, you can save the report to a floppy disk and print it from another computer. Compare the report created when the system was working correctly to the report created when conflicts existed, and note the differences.

Now that you have observed two devices in conflict, you remove one of the conflicting devices. When you remove a device, you should uninstall it in Device Manager before removing it from your system. If you don't, when you want to install a similar or the same device later, you end up with two devices installed under Device Manager, which can cause the new device not to work.

Follow these steps to uninstall the device in Device Manager and then remove it:

1. In Windows 2000/XP, right-click the device, and then click **Uninstall** in the shortcut menu. In the Confirm Device Removal dialog box that opens, click **OK**. In Windows 9x, click to select the problem device in Device Manager and click **Remove**. If prompted to restart the computer, click **No**.

2. Close Device Manager and shut down the system.

3. Remove the device you installed earlier.

4. Restart the computer, open Device Manager, and verify that no conflicts exist.

## REVIEW QUESTIONS

1. What symbol in Device Manager indicates that a component isn't working correctly?

   _____

2. What two devices in your system were in conflict?

   _____

3. What resources were causing a conflict?

   _____

   _____

4. Before physically removing a device from a system, what should you do?

   _____

5. What would happen if you didn't uninstall the device before removing it from your system?

   _____

# LAB 9.3 SIMULATE SERIAL PORT COMMUNICATION

## OBJECTIVES

The goal of this lab is to show how serial communication works by using a game. After completing this lab, you will be able to:

- Identify pin arrangements
- Explain which pins are used for handshake and data transfer

## MATERIALS REQUIRED

This lab requires the following:

- Seven pieces of string, each approximately 4 feet long
- A workgroup of 8 students

## LAB PREPARATION

Before the lab begins, the instructor or lab assistant needs to do the following:

- Divide the class into groups of 8 students.
- Give each group of students seven 4-foot pieces of string.

## ACTIVITY BACKGROUND

RS-232 standards specify cabling and communication methods for PCs. Among other things, they specify the sequence of signals that must travel across a serial cable to complete a handshake and transmit data between devices. In this lab, to keep things simple, you simulate a handshake and data transfer on a null modem cable. You and your fellow students play the part of the serial ports, using pieces of string for the cable.

**ESTIMATED COMPLETION TIME: 30 minutes**

**Activity**

Follow these steps to simulate a cable connection between two devices:

1. Position eight students in two rows facing each other, with four on each side. Designate the students on one side as Students A through D and the students on the other side as Students E through H. Students E and A should be facing each other, as should Students B and F, and so on down the line. The two groups of students make up Computer ABCD and Computer EFGH.

2. Stretch seven strings between the eight students, as shown in Figure 9-1. Student A's left hand and Student E's right hand are Pin 1 on their respective serial ports. The numbers should proceed down the line until Pin 8 is Student D's right hand and Student H's left hand. Table 9-4 describes the null modem cable communication your workgroup is simulating. Notice that Pins 1 and 9 aren't used in null modem cable communication and are, therefore, omitted from this simulation.

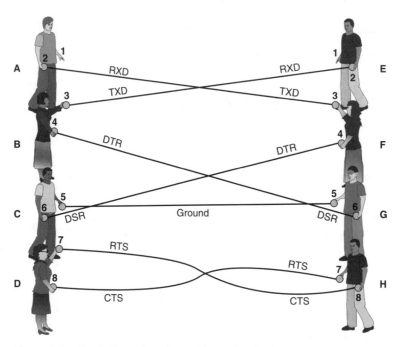

**Figure 9-1**   Simulating null modem cable communication

| Pin number on one connector | Pin number on the other connector | How the wire connecting the two pins is used |
|---|---|---|
| 1 | 1 | Not used |
| 2 (RXD) | 3 (TXD) | Data sent by one computer is received by the other |
| 3 (TXD) | 2 (RXD) | Data received by one computer is sent by the other |
| 4 (DTR) | 6 (DSR) | One end says to the other end "I'm able to talk" |
| 5 (Ground) | 5 (Ground) | Both ends are grounded |
| 6 (DSR) | 4 (DTR) | One end hears the other end say "I'm able to talk" |
| 7 (RTS) | 8 (CTS) | One end says to the other "I'm ready to talk" |
| 8 (CTS) | 7 (RTS) | One end hears the other say "I'm ready to talk" |
| 9 | 9 | Not used |

**Table 9-4**   Pin connections for a 9-pin null modem cable

Here are the meanings of the abbreviations in the table and figure:

- *RXD*—Receive data
- *TXD*—Transmit data
- *DTR*—Data terminal ready
- *DSR*—Data set ready
- *CTS*—Clear to send
- *RTS*—Request to send

Follow these steps to perform the handshake and then send and receive data. Suppose that Computer EFGH has initiated communication to Computer ABCD, and Computer ABCD is ready to receive data from Computer EFGH.

1. Student G raises his left hand indicating that he's able to talk (DSR high).

2. Student B raises her hand on the other end of the same string to indicate that she has received Student G's communication.

3. Student C raises his right hand, indicating he understands that Computer EFGH is able to talk (DTR high).

4. Student F raises her left hand, indicating she has received the communication.

5. Student H raises his right hand, indicating he's ready to talk (RTS high).

6. Student D raises her right hand, indicating she has received the communication.

7. Student D raises her left hand, indicating she's ready to receive data from Computer EFGH.

8. Student H raises his left hand, indicating he has received the communication.

   Computer ABCD has just indicated that it's able and ready to have a conversation. (DTR indicates that Computer ABCD is open to having a conversation, and RTS tells Computer EFGH to go ahead and start talking.) Computer EFGH is now ready to start talking to Computer ABCD.

9. Student F repeatedly raises and lowers her hand—which represents the TXD pin—to indicate that data is being sent. (Each raise of the hand represents one bit transmitted.)

10. Student A sees this signal and repeatedly raises and lowers his right hand—which represents the RXD pin—to indicate the reception of each bit.

    Now suppose that computer EFGH has been transmitting for a while and Computer ABCD has noticed that its buffer is getting full. (That is, it has to process what Computer EFGH has said.) This capability of the receiving computer to stop a transmission so that it can catch up is called flow control.

11. Student D lowers her left hand (RTS) to indicate that Computer ABCD is processing and doesn't want to hear any more right now.

12. Student H quits receiving CTS high and lowers his hand to indicate he has received the communication.

13. Other students keep their hands raised, indicating that the conversation still isn't over.

14. Student F quits sending data and keeps her hand down.

    At this point, Computer EFGH has quit talking but hasn't yet finished sending all the data. After a pause, Computer ABCD finishes processing and the buffer is empty. Computer ABCD is now ready to listen again.

15. Student D raises her left hand, indicating RTS high.

16. Student H raises his hand, indicating CTS high. In response, Student F starts sending data again until all data is sent.

17. Students H and G lower their hands, indicating that Computer EFGH has nothing more to say and wants to end the conversation.

18. All students then lower their hands in response to Students H and G. The conversation is ended.

Now that you have seen how Computer EFGH sends data to Computer ABCD, answer the following questions about communication from Computer ABCD to Computer EFGH:

▲ Which hands should be raised to indicate that Computer EFGH is able to communicate with Computer ABCD?

_____

▲ Which hands should be raised to indicate that Computer EFGH is ready to receive data?

_____

▲ Which hands should be raised to indicate data flowing from Computer ABCD to Computer EFGH?

_____

▲ Which hands should be lowered when Computer EFGH's buffers are full?

_____

▲ Which hands should be lowered when the communication is finished?

_____

19. Now raise and lower your hands to simulate communication from Computer ABCD to Computer EFGH.

## REVIEW QUESTIONS

1. What does a signal raised on Pin 8 indicate?

_____

2. Pin 4 on one end of the cable is connected to Pin _____ on the other end of the cable.

3. Data passes from Pin _____ on one end of the cable to Pin _____ on the other end of the cable.

4. What is the sole purpose of Pin 5's participation in network communication?

_____

# LAB 9.4 DIAGNOSE SIMPLE HARDWARE PROBLEMS

## OBJECTIVES

The goal of this lab is to give you practice diagnosing and repairing simple hardware problems. After completing this lab, you will be able to:

▲ Start with a functioning PC, introduce a problem, and remedy the problem

▲ Diagnose a problem caused by someone else

▲ Record the troubleshooting process

## MATERIALS REQUIRED

This lab requires the following:

◢ Windows 2000/XP or Windows 9x operating system

◢ A PC toolkit including screwdrivers and an antistatic ground strap

◢ Pen and paper

◢ The documentation notebook you began creating in Lab 9.1

◢ A workgroup of 2 to 4 students

## LAB PREPARATION

Before the lab begins, the instructor or lab assistant needs to do the following:

◢ Verify that Windows starts with no errors.

## ACTIVITY BACKGROUND

If you have worked in a computer repair shop dealing with the general public, you know that about half the problems you see are the result of an inexperienced person making a slight mistake when configuring a system and lacking the knowledge to diagnose and remedy the problem. Unless you're very skilled and lucky, you'll make many of the same mistakes from time to time. Your advantage is that you'll have the experience to narrow down and identify the problem and then fix it. This lab gives you experience troubleshooting and repairing simple problems. Before you begin, team up with another workgroup in your class. Your team works with this other group throughout the lab.

### ESTIMATED COMPLETION TIME: 60 minutes

 **Activity**

1. Verify that your team's system is working correctly. Also, verify that you have the completed charts for your system from Lab 9.1.

2. Make one of the following changes to your team's system:

   ◢ Remove the power cable from the hard drive on the primary interface or highest SCSI ID.

   ◢ Reverse the data cable for the floppy drive.

   ◢ Remove the RAM and place it safely inside the case so that the other team can't see it.

   ◢ Disable IDE, SCSI, or serial ATA controllers in CMOS.

   ◢ Remove the power-on wire from the motherboard connection.

   ◢ Partially remove the data cable from the hard drive.

   ◢ For IDE drives, swap master/slave jumper assignments or set both drives to the same setting.

3. Switch places with the other team, and then diagnose and remedy the problem on your team's PC. Record the troubleshooting process on a separate sheet of paper, making sure you answer the following questions:

   ◢ Describe the problem as a user would describe it to you if you were working at a Help desk.

   ◢ What is your first guess as to the source of the problem?

   ◢ What did you do that solved the problem and returned the system to good working order?

4. Repeat Steps 1 through 3, choosing items at random from the list in Step 2. Continue until your team has made all the changes listed in Step 2.

## CRITICAL THINKING (ADDITIONAL 30 MINUTES)

If time permits, try introducing two changes at a time. This procedure can prove much more difficult.

## REVIEW QUESTIONS

1. What problems resulted in a "non-system disk" error?

*boot CD.*

*~~Data cable does not plug in well~~ if you don't have*

2. Typically, what's the first indication that RAM has been removed?

*6 sound. (~~bits~~) beeps*

3. What was the first indication of a problem with drive assignments?

*drive will not show up*

4. Name three problems resulting in symptoms similar to those for a problem with the primary slave drive:

5. What was the first indication of a floppy drive problem?

*disk drive 0 failure*

# LAB 9.5 USE A MULTIMETER TO INSPECT CABLES

## OBJECTIVES

The goal of this lab is to teach you how to use a multimeter to test cables. After completing this lab, you will be able to:

▲ Set up a multimeter to measure resistance

▲ Test cables for resistance to determine pin arrangements

▲ Test cables for broken connections

▲ Measure resistance in a resistor

## MATERIALS REQUIRED

This lab requires the following:

▲ A multimeter

▲ Three assorted cables

◢ Assorted resistors

◢ *Optional*: Internet access

◢ A workgroup of 2 to 4 students

## LAB PREPARATION

Before the lab begins, the instructor or lab assistant needs to do the following:

◢ Provide students with the required multimeter, cables, and resistors.

◢ *Optional*: Verify that Internet access is available.

## ACTIVITY BACKGROUND

One of a multimeter's many uses is to determine whether a cable is good or bad. You can also use a multimeter to determine a cable's pin arrangement. Both are done by measuring resistance in the cable. Resistance is measured in ohms. Infinite ohms (resistance) indicate that no electricity can flow; a measure of zero ohms means that electricity can flow (a state referred to as continuity). A resistor is a device that resists or controls the flow of electricity in a circuit, and a multimeter can be used to measure a resistor. You begin the lab by setting up and testing your multimeter. Then you measure resistance in cables and resistors.

**ESTIMATED COMPLETION TIME: 45 minutes**

 **Activity**

Follow these steps to set up and test your multimeter:

1. Set the multimeter to measure resistance (sometimes represented by the symbol $\Omega$).

2. With the probes not in contact with anything, observe the reading on the meter. The reading should be infinity, open, 99999.99999, or similar.

3. With the probes touching each other, observe the reading on the meter. The reading should be 0 or similar.

Now that you have verified that your multimeter is working correctly, you can use it to measure the resistance or continuity in a cable. Examine the cables your instructor supplied. In the following steps, you use your multimeter to discover the pin-outs for each cable:

1. On a separate piece of paper, create a table for each cable indicating the cable's pin-outs. Can you identify the cable from your table and your knowledge of cables?

2. For Cable 1, complete the following:

◢ Description of cable connectors:

_____

◢ Number of pins on each end of the cable:

_____

◢ Number of pins on each end of the cable that are used:

_____

◢ Type of cable:

_____

3. For Cable 2, complete the following:
   ▲ Description of cable connectors:

   _____

   ▲ Number of pins on each end of the cable:

   _____

   ▲ Number of pins on each end of the cable that are used:

   _____

   ▲ Type of cable:

   _____

4. For Cable 3, complete the following:
   ▲ Description of cable connectors:

   _____

   ▲ Number of pins on each end of the cable:

   _____

   ▲ Number of pins on each end of the cable that are used:

   _____

   ▲ Type of cable:

   _____

Suppose a user comes to you with a problem. He has a cable that connects his computer's serial port to a serial printer. He needs to order more of the same cable but doesn't know whether it's a regular serial cable or a specialized cable made specifically for this printer. One connector on the cable is 9-pin, and the other connector is 25-pin. Using this information, answer the following:

1. Describe how to determine what kind of cable he needs to order:

   _____

   _____

   _____

   _____

2. Suppose the cable is not a regular serial cable but a specialized cable. How might you give the user the pin-outs necessary to order new custom-made cables?

   _____

   _____

   _____

   _____

So far you have used a multimeter to discover cable specifications. Next, you use the multimeter to measure the resistances of several resistors.

1. Measure each resistor and record the results in the following chart. Note that resistors have colored bands indicating their intended resistance. If you're testing more than four resistors, use a separate piece of paper to record your results.

| Resistor | Resistance reading |
|---|---|
|  |  |
|  |  |
|  |  |
|  |  |

## CRITICAL THINKING (ADDITIONAL 45 MINUTES)

On an Ethernet network, a patch cable is used to connect a PC to a hub or other network device, but a crossover cable is used for PC-to-PC or hub-to-hub connections. Answer the following questions:

1. How many pins does an RJ-45 patch cable or crossover cable have?

_____

2. Research the Internet for the pin-outs of a crossover cable and a patch cable. Draw a diagram of each cable's pin-outs.

3. Have your instructor give you one patch cable and one crossover cable. Can you tell which cable is which by examining them physically?

_____

4. Use your multimeter to confirm which cable is the patch cable and which is the crossover cable. Which pins did you examine?

_____

## REVIEW QUESTIONS

1. When a multimeter is set to measure resistance, what reading would you expect when the probes are touching?

_____

2. When a multimeter is set to measure resistance, what reading would you expect when the probes aren't touching anything?

_____

3. Suppose all pins match pin-outs except one at each end, and these nonmatching pins have no continuity with any other pin. What is the likely condition of the cable?

_____

_____

4. What do the colors on resistors indicate?

5. When you're measuring resistance, is there enough electricity in the wire to cause you harm?

# LAB 9.6 CRITICAL THINKING: SABOTAGE AND REPAIR A SYSTEM

## OBJECTIVES

The goal of this lab is to learn to troubleshoot a system by recovering from a sabotaged system.

## MATERIALS REQUIRED

This lab requires the following:

▲ A PC (containing no important data) that has been designated for sabotage

▲ A workgroup of 2 to 4 students

## LAB PREPARATION

Before the lab begins, the instructor or lab assistant needs to do the following:

▲ Verify that Windows starts with no errors.

▲ Verify that students' PCs contain no important data and can be sabotaged.

## ACTIVITY BACKGROUND

You have learned about several tools and methods you can use to troubleshoot and repair a failed system or failed hardware devices. This lab gives you the opportunity to use these skills in a simulated troubleshooting situation. Your group will work with another group to sabotage a system and then repair another failed system.

**ESTIMATED COMPLETION TIME: 45 minutes**

 **Activity**

1. If the hard drive contains important data, back it up to another medium. Back up anything else you would like to save before another group sabotages the system and note it here:

2. Trade systems with another group and sabotage the other group's system while that group sabotages your system. Do one thing that will cause the system to fail to work or give errors after booting. Use any of the problems listed in Lab 9.4 or introduce a new problem. (Do *not* alter the operating system files.) What did you do to sabotage the other team's system?

3. Return to your system and troubleshoot it.

4. Describe the problem as a user would describe it to you if you were working at a help desk:

_____

_____

5. What is your first guess as to the source of the problem?

_____

6. List the steps you took in the troubleshooting process:

_____

_____

_____

_____

_____

_____

7. What did you do that finally solved the problem and returned the system to good working order?

_____

_____

## REVIEW QUESTIONS

1. Thinking back on this troubleshooting experience, what would you do differently the next time you encounter the same symptoms?

_____

_____

2. What software utilities did you use or could you have used to solve the problem?

_____

3. What third-party software utility or hardware device might have been useful in solving this problem?

_____

4. In a real-life situation, what might cause this problem to occur? List three possible causes:

_____

_____

_____

# Multimedia Devices and Mass Storage

**Labs included in this chapter:**

- **Lab 10.1:** Install a Sound Card
- **Lab 10.2:** Install a PC Video Camera
- **Lab 10.3:** Compare CD and DVD Technologies
- **Lab 10.4:** Install Dual Monitors in Windows XP
- **Lab 10.5:** Research Digital Cameras
- **Lab 10.6:** Explore Windows XP Audio Features

## LAB 10.1 INSTALL A SOUND CARD

### OBJECTIVES

The goal of this lab is to help you learn how to install a sound card. After completing this lab, you will be able to:

◢ Physically install a sound card

◢ Install device drivers

◢ Test the card and adjust the volume

### MATERIALS REQUIRED

This lab requires the following:

◢ Windows 2000/XP operating system

◢ Windows 2000/XP installation CD or installation files

◢ An empty expansion slot

◢ A compatible sound card with speakers or headphones

◢ Sound card device drivers

◢ Motherboard documentation, if your system uses embedded audio

◢ A PC toolkit with antistatic ground strap

◢ *Optional*: Internet access

### LAB PREPARATION

Before the lab begins, the instructor or lab assistant needs to do the following:

◢ Verify that Windows starts with no errors.

◢ Verify access to motherboard and sound card documentation.

◢ *Optional:* Verify that Internet access is available.

◢ Provide each student with access to the Windows installation files, if needed.

### ACTIVITY BACKGROUND

Two of the most popular multimedia devices are the sound card and the embedded audio device. A sound card enables a computer to receive sound input and to output sound, as when playing a music CD. Many newer systems have audio embedded on the motherboard. As an A+ computer technician, you need to know how to install a sound card, whether you're putting together a computer from scratch, repairing a failed device, or upgrading components on an existing system. In this lab, you install, configure, and test a sound card.

**ESTIMATED COMPLETION TIME: 45 minutes**

 **Activity**

First, you need to find out whether your system has a sound card, an embedded audio device, or perhaps both or neither. Use the skills you have learned to discover and describe what audio configuration your system currently has. Describe the configuration, and then work through the steps to complete the lab in the following general order:

◢ Disable any existing audio devices in Windows.

◢ Remove or disable the hardware device(s).

⊿ Verify that the audio is disabled.

⊿ Physically install the sound card.

⊿ Install the drivers in Windows.

⊿ Verify the function of audio features.

⊿ Return the system to its original state (optional, per instructor's directions).

Follow these steps to uninstall a sound card or embedded audio device in Windows:

1. After you have logged on as an administrator, open Control Panel.

2. Click **Add/Remove Hardware** to start the Add/Remove Hardware Wizard.

3. Click the **Uninstall/Unplug a device** option button, and then click **Next** to continue.

4. In the Choose a Removal Task window, click the **Uninstall a device** option button, as shown in Figure 10-1, and then click **Next** to continue.

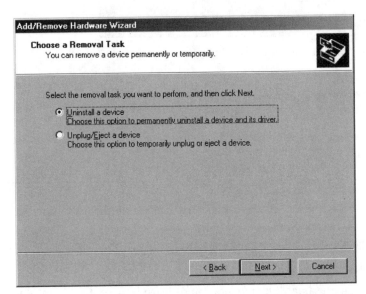

**Figure 10-1**    Use the Uninstall a device option to uninstall the sound card or embedded audio device

5. In the Devices list box, scroll down until you locate your audio device. Click your device to select it, and then click **Next** to continue.

6. Click the **Yes, I want to uninstall this device** option button, as shown in Figure 10-2, and then click **Next** to continue.

7. When the Add/Remove Hardware Wizard reports that you have uninstalled your audio device successfully, click **Finish** to close the window.

8. Close any open windows, log off, and shut down your computer.

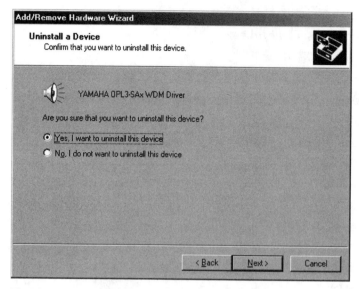

**Figure 10-2** Confirm that this device should be uninstalled

Follow these steps to remove the sound card:

1. Disconnect all external cables from the case.

2. Remove the case cover and locate the sound card. List any cables connected to the sound card:

   _____

3. Disconnect any cables from the sound card and secure them. Remove the sound card and place it in a safe place.

4. Reassemble the system and boot to Windows to verify that the audio doesn't function.

Follow these steps to disable the embedded audio device:

1. Consult the motherboard documentation to learn how to disable the embedded audio device. Also, take note of any internal audio cables. The way to disable the device is often a jumper setting, but sometimes you might have to disable the device in the CMOS setup utility. If you must disable the device in CMOS, describe the steps you took on the following lines, and then complete Steps 2 and 3:

   _____

   _____

   _____

2. Disconnect all external cables. Remove the case cover and locate the way to disable the embedded audio (if applicable). List the steps, and then remove and secure any internal audio cables:

   _____

   _____

3. Reassemble the system and boot to Windows to verify that the audio doesn't function.

Follow these steps to physically install a sound card:

1. Shut down the computer and disconnect all external cables from the case.

2. Remove the case cover.

3. Locate an empty expansion slot that you can use for the sound card. On some systems, expansion cards are attached to a riser card, which you might have to remove at this time. If necessary, remove the expansion slot faceplate on the case so that the sound card fits into the expansion slot.

4. Insert the sound card into the expansion slot on the motherboard (or insert the sound card into the riser card and the riser card into the motherboard). Line up the sound card on the slot and press it straight down, making sure the tab on the backplate (the metal plate on the rear of the card where sound ports are located) fits into the slot on the case. Normally, seating the card requires a little effort, but don't force it. If you can't insert the card with just a little effort, something is preventing it from seating. Check for obstructions and try again, removing components that are in the way, if needed.

5. After the card is installed, secure it with a screw. The screw goes through a hole in the card's backplate, securing the backplate to the case.

6. Attach any cable required to carry an audio signal from other multimedia devices, such as a CD-ROM drive.

7. Replace any components you removed while installing the sound card, and replace and secure the cover on the case.

8. Reattach all cables from external devices to the correct ports. Attach speakers or headphones. (Some speakers receive power from the computer, and others have to be plugged into an external power source, such as a wall outlet.)

Next, you configure the drivers and other software for your sound card. If you have the documentation for your sound card, follow those instructions. Otherwise, follow these general steps to install software for most sound cards, keeping in mind that your sound card might require a slightly different procedure:

1. Start the computer, and log on as an administrator. The Found New Hardware dialog box opens, attempts to determine what type of new hardware is present, and displays the result.

2. The New Hardware Wizard launches, informing you that it will help you install a driver. Click **Next** to continue.

3. The New Hardware Wizard displays a message asking how you want to install the software. Click the **Search for a suitable driver for my device (Recommended)** option button, and then click **Next** to continue.

4. The New Hardware Wizard displays a message asking where the drivers for the new device are located (see Figure 10-3). Insert the floppy disk or CD containing the drivers, and click the check box to indicate the location of the drivers. (If the CD Autorun program launches when you insert the CD, close it.) Click **Next** to continue. If your files aren't located on removable media, click the **Specify a location** check box. A dialog box opens, prompting you to type the path or browse to the file location. Use either method you prefer, and when you finish, click **OK** to continue.

5. If the New Hardware Wizard can locate the correct driver, it displays a message identifying the sound card model name, driver location, and driver file name. Click **Next** to continue and then skip to Step 7. If the wizard reports that it is unable to find the drivers, proceed to Step 6.

6. If the New Hardware Wizard reports that it was unable to locate the drivers, click **Back** and repeat Step 4, but this time click the **Specify Location** option, and then click **Browse** to open the Browse for a Folder dialog box.

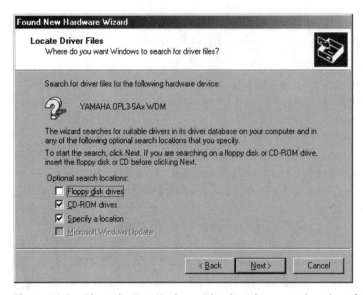

**Figure 10-3**  Direct the New Hardware Wizard to the correct location of the drivers

Browse to the location of the setup files, expanding folders as needed, and look for a folder named Win2000, Win2k, or similar. (If you aren't sure which .inf file to choose, consult the Readme.txt file, which should include instructions and last-minute information. Don't be surprised if you're instructed to use Windows NT 4 drivers for some devices!) After you select the correct folder, click **OK** to close the Browse for a Folder dialog box, and then click **Next** in the New Hardware Wizard. If the wizard finds the driver, continue to Step 7; otherwise, consult the documentation again for the correct installation procedure.

7. After locating and installing the drivers, the New Hardware Wizard displays a message notifying you that the device installation is completed. Click **Finish** to close the wizard. At some point, you might be required to supply the location of the i386 directory holding Windows installation files.

8. After the sound card is completely installed, Windows might detect additional devices. Sound cards sometimes include embedded features, such as MIDI Wave Audio, SB16 Emulation, Game Port, and so on. The New Hardware Wizard launches as needed to install these devices separately. Follow the preceding steps to install each device.

9. When Windows finishes installing software, you might be prompted to reboot. If so, go ahead and reboot. You should hear the Microsoft sound (the default sound played on startup) after you log on.

Follow these steps to adjust the volume in Windows and then test the sound card:

1. Open Control Panel. In Windows XP, click **Sounds, Speech, and Audio Devices,** and then click **Sounds and Audio Devices**. The Sounds and Audio Devices Properties dialog box opens. In Windows 2000, double-click **Sounds and Multimedia**. The Sounds and Multimedia Properties dialog box opens.

2. In Windows XP, click the **Volume** tab. In the Device volume section, make sure the **Place volume icon in taskbar** check box is selected, and drag the volume slider all the way to High. In Windows 2000, click the **Sounds** tab, if necessary. Make sure the **Show volume control on the taskbar** check box at the bottom of the tab is selected, and then move the volume slider all the way to High (see Figure 10-4). Click **OK** to close the dialog box, close Control Panel, and reboot the system.

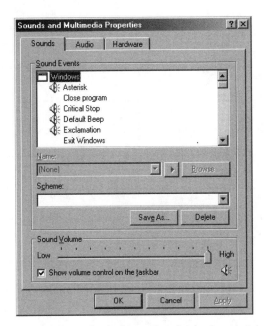

**Figure 10-4** Check the settings in the Sounds tab

3. On the right side of the taskbar, you should see the speaker volume setting represented by a speaker icon. Click the speaker icon. A pop-up window opens with a slider for adjusting speaker volume.

4. Drag the volume slider all the way to the top, and then click on the desktop to close the pop-up window.

5. Double-click the speaker icon. The Volume Control dialog box opens. Note that this dialog box gives you more control than the pop-up window you used in Step 4. Among other things, you can adjust the volume of various inputs, including the overall volume control, which controls the actual volume of the signal fed to the speakers. On the following lines, list the volume controls from left to right, and identify two settings (other than volume) that can be changed:

6. Set the volume slider on the far left to half volume, and then close the Volume Control dialog box.

7. Next, if you have Internet access, you can do a further test of your sound card. Use a search engine, locate a Lion.wav file, and play it to hear a lion's roar. What was the Web site where you found the file?

## REVIEW QUESTIONS

1. What Windows feature walks you through the process of installing drivers for a new device?

2. Other than driver files included with the sound card, what other information might Windows request when configuring a new sound card?

3. What other devices embedded on the sound card might Windows detect after the sound card installation is finished?

_____

_____

4. How does Windows handle the installation of these additional devices?

_____

_____

5. What Control Panel applet, and which tab in its Properties dialog box, do you use to adjust the volume in Windows?

_____

6. Besides output to the speakers on the sound card or embedded audio device interface, what other outputs and inputs are available on the sound card? What are their uses?

_____

_____

_____

# LAB 10.2 INSTALL A PC VIDEO CAMERA

## OBJECTIVES

The goal of this lab is to help you complete the process of installing and testing a PC camera. After completing this lab, you will be able to:

- Install a PC video camera
- Use Windows XP Movie Maker to test your PC camera
- Use Windows 98 NetMeeting to test your PC camera

## MATERIALS REQUIRED

This lab requires the following:

- Windows XP and Windows 98 operating systems
- Windows installation CD or installation files
- A USB-connected PC camera compatible with your system
- A spare USB port on the system
- Device drivers for the camera
- Sound card, speakers, and optional microphone
- _Optional_: Internet access

## LAB PREPARATION

Before the lab begins, the instructor or lab assistant needs to do the following:

⊿ Verify that Windows starts with no errors.

⊿ Provide each student with access to the necessary installation files or drivers.

⊿ *Optional:* Verify that Internet access is available.

## ACTIVITY BACKGROUND

PC cameras are becoming increasingly popular. Using these cameras, you can set up a video conference, record or send video images to your family and friends, and monitor your house over the Internet. You can even detach some PC cameras and use them to take still pictures while away from your system, uploading them to the computer when you return. Most PC cameras install via the USB port, making physical installation fairly simple. In this lab, you install, configure, and test a basic PC camera.

---
**ESTIMATED COMPLETION TIME: 45 minutes**
---

 **Activity**

In Windows XP, follow these steps to install a PC camera:

1. Start the computer and, if necessary, log on as an administrator.

2. Locate an unused USB port. Insert the PC camera's cable into the USB port. (Don't force the cable. If you can't insert it easily, flip the connector over, and try again; it should insert easily.)

3. Windows detects the new USB device and the Found New Hardware icon appears in the taskbar's notification area. A balloon tip above the icon informs you that new hardware has been found. Next, the balloon tip identifies the hardware as a camera, and then notifies you that it has identified the particular camera model. Finally, the balloon tip notifies you that the camera has been installed successfully. Windows XP probably won't give you the opportunity to use the camera manufacturer's device drivers. However, if requested, insert the camera installation CD or floppy disk. (If the Autorun program launches, close it.)

Next, you use My Computer to collect information about your camera by following these steps:

1. Open My Computer. Note the section title under which the camera is listed in the right pane of My Computer:

_____

2. Right-click the icon for your camera and click **Properties** in the shortcut menu. The *Cameraname* Properties dialog box opens. List the five types of information available in the Camera Status section of the General tab:

_____

_____

_____

3. Click the **Test Camera** button in the Diagnostics section. On the following lines, describe the results reported in the message box that opens, and then click **OK** to

close the message box. Click **OK** again to close the *Cameraname* Properties dialog box.

_____

_____

4. Now double-click the camera icon in My Computer. Record what happens and what tasks are available in the Camera Tasks section:

_____

_____

5. Use what you know about Windows and list two ways, other than My Computer or Windows Explorer but in Windows XP, where you can find information about the camera. Briefly describe any differences from My Computer on the amount of information available or the way it's presented:

_____

_____

_____

Next, you use Windows Movie Maker, a feature new to Windows XP, to put your camera to use. Complete the following steps:

1. Click **Start**, point to **All Programs**, point to **Accessories**, point to **Entertainment**, and then click **Windows Movie Maker**. Windows Movie Maker opens, as shown in Figure 10-5.

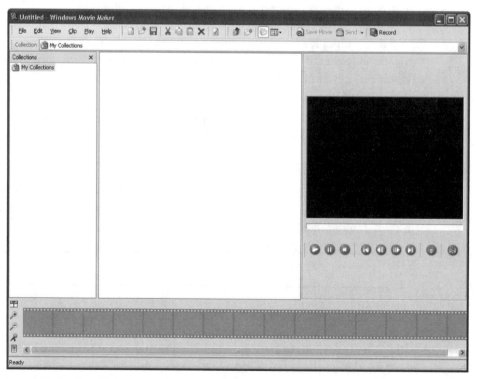

**Figure 10-5**   The Windows Movie Maker main window

2. On the Windows Movie Maker toolbar, click **Record**. The Record dialog box opens.

3. Click the **Record** list arrow, and list the choices you have for recording:

_____

_____

4. Click the **Change Device** button. The Change Device dialog box opens. What devices are currently selected?

_____

_____

5. Click the **Line** list arrow, and click the microphone on the camera. If your camera doesn't have a microphone, leave the default setting. Click **OK** to close the dialog box.

6. To record a video clip, click the **Record** button in the Record dialog box (see Figure 10-6). The Record button changes to Stop, and the Elapsed time counter starts ticking. Take several seconds of footage, and then click **Stop**. What's the name of the dialog box that opens? What is the default path in the new dialog box?

_____

_____

---

**✎ Notes**

If the Video Capture Wizard starts, go through the steps to select a device and so forth. Also, note that steps and screens might differ slightly for you, depending on the version of Windows XP you're using.

---

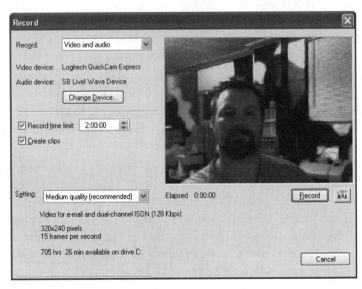

**Figure 10-6** The Record dialog box for Windows Movie Maker

7. Save your file as a test with the default extension. The Record dialog box closes, and the Creating Clips dialog box opens to show the save progress. When the clip is saved, the Creating Clips dialog box closes automatically. Where does your clip appear in the Windows Movie Maker window?

_____

_____

8. When you click a clip to select it, you can play that clip in the interface on the right side of the window. In addition, you can drag a clip to the Timeline/Storyboard interface at the bottom of Windows Movie Maker to edit it. Take a few minutes to explore Windows Movie Maker, and then record and save a clip describing what features you find interesting about the capability to record and edit video on your system.

In Windows 98, follow these steps to install a PC camera:

1. Start the computer and log on, if necessary.

2. Insert the PC camera's installation CD or floppy disk. (If the CD Autorun program launches, close it.)

3. Locate an unused USB port. Insert the PC camera's cable into the USB port. (Don't force the cable. If you can't insert it easily, flip the connector over and try again; it should insert easily.)

4. Windows detects the new USB device and the Found New Hardware dialog box opens, informing you that a USB device has been detected. A second dialog box opens, informing you that Windows is forming a New Driver Database; when the new database is finished, the second dialog box closes as well as the Found New Hardware dialog box. (If Windows doesn't detect the camera, check Device Manager or BIOS settings to discover whether the USB controller has problems or has been disabled. If necessary, enable the USB controller in Device Manager and CMOS setup, and begin again with Step 1.)

5. The New Hardware Wizard opens and indicates that it will begin searching for drivers for a USB device. Click **Next** to continue.

6. The wizard prompts you to specify a driver or search for the best driver. Click the **Search for the best driver for your device (Recommended)** option button, and then click **Next** to continue.

7. Locate the installation files, as you learned how to do in Lab 10.1, and click **Next**.

8. The wizard indicates that it has found the driver for the PC camera and displays the driver's location and file name. Click **Next** to continue.

9. The wizard copies all necessary files and displays a message indicating that the installation is complete. Click **Finish** to close the wizard. Many PC cameras have built-in microphones as well as other devices. If this is the case, the wizard might start again for each device. In addition, during any installation, the wizard might prompt you to provide the location of Windows 98 installation files.

Now you use Windows 98 NetMeeting to test your camera. NetMeeting is video conferencing software included with Windows 98. To conduct a full video conference with two or more people, you can use a directory server, an online database that NetMeeting uses to locate participants in a NetMeeting conference. One directory server is Microsoft Internet Directory. When you install NetMeeting, you're prompted to enter information about yourself and are then given the opportunity to be added to Microsoft Internet Directory. The following steps tell you to use the Microsoft Internet Directory, although your instructor might ask you to use a different directory server. Follow these steps to install NetMeeting if it's not already installed:

1. Open Control Panel, open the Add or Remove Programs applet, and then click the **Windows Setup** tab. Windows searches for Windows components.

2. Double-click the **Communications** group in the Components list box. The Communications dialog box opens.

3. Scroll down the Components list box, click the **Microsoft NetMeeting** check box, and then click **OK**. The Communications dialog box closes.

4. Click **OK** to close the Add or Remove Properties dialog box. The Copying Files dialog box opens, indicating that the copying process has begun. If prompted, supply the

location of Windows 98 installation files. When the files are copied, the Copying Files dialog box closes. Restart your PC if prompted to do so.

Follow these steps to start and configure Windows 98 NetMeeting:

1. Click **Start**, point to **Programs**, and then look for Microsoft NetMeeting on one of the submenus. You might find it under Internet Explorer or Accessories, Communications.

2. Click **Microsoft NetMeeting**.

3. Microsoft NetMeeting begins configuring your connection. Click **Next** to continue.

4. In the NetMeeting dialog box shown in Figure 10-7, accept Microsoft Internet Directory as the server name (unless your instructor gives you different directions), and then click **Next**.

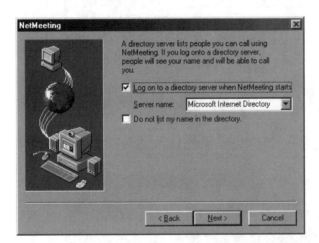

**Figure 10-7**   By default, installing NetMeeting adds you to Microsoft Internet Directory

5. Supply the requested identification information, including your name and e-mail address, and then click **Next** to continue. (Keep in mind that your identification information will be available to other NetMeeting users on the directory server.)

6. What you see on the next screen depends on the version of NetMeeting that's installed. You might see a screen asking you what category to use for your personal info (personal use for all ages, business use for all ages, or adults-only use). Select a category, and then click **Next**. For some versions of NetMeeting, the screen gives you the option of selecting a directory server. In this case, the default is Microsoft Internet Directory. Leave the default selected, and then click **Next**.

7. On the next screen, you're asked to specify your connection speed. Click **Local Area Network** (or other speed specified by your instructor), and then click **Next** to continue.

8. Next, you're asked to specify your video capturing device. Click your camera in the drop-down list, if it's not already selected, and then click **Next** to continue.

9. NetMeeting informs you that it will help tune your audio settings. Click **Next** to continue.

10. Set and test your audio settings. When they are satisfactory, click **Next** to continue.

11. When the installation is completed, click **Finish**. NetMeeting launches.

12. Click **Current Call**, and then click the **Play** button in the My Video frame. You should be able to see video supplied by your PC camera in the My Video frame, which indicates that your video camera was installed correctly.

## CRITICAL THINKING (ADDITIONAL 20 MINUTES)

If others in the lab are connected to NetMeeting and you have access to a sound card, speakers, and microphone, join someone else in a video conference. To make the connection, you can use an IP address of another computer on the LAN, instead of using a directory server. To use Windows 98 to determine a workstation IP address, type winipcfg in the Run dialog box, and then click the network adapter in the drop-down list. Figure 10-8 shows a full NetMeeting video conference complete with a shared whiteboard, chat window, and video window.

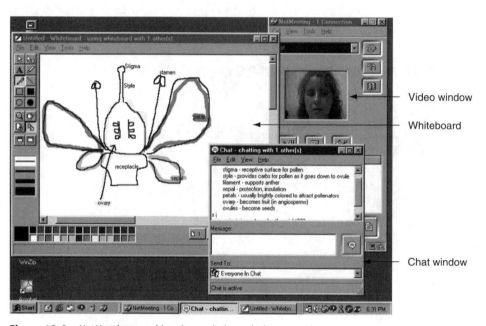

**Figure 10-8**    NetMeeting provides three windows during a session

## REVIEW QUESTIONS

1. Typically, via what type of port do PC cameras attach to a system?

2. What type of audio device might be embedded in a PC camera?

3. Do you have to power down the system before connecting a USB camera? Why or why not?

4. What feature of Windows XP is designed to create video content?

5. What application can you use to test the video supplied by your PC camera?

6. When would using a PC camera be beneficial to you?

_____

_____

## LAB 10.3 COMPARE CD AND DVD TECHNOLOGIES

### OBJECTIVES

The goal of this lab is to help you use the Internet to research CD and DVD standards. After completing this lab, you will be able to:

▲ Recognize CD and DVD specifications

### MATERIALS REQUIRED

This lab requires the following:

▲ Internet access

### LAB PREPARATION

Before the lab begins, the instructor or lab assistant needs to do the following:

▲ Verify that Internet access is available.

### ACTIVITY BACKGROUND

Many multimedia PCs include CD or DVD drives (and sometimes both). These drives can be of three types: read-only (ROM), write/record (R), or write/record and rewrite (RW or RAM). (The last two types can write and record only to specialized disks.) You research the features and limitations of CD and DVD standards in this lab.

**ESTIMATED COMPLETION TIME: 60 minutes**

### Activity

Use the Internet and your favorite search sites, such as Google (*www.google.com*) or Yahoo! (*www.yahoo.com*), to answer the following questions on CD standards. Print the source page or pages supporting your answers.

1. What is the maximum storage capacity of a CD?

_____

2. Briefly, how is information recorded on a CD-ROM disk?

_____

_____

3. Are CDs capable of storing data on both sides of the disk?

_____

4. What type or color of laser is used in a CD drive?

_____

5. What is a limitation of a CD-R drive that isn't an issue with a CD-RW drive?

_____

6. What kind of problems might occur if you tried to use an older CD-ROM drive or a CD player to play a CD-R or CD-RW disk?

_____

_____

7. Define "constant angular velocity" and explain how it applies to CD standards:

_____

_____

8. Define "constant linear velocity" and explain how it applies to CD standards:

_____

_____

9. What term is used for the process of writing data to a disk?

_____

10. Can any CD hold video data? Explain:

_____

11. On a CD, is data written in concentric circles or a continuous spiral track?

_____

12. What are three common standards CD drives use to interface with a system?

_____

_____

13. What does the X factor of a drive indicate? What is the specification of one X?

_____

_____

14. Briefly describe how a CD-RW writes data to a disk and how it's able to rewrite data:

_____

_____

_____

_____

15. How much would you pay for a package of CD-Rs? How much for a package of CD-RWs? How many discs are in a package of each type?

_____

_____

Use the Internet and your favorite search sites to answer the following questions on DVD standards. Print the source page or pages supporting your answers.

1. What is the maximum storage capacity of a DVD?

_____

2. What two characteristics give a DVD more storage capacity than a CD?

_____

_____

3. Describe the difference between DVD-R and DVD-RAM:

_____

_____

_____

4. Besides DVD-R, what other standards are available for burning DVDs?

_____

_____

5. Explain how DVD audio and CD audio differ:

_____

_____

_____

6. How many CDs worth of data can a single DVD hold?

_____

7. How many layers of data can be stored on one side of a DVD?

_____

8. How many data areas are on a single side of a DVD-R?

_____

9. List the versions and maximum capacities of DVD-RAM:

_____

_____

10. Can DVDs be used in CD devices? Explain:

_____

**11.** Explain the use of the UDF file system and how it applies to a DVD:

_____

_____

_____

_____

_____

## REVIEW QUESTIONS

**1.** What factors, other than storage capacity, would you consider when choosing between a DVD drive and a CD drive?

_____

_____

_____

**2.** What characteristics do DVD and CD drives share?

_____

_____

**3.** If you wanted to create a disc that would never need to be altered and could be used on the maximum number of systems, what type of disc would you use and why?

_____

_____

_____

**4.** Why do you think motion pictures are released on DVDs instead of CDs?

_____

_____

# *LAB 10.4 INSTALL DUAL MONITORS IN WINDOWS XP*

## OBJECTIVES

The goal of this lab is to help you set up a second monitor on a system. After completing this lab, you will be able to:

▲ Install a display adapter and its drivers

▲ Attach a second monitor

▲ Configure the system to use both monitors at the same time

## MATERIALS REQUIRED

This lab requires the following:

⊿ Windows XP operating system

⊿ A PC toolkit with antistatic ground strap

⊿ A second display adapter with drivers

⊿ A second monitor

## LAB PREPARATION

Before the lab begins, the instructor or lab assistant needs to do the following:

⊿ Verify that Windows starts with no errors.

## ACTIVITY BACKGROUND

Having two monitors on a system is often quite handy. For instance, you can have a Web browser displayed on one and a video-editing application on the other. Using two monitors has the effect of making your desktop larger and making it easier to work with multiple applications simultaneously, which is often useful when developing multimedia presentations. In this lab, you install and configure a second monitor on a computer.

**ESTIMATED COMPLETION TIME: 45 minutes**

### Activity

It's important to verify that the original hardware is working correctly before you try to add a second display adapter and monitor. That way, if a problem comes up after you install new hardware, you can be fairly sure something is amiss with the newly added components rather than the original equipment. Also, you should make sure the hardware is on the Windows XP HCL (recommended) or, at the very least, the device manufacturer offers drivers and specific instructions for use with Windows XP.

Follow these steps to physically install the second display adapter:

1. Check to make sure the original display adapter uses the PCI or AGP standard, and decide whether it will be the primary or secondary monitor.

2. Install the second adapter card in the PCI slot nearest to the AGP slot (if the original is an AGP adapter) or the PCI slot immediately next to the original PCI adapter (if the original is a PCI adapter). If you need additional guidance on installing a card, refer to Lab 10.1.

3. Attach the second monitor to the port on the back of the display adapter.

4. Boot your PC and enter CMOS setup. If your setup has display settings for dual monitors, adjust them so that the primary display adapter is initialized first. If you don't see this setting, your BIOS doesn't support it, so you can exit CMOS setup and wait for your system to reboot.

5. Enter CMOS setup again. If you see settings for dual monitors, for a system with an AGP slot, make sure the AGP adapter is selected as the primary adapter and the PCI adapter as the secondary adapter. For a system that uses two PCI adapters, it doesn't matter which adapter is the primary one; you can leave the setting as is. For additional guidance on adjusting BIOS settings, refer to Lab 6.1. Exit CMOS setup and wait for your system to reboot.

Follow these steps to install device drivers and adjust Windows display settings:

1. When the system reboots, log on as an administrator. Windows XP recognizes the new adapter and displays a Found New Hardware icon in the taskbar's notification area. Above the Found New Hardware icon, a balloon tip appears with the notification.

2. At this point, Windows might install the drivers automatically for you (if the drivers were available when XP was published) or launch the New Hardware Wizard if the adapter is new enough that XP isn't aware of the correct drivers. Complete the steps in the wizard to install the adapter. When the installation is completed, reboot. Refer to Lab 10.1 if you need additional information on using the wizard.

Before you use a second monitor, you must activate it. To do so, follow these steps:

1. Log on as an administrator, open Control Panel, and click **Appearance and Themes.** Then click the **Display** link to open the Display Properties dialog box.

2. Click the **Settings** tab in the Display Properties dialog box, as shown in Figure 10-9. The area at the top of the Settings tab now displays two monitors. Click the image of the monitor with the number 2, or in the Display list box, click the video adapter you just installed.

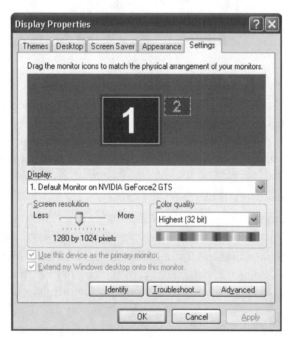

**Figure 10-9**   You must activate a second monitor before Windows can use it

3. Adjust the resolution and color settings to your preference, and then click the **Extend my Windows desktop onto this monitor** check box.

4. Click **Apply** to apply the settings. The second monitor displays the desktop.

Follow these steps to test your dual-monitor configuration:

1. Open Paint, and then drag it to the second monitor. Does your desktop extend to the second monitor as expected?

2. Open Windows Explorer, and maximize it on the original monitor. Can you see your mouse move as expected from one monitor to the next? Does the mouse interact with applications on each monitor?

3. Close Paint and Windows Explorer, and open Device Manager.

Follow these steps to remove the second adapter and return to a single-monitor configuration:

1. Open Device Manager, find the second display adapter, and click to select it. (Make sure you're looking at the second adapter, not the first.)

2. Click **Uninstall**. If prompted, verify that you do want to remove the device, and when asked if you want to restart the computer, click **No**.

3. Shut down the computer. Don't restart the computer at this time.

4. Remove the second monitor and adapter card. If necessary, reverse any BIOS changes you made that affect the display initialization sequence, and reboot the system to verify that the system no longer recognizes the adapter card.

## REVIEW QUESTIONS

1. Before installing a second monitor, why is it important to know whether your existing configuration is working correctly?

2. Why might it be necessary to change the sequence in which the system initializes display adapters?

3. In Display Properties, what is one way to select the monitor you want to adjust?

4. What would probably happen if the new adapter was on the Windows XP HCL and was in production before the release of Windows XP?

5. Does adjusting the settings of one monitor affect the settings of the other?

6. Why might you want to install multiple monitors on a system?

7. Which would be less expensive: adding a second 17-inch monitor to an existing system or buying a 21-inch monitor in single-monitor mode?

8. How did you arrive at your answer to Question 7?

_____

_____

# LAB 10.5 RESEARCH DIGITAL CAMERAS

## OBJECTIVES

The goal of this lab is to help you research digital cameras and learn how you can integrate them with a multimedia PC. In this lab, you will research:

◢ Camera picture quality and compatibility

◢ Camera storage technology

◢ Methods of transferring images to a PC

## MATERIALS REQUIRED

This lab requires the following:

◢ Internet access

## LAB PREPARATION

Before the lab begins, the instructor or lab assistant needs to do the following:

◢ Verify that Internet access is available.

## ACTIVITY BACKGROUND

As digital cameras have become more common and popular, they have also become more sophisticated. Their special features, image quality, methods of file storage, and methods of transferring image data to the PC have improved over earlier models. Also, the prices of digital cameras have decreased dramatically. In this lab, you research digital cameras and learn how they are used with multimedia PCs.

**ESTIMATED COMPLETION TIME: 60 minutes**

 **Activity**

Research digital photography on the Internet. Try searching for "digital camera" or "digital photography" on your favorite search engine. Web sites that might be useful include the following:

◢ CNET Networks, Inc., _www.cnet.com_

◢ Digital Photography Review, _www.dpreview.com_

◢ Shutterline, _www.shutterline.com_

◢ KeyWorlds.com, _www.keyworlds.com/d/digital_photography.htm_

Answer these questions about general camera topics. Print the Web page or pages supporting your answer.

1. How is image quality measured? Do all digital cameras produce the same image quality?

_____

_____

2. What are three storage technologies that digital cameras might use to store images in a camera?

_____

_____

_____

3. Name four technologies a camera might use to transfer images to a PC. What requirements must a PC meet for each?

_____

_____

_____

_____

4. Find and print information about at least two digital cameras that offer features such as changeable lenses, manual focus, aperture settings (f-stops), and shutter-speed settings (exposure). List the two digital cameras you selected on the following lines:

_____

_____

Answer these questions on basic image characteristics:

1. What three file types might a digital camera use to store images?

_____

2. Name three factors that affect the number of images that a camera can store on a single storage device:

_____

_____

_____

3. Do most digital cameras offer the capability to control image quality? Explain:

_____

4. Can you remove an image you don't like from a camera without transferring the image to a PC? Explain:

_____

_____

5. What are three means of printing a photo taken by a digital camera?

_____

_____

6. Can digital cameras record images other than still shots?

_____

Answer these questions about how cameras transfer images to a PC:

1. Which transfer method offers the highest transfer speed? What is that speed?

_____

2. Which transfer method requires the least specialized hardware on a PC?

_____

3. Which storage technologies allow direct image transfer by removing the storage device from the camera and inserting it into the PC?

_____

_____

4. What devices can be added to a PC to allow it to read flash memory cards directly?

_____

_____

5. What image transfer method doesn't require removing a device from the camera or using cabling to the PC?

_____

6. Does image resolution have any effect on transfer speed? Explain:

_____

_____

_____

Answer these questions about photo-quality printers:

1. What resolution would you recommend for a printer capable of reproducing digital pictures?

_____

2. Do you need special paper to get the best quality in photo printing? Explain:

_____

3. Describe one way you could get pictures from your digital camera to the printer:

_____

_____

## REVIEW QUESTIONS

1. What are three advantages of a digital camera over a 35mm camera?

_____

_____

_____

2. What are some disadvantages of a digital camera compared with a 35mm camera?

_____

_____

_____

3. What are some features you would like on a digital camera? Explain your choices:

_____

_____

_____

4. What can you do to maximize the number of images stored on a camera without modifying the storage device capacity?

_____

_____

_____

5. Would all 3.1 megapixel cameras have the same picture quality? Why or why not?

_____

_____

6. What factors should you consider when purchasing a photo printer?

_____

_____

## LAB 10.6 EXPLORE WINDOWS XP AUDIO FEATURES

### OBJECTIVES

The goal of this lab is to give you the opportunity to experiment with different audio features and capabilities of Windows XP. After completing this lab, you will be able to:

▲ Identify audio media types

▲ Download and install Nullsoft Winamp, a third-party sound application

◢ Control audio CD playback with Windows Media Player and Nullsoft Winamp

◢ Customize sounds that Windows plays for events

## MATERIALS REQUIRED

This lab requires the following:

◢ Windows XP operating system

◢ Windows XP installation CD or installation files

◢ Internet access

◢ CD-ROM drive and an audio CD

## LAB PREPARATION

Before the lab begins, the instructor or lab assistant needs to do the following:

◢ Verify that Windows starts with no errors.

◢ Provide each student with access to the Windows XP installation files, if needed.

◢ Verify that Internet access is available.

## ACTIVITY BACKGROUND

Windows XP offers features that let you use audio files in different ways. For example, Windows events can be configured to play a certain sound when the event occurs. These features can be used simply to make using Windows more enjoyable for average users, but to a sight-impaired user, they can be vital tools.

Windows XP provides Windows Media Player to play audio CDs as well as other multimedia types. Some people also install third-party media players with additional features, such as built-in codecs. In this lab, you experiment with Windows audio capabilities and use Nullsoft Winamp, a third-party sound application.

**ESTIMATED COMPLETION TIME: 40 minutes**

 **Activity**

Follow these steps to control which sounds play for certain Windows events:

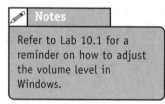
Refer to Lab 10.1 for a reminder on how to adjust the volume level in Windows.

1. Open Control Panel, click **Sounds, Speech, and Audio Devices**, and then click **Sounds and Audio Devices**. The Sounds and Audio Devices Properties dialog box opens. Click the **Sounds** tab, and scroll down the Program events list box; note that each event with a speaker icon has a sound assigned that plays when the event occurs, as shown in Figure 10-10.

**Figure 10-10**  A speaker icon indicates which events have sounds associated with them

2. Fill in the following chart by clicking each event in the table and writing down the sound associated with it. (The sound file associated with the selected event is displayed in the Sounds text box.) Also, note that not all Windows events are assigned a sound.

| Event | Sound name |
| --- | --- |
| Critical Stop | |
| Exit Windows | |
| Empty Recycle Bin | |

3. Click **Start Windows** in the Program events list box, and then click the **Play sound** button (to the left of the Browse button). The Windows XP Startup sound plays. If you don't hear the sound, check your volume levels and make sure the volume is not muted.

4. In the Sounds drop-down list, select and play several different sounds for Start Windows until you find one you like better than the Windows default. Click the **Save As** button at the top, type **Custom** in the dialog box that opens, and click **OK** to save the new settings. (You could also apply the Windows Default scheme by selecting it in the Sound scheme drop-down list.)

5. Click **OK** to apply and save the sound properties. To test the new sound, restart Windows and log on to the same account.

6. After you have verified that the new sound plays, repeat the process and return the sound to the original settings.

Follow these steps to play an audio CD with Windows Media Player:

1. Insert the audio disc in the CD-ROM drive. In the Audio CD dialog box that opens, click **Play Audio CD using Windows Media Player**, and then click **OK** to close the dialog box.

2. Windows Media Player should start and begin playing the CD automatically. Adjust the volume so that it's not distracting to others.

3. The right pane of Windows Media Player lists the tracks on the CD. The center section displays different images to accompany the audio output. Experiment with customizing this image by right-clicking this section and selecting another choice in the shortcut menu. List three of your favorite selections:

_____

_____

_____

4. Windows Media Player has the standard set of control features you would expect with a CD player. At the left are a number of other features. Experiment with Windows Media Player and answer the following questions:

◢ Which feature changes the appearance of the entire Windows Media Player interface?

_____

◢ What are some featured stations in Radio Tuner?

_____

◢ What types of information are available via Media Guide?

_____

Follow these steps to install Winamp and use it to play the audio CD. Bear in mind that new versions of software are released often, so these directions might differ slightly, depending on the latest release:

1. Open your Web browser, and go to **www.winamp.com**. Click the **Download Now!** icon, and download the default version of Winamp. What is the name of the file you found to download?

_____

2. Open Windows Explorer, find your download location, and double-click the file you downloaded to launch Winamp Setup and begin the installation process. Winamp Setup is similar to other installation wizards you have used. Step through the installation, using default settings for everything. If you don't want to receive e-mail from Nullsoft, click the **Stop Bugging Me** check box if it appears on the information screen for Winamp Setup. When prompted, click **Run Winamp** to launch Winamp, which then downloads additional information in the Winamp browser.

3. Close Winamp and the Winamp browser. Remove the audio CD, and then insert it again. This time, when the Audio CD dialog box opens, click **Play Audio CD using Winamp**. Winamp starts again and begins playing your audio CD.

4. Experiment with Winamp to answer these questions:

◢ Does Winamp have the same basic features as Windows Media Player?

_____

◢ What feature does Winamp have for customizing the sound tone?

_____

◢ Name three popular music file types that Winamp supports:

_____

◢ Could you set up a playlist for playing files on your CD in an order you choose, instead of first to last? Explain your answer:

_____

_____

_____

## REVIEW QUESTIONS

1. What Control Panel applet, and which tab in its Properties dialog box, do you use to change the sound that plays for an event?

_____

2. What feature of Windows Media Player enables you to listen to streaming audio content?

_____

3. What is the default sound played during Windows XP startup?

_____

4. Which audio player provided more features, and which was easier to use? Explain your answers:

_____

_____

_____

# Installing Windows 2000/XP

**Labs included in this chapter:**

- **Lab 11.1:** Install or Upgrade to Windows 2000
- **Lab 11.2:** Install and Use Windows 2000 Support Tools
- **Lab 11.3:** Use the Windows 2000 Setup Manager Wizard
- **Lab 11.4:** Determine Hardware Compatibility with Windows XP
- **Lab 11.5:** Install or Upgrade to Windows XP

# LAB 11.1 INSTALL OR UPGRADE TO WINDOWS 2000

## OBJECTIVES

The goal of this lab is to help you to install or upgrade to Windows 2000 Professional. After completing this lab, you will be able to:

◢ Plan an upgrade or installation

◢ Identify the benefits of an upgrade or a new installation

◢ Install or upgrade to Windows 2000 Professional

## MATERIALS REQUIRED

This lab requires the following:

◢ Windows 98 operating system

◢ Access to drivers or Internet access for downloading drivers

◢ Windows 2000 Professional installation files or installation CD

◢ Key from installation CD

## LAB PREPARATION

Before the lab begins, the instructor or lab assistant needs to do the following:

◢ Verify that Windows starts with no errors.

◢ Provide each student with access to the Windows 2000 installation files or CD and key.

◢ Verify that any necessary Windows 2000 drivers are available.

## ACTIVITY BACKGROUND

Many people are intimidated at the thought of installing or upgrading an operating system. The process doesn't need to be difficult. In fact, if you plan your installation carefully and are prepared to supply required information and device drivers, your main complaint might be that the process is time consuming. Even that annoyance can be minimized, using techniques designed to reduce the total installation time. In this lab, you plan and prepare for an installation or an upgrade to Windows 2000 Professional, and then perform the upgrade or installation.

**ESTIMATED COMPLETION TIME: 120 minutes**

 **Activity**

Follow these steps to plan and prepare for a Windows 2000 Professional installation on your computer:

1. Obtain a list of devices in the system and detailed system specifications, such as processor speed and drive capacity. If no list currently exists, you can use Device Manager or SiSoftware Sandra (installed in Lab 1.3) to compile one.

2. Make another list of important applications, and check to see whether they are compatible with Windows 2000. If you find any that aren't, check to see whether any patches or upgrades are available to make them compatible.

3. Check each system specification and device against the Hardware Compatibility List (HCL) and the system requirements list for Windows 2000 on the Microsoft Web site (*www.microsoft.com*). Your system will probably be compatible with Windows 2000.

However, when working on other systems, you might discover significant incompatibilities. In that case, you would have to decide whether upgrading to Windows 2000 is really an option. If you decide to go ahead with the upgrade, you would have to decide which applications or hardware you need to upgrade before upgrading the operating system. The Windows 2000 installation CD offers a Check Upgrade Only mode that you can use to check for incompatibility issues in your system before you actually install the OS; however, the information on the Microsoft Web site, which you're using in this step, is often more current and easier to access. Answer the following:

◢ Does your system qualify for Windows 2000?

_____

◢ If not, what hardware or application doesn't qualify?

_____

◢ Will you install using FAT32 or NTFS? Explain your decision:

_____

_____

_____

4. Download or otherwise obtain all necessary drivers, service packs, and application patches from the manufacturer's or Microsoft Web site for installed applications and hardware. Record a summary of the components you were required to install to make your system compatible with Windows 2000:

_____

_____

_____

_____

5. Gather any network-specific information in preparation for the installation. If you're connected to a network, answer the following:

◢ If you're using a TCP/IP network, how is your IP address configured?

_____

◢ For a static IP address, what is the IP address?

_____

◢ What is the workgroup name or domain name of the network?

_____

◢ What is your computer name?

_____

6. Make sure you have the correct CD key for your installation CD. The CD key, provided with the Windows 2000 installation CD, usually consists of a set of alphanumeric

characters. You must enter the CD key to complete the installation—even if you're installing the operating system from setup files located somewhere other than on the installation CD.

7. Review the information you have collected so far, and then decide whether to do a fresh installation or an upgrade. For instance, if all the important applications on your system are compatible with Windows 2000, an upgrade will probably save time because it leaves compatible applications in working condition. On the other hand, if you know you'll have to install new applications anyway because of incompatibilities, you might choose to perform a fresh installation. In many ways, a fresh installation is preferable because it ensures that no misconfigured system settings are carried over to the new operating system.

▲ Will you perform a clean install or an upgrade?

_____

▲ Give a brief explanation of why you chose that option:

_____

_____

8. Back up any critical data files (that is, any work you or others have stored on your computer that you can't afford to lose during the installation process).

▲ If you have critical data files on the PC, where did you back them up to?

_____

You're ready to begin installing Windows 2000 Professional. This lab assumes that you have Windows 98 installed and running. This is not the only situation in which you would install or even upgrade to Windows 2000, but it's common. Installing the operating system is possible using files on the installation CD, a network drive, or a local hard disk. To speed up the installation process, consider copying the setup files from the installation CD (or from a network drive) to a local hard disk. This method takes extra time at first but is faster overall.

▲ Are you performing the installation from the Windows 2000 CD, files stored on your hard drive, or a network drive?

_____

The following steps are representative of a typical installation. Your installation will probably vary in minor ways, depending on the installation options you choose, your system's hardware configuration, and other factors. The following steps are a general guide to let you know what to expect during the process. Don't become alarmed if your experience differs slightly. Use your knowledge to solve any problems on your own, and ask your instructor for help if you get stuck. You might want to record any differences between these steps and your own experience. Also, record any decisions you make and any information you enter during the installation process.

1. Before you insert the installation CD or run the setup files from a location on your hard drive or network, use antivirus software to scan the computer's memory and hard drive for viruses. After the scan is finished, make sure to disable any automatic scans and close the antivirus program before beginning installation.

2. The Setup program starts. This program guides you through the actual installation. If it doesn't begin automatically, click **Start, Run**, and run WINNT32.exe from the \I386 folder.

▲ Did Setup start automatically for you, or did you have to use the Run command?

_____

3. Setup informs you that you're running an older version of Windows and asks whether you want to upgrade to Windows 2000. Click **Yes** to continue and follow the instructions in the Setup program. Note that although Setup initially uses the word "upgrade," you're given the option of doing an upgrade from Windows 98 or a fresh installation of Windows 2000.

4. Accept the end user license agreement (EULA) and click **Next**.

5. When prompted, enter the CD key and click **Next**.

6. Setup examines your system and reports any situations that could cause problems during installation. You're given the opportunity to print the report and exit Setup to correct the problems. Even if some problems are reported, you have done your homework during planning and probably have the solution, so continue the installation.

7. You're given the opportunity to review the Hardware Compatibility List. If you want to review it again, do so and click **Next** to continue.

8. Specify your file system as NTFS and click **Next**. The system begins to copy files for the installation. Then the text portion of the installation, which has a command-line interface rather than a Windows GUI, begins. The text portion includes the following:

- Examining hardware
- Deleting old Windows files, if applicable
- Copying Windows 2000 operating system files
- Rebooting your computer automatically

After your computer reboots, the Windows 2000 Setup portion begins, which includes the following:

- Verifying the file system
- Checking the file structure
- Converting the file system to NTFS
- Rebooting automatically

> **Notes**
>
> Windows 98 doesn't support NTFS, so if you were setting up a dual-boot system that used that operating system, you should choose FAT32 as the file system.

1. Click **Windows 2000 Professional** in the startup menu. Because you converted your file system to NTFS, you should see a message indicating that the conversion was successful.

2. The system installs software for detected devices. When prompted, enter the requested network information. After you have specified how your network is configured, Setup performs some final setup tasks, including the following:

- Configuring the startup menu
- Registering components
- Upgrading programs and system settings
- Saving settings
- Removing temporary files

4. The computer reboots one more time. Now you can log on as an administrator and install any new applications or devices.

5. Verify that the system is working correctly.

On the following lines, record any differences you noted between these installation steps and your own experience. Also, record any decisions you made and any information you entered during the installation process:

_____

_____

_____

_____

_____

_____

## REVIEW QUESTIONS

1. List five things you should do before starting the installation process:

   _____

   _____

   _____

   _____

   _____

   _____

2. How can you find out whether your video card will work with Windows 2000?

   _____

3. What type of installation can save time because it usually retains system settings and leaves applications in working condition?

   _____

   _____

4. What step is critical to ensure that you don't lose important data during installation?

   _____

5. What step can you take to speed up the actual installation process?

   _____

# LAB 11.2 INSTALL AND USE WINDOWS 2000 SUPPORT TOOLS

## OBJECTIVES

The goal of this lab is to help you install and become familiar with Windows 2000 Support Tools. After completing this lab, you will be able to:

◢ Install Support Tools

◢ Access Support Tools

◢ Use Error and Event Messages Help to investigate Event Viewer events

◢ Use the Windows 2000 Support Tools Help feature to find out about other tools

◢ Use the Windows 2000 System Information tool to access software information

## MATERIALS REQUIRED

This lab requires the following:

◢ Windows 2000 Professional operating system

◢ Windows 2000 Professional installation files or installation CD

## LAB PREPARATION

Before the lab begins, the instructor or lab assistant needs to do the following:

◢ Verify that Windows starts with no errors.

◢ Provide each student with access to the Windows 2000 installation files, if needed.

## ACTIVITY BACKGROUND

Windows 2000 provides support tools you can use to prepare to install Windows 2000, to customize and configure Windows 2000, and to find information on Windows 2000. In this lab, you install these tools and then practice using some of them.

**ESTIMATED COMPLETION TIME: 30 minutes**

 **Activity**

Follow these steps to install Windows 2000 Support Tools:

1. Log on as an administrator.

2. Open Windows Explorer, navigate to the **Support\Tools** directory in the Windows 2000 installation files on your hard drive, or click **Browse This CD** on the Windows 2000 setup CD. Then double-click **Setup.exe**. The Setup Wizard launches.

3. Click **Next** to continue.

4. In the User Information window, enter your name and organization in the corresponding text boxes, and then click **Next** to continue.

5. In the Select an Installation Type window, click **Typical Installation**, and then click **Next** to continue.

6. The Begin Installation window is displayed to let you know the wizard is ready to begin copying files. Click **Next** to continue.

7. The Installation Progress window displays a progress bar. When the installation is completed and the Start menu is set up, the wizard indicates that the installation was successful. Click **Finish** to exit the wizard.

From a student's point of view, one of the most useful support tools is the Error and Event Messages Help tool. This tool gives information on error messages and tells you what steps to take to correct the problems that caused the error messages. Another useful tool is Event Viewer, which you learn more about in Lab 12.3. In Event Viewer, events are assigned event ID numbers. These ID numbers are also used in the Error and Event Messages Help tool, which allows you to search by event ID number for more information on the event. To familiarize yourself with the Error and Event Messages Help tool, follow these steps:

1. In Control Panel, double-click the **Administrative Tools** icon. The Administrative Tools window opens.

2. Double-click the **Event Viewer** icon to launch Event Viewer.

3. In the left pane of Event Viewer, click **System** and view the event entries in the right pane.

4. If you see any warning or error events, double-click one. Otherwise, double-click an information event. When you double-click any event, the Event Details dialog box

opens. Read the information in this window, and record the event ID number and description:

_____

_____

_____

5. Click **Start**, point to **Programs**, point to **Windows 2000 Support Tools**, and then click **Error and Event Messages**. The Error and Event Messages Help window opens.

6. Click the **Search** tab.

7. Click the **Type in word(s) to search for** text box, and then type the event ID number you recorded in Step 4. (Type the number only; don't type the number sign or the words "ID number.") Then click the **List Topics** button. The Select Topic list box displays all Help topics that refer to this event ID number.

8. In the Select Topic list box, click to highlight the item with a title matching the event description you recorded in Step 4.

9. Click the **Display** button. Information about the highlighted item is displayed in the right pane. Record the explanation of the event and the related user action, if that information is available:

_____

_____

_____

_____

You already know how to use Windows Help to locate information about the operating system. When you need information specifically about Windows 2000 Support Tools, you can use Tools Help. Follow these steps to find and print information about a particular support tool:

1. Click **Start**, point to **Programs**, point to **Windows 2000 Support Tools**, and then click **Tools Help**. Tools Help opens in a familiar Help window.

2. Next, you find information about the executable file for the Windows 2000 System Information tool, which provides information on the hardware resources and software environment for your system. The name of this file is msinfo32.exe. Click the **Search** tab (if necessary), type **msinfo32.exe** in the Type in the word(s) to search for text box, and then click **List Topics**. Topics related to msinfo32.exe are displayed in the Select topic pane.

3. Double-click the topic ranked second. Information on msinfo32.exe is displayed in the right pane.

4. Click **Options, Print** from the Tools Help menu. The Print dialog box opens. If necessary, select a printer and change any settings as required.

5. Click **Print** to print the information on msinfo32.exe. Keep the printed information handy so that you can refer to it in the next part of this lab.

In the following steps, you use the System Information tool (msinfo32.exe). Follow these steps to record information about your system's software environment:

1. Launch System Information, following directions in the Help information you printed earlier in Step 5.

2. In the left pane, double-click the **Software Environment** category to display a list of subcategories, and record them on the following lines:

_____

_____

_____

_____

_____

3. In the left pane, click **Program Groups**. The program groups for Windows are displayed, showing the software installed on the system. What five program groups are always added for each user?

_____

_____

_____

_____

_____

4. In the left pane, click **Startup Programs**. Are the programs listed associated with your Start menu, or do they launch automatically when you log on to the system? Explain:

_____

_____

_____

## REVIEW QUESTIONS

1. What directory contains the files needed to set up Windows 2000 Support Tools?

_____

2. What support tool enables you to search for information based on the event ID numbers used in Event Viewer?

_____

3. What Windows 2000 Support Tool offers information about all other Support Tools?

_____

4. What is the executable file for the System Information tool?

_____

5. Can you run all the Support Tools from the Start menu?

_____

# LAB 11.3 USE THE WINDOWS 2000 SETUP MANAGER WIZARD

## OBJECTIVES

The goal of this lab is to help you use the Windows Setup Manager Wizard to create an answer file and distribution folder for unattended Windows 2000 installations. After completing this lab, you will be able to:

- ◢ Install Windows 2000 Setup Manager
- ◢ Use the Windows 2000 Setup Manager Wizard to create an answer file and distribution folder

## MATERIALS REQUIRED

This lab requires the following:

- ◢ Windows 2000 Professional operating system
- ◢ Windows 2000 installation files or installation CD
- ◢ WinZip or another similar file compression utility

## LAB PREPARATION

Before the lab begins, the instructor or lab assistant needs to do the following:

- ◢ Verify that Windows starts with no errors.
- ◢ Provide each student with access to the Windows 2000 installation files, if needed.
- ◢ Verify that a file compression utility that can open .cab files is available.

## ACTIVITY BACKGROUND

Windows 2000 Professional (and other versions of Windows) enables you to perform an unattended installation. This type of installation can be a time-saver, especially if you're installing Windows on a number of machines. As you know, several pieces of information must be entered during installation to configure the operating system correctly. During an unattended installation, this information is supplied by an answer file. In the past, creating an answer file meant typing or editing a text file saved in a specific text format. To speed up the process of setting up an unattended installation and creating an answer file, Windows 2000 and XP offer a wizard designed to guide you through the process, the Windows Setup Manager Wizard. In this lab, you install and use this wizard.

> **ESTIMATED COMPLETION TIME: 30 minutes**

**🖐 Activity**

Follow these steps to install Windows 2000 Setup Manager:

1. Open Windows Explorer and click the **C:** drive. Create a new folder named **Deploy**.
2. Using Windows Explorer, navigate to the **Support\Tools** directory in the Windows 2000 installation files on your hard drive or the Windows 2000 setup CD.
3. Double-click **Deploy.cab**, and follow the directions on the screen to copy **contents of Deploy.cab** to the Deploy directory on drive C.

Now that you have installed Windows 2000 Setup Manager, you can use the Windows 2000 Setup Manager Wizard to create an unattended installation answer file. Follow these steps:

1. Verify that the C:\Deploy directory is still open in Windows Explorer, and then double-click **setupmgr.exe**. The Windows 2000 Setup Manager Wizard starts and displays a welcome message.

2. Click **Next** to continue.

3. In the New or Existing Answer File window, click **Create a new answer file**, and then click **Next**.

4. In the Product to Install window, click **Windows 2000 Unattended Installation**. What other types of products does this wizard support?

   _____

   _____

5. Click **Next** to continue.

6. In the Platform Type window, click **Windows 2000 Professional**, and then click **Next** to continue.

7. In the User Interaction Level window, click **Fully Automated**, and then click **Next** to continue.

8. In the License Agreement window, accept the EULA, and then click **Next** to continue.

9. In the Customize the Software window, enter the user name and organization name, and then click **Next** to continue.

10. In the Computer Names window, type the computer name and then click **Add**. Note that you could use the answer file you're creating to install Windows 2000 on several computers, as long as the computers' hardware configurations are identical.

11. Click **Next** to continue.

12. In the Administrator Password window, enter the Administrator password for this computer, confirm the password, and then click **Next** to continue.

13. In the Display Settings window, specify your preferences for video settings. These settings include color, screen area, and refresh rate and depend on the settings supported by the video card in the computer where you're performing an unattended installation.

14. Click **Next** to continue.

15. In the Network Settings window, click the correct network type and settings for your network, and then click **Next**.

16. In the Workgroup or Domain window, specify whether the computer is part of a workgroup or domain. If the computer is a part of a domain, enter the Administrator user name and password account.

17. Click **Next** to continue.

18. In the Time Zone window, specify your time zone, and then click **Next**.

19. In the Additional Settings window, you could select settings required for other devices, such as telephone information, regional settings (country and currency, for example), preferred language for menus and other operating system features, and printers that you might want to install automatically. For this lab, however, click the **No, do not edit the additional settings** option button, and then click **Next** to continue.

20. In the Distribution Folder window, you can choose whether you want to install the operating system from a CD or create a distribution folder, typically on a network

location. When you use a distribution folder, all necessary source files are copied to that location. For this lab, however, click the option button indicating installation from a CD, and then click **Next** to continue.

21. In the Answer File Name window, specify the name (Sysprep.inf) and location for the answer file you're creating (the Sysprep folder at the root level of the drive on which Windows will be installed). Click **Next** to continue.

22. Click **Finish** to exit the wizard and close Windows 2000 Setup Manager. The wizard creates the answer file in the specified location.

## CRITICAL THINKING: USING THE ANSWER FILE (ADDITIONAL 120 MINUTES)

Install Windows 2000 using the answer file you just created, and then answer these questions:

◢ Where were the installation files located?

_____

◢ How did you launch the installation process?

_____

_____

◢ How did you tell Setup to use your answer file?

_____

_____

◢ What, if anything, did you have to do while the installation was in progress?

_____

◢ What error messages, if any, did you see? What did you do about them?

_____

_____

_____

## REVIEW QUESTIONS

1. What type of file does the Windows 2000 Setup Manager Wizard create, and what is this file used for?

_____

_____

2. Before the wizard was developed, how was this type of file created?

_____

3. What other operations does this wizard support?

_____

_____

4. Could you use the Windows 2000 Setup Manager Wizard to create a file to assist an unattended installation that automatically creates an account on a Windows domain? Explain:

_____

_____

5. If you choose to create a distribution folder, why isn't the Windows 2000 Professional installation CD necessary during the unattended installation?

_____

_____

## LAB 11.4 DETERMINE HARDWARE COMPATIBILITY WITH WINDOWS XP

### OBJECTIVES

The goal of this lab is to help you determine whether your hardware is compatible with Windows XP. After completing this lab, you will be able to:

- Use Windows to identify system components
- Find and use the Microsoft Hardware Compatibility List (HCL)

### MATERIALS REQUIRED

This lab requires the following:

- Windows 9x or Windows 2000 operating system
- Internet access

### LAB PREPARATION

Before the lab begins, the instructor or lab assistant needs to do the following:

- Verify that Windows starts with no errors.
- Verify that Internet access is available.

### ACTIVITY BACKGROUND

You can't assume that an operating system will support your hardware, especially with older devices, because software developers focus on supporting the most capable and popular devices. To verify that Microsoft operating systems support your hardware, you can check the Microsoft Hardware Compatibility List (HCL) at *www.microsoft.com/whdc/hcl/default.mspx*. The HCL includes devices that have drivers written by Microsoft or devices that have drivers tested and approved by Microsoft. In this lab, you use Device Manager to inventory devices in a system. Then you check the HCL to see whether Windows XP supports the system's devices.

**Activity**

To use Device Manager to inventory your system, follow these steps:

1. Open Control Panel and double-click the **System** icon.

2. In Windows 2000, click the **Hardware** tab, and then click the **Device Manager** button. In Windows 9x, click the **Device Manager** tab. The Device Manager window opens.

3. In Device Manager, devices are arranged by category. To see what kind of video adapter is installed on your system, click the **+** (plus sign) to the left of Display Adapters.

4. Click your video adapter and click the **Properties** button. Record the information about the model and manufacturer that's displayed:

_____

_____

_____

5. Use Device Manager to find similar information for your network adapter, modem card, or sound card, and record that information here:

_____

_____

_____

Now that you have a list of devices installed on your system, check the HCL to see whether Windows XP supports these devices. Web sites change often, so the following steps might have to be adjusted to accommodate changes. If you have difficulty following these steps because of Web site changes, see your instructor for help.

1. Open your browser and go to **www.microsoft.com/whdc/hcl/default.mspx**. Click the **Windows XP: See Windows Catalog** link.

2. Click the **Hardware** tab. At the left under Hardware, point to **Cameras and Video**, and then click **Video Cards**. Using the information about your video adapter you recorded previously in Step 4, find your video card by scrolling the list or using the search box in the upper-left corner. If you don't find your adapter, try using a more general description of it. For example, if "Intel 82810E" doesn't return a result, try typing "Intel."

3. Confirm that you have found your device by verifying that the correct manufacturer and model are listed.

4. Look to the right for an XP logo or a compatible symbol under the XP column. Either one indicates that the device is compatible with XP.

5. Add a note to your list of devices indicating whether the device is compatible with Windows XP.

6. Check the other devices in your list, and note whether they are compatible with Windows XP.

## REVIEW QUESTIONS

1. Explain how to compile a list of devices installed on your system:

   _____

   _____

   _____

2. How are devices grouped in Device Manager?

   _____

3. Where can you find the HCL?

   _____

4. If a device isn't listed in the HCL, what are your options when installing Windows XP? List at least two possibilities:

   _____

   _____

5. Does the hardware in your system qualify for Windows XP? If it doesn't, explain why:

   _____

   _____

## *LAB 11.5 INSTALL OR UPGRADE TO WINDOWS XP*

### OBJECTIVES

The goal of this lab is to help you install or upgrade to Windows XP Professional. After completing this lab, you will be able to:

- Plan an upgrade or installation
- Identify the benefits of an upgrade or new installation
- Install or upgrade to Windows XP Professional

### MATERIALS REQUIRED

This lab requires the following:

- Windows 98SE operating system
- Access to drivers or Internet access for downloading drivers
- Windows XP Professional installation CD or installation files
- Key from installation CD
- A storage medium for updated device drivers

## LAB PREPARATION

Before the lab begins, the instructor or lab assistant needs to do the following:

◢ Verify that Windows starts with no errors.

◢ Provide each student with access to the Windows XP installation files and key.

◢ Verify that any necessary Windows XP drivers are available.

## ACTIVITY BACKGROUND

Windows XP is designed to be reliable and has a new user interface to give you a more personalized computing experience. The operating system's updated look uses more graphics to simplify the user interface. It has a task-oriented design, which gives you options specifically associated with the task or file you're working on. You can upgrade your computer's operating system to Windows XP Professional from Windows 98/98SE, Windows Me, Windows NT Workstation 4.0, Windows 2000, or Windows XP Home Edition. For this lab, you upgrade from Windows 98SE. Installing or upgrading an operating system isn't difficult. Careful planning can minimize or eliminate many of the headaches some users have experienced when upgrading to Windows XP.

> **ESTIMATED COMPLETION TIME: 90 minutes**

 **Activity**

Your lab system will likely be compatible with Windows XP. However, when working on other systems, you might discover significant incompatibilities. In that case, you have to decide whether upgrading to Windows XP Professional is really an option. Many users have had major problems with device drivers when upgrading to Windows XP. For this reason, it's essential to do your research and download device drivers that are compatible with Windows XP Professional before you install the upgrade. You might need to visit the manufacturer Web sites for all your devices, such as scanners, printers, modems, keyboards, mouse, camera, and so on, to see whether they are compatible with Windows XP Professional. If the manufacturer provides an updated device driver to support Windows XP Professional, you need to download the files to a storage medium. Also, when planning an upgrade, recording information in a table, such as Table 11-1, is helpful. Follow these steps to create a plan and prepare for a Windows XP Professional upgrade on your computer:

1. Use Device Manager or SiSoftware Sandra (installed in Lab 1.3) to compile the information in the first row of Table 11-1.

| Things to do | Further information |
|---|---|
| **Does the PC meet the minimum or recommended hardware requirements?** | **CPU:**<br>**RAM:**<br>**Hard drive size:**<br>**Free space on the hard drive:** |
| **Have you checked all your applications to verify that they qualify for Windows XP or need patches to qualify?** | **Applications that need to be upgraded:** |

**Table 11-1**    Things to do and information to collect when planning a Windows upgrade

| Things to do | Further information |
|---|---|
| Have you checked the Microsoft Web site to verify that all your hardware qualifies? | Hardware that needs to be upgraded: |
| Have you decided how you will join a network? | Workgroup name:<br>Domain name:<br>Computer name: |
| Do you have the product key available? | Product key: |
| Have you backed up critical data? | Location of backup files: |
| Is your hard drive ready? | Size of the hard drive partition:<br>Free space on the partition:<br>File system you plan to use: |

**Table 11-1**  Things to do and information to collect when planning a Windows upgrade (continued)

2. Compare your information to the Windows XP requirements in Table 11-2.

   ◢ Does your system meet the minimum requirements?

   _____

   ◢ Does your system meet the recommended requirements?

   _____

| Component or device | Minimum requirement | Recommended requirement |
|---|---|---|
| One or two CPUs | Pentium II 233 MHz or better | Pentium II 300 MHz or better |
| RAM | 64 MB | 128 MB up to 4 GB |
| Hard drive partition | 2 GB | 2 GB or more |
| Free space on the hard drive partition | 640 MB (bare bones) | 2 GB or more |
| CD-ROM drive | 12x | 12x or faster |
| Accessories | Keyboard and mouse or other pointing device | Keyboard and mouse or other pointing device |

**Table 11-2**  Minimum and recommended requirements for Windows XP Professional

3. Make a list of important applications on your system and verify whether they are compatible with Windows XP Professional. If you find any that aren't, check to see whether patches or upgrades are available to make them compatible. List in Table 11-1 any applications that don't qualify or that need patches to qualify. List any software upgrades or patches you downloaded to prepare your applications for Windows XP:

   _____

   _____

4. Install any application upgrades or patches you have downloaded.

5. Check each hardware device against the Hardware Compatibility List and the System Requirements list for Windows XP Professional on the Microsoft Web site (*www.microsoft.com*). List in Table 11-1 any hardware devices that need updated drivers.

6. Download or otherwise obtain all necessary drivers from the manufacturers' Web sites or the Microsoft site for your hardware. List any drivers you were required to install to make your hardware compatible with Windows XP Professional:

7. Gather any network-specific information in preparation for the installation. If you're connected to a network, answer the following:

   ◢ If you're using a TCP/IP network, how is your IP address configured?

   ◢ For a static IP address, what is the IP address?

   ◢ What is the workgroup name or domain name of the network?

   ◢ What is your computer name?

   Record the workgroup or domain name and the computer name in Table 11-1.

8. Based on the information you have collected in Table 11-1, answer the following:

   ◢ Does your system qualify for Windows XP Professional?

   ◢ If not, what hardware or application doesn't qualify?

9. Make sure you have the correct CD key for your installation CD and record it in Table 11-1. The CD key, provided with the Windows XP Professional installation CD, usually consists of a set of alphanumeric characters. You must enter the CD key to complete the installation, even if you're installing the operating system from setup files located somewhere other than the installation CD.

10. Review the information you've collected so far, and then decide whether to do a fresh installation or an upgrade. For instance, if all the important applications on your system

are compatible with Windows XP Professional, an upgrade will probably save time because it leaves compatible applications in working condition. On the other hand, if you know you have to install new applications because of incompatibilities, you might choose to perform a fresh installation. In many ways, a fresh installation is preferable because it ensures that no misconfigured system settings are carried over to the new operating system.

11. Back up critical data files (that is, any work you or others have stored on your computer that you can't afford to lose during the installation process).

12. If you have critical files on the PC, to what location did you back them up? Record that information in Table 11-1.

13. The hard drive partition that is to be the active partition for Windows XP must be at least 2 GB and have at least 2 GB free. Record the size of the hard drive partition and the amount of free space on that partition in Table 11-1. Answer these questions:

◢ What Windows utilities or commands did you use to determine the size of the active partition?

_____

_____

◢ What Windows utilities or commands did you use to determine how much free space is on that partition?

_____

_____

14. When installing Windows XP, you have a choice of using the FAT or NTFS file system. For this installation, use the NTFS file system already installed. Record that information in Table 11-1.

You're ready to begin installing Windows XP Professional. This lab assumes that you have Windows 98SE installed and running. This is not the only situation in which you would install or upgrade to Windows XP Professional, but it's common. Installing Windows XP is possible using setup files stored on the installation CD, a network drive, or a local hard disk.

The following steps are representative of a typical upgrade. Your installation will probably vary in minor ways, depending on the installation options you choose, your system's hardware configuration, and other factors. The following steps are a general guide to let you know what to expect during the process. Don't become alarmed if your experience differs slightly. Use your knowledge to solve any problems on your own, and ask your instructor for help if you get stuck. You might want to record any differences between these steps and your own experience. Also, record any decisions you make and any information you enter during the installation process.

1. Before you insert the installation CD or run the installation files from a location on your hard drive or network, use antivirus software to scan the computer's memory and hard drive for viruses. After the scan is finished, make sure you disable any automatic scans and close the antivirus program before beginning the installation.

2. Insert the Windows XP Professional CD. The Setup program starts. This program guides you through the actual installation. If it doesn't begin automatically, click **Start**, **Run** and browse for the Setup.exe file to begin the installation.

3. The Welcome to Microsoft Windows XP window opens with three options. What options do you see?

_____

_____

_____

4. Click **Install Windows XP**. The Setup program begins collecting information, and the Welcome to Windows Setup window opens with Installation Type: Upgrade (Recommended) in the text box. Click **Next**.

5. Accept the EULA, and then click **Next**.

6. When prompted, enter the CD key, and then click **Next**.

7. The Windows Setup Upgrade Report window opens. If necessary, click the **Show me hardware issues and a limited set of software issues (Recommended)** option, and then click **Next**.

8. The Windows Setup Get Updated Setup Files window opens. Because you can check for updates later and are focusing on upgrading for now, click **No, skip this step and continue installing Windows,** and click **Next**.

9. Windows is now preparing the installation of Windows XP Professional by analyzing your computer. This setup takes approximately 60 minutes. Read the informational screens as they're displayed. You can gain a lot of knowledge of Windows XP through this mini tutorial. Your computer restarts several times during the installation and setup process.

10. When the installation is finished and Windows XP has restarted for the last time, the Welcome to Microsoft Windows window opens. Click **Next** to continue.

11. In the Ready to Register with Microsoft window, click **No, not at this time**, and then click **Next**.

12. Now you're ready to enter your user information. You can type the name of each person who will use this computer. Windows creates a separate user account for each person, so you can personalize the way you want Windows to organize and display information, protect your files and computer settings, and customize the desktop. The user names you enter appear in the Welcome window in alphabetical order. When you start Windows, you simply click your name in the Welcome window to begin working in Windows XP Professional. For now, enter only your first name, and then click **Next**.

13. When you see a Thank You message, click **Finish** to continue.

14. You can also set a password for all Windows XP accounts. Enter a password to be used for all the listed accounts. If you want to change the passwords later, go to the User Accounts applet in Control Panel.

15. To begin using Windows XP, click your user name and enter your password. A Welcome window appears. Wait while Windows XP loads your personal settings. The first time you start Windows XP, the Start menu is displayed until you click something else. Thereafter, you open the Start menu by clicking the Start button at the left of the taskbar.

16. Remove the installation CD from the drive and return it to the instructor.

## REVIEW QUESTIONS

1. Was the Windows XP upgrade a success? If so, what did you find to be most challenging about the upgrade process?

   _____

   _____

2. Describe the Windows XP desktop:

   _____

   _____

   _____

3. By default, which icon appears on the Windows XP desktop?

   _____

4. At first glance, what is your impression of the user interface?

   _____

5. How does Windows XP offer to help you learn about its exciting new features?

   _____

   _____

**CHAPTER 12**

# Maintaining Windows 2000/XP

**Labs included in this chapter:**

# LAB 12.1 NAVIGATE AND CUSTOMIZE WINDOWS XP

## OBJECTIVES

The goal of this lab is to help you become familiar with navigating and customizing the Windows XP user interface. After completing this lab, you will be able to:

◢ Customize the taskbar

◢ Work with a program shortcut

◢ Customize the Start menu

◢ Clean up the Windows XP desktop

◢ Locate essential system information

## MATERIALS REQUIRED

This lab requires the following:

◢ Windows XP Professional operating system

## LAB PREPARATION

Before the lab begins, the instructor or lab assistant needs to do the following:

◢ Verify that Windows starts with no errors.

## ACTIVITY BACKGROUND

Becoming proficient at navigating a new operating system can require some time and effort. Upgrading from Windows 98SE to Windows XP Professional is a giant step, especially after you look at the differences in the user interface. From the redesigned Start menu to the new task links in folder windows, just about everything looks a bit different in Windows XP, and locating previously used utilities might prove a challenge. In this lab, you explore how Windows XP handles some routine tasks.

**ESTIMATED COMPLETION TIME: 30 minutes**

 **Activity**

To work with the taskbar, follow these steps:

1. Place the mouse pointer over an empty part of the taskbar, and drag the taskbar to the right side of the screen.

   ◢ Were you able to move the taskbar? If not, what do you think the problem might be?

   _____

   _____

2. Right-click an empty area of the taskbar. Click **Lock the Taskbar** to deselect this option. Now try to move the taskbar to the right side of the screen. Return the taskbar to its default position.

   ◢ Were you able to move the taskbar?

   _____

You can create shortcuts and place them on the desktop to provide quick access to programs. You can also rename and delete a shortcut on your desktop. To create, rename, and delete a desktop shortcut, follow these steps:

1. Click **Start**, point to **All Programs**, and point to **Accessories**.

2. Right-click **Calculator**. In the menu that opens, point to **Send To**, and then click **Desktop (create shortcut)**. Windows adds the shortcut to your desktop. (You might need to minimize any open windows to see it.)

3. Right-click the shortcut, and click **Rename** in the shortcut men.

4. Type a new name for the shortcut, and press **Enter**.

5. To delete a shortcut icon from the desktop, right-click it, and click **Delete** in the shortcut menu. In the Confirm File Delete dialog box that opens, click **Yes**. The shortcut is deleted from the desktop.

The Start menu has been redesigned in Windows XP to give you easy access to programs. When it first opens, it looks something like Figure 12-1. When you install most programs, they are added automatically to the Start menu. If a program isn't added during installation, you can add it yourself. Windows XP enables you to "pin" a program to your Start menu. To customize the Start menu, follow these steps:

1. First, you need to find a program to pin to the Start menu. Because performing a backup is essential in maintaining your PC, you'll pin the Backup utility to the Start menu. Click **Start**, point to **All Programs**, point to **Accessories**, and click **System Tools**.

2. Right-click **Backup**, and click **Pin to Start Menu** in the shortcut menu. The program is added to your Start menu. Write the steps you would take to unpin the Backup utility from the Start menu:

_____

_____

_____

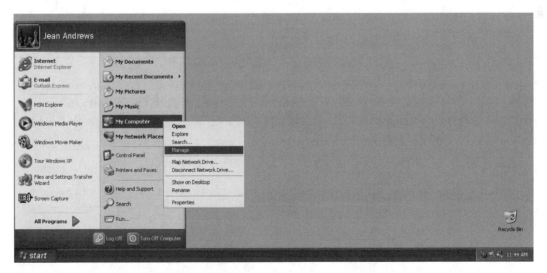

**Figure 12-1**   The Windows XP desktop and Start menu

If you're accustomed to the Windows 9x/2000 Start menu style, now called the Classic menu, you might find that changes to the Start menu take some getting used to. Giving the new Start menu a try is recommended, however, because it was designed to increase efficiency. If you're unable to adjust, you can revert to the Classic version of the Start menu by following these steps:

1. Right-click **Start** and click **Properties** in the shortcut menu. If necessary, click the **Start Menu** tab.

2. Click the **Classic Start menu** option button, and then click **Apply**. Click **OK**.

3. Which Start menu version do you prefer, and why?

_____

_____

The Desktop Cleanup Wizard helps you clean up your desktop by moving rarely used shortcuts to a desktop folder called Unused Desktop Shortcuts. This folder is a temporary holding area for shortcuts you aren't using. You can restore shortcuts from this folder or delete the entire folder. To use the Desktop Cleanup Wizard to remove rarely used shortcuts, follow these steps:

1. Right-click any open area of the desktop, point to **Arrange Icons By**, and then click **Run Desktop Cleanup Wizard**. The Desktop Cleanup Wizard starts.

2. Click **Next** to open the Shortcuts dialog box. The Shortcuts to Clean Up list is displayed along with the Date Last Used.

3. To leave a shortcut on your desktop, click to clear its check box. Only those shortcuts with a check mark in the box are moved to the Unused Desktop Shortcuts folder. Click a shortcut in your list, and then click **Next**.

4. You see a confirmation message indicating which shortcuts will be moved. Click **Finish**.

5. Click **Yes to All**. You're returned to the Windows desktop. You should see a new folder called Unused Desktop Shortcuts.

6. Next, you move the entire folder to the Recycle Bin. Before you do, however, take notice of the Recycle Bin icon. Now drag the new folder to the Recycle Bin.

   ◢ Did the appearance of the Recycle Bin icon change? If so, explain the change:

_____

_____

By now, you might have noticed quite a few changes to the way you view and navigate Windows XP compared to Windows 98SE. In the next steps, you locate essential system information using My Computer and Control Panel. Remember, however, with the new interface, locating some items might not be as easy.

1. Click **Start, My Computer**.

   ◢ How does the way Windows XP displays information in My Computer differ from Windows 98?

_____

_____

   ◢ What happens when you click the drive C icon?

_____

_____

2. Double-click the drive **C** icon.

◢ Describe how Windows XP displays information about your hard drive:

_____

_____

◢ What happens when you click Show the contents of this drive?

_____

_____

3. Click the **Back** button on the Standard toolbar (the bar below the menu bar). Close the My Computer window.

4. Click **Start, Control Panel.**

◢ What categories of information are displayed in Control Panel?

_____

_____

_____

◢ List the steps you would take to view information or make changes to your mouse settings:

_____

_____

_____

_____

5. Close Control Panel and return to the Windows XP desktop.

## REVIEW QUESTIONS

1. What steps must you take to locate My Computer?

_____

2. Using the Help and Support feature in Windows XP, locate information on installing new or updated printer drivers. How did you find the information?

_____

_____

_____

3. What Windows XP utility can you use to transfer user files and preferences from one computer to another?

_____

4. Why does Windows XP allow you to change to a Classic Start menu?

5. What Windows XP tool can be used to remove unused shortcuts from the desktop?

# *LAB 12.2 USE WINDOWS MEDIA PLAYER*

## OBJECTIVES

The goal of this lab is to give you experience managing audio and video with Windows Media Player. After completing this lab, you will be able to:

◢ Launch Windows Media Player

◢ Change Windows Media Player options

◢ Create and use a music playlist

## MATERIALS REQUIRED

This lab requires the following:

◢ Windows XP Professional operating system

◢ Internet access

◢ A music CD

## LAB PREPARATION

Before the lab begins, the instructor or lab assistant needs to do the following:

◢ Verify that Windows starts with no errors.

◢ Verify that Internet access is available.

**Notes**

If you've used Media Player before, it might open in full mode by default. To switch modes at any time, right-click anywhere on the player, and then click Switch to Full (or Skin) Mode.

## ACTIVITY BACKGROUND

Many people enjoy playing music or videos on their computers. With Windows Media Player, you can have an entertainment center right on your desktop. Windows XP Professional comes with Windows Media Player 8, which you can use to play, copy, and catalog audio and video files from your computer, CDs, DVDs, or the Internet. You can display Media Player in one of two modes: full mode or skin mode. By default, Media Player opens in skin mode.

**ESTIMATED COMPLETION TIME: 30 minutes**

**Activity**

To launch Windows Media Player, follow these steps:

1. If necessary, log on to Windows XP.

2. Click **Start**, point to **All Programs**, and then click **Windows Media Player**. The Windows Media Player window opens. A sample playlist will probably open and start playing the first selection. The display area shows the default visualization.

3. In the task pane on the left, click **Now Playing**, if necessary, to display the current playlist. To play a song, double-click a song in the list.

Visualizations are shapes and colors displayed in the Windows Media Player window to enhance the audio while songs are playing. You can change the visualization options by following these steps:

1. Click the **Select visualization or album art** button (round button with a * labeled in Figure 12-2), point to **Visualizations**, point to **Spikes**, and then click **Spike** in the menu. You can also select visualizations by clicking **View** on the menu, pointing to **Visualizations**, and clicking the visualization you want.

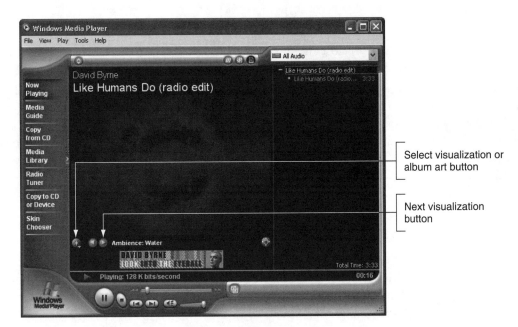

**Figure 12-2**   Selecting a visualization in Windows Media Player

2. Click the **Next visualization** button (the button with a right-facing arrow) to move to the next Spikes option, Spikes: Amoeba.

3. Click the **Next visualization** button to view other available options. List five of these options here:

_____

_____

_____

_____

_____

Using Windows Media Player, you can browse the Internet for songs. Do the following:

1. In the task pane on the left, click **Media Guide**. If you're connected to the Internet, the Windows Media Web site opens.

2. Browse through the Web site to see what it has to offer.

3. In the task pane on the left, click **Radio Tuner**. The Radio Tuner opens with a list of featured stations displayed.

4. In the Featured Stations list, click through the radio stations until you find one that has a Play button.

5. Click the **Play** button to hear the station. The radio station's Web site opens in a new window in the background.

6. Describe how the Web site is set up so that you can choose the music you want to hear:

_____

_____

_____

7. Click **Close** to close the Windows Media Player window, and then close the window displaying the radio station's Web site.

Those who have used Media Player and taken advantage of downloading files to their hard disks soon find that they have accumulated hundreds of songs. Just as managing data files on your hard drives is important, you should also practice good file management of music files you accumulate. Windows XP helps solve the problem of scrolling through endless lists of files searching for the next song you want to hear by creating playlists. A playlist is a list of digital media files, such as songs, video clips, and links to radio stations. You can create a playlist as a collection, which allows you to play, copy, or burn it to a CD.

To create a music playlist and add a song to it, follow these steps:

1. Open the Windows Media Player window.

2. In the task pane on the left, click **Media Library**, and then click **Playlists, New Playlist** from the menu at the upper left. The New Playlist dialog box opens.

3. Type **MyBestSongs** in the Playlist Name text box, which will be a subgroup under MyPlaylists. Click **OK**. MyBestSongs is then listed under My Playlists. If you click MyBestSongs, no songs are listed.

Next, you copy two songs from a CD to your hard drive and then add one song to your playlist, MyBestSongs. Do the following:

1. Insert a music CD in the CD-ROM drive; the music CD might start playing. Click **Copy from CD** in the task pane on the left. A list of songs on the CD is displayed, and all songs on the CD are selected for copying. Clear the check boxes next to all except two songs.

2. Click **Copy Music** at the top of the window to copy the two selected songs to your hard drive.

3. If the CD is copy protected, you might have to click a check box saying you understand the conditions, and then step through a few additional dialog boxes.

4. The two selected songs are copied to your My Music folder and also listed under Media Library. When the copying is finished, click **Media Library**. The two songs are listed in the right pane.

5. Drag one of the songs to the **MyBestSongs** playlist under My Playlists. Then click the MyBestSongs folder in the pane on the left, where you'll see that song listed in your custom playlist. Double-click the song to play it.

6. Stop the current selection from playing and close Windows Media Player.

There's a simple way to listen to songs you have put into your My Music folder. Do the following:

1. Click **Start, My Music**.

2. Locate the song in the folder or its subfolder and double-click the song.

▲ What application launches to play the song?

## REVIEW QUESTIONS

1. Describe how Windows Media Player uses visualizations:

_____

_____

2. Using Windows Media Player, is it possible to copy music files to a CD? If so, explain how you would accomplish that task:

_____

_____

3. When you first open Windows Media Player, it appears in skin mode. How many other skins are available? Explain how you change the skin in Media Player:

_____

_____

4. Explain how you switch from full mode back to skin mode:

_____

_____

# LAB 12.3 USE THE MICROSOFT MANAGEMENT CONSOLE

## OBJECTIVES

The goal of this lab is to help you add snap-ins and save settings using the Microsoft Management Console (MMC) to create a customized console. After completing this lab, you will be able to:

▲ Use the MMC to add snap-ins

▲ Save a customized console

▲ Identify how to launch a console from the Start menu

## MATERIALS REQUIRED

This lab requires the following:

▲ Windows 2000/XP Professional operating system

## LAB PREPARATION

Before the lab begins, the instructor or lab assistant needs to do the following:

▲ Verify that Windows starts with no errors.

## ACTIVITY BACKGROUND

The Microsoft Management Console (MMC) is a standard management tool you can use to create a customized console by adding administrative tools called snap-ins. You can use snap-ins provided by Microsoft or other vendors. Many of the administrative tools you have already used (such as Device Manager) can be added to a console as a snap-in. The console itself serves as a convenient interface that helps you organize and manage the administrative tools you use most often. In this lab, you use the MMC to create a customized console.

**ESTIMATED COMPLETION TIME: 30 minutes**

 **Activity**

Follow these steps to build a customized console:

1. Log on as an administrator.

2. Click **Start, Run**. The Run dialog box opens.

3. In the Open text box, type **mmc**, and then click **OK**. An MMC window named Console 1 opens with another window named Console Root within it, which is used to display the console's contents.

4. From the Console 1 menu, click **File, Add/Remove Snap-in**. The Add/Remove Snap-in dialog box opens. Console 1 is currently empty—that is, it doesn't contain any snap-ins yet. As you can see in the Snap-ins added to list box, any new snap-ins are added to the Console Root folder.

5. Click **Add**. The Add Standalone Snap-in dialog box opens, displaying a list of available snap-ins. Note that this list includes some administrative tools you have already used, such as Device Manager and Event Viewer.

6. Click **Device Manager**, and then click **Add**.

7. The Device Manager dialog box opens, where you specify which computer you want this Device Manager snap-in to manage. You want it to manage the computer you're currently working on, so verify that the **Local computer** option button is selected (see Figure 12-3), and then click **Finish**. Device Manager on the local computer is added to the Add/Remove Snap-in dialog box. The Add Standalone Snap-in dialog box remains open.

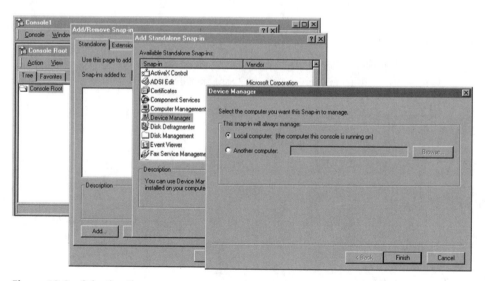

**Figure 12-3**   Selecting the computer you want the snap-in to manage

8. Next, you add Event Viewer as a snap-in. Click **Event Viewer** in the Add Standalone Snap-in dialog box, and then click **Add**. The Select Computer dialog box opens.

9. Verify that the **Local computer** option button is selected, and then click **Finish**. The Select Computer dialog box closes, and Event Viewer (Local) is added in the Add/Remove Snap-in dialog box. The Add Standalone Snap-in dialog box remains open.

You have finished adding snap-ins for the local computer to your console. Next, you add another Event Viewer snap-in to be used on a network computer. If your computer isn't connected to a network, you can read the following set of steps, but don't attempt to perform them. If your computer is connected to a network, follow these steps:

1. Add another Event Viewer snap-in, and then click the **Another computer** option button in the Select Computer dialog box. Now you need to specify the name of the computer to which you want this Event Viewer snap-in to apply. You could type the name of the computer, but it's easier to select the computer by using the Browse button.

2. Click the **Browse** button. A different Select Computer dialog box opens and begins searching the network for eligible computers. Eventually, it displays a list of eligible computers.

3. Click the name of the computer to which you want to apply this Event Viewer snap-in, and then click **OK**. The second Select Computer dialog box closes, and you return to the first Select Computer dialog box.

4. Click **Finish**. The Select Computer dialog box closes, and a second Event Viewer snap-in is added to the Add/Remove Snap-in dialog box. The new Event Viewer listing is followed by the name of the remote computer in parentheses.

At this point, regardless of whether your computer is connected to a network, the Add Standalone Snap-in dialog box should be open. You're finished adding snap-ins and are ready to return to the Console1 window and save your new, customized console so that you can use it whenever you need it. Follow these steps:

1. Click **Close** in the Add Standalone Snap-in dialog box. You return to the Add/Remove Snap-in dialog box.

2. Click **OK**. The Add/Remove Snap-in dialog box closes, and you return to the Console1 window. The left pane of the Console Root window (within the Console1 window) now contains the following items: Device Manager (Local), Event Viewer (Local), and Event Viewer (*remote computer name*).

3. In the Console1 window, click **File, Save As** from the menu. The Save As dialog box opens with the default location set to C:\Documents and Settings\Administrator \Start Menu\Programs\Administrative Tools. If you save your customized console in this location, Administrative Tools is also added to the Start menu. Instead, use the Save in drop-down list box to choose C:\Documents and Settings\Administrator \Start Menu\Programs for the save location. Be sure to double-click **Programs** so that the file goes in the Programs folder.

4. Name the console **Custom.msc**, and then click **Save**. The Save As dialog box closes.

5. Close the Console1 window.

Follow these steps to open and use your customized console:

1. Click **Start**, point to **All Programs** (**Programs** in Windows 2000), and click **Custom**. Your customized console opens in a window named Custom - [Console Root].

2. Maximize the console window, if necessary.

3. In the left pane, click **Device Manager on local computer** and observe the options in the right pane.

4. In the left pane, click the + (plus sign) next to Event Viewer (Local). Subcategories are displayed below Event Viewer (Local). List the subcategories you see:

_____

_____

_____

5. Click **Event Viewer** (*remote computer name*), and observe that the events displayed are events occurring on the remote computer.

6. From the Custom - [Console Root] menu, click **File, Exit**. A message box opens, asking if you want to save the current settings.

7. Click **Yes**. The console closes.

8. Launch the customized console from the Start menu again, and record the type of information displayed in the right pane when the console opens:

_____

## REVIEW QUESTIONS

1. What term is used to refer to the specialized tools you can add to a console with the MMC? What are they used for?

_____

_____

2. Suppose you haven't created a customized MMC yet. How would you start MMC?

_____

_____

3. How can a customized console be used to manage many computers from a single machine?

_____

_____

4. What information do you see when you open a customized console?

_____

_____

5. How do you add a customized console to the Start menu?

_____

_____

# LAB 12.4 ANALYZE A SYSTEM WITH WINDOWS 2000/XP EVENT VIEWER

## OBJECTIVES

The goal of this lab is to help you learn to work with Windows 2000/XP Event Viewer. After completing this lab, you will be able to use Event Viewer to:

◢ View normal startup events

◢ View failed events

◢ Record event logs

◢ Compare recent events to logged events

## MATERIALS REQUIRED

This lab requires the following:

◢ Windows 2000/XP Professional operating system

◢ Network access using the TCP/IP protocol suite

◢ An administrator account and password

## LAB PREPARATION

Before the lab begins, the instructor or lab assistant needs to do the following:

◢ Verify that Windows starts with no errors.

## ACTIVITY BACKGROUND

Most of the things that happen to your computer while running Windows 2000/XP are recorded in a log. In Windows, you can look at these events with a tool called Event Viewer, an application that provides information on various operations and tasks (known as events) in Windows. Event Viewer notes the occurrence of various events, lists them chronologically, and gives you the option of saving the list so that you can compare it to a future list. You can use Event Viewer to find out how healthy your system is and to diagnose nonfatal startup problems. Fatal startup problems don't allow you into Windows far enough to use Event Viewer.

**ESTIMATED COMPLETION TIME: 30 minutes**

 **Activity**

Follow these steps to begin using Event Viewer:

1. Boot the system and log on as an administrator.

2. Click **Start, Control Panel** (in Windows 2000, click **Start**, point to **Settings**, and click **Control Panel**) to open the Control Panel window.

3. In Windows XP, click **Performance and Maintenance**, and then click **Administrative Tools**. In Windows 2000, double-click the **Administrative Tools** icon. The Administrative Tools applet opens.

4. Double-click **Event Viewer** to open the Event Viewer window, with the latest events displayed in chronological order from most recent to oldest (see Figure 12-4). The symbols to the left of each event indicate important information about the event.

For example, the red "X" indicates an error (a failed event), a lowercase "i" in a circle indicates an event providing information about the system, and an exclamation mark in a triangle indicates a warning, such as a disk being near its capacity. The listing for each event includes a brief description and the time and date it occurred.

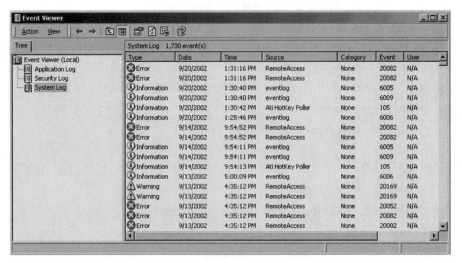

**Figure 12-4**  Event Viewer tracks failed and successful events

5. Locate the listings for the four most recent events on your system. For each event, list the source (what triggered the event), time, and date:

_____

_____

_____

_____

6. Double-click the top (most recent) event. The Event Properties dialog box opens. What additional information does this dialog box provide? Note that you can also see an event's properties by clicking an event to select it, and then clicking **Action, Properties** from the menu.

_____

_____

_____

7. Close the Event Properties dialog box.

You can save the list of events shown in Event Viewer as a special file called a log file. When naming a log file, it's helpful to use the following format: EV*mm-dd-yy*.evt (*mm* = month, *dd* = day, and *yy* = year). For example, you would name a log file saved on January 13, 2007 as EV01-13-07.evt. After you create a log file, you can delete the current list of events from Event Viewer, allowing the utility to begin creating an entirely new list of events. Follow these steps to save the currently displayed events as a log file, and then clear the current events:

1. Open Windows Explorer, and create a folder called **Logs** in the root directory of drive C.

2. Open Event Viewer (if it's not already open), and click somewhere on the Event Viewer window so that no event is selected. Then click **Action, Export List** from the menu.

3. Click the **Logs** folder created in Step 1, name the file **EV*mm-dd-yy*.evt**, and then click **Save**. Now you're ready to clear the current list of events from Event Viewer.

4. Click **Action, Clear all Events** from the menu.

5. When asked if you want to save the System log, click **No**. The Event Viewer window no longer displays any events.

6. Close Event Viewer.

Next, you try to create an intentional problem by attempting to remove a system file. Recall that the Windows File Protection feature doesn't allow you to delete or rename a system file. If you try to do that, the event is recorded in Event Viewer. To attempt to delete a system file, do the following:

1. Open Windows Explorer, and locate the Tcpip.sys file in the \WINNT\system32\drivers folder.

2. Click **tcpip.sys** and press **Delete**. When you're asked to confirm sending this file to the Recycle Bin, click **Yes**. It appears as though Tcpip.sys is deleted. The file makes it possible for the computer to communicate over the network and is a protected system file, so Windows immediately replaces the file. (You learn more about TCP/IP in later chapters.)

3. Close Windows Explorer and open Event Viewer. Double-click the **Windows File Protection** event, and answer these questions:

   ◢ What is the description of the event?

   _____

   _____

   _____

   ◢ What is the type assigned to this event?

   _____

4. Close the Event Properties dialog box.

5. Open Windows Explorer. Is Tcpip.sys in the \WINNT\system32\drivers folder?

   _____

Next, you create an intentional problem by disconnecting the network cable from your PC, and then see how the resulting errors are recorded in Event Viewer. Do the following:

1. Carefully disconnect the network cable from the network port on the back of your PC.

2. Restart the computer and log on as an administrator. Record any messages you receive, if any:

   _____

   _____

3. Open My Network Places. Are you able to browse the network?

   _____

4. Close My Network Places, and then open Event Viewer. How many events are displayed?

   _____

5. List the source, date, and time for any error events (indicated by a red "X") you see:

_____

_____

_____

_____

6. Click each error or warning event, and read the details. For each event, write a summary of the information in the Description text box. (In the Event Properties dialog box, click **Close** to exit after you have read the description for each event, or use the arrow buttons to scroll through and locate the next error.)

_____

_____

_____

_____

_____

_____

_____

When troubleshooting a system, comparing current events with a list of events you previously stored in a log file is often helpful because you can spot the time when a particular problem occurred. Follow these steps to compare the current list of events to the log you saved earlier:

1. Open another instance of Event Viewer (that is, open a second Event Viewer window without closing the first one).

2. In the new Event Viewer window, click a blank area of the window so that no event is selected. Then click **Action, Open Log File** from the menu.

3. Open the **Logs** folder, and click the log file you created earlier. Under Log Type, click **System** and then click **Open**. If a message box appears asking you to confirm opening the file, click **OK**.

4. To position the two instances of Event Viewer on your desktop so that you can compare them, right-click a blank spot on the taskbar. A shortcut menu opens, giving you options for how to arrange all open windows—cascading the windows or tiling them horizontally or vertically. Click **Tile Vertically** to position the two open windows side by side. You might notice that the current list of events contains one more successful event than the log of previous events. One of these successful events might be the cause of a failed event. For instance, a service starting and allocating resources that another component was previously using would be listed as a successful event. However, allocating resources currently in use would cause the component that had been using the resources to fail, thereby resulting in a failed event. Judging by the log file you created earlier, how many events occur in a normal startup?

_____

To restore the network connection and verify that the connection is working, follow these steps:

1. Reconnect the network cable to the network port on the back of your computer, restart your computer, and log on. Did you receive any messages after you started Windows this time?

_____

2. Open Event Viewer and verify that no errors occurred during startup.

3. Open another instance of Event Viewer, open the log you saved earlier (in the Logs folder), and verify that the same events occurred in both windows.

4. Close both Event Viewer windows.

## CRITICAL THINKING (ADDITIONAL 30 MINUTES)

Using the Internet for research, find answers to the following questions. Be sure to list the URLs that support your answers.

1. Which version of Windows introduced Windows File Protection? Explain what Windows File Protection does:

_____

_____

2. Does Windows 2000/XP need DOS to run? Explain your answer:

_____

_____

3. Name two benefits to upgrading to Windows XP and explain your answers:

_____

_____

## REVIEW QUESTIONS

1. Judging by the path to Event Viewer using the Start menu, what type of tool is Event Viewer?

_____

2. Based on what you learned in this lab, what might be your first indication that a problem occurred after startup?

_____

3. How can you examine events after you have cleared them from Event Viewer?

_____

_____

4. Explain how to compare a log file with the current set of listed events:

_____

_____

5. Why might you like to keep a log file of events that was made when your computer started correctly? List the steps to create this log of a successful startup:

_____

_____

_____

_____

_____

# LAB 12.5 USE TASK MANAGER

## OBJECTIVES

The goal of this lab is to help you use Task Manager to examine your system. After completing this lab, you will be able to:

▲ Identify applications that are currently running

▲ Launch an application

▲ Display general system performance and process information in Task Manager

## MATERIALS REQUIRED

This lab requires the following:

▲ Windows 2000/XP Professional operating system

▲ Installed CD drive, installed sound card, and audio CD

## LAB PREPARATION

Before the lab begins, the instructor or lab assistant needs to do the following:

▲ Verify that Windows starts with no errors.

▲ Verify that a CD drive and sound card have been installed on student computers.

## ACTIVITY BACKGROUND

Task Manager is a useful tool that allows you to switch between tasks, end tasks, and observe system use and performance. In this lab, you use Task Manager to manage applications and observe system performance.

**ESTIMATED COMPLETION TIME: 30 minutes**

 **Activity**

Follow these steps to use Task Manager:

1. Log on as an administrator.

2. Press **Ctrl+Alt+Del** to open Task Manager, or right-click any blank area on the taskbar and click **Task Manager** in the shortcut menu. The Task Manager dialog box opens,

with tabs you can use to find information about applications, processes, and programs running on the computer and information on system performance.

3. If necessary, click the **Applications** tab. What information is currently listed in the Task list box?

_____

_____

_____

4. Use the Start menu to open Windows Help and Support (in Windows 2000, open Windows 2000 Help), and then observe the change to the Task list in the Applications tab. What change occurred in the Task list?

_____

5. Right-click the new task and click **Go to process**. What process is associated with this task?

_____

6. In the Applications tab, click the **New Task** button. The Create New Task dialog box opens, which is almost identical to the Run dialog box you open from the Start menu.

7. In the Open text box, type **command.com**, and then click **OK**. A command prompt window opens. Examine the Application tab in Task Manager, and note that \WINNT\system32\command.com now appears in the Task list.

8. Click the title bar of the command prompt window. It's now the active window, but notice that Task Manager remains on top of all other open windows. This ensures that you can keep track of changes in the system while opening and closing applications.

You can customize Task Manager to suit your preferences. Among other things, you can change the setting that keeps Task Manager on top of all other open windows and change the way information is displayed. To learn more about changing Task Manager settings, make sure the command prompt window is still open, and follow these steps:

1. In Task Manager, click **Options** on the menu bar. A menu with a list of options opens. Note that the check marks indicate which options are currently applied. The Always On Top option is currently selected, which keeps the Task Manager window on top of all other open windows. List the available menu options here:

_____

_____

_____

2. Click **Always On Top** to clear the check mark, and then click the command prompt window. What happens?

_____

_____

_____

3. Click **Options** on the Task Manager menu bar, and then click **Always On Top** to select it again.

4. On the Task Manager menu bar, click **View**. You can use the options on this menu to change the way information is displayed in the Task Manager window. Selected settings are indicated by a dot. List the available and current settings:

_____

_____

_____

5. Click **Large Icons** to select this setting. Note how it affects the way information is displayed in Task Manager.

6. Return the view to the **Details** setting.

Follow these steps in Task Manager to end a task and observe system use information:

1. In the Applications tab, notice that three types of information are listed in the bar at the bottom of Task Manager. What three types of information do you see, and what are their values?

_____

_____

_____

2. While observing these three values, move your mouse around the screen for several seconds and then stop. Which value changed?

_____

3. In the Task list, click **Windows Help and Support** (in Windows 2000, click **Windows 2000 Help**), and then click the **End Task** button.

4. Compare the number of processes, CPU usage, and commit charge (memory usage) to the information recorded in Step 1. How much memory was Windows Help and Support (or Windows 2000 Help) using?

_____

Follow these steps in Task Manager to observe process and performance information:

1. In Task Manager, click the **Processes** tab. This tab lists current processes in the Image Name column and displays information about each process, such as Process ID (PID), CPU Percent Used By (CPU), a running total of CPU time (CPU Time), and Memory Usage (Mem Usage), depending on which operating system you're running.

2. Scroll down and examine each process. What process is currently using the highest percentage of CPU resources?

_____

3. Use the Start menu to start Windows Help and Support (or Windows 2000 Help).

4. Drag the Help window to position it as shown in Figure 12-5, so that the left pane is visible to the left of the Task Manager window.

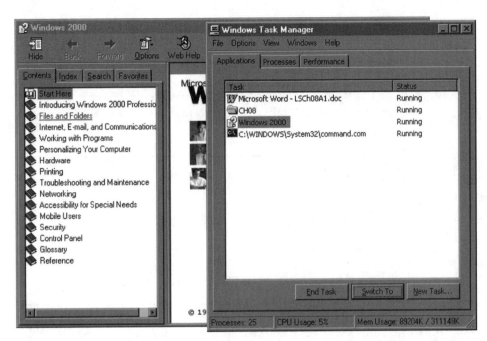

**Figure 12-5** Position the Windows 2000 Help window to the left of the Task Manager window

5. Verify that the Help window is the active window, and then observe the process information in Task Manager as you move the mouse pointer up and down over the topics in the left pane of the Help window. Which process or processes begin to use more CPU resources as the mouse moves from topic to topic?

_____

6. In the Processes tab of Task Manager, click **HelpSvc.exe** (**hh.exe** in Windows 2000), and then click **End Process**. What message is displayed?

_____

_____

_____

7. In addition to processes for optional user applications, the Processes tab displays and allows you to end core Windows processes. *Caution*: Be careful about ending tasks; ending a potentially essential task (one that other processes depend on) could have serious consequences. Because Windows Help and Support (or Windows 2000 Help) is not critical to core Windows functions, it's safe to end this task. Click **Yes** to end.

8. Click the **Performance** tab, which displays CPU usage and PF (page file) usage (memory in Windows 2000) in bar graphs. This tab also shows a running history graph for both CPU usage and page file usage (memory in Windows 2000). What other four categories of information are displayed in the Performance tab?

_____

_____

9. Insert an audio CD. Configure it to begin playing, if necessary. Observe the CPU and page file or memory usage values, and record them here:

_____

10. Stop the CD from playing, and again observe the CPU usage and page file or memory usage. Compare these values to the values from Step 9. Which value changed the most?

_____

## REVIEW QUESTIONS

1. Explain one way to launch Task Manager:

_____

2. Which Task Manager tab do you use to switch between applications and end a task?

_____

3. Why could it be dangerous to end a process with Task Manager?

_____

_____

4. How could you tell whether the processor had recently completed a period of intensive use but is now idle?

_____

5. Did the playback of an audio CD use more system resources than moving the mouse? Explain:

_____

_____

# *LAB 12.6 MONITOR THE MEMORY COUNTER*

## OBJECTIVES

The goal of this lab is to help you monitor the memory counter to investigate a possible memory shortage. After completing this lab, you will be able to:

◢ Add memory counters to System Monitor

◢ Analyze memory usage during defragmentation

## MATERIALS REQUIRED

This lab requires the following:

◢ Windows XP Professional operating system

## LAB PREPARATION

Before the lab begins, the instructor or lab assistant needs to do the following:

◢ Verify that Windows starts with no errors.

## ACTIVITY BACKGROUND

In Windows XP, you can use the System Monitor utility to observe system performance and add counters to collect data about the system. In this lab, you add and monitor counters that measure available memory, memory paging, and the read and write times for disk access. These counters can help you determine how much of the total system resources a particular process (such as defragmenting the hard drive) is using.

**ESTIMATED COMPLETION TIME: 15 minutes**

 **Activity**

Follow these steps to add counters to System Monitor:

1. Click **Start**, point to **All Programs**, point to **Administrative Tools**, and then click **Performance**. (If Administrative Tools doesn't appear on your All Programs menu, you need to add it. To do this, right-click **Start**, click **Properties**, click the **Start Menu** tab in the Properties dialog box, click **Customize**, click the **Advanced** tab in the Customize dialog box, scroll down to **System Administrative Tools**, click **Display** on the All Programs menu, and then click **OK** in both dialog boxes. After adding Administrative Tools to the All Programs menu, start again at the beginning of this step.)

2. The Performance console opens. Make sure that System Monitor is selected in the left pane. In the right pane, right-click in the blank area, and then click **Add Counters** in the shortcut menu.

3. The Add Counters dialog box opens. In the Performance object drop-down list, click the **Memory** object. Scroll down the list box labeled Select counters from list, click the **Available Bytes** counter, and then click the **Add** button to add the selected Available Bytes counter to the Performance console.

4. Click the **Explain** button and record the explanation of the Available Bytes counter:

   _____

   _____

5. Repeat Step 3 to add the **Pages/sec** counter for the Memory object, the **Processor Time** counter for the Processor object, and the **Disk Read Time** and **Disk Write Time** counters for the Physical Disk object. Record the explanations of each counter:

   _____

   _____

   _____

   _____

6. Click the **Close** button in the Add Counters dialog box. You return to the Performance Console, where the counters you added are listed in the right pane. Look in the Color column, and make sure each counter is monitored with a different color. (If you find

a color difficult to read, you can change it by clicking the counter to select it, then right-clicking it, and clicking **Properties** from the shortcut menu. In the Properties dialog box, click a color in the Color drop-down list, and then click **OK**.)

Follow these steps to monitor the counters for two different applications:

1. With the Performance console still open, open the Notepad application. Wait a few seconds, and then close it again.

2. In the Performance console, click the **Freeze Display** button (a red circle with a white "X"), and then click the highlight button (a lightbulb). Click the up and down arrows to move between counters in the list below the performance display.

   ▲ How did the display change when you highlighted a particular counter?

   _____

   ▲ Which resources did Notepad use primarily? What other resources did it use?

   _____

   _____

3. Leave the Performance console open. Click **Start**, point to **All Programs**, point to **Administrative Tools**, and then click **Computer Management**.

4. The Computer Management console opens. Under Storage in the left pane, click **Disk Defragmenter**, and then click **Analyze** in the right pane. What message appears when the analysis is completed?

   _____

5. Click **Close** to close the message box.

6. Close the Computer Management console and return to the Performance console. Click the **Freeze Display** button and the highlight button as you did for Notepad. Which resources did Disk Defragmenter use primarily? Which other resources did it use?

   _____

   _____

## REVIEW QUESTIONS

1. Did Notepad and Disk Defragmenter use the same resources? Why or why not?

   _____

   _____

2. How do you think the performance display might have changed if both applications had been open at once?

   _____

   _____

3. What other counters could be useful for monitoring system performance?

   _____

   _____

4. What system resources that you were monitoring might have been used if you had actually defragmented your hard drive?

_____

_____

5. If you were considering whether to upgrade your system's memory or processor, which counters would you choose to monitor, and why? How would you decide whether you needed to make the upgrade?

_____

_____

_____

# LAB 12.7 MANAGE VIRTUAL MEMORY

## OBJECTIVES

The goal of this lab is to learn to manage virtual memory. After completing this lab, you will be able to:

◢ Locate the Windows tool for adjusting virtual memory settings

◢ Change the size of the paging file

◢ Move the location of the paging file

## MATERIALS REQUIRED

This lab requires the following:

◢ Windows 2000/XP Professional operating system

◢ Internet access

◢ A printer

## LAB PREPARATION

Before the lab begins, the instructor or lab assistant needs to do the following:

◢ Verify that Windows starts with no errors.

◢ Verify that Internet access is available.

## ACTIVITY BACKGROUND

Virtual memory allows the OS to make use of an HDD (hard drive) to simulate RAM. This option can be useful when, for instance, the OS is running a number of applications, and each requires an allocation of RAM reserved for its use. Ideally, the Virtual Memory Manager protects actual RAM for the most active applications by moving the data other applications use to a swap file on the hard drive. In Windows 2000/XP, the swap file is called a "paging file." The virtual memory default settings allow Windows to manage the paging file, increasing or decreasing the size as needed.

In most situations, allowing Windows to manage virtual memory with default settings works fine, but this practice can cause pauses in application response time when the OS switches to an application with data stored in the paging file. This delay is caused by longer access time when reading from a drive instead of reading from RAM. The access time increases especially if the file is on the boot partition or any other partition subject to heavy use. If performance has become a problem, you might want to specify virtual memory settings manually.

**ESTIMATED COMPLETION TIME: 30 minutes**

 **Activity**

Log on to your computer using an account with administrative privileges. Complete the following steps to gather information about your system:

In Windows XP, follow these steps:

1. Click **Start, Control Panel**. The Control Panel window opens.

2. In the Pick a category section, click **Performance and Maintenance**. The Control Panel window changes to Performance and Maintenance.

3. Click the **System** icon in Performance and Maintenance. The System Properties dialog box opens.

4. Review the information in the General tab, and note how much RAM is installed. Click **OK** to close the System Properties dialog box.

5. Click the **Administrative Tools** icon in Performance and Maintenance. The Performance and Maintenance window changes to Administrative Tools.

6. Double-click the **Computer Management** shortcut in Administrative Tools. The Computer Management console opens.

7. In the left pane, click **Disk Management**, and review the information in the right pane. List the required information on the following lines, and then close the Computer Management console and Administrative Tools window.

   ◢ Disks installed:

   _____

   ◢ Partitions and letters assigned:

   _____

   ◢ Partition designated as the system partition:

   _____

   ◢ Disk with unallocated space:

   _____

In Windows 2000, follow these steps:

1. Click **Start**, point to **Settings**, and then click **Control Panel**. The Control Panel window opens.

2. Double-click the **System** icon. The System Properties dialog box opens.

3. Review the information in the General tab, and note how much RAM is installed. Click **OK** to close the System Properties dialog box.

4. Double-click the **Administrative Tools** icon in Control Panel. The Control Panel window changes to Administrative Tools.

5. Double-click the **Computer Management** shortcut in Administrative Tools. The Computer Management snap-in appears in an MMC.

6. In the left pane, click **Disk Management**, and review the information in the right pane. List the required information on the following lines, and then close the MMC and Administrative Tools window.

◢ Disks installed:

_____

◢ Partitions and letters assigned:

_____

◢ Partition designated as the system partition:

_____

◢ Disk with unallocated space:

_____

Visit the Microsoft Web site at *http://support.microsoft.com* and search the Knowledge Base for the following articles:

◢ Article 123747: Moving the Windows Default Paging and Spool File

◢ Article 197379: Configuring Page Files for Optimization and Recovery

◢ Article 314482: How to Configure Paging Files for Optimization and Recovery in Windows XP

◢ Article 307886: How to Move the Paging File in Windows XP

Print and read these articles, and then answer the following questions:

1. What is the paging file's default or recommended size?

_____

2. What is a disadvantage of totally removing the paging file from the boot partition?

_____

_____

3. What performance-degrading issue is the paging file subject to if it's moved to a partition containing data?

_____

_____

4. What additional benefit is there to setting up a paging file on multiple hard drives?

_____

_____

5. According to Article 307886, how do you select the partition on which you want to modify paging file settings?

_____

_____

6. What is the minimum size of the paging file required to allow a memory dump in the event of a Stop error?

_____

Next, you work with the Virtual Memory dialog box to view and record paging file settings. The information about the paging file's recommended maximum size might not be clear. As you record your settings, notice that the maximum size is the same as the recommended size.

In Windows XP, follow these steps:

1. Click **Start, Control Panel**. The Control Panel window opens.

2. In the Pick a category section of Control Panel, click **Performance and Maintenance**. Control Panel changes to the Performance and Maintenance window.

3. Click the **System** icon in Performance and Maintenance. The System Properties dialog box opens.

4. In System Properties, click the **Advanced** tab.

5. In the Performance section of the Advanced tab, click **Settings**. The Performance Options dialog box opens.

6. In the Performance Options dialog box, click the **Advanced** tab, shown in Figure 12-6.

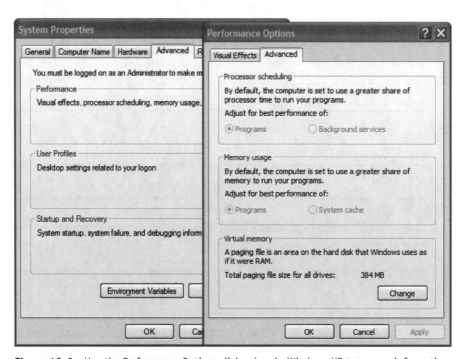

**Figure 12-6**   Use the Performance Options dialog box in Windows XP to access information on your computer's paging file

7. In the Virtual memory section, click the **Change** button. The Virtual Memory dialog box opens (see Figure 12-7). List the current settings on the following lines:

⊿ Does your computer have multiple paging files?

_____

⊿ Drive(s) where a paging file is located:

_____

⊿ Current size of the paging file:

_____

⊿ Recommended size:

_____

⊿ Currently allocated size:

_____

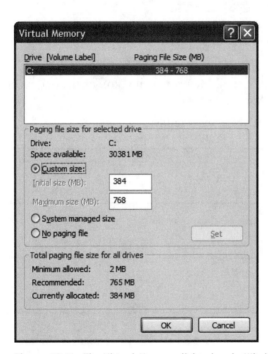

**Figure 12-7**  The Virtual Memory dialog box in Windows XP

In Windows 2000, follow these steps:

1. Click **Start**, point to **Settings**, and click **Control Panel**. The Control Panel window opens.

2. Double-click the **System** icon. The System Properties dialog box opens.

3. Click the **Advanced** tab. In the Performance section, click **Performance Options**. The Performance Options dialog box opens, as shown in Figure 12-8.

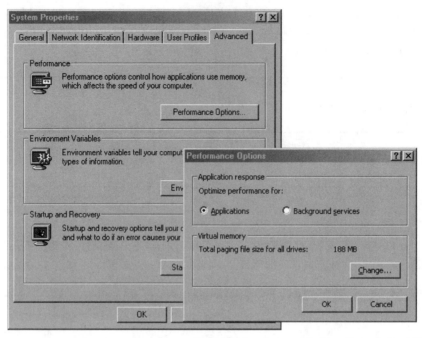

**Figure 12-8**    Use the Performance Options dialog box in Windows 2000 to access information on your computer's paging file

4. Click the **Change** button. The Virtual Memory dialog box opens (see Figure 12-9). List the current settings on the following lines:

▲ Does your computer have multiple paging files?

_____

▲ Drive(s) where a paging file is located:

_____

▲ Minimum allowed size:

_____

▲ Recommended size:

_____

▲ Currently allocated size:

_____

Based on information in the Knowledge Base articles and the data you have collected about your computer, answer the following questions:

1. Given your computer's current physical configuration, is the paging file set for optimal performance? Explain:

_____

_____

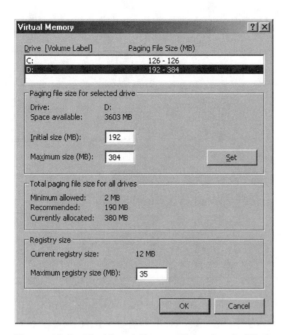

**Figure 12-9** The Virtual Memory dialog box in Windows 2000

2. What actions and paging file settings do you recommend to maximize performance? Explain:

_____

_____

3. Consider a computer with the following configuration:

   ◢ 512 MB RAM

   ◢ HDD0 C: (system) 17 GB NTFS with 2.8 GB unallocated disk space

   ◢ HDD1 D: (general storage) 20 GB NTFS with no unallocated disk space

   ◢ Paging file on the C drive with a custom size of 384 MB initial and 786 MB maximum

Based on what you've learned so far, what is your recommendation to maximize virtual memory performance while allowing the use of debugging information?

_____

_____

_____

_____

## REVIEW QUESTIONS

1. What is meant by the term "virtual memory"?

_____

_____

2. What is the swap file called in Windows XP?

_____

3. Why would you want to move the paging file off the boot partition?

_____

_____

4. When could fragmentation of the paging file occur?

_____

_____

5. What is the main reason for slight pauses in an application when retrieving information from the paging file?

_____

_____

6. *Bonus*: Because Microsoft acknowledges a performance advantage in locating the paging file off the boot partition, what's the main reason the boot partition is its default location?

_____

_____

# LAB 12.8 USE DR. WATSON

## OBJECTIVES

The goal of this lab is to help you troubleshoot program errors that occur when you're running Windows. After completing this lab, you will be able to:

▲ Use Dr. Watson to collect detailed information about the state of your operating system

▲ Use Dr. Watson to troubleshoot program errors

▲ Customize Dr. Watson

## MATERIALS REQUIRED

This lab requires the following:

▲ Windows 2000/XP Professional operating system

▲ Internet access

## LAB PREPARATION

Before the lab begins, the instructor or lab assistant needs to do the following:

▲ Verify that Windows starts with no errors.

▲ Verify that Internet access is available.

## ACTIVITY BACKGROUND

Dr. Watson for Windows is a program error debugger designed to detect problems caused by applications and stop them before the problems affect other applications. Technical support personnel can use the information Dr. Watson collects and logs to diagnose a program error for a computer running Windows. If an error occurs, Dr. Watson starts automatically. A text file (Drwatson.log) is created whenever an error is detected and can be distributed to support personnel by various methods.

**ESTIMATED COMPLETION TIME: 30 minutes**

**Activity**

Dr. Watson can't prevent errors from occurring, but the information recorded in the log file can be used to diagnose the problem. Dr. Watson (drwtsn32.exe) is installed in your system folder when you set up Windows. The default options are set the first time Dr. Watson runs, which can be when a program error occurs or when you start Dr. Watson yourself.

There are three ways to start Dr. Watson:

- Enter the program name (drwtsn32) in the Run dialog box.
- Enter the program name (drwtsn32.exe) in a command prompt window.
- Use the Tools menu of the System Information window. (To access the System Information window, click Start, point to All Programs (Programs in Windows 2000), point to Accessories, and click System Tools.)

In this lab, you start Dr. Watson by using the first method. Do the following:

1. Click **Start, Run**. The Run dialog box opens. Type **drwtsn32**, and then click **OK**. The Dr. Watson for Windows dialog box opens, and an icon for Dr. Watson is displayed on the taskbar.

2. Click the **Browse** button to the right of the Log File Path text box. What is the path to the log file?

   _____

3. Using Windows Explorer, look in this folder. Is a log file there? If so, what's the file size in bytes?

   _____

4. Double-click the log file. The file should open in Notepad. A sample log file is shown in Figure 12-10. Scroll through the file looking for dates that information was recorded to the file. What applications caused errors, and on what dates did these errors occur?

   _____

   _____

   _____

5. Close the log file.

Dr. Watson is available for Windows 98 and Windows 2000/XP, but the file name and path to the program file and log file differ in each OS. Research the information about these file names and paths, and fill in the following chart. You can get your information by searching the hard drives of computers with these OSs installed, or you can search the Microsoft Web site (*http://support.microsoft.com*) for the information.

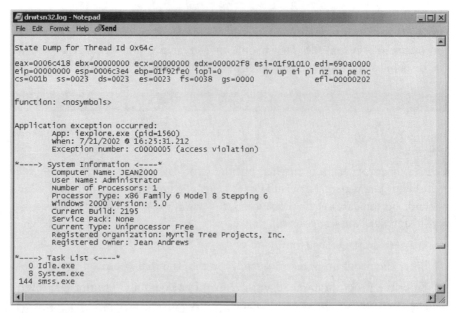

**Figure 12-10**    A sample Dr. Watson log file

| Operating system | Path and filename to the Dr. Watson program | Path and filename to the Dr. Watson log file |
|---|---|---|
| Windows 98 | | |
| Windows 2000 | | |
| Windows XP | | |

## REVIEW QUESTIONS

1. Describe the purpose of the Dr. Watson utility:

   _____

   _____

2. Who might find the information recorded in the Dr. Watson log file or dump file useful?

   _____

3. What is the name of the Dr. Watson log file used by Windows 98?

   _____

4. What is the name of the Dr. Watson log file used by Windows XP?

   _____

5. What type of event causes Dr. Watson to start automatically?

   _____

# Supporting Windows 2000/XP Users and Their Data

## *LAB 13.1 ALLOW TWO USERS TO LOG ON SIMULTANEOUSLY*

### OBJECTIVES

The goal of this lab is to help you understand Windows XP support for multiple logons. After completing this lab, you will be able to:

- Create a user account
- Log on as two different users simultaneously
- Customize desktop settings for both users
- Switch between two user accounts that are both logged on to the system

### MATERIALS REQUIRED

This lab requires the following:

- Windows XP Professional operating system
- A user account with administrative privileges

### LAB PREPARATION

Before the lab begins, the instructor or lab assistant needs to do the following:

- Verify that Windows starts with no errors.

### ACTIVITY BACKGROUND

Windows XP includes a new feature that allows more than one user to be logged on to the same computer at the same time, each with his or her own preferences set and programs open. This feature is useful when more than one person needs to use the same computer. In this lab, you create a new user account, log on to that account, open a program, change desktop settings, switch back to your own account, and observe the effects of switching between the two user accounts.

**ESTIMATED COMPLETION TIME: 30 minutes**

 **Activity**

Follow these steps to create a new user account and open an application using the new account:

1. Log on to your computer with your user account, which should have administrative privileges.
2. Click **Start**, right-click **My Computer**, and click **Manage** in the shortcut menu.
3. The Computer Management console opens. Click the **+** (plus sign) next to Local Users and Groups to expand it.
4. Under Local Users and Groups, right-click the **Users** folder and click **New User** in the shortcut menu. The New User dialog box opens.
5. In the New User dialog box, enter a user name, full name, description, and password for your new user. Click to clear the **User must change password at next logon** check box, and then click to select the **User cannot change password** and **Password never**

**expires** check boxes. (The remaining check box disables the account, which you don't need to do at this time.) Record the user name, full name, and password here:

_____

_____

6. Click the **Create** button to create the new user account, and then click **Close** to close the New User dialog box.

7. Double-click the **Users** folder so that the list of users on your computer appears in the right-hand pane of the Computer Management console, and verify that the new user is listed.

8. Open Microsoft Word, WordPad, or some other application.

Follow these steps to switch between users and make changes as the new user:

1. Click **Start, Log Off**, and then answer these questions:

   ◢ What options does the Log Off Windows dialog box provide?

   _____

   ◢ Hold your mouse pointer over the **Switch User** icon. If balloon text is enabled on your system, write down the keyboard shortcut for switching users:

   _____

2. Click the **Switch User** icon. The logon window opens, just as it does when you first turn the computer on and log on to your account. The new user you just created should be listed. Click the icon for that user's name, and enter the password for the user when prompted.

3. Now that you're logged on as the new user, right-click an empty area of the desktop, and then click **Properties**. The Display Properties dialog box opens. Click the **Desktop** tab, and then change the desktop background for this user. Next, open an application other than the one you opened earlier (such as Microsoft Excel, for instance).

4. Click **Start, Log Off** again, and then click **Switch User** to display the logon window.

   ◢ What information is listed under your user name and the new user's name?

   _____

5. Switch back to your user name, and then switch back to the new user again.

   ◢ Does the desktop background change for each user? Do the user's programs remain open?

   _____

6. While logged on as the new user, click **Start, Turn Off Computer**, and then click the **Turn Off** button.

   ◢ What message do you receive?

   _____

7. Click **No** in the message box that opens when you tried to turn off the computer. You return to the new user's desktop.

8. Now you're ready to log off. To do that, click **Start, Log Off** again. In the Log Off Windows dialog box, click **Log Off** instead of Switch User. The logon window reopens.

◢ What information appears under your user name now? What information appears under the new user's name?

_____

_____

## REVIEW QUESTIONS

1. How do you think the process of switching between users would have been different if you didn't assign the new user a password? How would it have been different if you had required the user to change the password at the next logon?

_____

_____

2. When multiple users are logged on to the same computer, does the logon window show which programs each user has open? Why or why not?

_____

_____

3. What are three advantages of multiple logons?

_____

_____

_____

4. List the steps to render the new user's account inactive without deleting it. After the account has been rendered inactive, would the user still be listed in the logon window? Explain:

_____

_____

_____

_____

5. In what situation might disabling a user account be appropriate?

_____

_____

# LAB 13.2 MANAGE USER ACCOUNTS IN WINDOWS XP

## OBJECTIVES

The goal of this lab is to give you experience adding and modifying user accounts by using Computer Management. After completing this lab, you will be able to:

▲ Add users

▲ Reset passwords

▲ Control password policies

## MATERIALS REQUIRED

This lab requires the following:

▲ Windows XP Professional operating system

▲ An administrator account and password

## LAB PREPARATION

Before the lab begins, the instructor or lab assistant needs to do the following:

▲ Verify that Windows starts with no errors.

## ACTIVITY BACKGROUND

Windows XP needs just a few pieces of information to set up a user account: a unique user name, the user's full name, a description of the user (typically title and department), and a password. Managing users can take quite a bit of administrative time, however. Much of this time is spent helping users who have forgotten their passwords or entered their passwords incorrectly multiple times, causing Windows XP to lock their accounts. In this lab, you practice managing user accounts and passwords in Computer Management.

**ESTIMATED COMPLETION TIME: 30 minutes**

 **Activity**

To examine the user account information available via Computer Management, follow these steps:

1. Log on as an administrator.

2. Click **Start, Control Panel**, and then click **Performance and Maintenance**.

3. Click **Administrative Tools** and double-click **Computer Management**. The Computer Management window opens, similar to the one in Figure 13-1. (You can also right-click My Computer and click Manage in the shortcut menu, as you did in Lab 13.1.)

4. Click the **+** (plus sign) next to Local Users and Groups to expand the category. Examine the Computer Management window and answer the following questions:

   ▲ Based on your knowledge of Windows XP, what two user accounts are included on a Windows XP system by default?

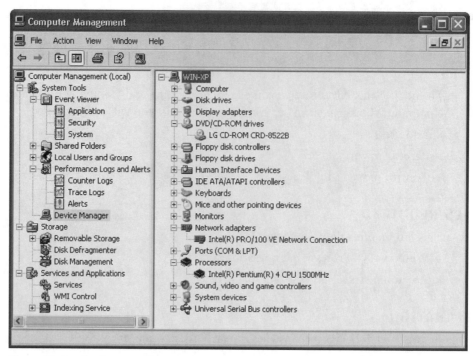

**Figure 13-1** The Computer Management console

▲ Does your system contain any personal user accounts? If so, list them here:

_____

_____

▲ What user groups are included on your Windows XP system?

_____

_____

In Computer Management, you can add and configure users on a local computer by following these steps:

1. In the left pane under Local Users and Groups, click the **Users** folder to display a list of current user names.

2. Right-click **Users** and click **New User** in the shortcut menu. The New User dialog box opens.

3. In the User name text box, type **James**.

4. In the Full name text box, type **James Clark**.

5. In the Description text box, type **Supervisor**.

6. In the Password text box, type **newuser**.

7. Confirm the password, make sure the **User must change password at next logon** and **Account is disabled** check boxes are cleared, and then click **Create**.

   ▲ What other check box could you select?

   _____

   _____

8. Close all open windows.

When Windows XP creates a new user, that user is automatically added to the Limited group, which means the account can't create, delete, or change other accounts; make systemwide changes; or install software. To give the account administrative privileges, do the following:

1. Open Control Panel and click **User Accounts**. The User Accounts window opens with a list of all accounts.

2. Click **Change an account,** and then click the **James Clark** account. The User Accounts window changes so that you can change the account.

◢ What are the five things you can do to an account in this window?

_____

_____

_____

_____

_____

3. Click **Change the account type**.

4. In the next window, click the **Computer administrator** option button, and then click the **Change Account Type** button. Click the **Back** button to return to the opening window.

5. Log off your computer and log on as James Clark. List the steps you took to accomplish that task:

_____

_____

_____

## REVIEW QUESTIONS

1. Besides adding and deleting users, what other tasks can you perform with Computer Management in the Local Users and Groups category?

_____

2. List the five types of Windows XP user groups created when Windows XP is first installed, and explain what each group can do:

_____

_____

_____

_____

_____

3. List the steps to change the group to which an account belongs:

_____

_____

_____

_____

4. List the steps to delete a user account:

_____

_____

_____

5. Why is it a good idea to have users change their passwords the first time they log on?

_____

# LAB 13.3 SET DISK QUOTAS

## OBJECTIVES

The goal of this lab is to show you how to set and monitor disk quotas. After completing this lab, you will be able to:

- Convert a logical drive from FAT to NTFS
- Set disk quotas for new users
- Monitor quota logs
- Identify when quotas have been exceeded

## MATERIALS REQUIRED

This lab requires the following:

- Windows XP Professional operating system
- A computer containing a partition (which can be the partition where Windows XP is installed) that has no important information

## LAB PREPARATION

Before the lab begins, the instructor or lab assistant needs to do the following:

- Verify that Windows starts with no errors.

## ACTIVITY BACKGROUND

When a system is used by more than one account or when server storage space is limited, setting storage limits for each user is often a good idea. No one account should monopolize storage space by filling up the server and preventing other users from storing data. Note, however, that you can impose disk quotas only on drives formatted with NTFS. In this lab, you use disk quotas to limit user storage space.

### Activity

In the following steps, you set very small disk quotas for all users. That way, you can easily exceed the disk quota limit later and observe the results. Do the following to verify that you're using the NTFS file system:

1. Log on as an administrator.

2. Open Windows Explorer, right-click drive **C** (or another logical drive designated by your instructor), and click **Properties** in the shortcut menu. The Local Disk (C:) Properties dialog box opens. (If you selected another drive letter, the dialog box name will be different.) On the General tab, verify that the drive is using the NTFS file system.

If you currently have the FAT32 file system and need to convert to NTFS, use the following steps, and then open the Local Disk (C:) Properties dialog box again. If you already have NTFS, skip the next three steps.

1. Open a command prompt window.

2. At the command prompt, type **convert C: /fs:ntfs** and press **Enter**. (If necessary, substitute the drive letter for another logical drive in the command, as specified by your instructor.)

3. After the command runs, reboot your computer to complete the conversion to NTFS.

To enable disk quotas, do the following:

1. In the Local Disk (C:) Properties dialog box, click the **Quota** tab.

2. Click the **Enable quota management** check box. This option allows you to set and change quotas.

3. Click the **Deny disk space to users exceeding quota limit** check box. This option prevents users from using more disk space after reaching their quota.

4. Verify that the **Limit disk space to** option button is selected and that **1** appears in the text box to the right. Then click **MB** in the drop-down list to set the disk quota to 1 MB of storage space.

5. In the Set warning level to text box, type **500**, and then verify that **KB** is displayed in the text box to the right. This setting ensures that users receive warnings after they have used 500 KB of disk space.

6. Click **Log event when a user exceeds their quota limit**. This option ensures that a record is made when a user exceeds the quota limit.

7. Click **Log event when a user exceeds their warning level**. This option ensures that a record is made when users reach their warning limit. (You can view these records in the Local Disk (C:) Properties dialog box.)

8. Click **OK** to apply the new settings and close the Local Disk (C:) Properties dialog box.

Follow these steps to exceed the quota limits you have just set:

1. Using what you learned in Lab 13.1, create a new restricted user called **Quota Test**.

2. Create a directory called **Quota** in the root of the NTFS drive.

3. Log off as an administrator, and log on as **Quota Test**.

4. In Windows Explorer, open the **Windows** or **WINNT** folder, and click the **Show the contents of this folder** link. One at a time, copy (*do not cut*) all .gif and .bmp files in the Windows or WINNT folder, and paste them into the Quota folder.

◢ What happens when you exceed the warning level and then the storage quota?

_____

_____

5. Log off as the Quota Test user.

Because of the options you selected when you created the disk quota, logs were created when you exceeded the warning level and the storage quota. To view these quota logs, follow these steps:

1. Log on as an administrator.

2. Open the Local Disk (C:) Properties dialog box, click the **Quota** tab, and then click the **Quota Entries** button. The Quota Entries dialog box opens, displaying the log of quota entries for certain events.

◢ What types of information are displayed for each entry?

_____

_____

3. Double-click an entry for Quota Test. The Quota Settings dialog box for that user opens. Note that you can raise or lower the user's disk quotas.

4. Check the quota settings for each entry, and record any entry for which you were unable to adjust settings:

_____

_____

## REVIEW QUESTIONS

1. How would you set up disk quotas on a drive formatted with FAT32?

_____

_____

2. Why might you want to impose disk quotas?

_____

3. What option must be selected to specify a warning level?

_____

_____

4. What options must be selected to prevent users from exceeding their quotas?

_____

_____

5. Explain how to monitor and change disk quotas:

_____

_____

## LAB 13.4 BACK UP AND RESTORE FILES IN WINDOWS 2000/XP

### OBJECTIVES

The goal of this lab is to help you use the Windows 2000/XP Backup and Recovery Tools to back up and recover lost files. After completing this lab, you will be able to:

◢ Back up files

◢ Delete files

◢ Recover deleted files

### MATERIALS REQUIRED

This lab requires the following:

◢ Windows 2000/XP operating system

### LAB PREPARATION

Before the lab begins, the instructor or lab assistant needs to do the following:

◢ Verify that Windows starts with no errors.

### ACTIVITY BACKGROUND

Windows 2000/XP provides the Backup and Recovery Tools to help you safeguard data in Windows system files. Using these tools, you can back up a single file or even an entire drive from the local or remote computer. Backups, compressed into a single file, can be saved to a location of your choice, without the need for a dedicated backup device, such as a tape drive. In this lab, you back up, delete, and restore data files using the Backup and Recovery Tools.

**ESTIMATED COMPLETION TIME: 45 minutes**

 **Activity**

Follow these steps to select the files or folders you want to back up:

1. Log on to an account in the Power Users group.

2. Create folders called **C:\Backups** and **C:\BackMeUp**, and then create several text files in the C:\BackMeUp folder.

3. Click **Start**, point to **All Programs** (in Windows 2000, **Programs**), point to **Accessories**, point to **System Tools**, and then click **Backup**. In Windows XP, click **Advanced Mode**.

The Windows Backup and Recovery Tools utility opens. What three options are available on the Welcome tab?

_____

_____

_____

4. Click the **Backup** tab. In the left pane, click the **+** (plus sign) next to drive C. The right pane displays all the items you can back up.

5. First, you back up an entire folder. Click the check box next to the **BackMeUp** folder in the right pane, which indicates you want to back up the entire contents of that folder.

6. Instruct the system to back up the entire contents of the Documents and Settings folder. Explain how you performed this task:

_____

_____

_____

7. In addition to the folders you just selected for backup, you'll select a single file, Notepad.exe, for backup. Double-click the **Windows** folder in the right pane. The Windows folder is highlighted in the left pane, and its contents are displayed in the right pane.

8. Click the **Notepad.exe** check box to specify that you want to back up this file.

9. In the Backup media or file name text box, type **C:\Backups\Lab13.bkf**, which specifies the name and location of the backup file you're creating.

Follow these steps to start the backup process:

1. In the Backup tab, click **Start Backup**. The Backup Job Information dialog box opens. The Backup description text box displays date and time information about this backup. This information is displayed later to help you identify the backup during a recovery process. If you need to perform many backup operations (and, therefore, have to keep track of multiple backup sets), you should always use this text box to describe the files in this set. Alternatively, you might want to keep a backup log book and refer to an entry number that describes in detail what's in this backup set. Because this is your initial backup, you can ignore the other sections of the dialog box and click **Start Backup**.

2. The Backup Schedule dialog box briefly opens and then closes. Next, the Backup Progress dialog box opens. Quickly click **Cancel** in this dialog box.

3. The Backup dialog box opens and displays a message asking if you want to complete the backup. Click the title bar of the Backup dialog box and drag it aside so that you can view the Backup Progress dialog box. Answer these questions:

   ◢ What three items give you an idea of how the backup is progressing?

_____

_____

_____

◢ Can you tell how many files must be backed up?

_____

◢ Can you tell which files have already been completed or are currently being processed?

_____

◢ What information continues to change even when the backup process is paused?

_____

4. Click **Yes** in the Backup dialog box to indicate that you want to continue the backup, and watch as the backup process is completed.

5. When the backup is finished, click **Report** in the Backup Progress dialog box to open the Backup log in Notepad.

6. Print and examine the report. What errors and causes are reported?

_____

_____

_____

Follow these steps to delete files and observe the effects:

1. Log off and log on as a different user. Right-click **Recycle Bin** on the desktop, and click **Empty Recycle Bin** in the shortcut menu. Click **Yes** to confirm that you want to empty the Recycle Bin.

2. Open a command prompt window. At the command prompt, type **DEL C:\BackMeUp\*.*** and press **Enter** to delete all files in the C:\BackMeUp directory. Confirm the deletion when prompted. Close the command prompt window.

3. In Windows Explorer, delete **Notepad.exe** in the \Windows folder.

4. Double-click **Recycle Bin** and note which files are displayed.

◢ Of the files you deleted, which ones are not displayed in the Recycle Bin?

_____

_____

◢ Why do you think these files are missing?

_____

_____

◢ Of the files you deleted, which files can you restore without using your backups and why?

_____

_____

5. Empty the Recycle Bin again and then, in Windows Explorer, look for your text files in C:\BackMeUp to confirm that they are gone.

6. Click **Start**, point to **All Programs** (**Programs** in Windows 2000), point to **Accessories**, and then click **Notepad**. Record the results on the following lines, and then click **Cancel** to close the dialog box.

_____

_____

Follow these steps to restore the deleted files:

1. Log off and log on as an administrator. (Power Users don't have permission to restore files.)

2. Click **Start**, point to **All Programs** (**Programs** in Windows 2000), point to **Accessories**, point to **System Tools**, and then click **Backup**. The Backup window opens.

3. Click the **Restore and Manage Media** tab (**Restore** in Windows 2000). In the left pane, click the **+** (plus sign) to expand the file symbol, and then click to expand **Media Created** *Date and Time*. Now attempt to expand the "**?**" folder on drive C. This opens the Backup File Name dialog box.

4. In the Backup File Name dialog box, click **Browse**.

5. Click **Lab13.bkf** in the C:\Backups folder, and then click the **Open** button. The Select File to Catalog dialog box closes, and the Backup File Name dialog box opens with the Operations Status dialog box beneath it.

6. Click **OK** in the Backup File Name dialog box. The Operations Status dialog box, which opened previously, closes when the cataloging process is completed. Your backup is displayed in the left pane of the Restore and Manage Media (Restore in Windows 2000) tab.

7. To restore files and folders, click the necessary check boxes, and then click **Start Restore**. Do you think you could choose to restore only part of the information? If so, how?

_____

_____

8. The Confirm Restore dialog box opens. Click **OK** to continue.

9. The Enter Backup Filename dialog box opens and displays your backup file. Click **OK** to continue.

10. The Restore Progress dialog box opens. When the restore operation is finished, click **Close** to close the Restore Progress dialog box.

11. To confirm that the restore is complete, look for your text files, and start Notepad from the Start menu.

## CRITICAL THINKING (ADDITIONAL 15 MINUTES)

Assign a Power User to a specific group (not the Administrators group), which reduces the errors you encountered during the backup. Log on as this user, perform a backup called

Lab13b.bkf, and then view and print the backup file. Are members of the group to which you assigned the Power User allowed to restore files? How could you tell?

_____

_____

_____

## REVIEW QUESTIONS

1. Is it more important to back up Windows system files or data files? Why?

_____

_____

2. What is the Start menu path for launching Windows Backup and Restore Tools?

_____

3. What features of Windows Backup and Restore Tools can you use if you're unfamiliar with the backup and restore process?

_____

_____

4. What does the Backup Job Information dialog box allow you to define? Why is this function useful?

_____

_____

_____

5. If time is a factor when restoring critical data files, what could you specify (or decide not to specify) in the left pane of the Restore tab to speed up the restoration?

_____

_____

## LAB 13.5 RESEARCH DATA RECOVERY SERVICES

### OBJECTIVES

The goal of this lab is to help you research data recovery services. After completing this lab, you will be able to:

▲ Find tips on how to make recovery services less necessary

▲ Explain how to minimize data loss

▲ Describe some recovery options

## MATERIALS REQUIRED

This lab requires the following:

◢ Internet access

## LAB PREPARATION

Before the lab begins, the instructor or lab assistant needs to do the following:

◢ Verify that Windows starts with no errors.

◢ Verify that Internet access is available.

## ACTIVITY BACKGROUND

You've probably deleted or overwritten an important file accidentally. To make matters worse, you probably couldn't replace the file unless you had backed it up previously. Now imagine if the lost file consisted of financial information that could affect the success or failure of a business with 100 employees or contained a creative work that took months to produce. You would certainly try to recover the data yourself, but if you couldn't, you might decide to seek the help of a professional data recovery service. In this lab, you research sites offering these services.

**ESTIMATED COMPLETION TIME: 45 minutes**

 **Activity**

Use your favorite search engine to research data recovery services, or search these Web sites and answer the following questions:

◢ *www.datarecoveryclinic.com*

◢ *www.savemyfiles.com*

◢ *www.drivesavers.com*

◢ *www.adv-data.com*

◢ *www.atl-datarecovery.com*

◢ *www.datarecovery.net*

1. Name two Web sites that offer a do-it-yourself data recovery option in addition to professional recovery services:

   _____

   _____

2. Give an example of a service that offers data recovery in a Linux environment:

   _____

3. Give two examples of services that recover data from striped sets or volume sets:

   _____

   _____

4. From what type or types of media can files be recovered? Circle the correct answer(s):

   a. tape

   b. CD-ROM

   c. Zip disk

   d. floppy disk

   e. hard disk

5. Give two examples of companies that don't charge you if they are unable to recover your important data:

   _____

   _____

6. List two general levels of turnaround time for data recovery:

   _____

   _____

7. What measures are taken when recovering ultrasensitive (secure) data?

   _____

   _____

   _____

8. Besides natural disaster and mechanical failure, what are four other common causes of data loss?

   _____

   _____

   _____

   _____

9. If you learn that you have lost data on drive D, what should you absolutely not do? Circle the correct answer(s):

   a. Install recovery software on drive C.

   b. Defragment drive D.

   c. Restore objects in the Recycle Bin.

   d. Install recovery software on drive D.

10. Give two examples of services designed to proactively prevent data loss:

   _____

   _____

11. List a few reasons that it might be impossible to recover some data:

 

 

 

12. Will you always be able to recover all the data you lose? Why or why not?

 

 

 

13. Why is performing hard drive data recovery in a clean room important?

 

 

 

14. What class of clean room should be used for data recovery?

 

15. In what formats can your recovered data be returned to you?

 

 

 

16. Give one example of a company that specializes in recovery from optical media:

 

17. What Web site (or sites) includes a "museum" of interesting recovery projects it has undertaken?

 

 

18. What circumstances might require the data recovery service to perform a recovery attempt at your site?

 

 

19. List two companies that recover data from flash cards or memory sticks:

 

13

20. Pick two of the companies you researched and list some other services and products they offer:

_____

_____

## REVIEW QUESTIONS

1. Based on your research, what impression do you get about how expensive data recovery services are? Explain your answer:

_____

_____

2. Based on your research, do you think individuals or companies would be more interested in using data recovery services? Why?

_____

_____

3. In general, do companies specialize in recovery from specific types of media, or do they tend to provide data recovery for all types of media?

_____

_____

4. Based on your research, what three factors affect the price you might pay for recovery services from a specific provider?

_____

_____

# *LAB 13.6 RECOVER DELETED FILES*

## OBJECTIVES

The goal of this lab is to help you explore options for recovering deleted files even after the Recycle Bin has been emptied. After completing this lab, you will be able to:

◢ Download and install File Recover by PC Tools
◢ Use File Recover to scan the hard drive for deleted files for possible recovery

## MATERIALS REQUIRED

This lab requires the following:

◢ Windows 2000/XP or Windows 9x operating system
◢ Internet access

## LAB PREPARATION

Before the lab begins, the instructor or lab assistant needs to do the following:

- ◢ Verify that Windows starts with no errors.
- ◢ Verify that Internet access is available.
- ◢ For labs that don't have Internet access, download this file to a file server or other storage media available to students in the lab:
  - The frinstall.exe file downloaded from *www.pctools.com/file-recover*

## ACTIVITY BACKGROUND

Probably nothing makes a computer user panic more than the prospect of losing important data. As a technician, you have to be prepared to recover data from a variety of storage media; most often, however, you're asked to recover it from a hard drive. Data on a hard drive can be lost for a variety of reasons, ranging from human error to a natural disaster that renders the drive inoperable. In this lab, you investigate how to recover files that have been deleted and emptied from the Recycle Bin.

If your lab doesn't have Internet access, ask your instructor for the location of the file downloaded previously for you to use. Write the path to the file here:

---

**ESTIMATED COMPLETION TIME: 30 minutes**

 **Activity**

Do the following to download and use File Recover:

1. Create a folder on the C drive named **Downloads**. Under this folder, create a folder named **FileRecover**. If you put all downloaded files into folders under C:\Downloads, it's easier to find them.

2. Open your Web browser and go to **www.pctools.com/file-recover**. Click the **Download File Recover** link. Follow instructions on-screen to download the file, and save it to C:\Downloads\FileRecover. What's the name of the downloaded file?

---

3. To install File Recover, double-click the file name. The installation process begins. Follow instructions on-screen to install the software.

Follow these steps to use the software:

1. Click **Start**, point to **All Programs** (**Programs** in Windows 2000), point to **File Recover**, and click **File Recover**. The File Recover main window opens (see Figure 13-2).

2. In the Select an Action section, click **Advanced Scan**. In the upper-right corner of the Scan & Recovery Settings window, you can select the drive to scan. Click **Scan Drive C:\** in the drop-down list, and then click **Scan**. The scanning process begins and shows its progress on-screen. Files that can be recovered are listed.

3. To select a file in the list to recover, click the check box to the left of the file name. What file did you select?

---

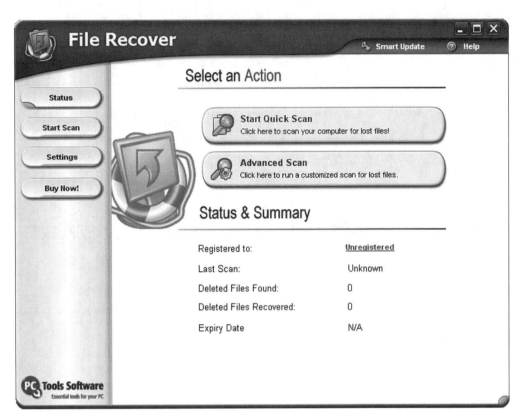

**Figure 13-2**  The File Recover main window

4. Click **Recover** to recover the file. What message did you see?

 

5. Close the File Recover window.

After you have evaluated software, if you don't want to purchase it, remove it from your system so that it doesn't take up space on your hard drive and clutter up your system. To uninstall the File Recover software, do the following:

1. Open Control Panel, and then open the Add or Remove Programs applet.

2. Click the **File Recover** software, and then click the **Change/Remove** button to remove it. Did you get any errors when you removed the software? If so, list them here:

 

## REVIEW QUESTIONS

1. If you delete a file by dragging it to the Recycle Bin, what's the easiest way to recover it?

 

2. Why does File Recover not allow you to use the free downloaded software to recover a file?

**3.** Why is it a good idea to uninstall software after you're finished with it?

_____

_____

**4.** What applet in Control Panel is used to uninstall software?

_____

_____

## LAB 13.7 USE DO-IT-YOURSELF DATA RECOVERY SOFTWARE

### OBJECTIVES

The goal of this lab is to help you explore options for recovering data from a malfunctioning hard drive. After completing this lab, you will be able to:

▲ Search _www.ontrack.com_ to learn about data recovery

▲ Use the EasyRecovery DataRecovery software to locate files for possible recovery

### MATERIALS REQUIRED

This lab requires the following:

▲ Windows 2000/XP or Windows 9x operating system

▲ Internet access

▲ Printer access

### LAB PREPARATION

Before the lab begins, the instructor or lab assistant needs to do the following:

▲ Verify that Windows starts with no errors.

▲ Verify that Internet access and printer access are available.

▲ For labs that don't have Internet access, download this file to a file server or other storage media available to students in the lab (note that the file is 34.5 MB):

• The Erdrt_610.exe file downloaded from _www.ontrack.com_

### ACTIVITY BACKGROUND

**Notes**

If you're using a dial-up connection to the Internet, the software download time might increase the time required for this lab.

In Lab 13.6, you worked with file recovery software available online. In this lab, you investigate other data recovery options and learn to use one of them.

If your lab doesn't have Internet access, ask your instructor for the location of the file downloaded previously for you to use. Write the path to the file here:

_____

**Activity**

Ontrack, Inc. is a major data recovery company that specializes in recovering files and e-mail. Follow these steps to explore the Ontrack Web site:

1. Open your Web browser and go to **www.ontrack.com**.

2. Answer the following questions, using the links on the Ontrack Web site. If you can't find all the answers at this site, use information from the sites you found in your research for Lab 13.5. Print pages from the site to support your answers.

◢ According to the information you found, what are the two top causes of data loss?

_____

_____

◢ What data recovery options are available?

_____

_____

_____

◢ What solutions work with your operating system?

_____

◢ What should you do if a hardware malfunction is detected?

_____

_____

◢ Is Internet access necessary for this recovery option?

_____

◢ Will this option work if you can't boot from the hard drive?

_____

◢ Each year, Ontrack publishes the top 10 strangest and funniest data disasters. List the top three:

_____

_____

_____

3. Return to the Ontrack home page.

4. Locate and follow the link that leads to information about the EasyRecovery DataRecovery software.

5. Using information on the EasyRecovery DataRecovery page, answer the following questions:

◢ Does this software need to be installed before the data loss?

_____

◢ Does this software require that your system be healthy enough to boot from the hard drive?

_____

◢ Can this product recover data from a deleted partition? Print the Web page supporting your answer.

_____

◢ Can this product recover data from removable media? If so, what types?

_____

_____

_____

Next, you download and use EasyRecovery Professional trial edition. Be aware that Web sites change often, so the links might not be the same as in the following steps. Do the following:

1. If you didn't do so in Lab 13.6, create a folder on your C drive named **Downloads**. Under this folder, create a folder named **EasyRecovery**.

2. On the Ontrack home page, click **Software**. In the list of DataRecovery software, click **EasyRecovery DataRecovery**. On the EasyRecovery DataRecovery page, click the **Free Trial** link.

3. The Download page opens. If you see a security warning, click **Save** to download the software. Also, if your browser is set to block pop-ups, you might see the message shown in Figure 13-3. To allow the Security Warning dialog box to open and the file to download, click the message and then click **Download File**, as shown in Figure 13-3.

4. Download the file, saving it to **C:\Downloads\EasyRecovery**. What's the name of the downloaded file?

_____

5. Close all open windows and open Windows Explorer. Double-click the file name. The EasyRecovery window opens.

6. To continue installing EasyRecovery, click **English** to select it as the language. The InstallShield Wizard starts.

7. Accept the end user license agreement (EULA).

8. Click **Next** several times to continue through the installation process, and accept the default settings.

9. When prompted, click **Yes, I want to restart my computer now**, and then click **Finish** to complete the EasyRecovery installation. Your PC restarts, and the EasyRecovery Professional shortcut is displayed on your desktop.

> **Notes**
>
> Installing EasyRecovery on the partition containing the data you want to recover might overwrite the lost data. To avoid this problem, you should install EasyRecovery on a separate partition or PC, and then create an EasyRecovery emergency boot disk. For the purpose of this lab, however, installing on your current partition is okay.

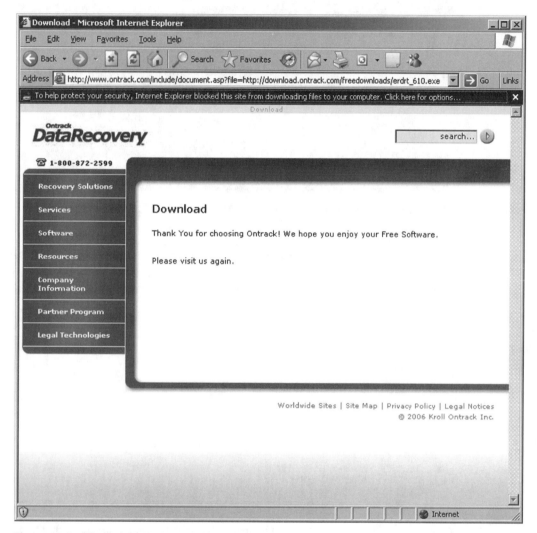

**Figure 13-3** If your browser is set to block pop-ups, a message is displayed under the address box

Follow these steps to use the software:

1. Double-click the **EasyRecovery Professional** shortcut on your desktop. An EasyRecovery notice opens and informs you that the edition can identify recoverable files, but you must purchase the full version to recover files. Click **OK** to close the notice. The Ontrack EasyRecovery Professional application launches.

2. Click the **Data Recovery** button, and then click **Advanced Recovery Option**. A warning message is displayed suggesting that you copy recovered data to a different medium, such as a Zip drive or floppy disk, if you suspect that all partitions on your hard drive might be damaged. Click **OK** to close the notice. The Data Recovery window is displayed (see Figure 13-4).

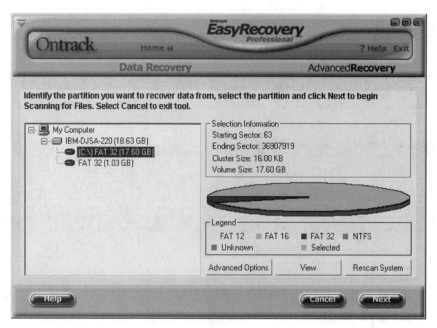

**Figure 13-4**    The Data Recovery window shows drives that can be scanned for missing or corrupt files

3. A list of drives on your system is displayed in the window. Notice that EasyRecovery displays partition information graphically along with a legend defining partition information and use. Click the item for drive C at the upper left, and answer the following questions:

▲ What is the starting sector for drive C?

_____

▲ What is the ending sector for drive C?

_____

▲ What is the cluster size for drive C?

_____

▲ What file system does drive C use?

_____

4. Click **Next** to begin scanning for files that the software can recover. The process might take some time because the software searches the entire drive. You can cancel the process at any time by clicking **Cancel** in the Scanning for Files dialog box. If you cancel the process, the message "Would you like to save the state of your recovery to resume at a later time?" is displayed. Click **No**.

5. A warning message appears stating that this trial version can't recover files. Click **OK** to close the message.

6. A list of files that the software can recover is displayed, with a condition status indicated for each file: G, D, X, S, B, or N. Click the **Filter Options** button and explain what each status means:

▲ The status G means: _____

▲ The status D means: _____

▲ The status X means: _____

13

◢ The status S means:

◢ The status B means:

◢ The status N means:

7. Click **OK** to close the Filter Options window.

8. In the left pane of the Data Recovery window, a hierarchical list of folders is displayed. The right pane shows recoverable files in those folders. You can select folders to search for a corrupted or lost file you're trying to recover. Open a folder on drive C, and select a file in that folder. Click **View File** to view the file's contents. Viewing the contents of a file can often help in locating the correct file.

9. If you were using the purchased version of the software, after you had located the files to recover, you could click **Next** and then specify a destination for the files. These files would then be copied from their current location to the specified destination. Notice that the Next button is grayed out because you're using the trial version.

10. Click **Cancel** to return to the main window. A message appears asking if you would like to save the state of your recovery. Click **No**.

11. Besides the AdvancedRecovery option on the main window, the following five options are available. Give a brief explanation of each option:

◢ DeletedRecovery

_____

_____

◢ FormatRecovery

_____

_____

◢ RawRecovery

_____

_____

◢ ResumeRecovery

_____

_____

◢ EmergencyDiskette

_____

_____

12. Using procedures you learned in earlier labs, print a screen shot of this EasyRecovery window.

13. Close the EasyRecovery window.

14. Your instructor might tell you to uninstall the EasyRecovery software. If so, uninstall the software with the Add/Remove Programs applet in Control Panel.

## REVIEW QUESTIONS

1. What are three causes of data loss?

   _____

   _____

2. Which of these causes would Remote Data Recovery and EasyRecovery fail to overcome?

   _____

3. Normally, is it possible to recover lost data that has been overwritten by other data? Explain:

   _____

   _____

4. What are some symptoms of a hardware malfunction that would result in data loss?

   _____

   _____

5. List some steps to prevent mechanical drive failure:

   _____

   _____

   _____

# LAB 13.8 PERFORM HARD DRIVE ROUTINE MAINTENANCE

## OBJECTIVES

The goal of this lab is to help you perform routine maintenance on a hard drive. After completing this lab, you will be able to:

▲ Delete unneeded files on a hard drive

▲ Defragment a hard drive

▲ Scan a hard drive for errors

## MATERIALS REQUIRED

This lab requires the following:

▲ Windows 2000/XP or Windows 9x operating system

## LAB PREPARATION

Before the lab begins, the instructor or lab assistant needs to do the following:

▲ Verify that Windows starts with no errors.

## ACTIVITY BACKGROUND

To ensure that your hard drive operates in peak condition, you should perform some routine maintenance tasks regularly. For starters, you need to ensure that your hard drive includes enough unused space (which it requires to operate efficiently). In other words, you should remove unnecessary files from the drive.

In addition, files on a hard drive sometimes become fragmented over time; defragmenting the drive can improve performance. Other routine maintenance tasks include scanning the hard drive for errors and repairing them. In this lab, you learn about three tools you can use for important disk maintenance tasks. You should use these tools on a scheduled basis, in the order given in this lab, to keep your hard drive error free and performing well.

**ESTIMATED COMPLETION TIME: 30 minutes**

 **Activity**

Follow these steps to delete unnecessary files on your hard drive:

1. Close all open applications.

2. Click **Start**, point to **All Programs** (**Programs** for Windows 2000/9x), point to **Accessories**, point to **System Tools**, and then click **Disk Cleanup**. The Select Drive dialog box opens.

3. Select the drive you want to clean up in the drop-down list, and click **OK** to close the Select Drive dialog box.

4. The Disk Cleanup dialog box opens, where you need to select the types of files you want Disk Cleanup to delete. Select all possible options. Depending on your system, these options might include Downloaded Program Files, Recycle Bin, Temporary files, and Temporary Internet files.

   ◢ How much disk space does each group of files take up?

   _____

   _____

   ◢ Based on information in the Disk Cleanup dialog box, what is the purpose of each group of files?

   _____

   _____

   _____

   _____

   ◢ What is the total amount of disk space you would gain by deleting these files?

   _____

5. Click **OK** to delete the selected groups of files.

6. When asked to confirm the deletion, click **Yes**. The Disk Cleanup dialog box closes, and a progress indicator appears while the cleanup is under way. The progress indicator closes when the cleanup is finished, returning you to the desktop.

The next step in routine maintenance is to use Windows 2000/XP Chkdsk or Windows 9x ScanDisk to examine the hard drive and repair errors.

In Windows 2000/XP, follow these steps:

1. Close any open applications.

2. Click **Start, Run**. Type **cmd** in the Run dialog box and press **Enter**. The command prompt window opens.

3. Several switches (options) are associated with the Chkdsk utility. To show all available switches, type **chkdsk /?** at the command prompt and press **Enter**. What are two switches used to fix errors that Chkdsk finds?

_____

4. To use the Chkdsk utility to scan the hard drive for errors and repair them, type **chkdsk c: /R** and press **Enter**.

In Windows 9x, do the following to use ScanDisk:

1. Click **Start**, point to **Programs**, point to **Accessories**, point to **System Tools**, and then click **ScanDisk**. The ScanDisk window opens.

2. ScanDisk offers two options: Standard and Thorough. The Standard option checks for errors in files and repairs them. The Thorough option does the same and also scans the hard drive surface for problems that might cause future errors. If a segment of the disk surface seems to be damaged, ScanDisk marks that segment so that it won't be used in the future. The Thorough option takes longer, but you should use it to get the most benefit from ScanDisk. Click **Thorough**, and then click **Start**.

3. If ScanDisk finds an error, it asks if you want to repair it. Click **OK** to repair any errors.

4. When the process is completed, ScanDisk reports what it found and corrected. Click **Close** in the report window. What errors, if any, did ScanDisk find?

_____

_____

_____

The last step in routine hard drive maintenance is to use the Disk Defragmenter tool to locate fragmented files and rewrite them to the hard drive in contiguous segments. In all versions of Windows, follow these steps:

1. Close all open applications.

2. Click **Start**, point to **All Programs** (**Programs** for Windows 2000/9x), point to **Accessories**, point to **System Tools**, and then click **Disk Defragmenter**. The Disk Defragmenter window opens.

3. Select the drive you want to defragment. In Windows 2000/XP, click **Defragment**. In Windows 9x, click **OK**. Disk Defragmenter begins defragmenting the drive, displaying a progress indicator of estimated fragmentation before and after it works.

**Notes**

Fully defragmenting your hard drive can take a few hours, depending on how fragmented it is. If you don't have time to wait, you can stop the process by clicking Stop. (In Windows 9x, you also have to click Exit in the confirmation dialog box to stop defragmenting.)

4. In Windows 9x, click **Show Details** to expand Disk Defragmenter to a full screen. With the Details view of Disk Defragmenter, you can observe a graphical representation of the defragmentation process.

5. To see what happens when you open an application while the hard drive is defragmenting, open Microsoft Word or another program. Use the program for a moment and then close it. Answer the following:

   ◢ In Windows 9x, what happened to Disk Defragmenter when you opened another application?

   _____

   ◢ In Windows 2000/XP, what happened to Disk Defragmenter when you opened another application?

   _____

6. When defragmentation is completed, close the Disk Defragmenter window.

## REVIEW QUESTIONS

1. Why do you need to begin your hard disk maintenance chores with Disk Cleanup?

   _____

2. Why should you finish your hard disk maintenance with Disk Defragmenter?

   _____

3. What is the Chkdsk equivalent to the Standard option in ScanDisk?

   _____

4. What happened when you tried to run another program while Disk Defragmenter was running? Why do you think it happened?

   _____

   _____

5. What types of files might you not want to delete during disk cleanup? Why?

   _____

# Troubleshooting Windows 2000/XP Startup

**Labs included in this chapter:**

- **Lab 14.1:** Use Windows Help and Troubleshooters
- **Lab 14.2:** Restore the System State
- **Lab 14.3:** Install the Recovery Console as an Option on the Boot Loader Menu
- **Lab 14.4:** Use the Recovery Console to Copy Files
- **Lab 14.5:** Critical Thinking: Sabotage and Repair Windows XP

# LAB 14.1 USE WINDOWS HELP AND TROUBLESHOOTERS

## OBJECTIVES

The goal of this lab is to demonstrate how to use Windows Help tools to find information and how to use Windows Troubleshooters to correct common problems. After completing this lab, you will be able to:

▲ Find information on various topics in Windows Help

▲ Use a Windows Troubleshooter

## MATERIALS REQUIRED

This lab requires the following:

▲ Windows 2000/XP Professional operating system

## LAB PREPARATION

Before the lab begins, the instructor or lab assistant needs to do the following:

▲ Verify that Windows starts with no errors.

## ACTIVITY BACKGROUND

You can use Windows Help to look up information on topics related to the operating system. To access Windows Help, use the Start menu or, with the desktop active, press F1. Help is useful when you need information. If you want help actually solving a problem, however, you can use the Windows Troubleshooters, which are interactive utilities that walk you through the problem of repairing a misconfigured system. Windows Troubleshooters are often launched automatically when Windows detects a problem. You can also start them manually from Windows Help.

**ESTIMATED COMPLETION TIME: 30 minutes**

 **Activity**

In the following steps, you learn to use the main features of Windows Help. Note that pressing F1 starts Help for whatever application happens to be active at that time. To start Windows Help, you need to close or minimize any open applications, thereby making the desktop active, and then you can press F1 to start Windows Help. To learn more, follow the procedure for your operating system.

In Windows XP, follow these steps:

1. Log on to your computer as an administrator.

2. Close or minimize any applications that start automatically so that the desktop is active.

3. Press **F1**. (Instead of activating the desktop and pressing F1, you could simply click **Start, Help and Support**.) Windows Help opens. As you can see, the Windows Help interface is similar to a Web browser. Answer the following questions:

   ▲ What four tasks are available in Windows Help?

   _____

   _____

◢ Which help topic could you use to learn how to set up and manage your computer resources?

_____

_____

4. Move the pointer over the **What's new in Windows XP** topic in the left pane, and note that the pointer becomes a hand, as it does in a Web browser when you move it over a link. When you point to a topic, it becomes underlined, like a hyperlink.

5. Click **What's new in Windows XP** in the left pane. This topic expands in the left pane, displaying subtopics.

6. Click **What's new**. Subtopics are displayed in the right pane.

7. Scroll the right pane to get a sense of what information is available, and then click **What's new with files and folders** in the right pane. The topic expands to show a description of the contents as well as links to more information.

8. Click **New ways for viewing files and pictures**. The topic expands to add a brief overview and additional subcategories. Click **Viewing files and folders overview**. The right pane displays a list of ways to arrange and identify your files. Record the possible view options here:

_____

_____

_____

9. The Windows Help toolbar has buttons similar to those in a Web browser, including a Back button (a left-facing arrow) you can use to display a previous topic. Click the **Back** button in Windows Help. The Tips for new users topic is displayed again in the right pane.

You can also look for topics in Windows Help by using the Search text box, where you type in keywords to locate the information you need. This feature is useful when you're familiar with Windows Help but don't know where to look for a specific topic in the Contents tab. Follow these steps to use the Search feature:

1. Type **lost files** in the Search text box. The list of topics should now include one on locating lost files. Click **locating lost files** to display the topic.

   ◢ What does Windows prompt you to do?

   _____

   _____

2. Click **The My Documents Folder**. How does Windows suggest you look in this location?

   _____

   _____

With the Add to Favorites button, you can record a list of topics you want to refer to again without having to search for them. Follow these steps:

1. Click the **Add to Favorites** button.

2. A pop-up window is displayed, stating that the page has been added to your favorites list.

Windows Help enables you to search for information on topics related to using Windows. Windows Troubleshooters provide information on how to fix problems with Windows and its applications. You can access Troubleshooters from Windows Help. In the following steps, you use a Troubleshooter to repair a nonfunctioning sound card:

1. Type **list of troubleshooters** in the Search text box.

2. In the left pane, locate and click **List of troubleshooters**.

3. A table appears in the right pane, with a list and description of Windows troubleshooting tools. In the table, click **sound**.

4. The Windows Troubleshooter for sound starts in the right pane of Windows Help. The Troubleshooter asks you for details about the problem you're troubleshooting so that it can provide a solution tailored to that problem. For this portion of the lab, assume the following:

   ◢ A sound appears to play, but you don't hear anything.

   ◢ Your speakers can't play system sounds.

   ◢ Your volume is not set too low, and audio is not muted.

5. To troubleshoot the problem, click the option buttons for the specified scenario. Click **Next** to advance through the Troubleshooter windows. Notice that the Troubleshooter includes buttons you can use to go back to a previous window and start over at the beginning of the process. What solution does the Troubleshooter offer for your problem?

   _____

   _____

6. Click the **Start Over** button to troubleshoot a slightly different problem. This time, assume the following:

   ◢ The sound is distorted or scratchy.

   ◢ You aren't using an excessively high volume level.

   ◢ You don't have a hardware device conflict.

7. Answer the following questions:

   ◢ What conclusion does the Troubleshooter reach?

   _____

   _____

   ◢ What options are offered to correct the problem?

   _____

   _____

In Windows 2000, follow these steps:

1. Log on to your computer as an administrator.

2. Close or minimize any applications that start automatically so that the desktop is active.

3. Press **F1**. (Instead of activating the desktop and pressing F1, you could simply click **Start, Help**.) Windows Help opens. As you can see, the Windows Help interface is similar to a Web browser. Answer the following questions:

   ◢ What four tabs are available in Windows Help?

   _____

   _____

◢ What are the five menu bar items?

_____

_____

4. If no one has used Windows Help on your computer before, the Contents tab is visible. If Help has been opened previously, the most recently used tab is visible. Click the **Contents** tab if it's not already visible.

5. Move the pointer over the **Introducing Windows 2000 Professional** in the left pane, and note that the pointer becomes a hand, as it does in a Web browser when you move it over a link. When you point to a topic, it becomes underlined, like a hyperlink.

6. Click **Introducing Windows 2000 Professional** in the left pane. This topic expands in the left pane, displaying subtopics.

7. Click **Tips for new users**. Subtopics are displayed in the right pane.

8. Scroll the right pane to get a sense of what information is available, and then click **locate lost files** in the right pane. The topic expands to show a description of the contents as well as links to more information.

9. Click **Overview for locating lost files**. The right pane displays a list of locations where lost files might be found along with steps for looking for files in each location. The list begins with the most likely locations for lost files, with less likely possibilities at the bottom. Record the possible locations for lost files:

_____

_____

_____

_____

_____

10. The Windows Help toolbar has buttons similar to those in a Web browser, including a Back button (a left-facing arrow) you can use to display a previous topic. Click the **Back** button in Windows Help. The Tips for new users topic is displayed again in the right pane.

You can also look for topics in Windows Help by using the Index and Search tabs, where you can type in keywords to locate the information you need. These features are useful when you're familiar with Windows Help but don't know where to look for a specific topic in the Contents tab. Follow these steps to use the Index and Search features:

1. Click the **Index** tab. If this is the first time the Index tab has been used, Help displays a small box with a flashlight icon and the message "Preparing index for first use." At the top of the Index tab is a text box where you can type keywords you want to search on. Below the text box is a list of all possible Help topics.

2. Type **los** in the text box.

◢ As you type, what happens to the list of topics?

_____

_____

3. Finish typing "lost files" (without the quotation marks) in the text box. The list of topics below the text box should now include one on lost files. Click to highlight the **lost files** topic, if necessary, in the list of topics. Click the **Display** button at the bottom to display the topic.

   ◢ What does Windows prompt you to do?

   _____

4. In the list of topics, click **locating**, and then click the **Display** button. The Topics Found dialog box opens, listing two topics. These topics should look familiar to you.

5. In the Topics Found dialog box, click **Locating lost files** to select it, if necessary, and then click the **Display** button. The Topics Found dialog box closes, and information on locating lost files is displayed in the Help window's right pane. How does the information currently displayed compare to the information you recorded earlier?

   _____

6. Now click the **Search** tab. It looks similar to the Index tab, except it doesn't display topics automatically. Search for Help is an alternative to browsing the Index for a topic. You simply type a topic in the Search text box and click the **List Topics** button. Keep search topic strings as short as possible to better focus your search.

7. Type **lost files** in the text box at the top, and then click the **List Topics** button. A list of topics is displayed below the text box. Did the Search feature return more or fewer topics than the Index feature?

   _____

8. Click **Tips for new users**, and then click the **Display** button. How does the display in the right pane change?

   _____

In the Favorites tab, you can record a list of topics you want to refer to again without having to search for them. Follow these steps:

1. Click the **Favorites** tab.

2. The topic "Tips for new users" is listed at the bottom below a blank pane. Click the **Add** button to add this item to your list of favorite topics.

Windows Help enables you to search for information on topics related to using Windows. Windows Troubleshooters provide information on how to fix problems with Windows and its applications. You can access Troubleshooters from Windows Help. In the following steps, you use a Troubleshooter to repair nonfunctioning DOS applications:

1. Click the **Contents** tab in the Help window.

2. In the left pane, locate and click **Troubleshooting and Maintenance**. A list of subtopics appears below "Troubleshooting and Maintenance" in the left pane.

3. In the list of subtopics, click **Windows 2000 troubleshooters**.

4. A table appears in the right pane, with a list and description of Windows troubleshooting tools. In the table, click **MS-DOS programs**.

5. The Windows Troubleshooter for MS-DOS programs starts in the right pane of Windows Help. The Troubleshooter asks you for details about the problem you're

troubleshooting so that it can provide a solution tailored to that problem. For this portion of the lab, assume the following:

◢ You have only one DOS application that isn't working.

◢ The NTVDM subsystem is working.

◢ The program works when it's the only program running.

6. To troubleshoot the problem, click the option buttons for the specified scenario. Click **Next** to advance through the Troubleshooter windows. Notice that the Troubleshooter includes buttons you can use to go back to a previous window and start over at the beginning of the process. What solution does the Troubleshooter offer for your problem?

_____

_____

7. Click the **Start Over** button to troubleshoot a slightly different problem. This time, assume the following:

◢ No DOS applications work.

◢ The NTVDM subsystem does work.

◢ The program doesn't run by itself.

◢ The program does run in Safe Mode.

8. Answer the following questions.

◢ What conclusion does the Troubleshooter reach?

_____

_____

◢ What two options are offered to correct the problem temporarily?

_____

_____

## REVIEW QUESTIONS

1. What type of program is Windows Help similar to in appearance?

_____

2. What can you do if you're not sure where to look for a specific topic?

_____

3. What are two ways to launch Windows Help?

_____

4. What tool accessible from Windows Help takes you step by step through the process of diagnosing and perhaps repairing common problems?

_____

5. Are Troubleshooters ever launched automatically? Explain:

_____

_____

## *LAB 14.2 RESTORE THE SYSTEM STATE*

### OBJECTIVES

The goal of this lab is to help you restore the system state on a Windows XP computer. After completing this lab, you will be able to:

◢ Create a restore point by using System Restore

◢ Change system settings

◢ Restore the system state with the restore point you created

### MATERIALS REQUIRED

This lab requires the following:

◢ Windows XP Professional operating system

### LAB PREPARATION

Before the lab begins, the instructor or lab assistant needs to do the following:

◢ Verify that Windows starts with no errors.

### ACTIVITY BACKGROUND

The System Restore tool in Windows XP enables you to restore the system to the state it was in when a snapshot, called a "restore point," was taken of the system state. The settings recorded in a restore point include system settings and configurations and files needed for a successful boot. When the system state is restored to a restore point, user data on the hard drive isn't affected, but software and hardware might be. Restore points are useful if, for example, something goes wrong with a software or hardware installation. In this lab, you create a restore point, make changes to system settings, and then use the restore point to restore the system state.

**ESTIMATED COMPLETION TIME: 30 minutes**

 **Activity**

To use the System Restore tool to create a restore point, follow these steps:

1. Click **Start,** point to **All Programs,** point to **Accessories,** point to **System Tools,** and then click **System Restore.**

2. The System Restore window opens with two choices: Restore my computer to an earlier time and Create a restore point. The first option restores your computer to an existing restore point. Read the information at the left and answer these questions:

   ◢ Can changes made by System Restore be undone? What type of data does System Restore leave unaffected?

   _____

   ◢ What is the term for the restore points the system creates automatically?

   _____

◢ As you've read, it's helpful to create a restore point before you install software or hardware. In what other situations might you want to create a restore point?

_____

_____

3. Click the **Create a restore point** option button, and then click **Next**.

4. In the next window, type a description of the restore point. The description should make it easy to identify the restore point later, such as "Restore *today's date*."

5. Click the **Create** button.

6. A message is displayed stating that the restore point was created and showing the date, time, and name of the restore point. Click the **Close** button.

Next, you make two changes to the system: uninstalling a Windows component and changing display settings. First, you uninstall the MSN (Microsoft Network) Explorer component. (If it isn't currently installed, ask your instructor which Windows component you should uninstall instead.)

1. In Control Panel, click **Add or Remove Programs**. The Add or Remove Programs window opens.

2. To see a list of Windows components, click the **Add/Remove Windows Components** icon on the left.

3. The Add or Remove Programs window remains open, and the Windows Components Wizard launches. In the list box in the middle, components that are checked are currently installed. Scroll down until you see the MSN Explorer component, and then click to clear the check box next to it.

4. A message box is displayed asking whether you want to uninstall this component. Click **Yes** to continue.

5. The MSN Explorer check box is cleared. Click **Next** to continue.

6. A progress window indicates the component the system is uninstalling. When the process is completed, a message is displayed stating that you have completed the Windows Components Wizard. Click **Finish**.

7. Click **Close** in the Add or Remove Programs window.

Next, you change some display settings:

1. In Control Panel, click **Appearance and Themes**, and then click **Display**. The Display Properties dialog box opens.

2. Click the **Desktop** tab. In the Background list box, click a background, and then click **OK**.

3. The Display Properties dialog box closes. Close the Control Panel window. Notice that the desktop background has changed to the one you selected.

Follow these steps to use the restore point you created to restore the system state:

1. Open the System Restore tool as explained earlier in this lab.

2. Click the **Restore my computer to an earlier time** option button, and then click **Next**.

3. A window opens showing a calendar of the current month, with the current date highlighted and all dates on which restore points were made in bold.

◢ How many restore points were created in the current month?

_____

◢ Click each bold date and list the reasons that the restore points were made:

_____

_____

_____

4. Click the current date. In the list on the right, click the name of the restore point you created earlier in the lab, and then click **Next**.

5. When a confirmation window is displayed, click **Next** to continue.

◢ Describe what happens when you click the Next button:

_____

_____

_____

6. After the system restarts, click your logon name to return to the Windows XP desktop. A message is displayed stating that the restoration is complete. Click **OK**.

◢ Did the display settings change back to their original settings?

_____

7. Start the Windows Components Wizard as you did earlier in this lab.

◢ Is MSN Explorer installed?

_____

## REVIEW QUESTIONS

1. List three situations in which you might want to create a restore point:

_____

_____

_____

2. What types of restore point are created by the system, and what types are created by users?

_____

_____

3. How often does the system create restore points automatically?

_____

4. Can more than one restore point be made on a specific date?

_____

5. Which of your changes was reversed when you used the restore point to restore the system state, and which change was not reversed? Explain why this happened:

_____

_____

_____

# LAB 14.3 INSTALL THE RECOVERY CONSOLE AS AN OPTION ON THE STARTUP MENU

## OBJECTIVES

The goal of this lab is to help you install the Recovery Console as a startup option. After completing this lab, you will be able to:

⊿ Install the Recovery Console

⊿ Open the Recovery Console from the Startup menu

## MATERIALS REQUIRED

This lab requires the following:

⊿ Windows XP Professional operating system

⊿ Windows XP Professional installation CD or installation files

## LAB PREPARATION

Before the lab begins, the instructor or lab assistant needs to do the following:

⊿ Verify that Windows starts with no errors.

⊿ Provide each student with access to the Windows XP installation files, if needed.

## ACTIVITY BACKGROUND

The Recovery Console tool in Windows XP allows you to start the computer when other startup and recovery options, such as System Restore, Safe Mode, and the Automated System Recovery (ASR) process, don't work. In the Recovery Console, you can use a limited group of DOS-like commands to format a hard drive, copy files from a floppy disk or CD to the hard drive, start and stop certain system processes, and perform other administrative tasks and troubleshooting tasks. If the Recovery Console isn't installed on your computer, you have to run it from the Windows XP installation CD. This lab shows you how to install the Recovery Console on your Windows XP computer so that it appears as an option when the computer starts.

**ESTIMATED COMPLETION TIME: 30 minutes**

 **Activity**

Follow these steps to install the Recovery Console as a startup option:

1. Insert the Windows XP installation CD into your CD-ROM drive. If the Autorun feature launches, close it. If your instructor has given you another location for the installation files, what drive letter do you use to access them?

_____

2. Click **Start, Run**. The Run dialog box opens. Type **cmd** and then click **OK**. A command prompt window opens.

3. To switch to your CD-ROM drive (or other drive with the installation files), type the drive letter followed by a colon, and then press **Enter**.

4. Next, you run the Windows XP setup program stored on this drive. The path to the program might vary, depending on the release of Windows XP you're using. Try the following possibilities until you locate the command that runs the program:

   ◢ Type **\i386\winnt32.exe /cmdcons** and press **Enter**.

   ◢ Type **\english\winxp\pro\i386\winnt32.exe /cmdcons** and press **Enter**.

   ◢ Type **\english\winxp\home\i386\winnt32.exe /cmdcons** and press **Enter**.

   ◢ Which command launched the setup program?

_____

5. A message box is displayed, asking if you want to install the Recovery Console. Click **Yes** to continue.

6. The Windows Setup window opens and shows that Setup is checking for updates. When the update check is finished, a progress indicator appears. When the installation is finished, a message box is displayed stating that the Recovery Console was installed successfully. Click **OK** to continue.

7. Restart your computer.

8. When the Startup menu is displayed, click **Microsoft Recovery Console** and press **Enter**. What do you see when the Recovery Console opens?

_____

_____

_____

_____

9. Type **1** (to log on to your Windows installation) and press **Enter**.

10. When prompted, type the administrator password for your computer and press **Enter**.

11. Type **help** and press **Enter** to see a list of commands available in the Recovery Console.

12. Type **exit** and press **Enter** to close the Recovery Console and restart the computer.

## REVIEW QUESTIONS

1. What is the advantage of being able to access the Recovery Console from your hard drive instead of the CD-ROM drive?

   _____

   _____

2. What is another way to exit the Recovery Console without logging on to your Windows installation?

   _____

3. In the Recovery Console, what command deletes a directory? What command can you use to list services that are running?

   _____

4. Name at least two tasks you might not be able to perform in the Recovery Console:

   _____

   _____

5. Why is an administrator password needed for access to the Recovery Console?

   _____

## LAB 14.4 USE THE RECOVERY CONSOLE TO COPY FILES

### OBJECTIVES

The goal of this lab is to help you learn how to copy files using the Recovery Console. After completing this lab, you will be able to:

⊿ Copy files from a storage medium to your hard drive using the Recovery Console

### MATERIALS REQUIRED

This lab requires the following:

⊿ Windows XP operating system

⊿ A floppy disk or other storage medium

### LAB PREPARATION

Before the lab begins, the instructor or lab assistant needs to do the following:

⊿ Verify that Windows starts with no errors.

### ACTIVITY BACKGROUND

The Windows XP Recovery Console is useful when you need to restore system files after they have been corrupted (perhaps by a virus) or accidentally deleted from the hard drive. In this lab, you use the Recovery Console (which you installed in Lab 14.3) to restore a system file, System.ini, from a floppy disk or other storage medium. (Windows XP doesn't need this file to boot; it's included in Windows XP for backward compatibility with older Windows software.)

**ESTIMATED COMPLETION TIME: 30 minutes**

**Activity**

Follow these steps to copy the file System.ini to a floppy disk and then copy it from the floppy to the hard drive using the Recovery Console:

1. Insert the floppy disk in the floppy drive.

2. Open Windows Explorer, and then locate and click the **System.ini** file (which is usually in the C:\Windows folder).

3. Copy the **System.ini** file to the floppy disk, and then eject the floppy disk from the drive.

4. Locate System.ini on your hard drive again and rename it as **System.old**. When prompted, click **Yes** to confirm that you want to rename the file.

5. Restart the computer and click the **Recovery Console** option.

6. Insert the floppy disk in the floppy disk drive. In the Recovery Console, log on with the administrator password. Type **copy a:\ system.ini c:\windows\system.ini** and press **Enter**. This command copies System.ini from the floppy disk to its original location (C:\Windows). What message does Recovery Console display?

> **Notes**
>
> In these steps, a floppy disk is used as the storage medium, but you can adapt the steps to whatever storage medium you're using.

_____

7. If C:\Windows is not the active directory, change to that directory and then use the **dir** command to view its contents. Verify that System.ini was copied to this directory. You might have to use the spacebar to scroll down.

8. Exit the Recovery Console and restart the computer.

## REVIEW QUESTIONS

1. You could have used the Recovery Console to rename the System.old file instead of copying the original version from the floppy disk. What command do you use to perform this task?

_____

2. Assume you moved the System.ini file to the My Documents folder. What command do you use in the Recovery Console to move it back to the C:\Windows folder?

_____

3. When might it be useful to be able to copy files from a CD to the hard drive by using the Recovery Console?

_____

4. Why does Windows XP include the System.ini file?

_____

5. When might you want to use the Recovery Console to copy files from the hard drive to a floppy disk?

_____

_____

# LAB 14.5 CRITICAL THINKING: SABOTAGE AND REPAIR WINDOWS 2000/XP

## OBJECTIVES

The goal of this lab is to learn to troubleshoot Windows 2000/XP by repairing a sabotaged system. After completing this lab, you will be able to:

◢ Troubleshoot and repair a system that isn't working correctly

## MATERIALS REQUIRED

This lab requires the following:

◢ Windows 2000/XP Professional installed on a PC designated for sabotage

◢ Windows 2000/XP Professional installation CD or installation files

◢ A workgroup of 2 to 4 students

## LAB PREPARATION

Before the lab begins, the instructor or lab assistant needs to do the following:

◢ Verify that Windows starts with no errors.

◢ Provide each workgroup with access to the Windows 2000/XP installation files, if needed.

## ACTIVITY BACKGROUND

You have learned about several tools and methods you can use to recover Windows 2000/XP when it fails. This lab gives you the opportunity to use these skills in a troubleshooting situation. Your group sabotages another group's system while that group sabotages your system. Then your group repairs its own system.

---

**ESTIMATED COMPLETION TIME: 45 minutes**

---

 **Activity**

1. If your system's hard drive contains important data, back it up to another medium. Is there anything else you would like to back up before another group sabotages the system? Record that item here, and then back it up:

   _____

2. Trade systems with another group, and sabotage the other group's system while it sabotages your system. Do one thing that will cause the system to fail to boot, display errors after the boot, or prevent a device or application from working. The following list offers some sabotage suggestions. Do something in the following list, or think of another option. (Do *not* alter the hardware.)

   > **Notes**
   >
   > Windows XP has several features designed to prevent sabotage, so you might find it a little challenging to actually prevent the system from booting by deleting or renaming system files.

   ◢ Find a system file in the root directory that's required to boot the computer, and rename it or move it to a different directory. (Don't delete the file.)

◢ Using the Registry Editor (Regedit.exe), delete several important keys or values in the Registry.

◢ Locate important system files in the \Windows directory, and rename them or move them to another directory.

◢ Put a corrupted program file in the folder that will cause the program to launch automatically at startup. Record the name of that program file and folder here:

_____

◢ Use display settings that aren't readable, such as black text on a black background.

◢ Disable a critical device driver.

3. Reboot the system and verify that a problem exists.

4. How did you sabotage the other team's system?

_____

_____

_____

5. Return to your system and troubleshoot it.

6. Describe the problem as a user would describe it to you if you were working at a help desk.

_____

_____

7. What is your first guess as to the source of the problem?

_____

8. List the steps you took in the troubleshooting process:

_____

_____

_____

9. How did you finally solve the problem and return the system to good working order?

_____

_____

_____

## REVIEW QUESTIONS

1. What would you do differently the next time you encountered the same symptoms?

_____

_____

## 14

2. What Windows utilities did you use or could you have used to solve the problem?

_____

_____

3. In a real-life situation, what might cause this problem to happen? List three possible causes:

_____

_____

_____

4. If you were the PC support technician responsible for this computer in an office environment, what could you do to prevent this problem from happening in the future or limit its impact on users if it did happen?

_____

_____

# chapter 15

# Using the Windows 9x/Me Startup Disk and Command Line

**Labs included in this chapter:**

- **Lab 15.1:** Create and Examine a Windows 98 Startup Disk
- **Lab 15.2:** Use the Microsoft Diagnostics Utility in Windows
- **Lab 15.3:** Create a Windows 9x Boot Disk Without Using Windows 9x
- **Lab 15.4:** Learn to Work from the Command Line
- **Lab 15.5:** Use the Diskcopy and Xcopy Commands
- **Lab 15.6:** Install and Partition a Hard Drive
- **Lab 15.7:** Format a Drive and Test it with ScanDisk

# LAB 15.1 CREATE AND EXAMINE A WINDOWS 98 STARTUP DISK

## OBJECTIVES

The goal of this lab is to learn how a Windows 98 startup disk is created and used. After completing this lab, you will be able to:

▲ Create a Windows 98 startup disk

▲ Describe the steps in booting from a startup disk

## MATERIALS REQUIRED

This lab requires the following:

▲ Windows 98 operating system

▲ Windows 98 installation CD or installation files

▲ A blank floppy disk

▲ A workgroup of 2 to 4 students

## LAB PREPARATION

Before the lab begins, the instructor or lab assistant needs to do the following:

▲ Verify that Windows starts with no errors.

▲ Provide each student with access to the Windows 98 installation files, if needed.

## ACTIVITY BACKGROUND

In Windows 98, you can create a startup disk, which is a helpful tool for troubleshooting and setup. A startup disk is a bootable disk containing several useful utilities and drivers. In this lab, you create and experiment with a startup disk. If you don't have access to a Windows 98 computer to create the startup disk, in Lab 15.3 you learn how to create the disk by downloading the necessary files from the Internet.

**ESTIMATED COMPLETION TIME: 30 minutes**

 **Activity**

1. Open Control Panel and double-click the **Add/Remove Programs** icon.

2. In the Add/Remove Programs applet, click the **Startup Disk** tab.

3. Click the **Create Disk** button, and follow the prompts to create the startup disk.

4. When the process is finished, close the Add/Remove Programs applet.

Answer the following questions about the startup disk:

1. What two files on the startup disk end in the .bat extension?

_____

2. What are the purposes of these files?

_____

3. What kind of information is provided in the Readme.txt file?

_____

_____

With the startup disk in the drive, reboot your computer and answer these questions:

1. What prompt do you see while the system boots?

_____

2. What type of drive is set up during the boot process?

_____

3. Why do you think this drive is set up?

_____

To continue exploring the startup disk, follow these steps:

1. Using the command prompt provided by the startup disk, access the hard drive by typing the command **C:** and pressing **Enter**.

2. The prompt you should see now is called the C prompt. Write the prompt here:

_____

3. Type **DIR** and press **Enter** to view the contents of the root directory of the C drive.

4. Keeping in mind that file names usually describe the file's function, record the names of the files listed as a result of the DIR command. Explain what you think the purpose of each file is:

_____

> ✎ **Notes**
> Keep your startup disk to use in later labs.

_____

_____

## REVIEW QUESTIONS

1. Why might you want to use a startup disk?

_____

_____

2. What icon in Control Panel do you use to create a startup disk?

_____

3. Why do you think you might need CD-ROM support when using the startup disk?

_____

_____

4. If you want to examine the files on the CD-ROM drive, what command do you issue at the command prompt?

_____

5. What three files must be on the startup disk to make the disk bootable?

_____

# LAB 15.2 USE THE MICROSOFT DIAGNOSTICS UTILITY IN WINDOWS

## OBJECTIVES

The goal of this lab is to observe the boot process. After completing this lab, you will be able to:

▲ Use the Microsoft Diagnostics (MSD) utility to examine your system

▲ Compare the results of using MSD in real mode and protected mode

## MATERIALS REQUIRED

This lab requires the following:

▲ Windows 98 operating system

▲ Bootable floppy disk or startup disk from Lab 15.1

▲ Windows 98 installation CD or installation files

## LAB PREPARATION

Before the lab begins, the instructor or lab assistant needs to do the following:

▲ Verify that Windows starts with no errors.

▲ In CMOS setup, verify that the boot sequence is the floppy drive and then the hard drive.

▲ Provide each student with access to the Windows 98 installation files, if needed.

## ACTIVITY BACKGROUND

The Microsoft Diagnostics (MSD) utility, included with DOS and all versions of Windows, examines your system and displays useful information about ports, devices, memory, and the like. The program file for Microsoft Diagnostics, Msd.exe, is in the Tools\OldMSDOS directory on your Windows 98 installation CD. In this lab, you install and use MSD. If you don't have the Windows 98 installation CD available, ask your instructor for the network path to these files. What is that path?

_____

**Activity**

Before you can begin using MSD, follow these steps to copy the program file to your hard disk:

1. Insert the Windows 98 installation CD into your CD-ROM drive or access the setup files at the location your instructor provided.

2. Copy the **MSD.EXE** file from the Windows 98 Tools\OldMSDOS directory to your hard drive, storing it in a subfolder named **\Tools**.

Now that you have copied the program file to your hard disk, you can start MSD. Follow these steps to use MSD in a real mode environment:

1. Reboot your computer using the bootable floppy disk or Windows 98 startup disk from Lab 15.1, which starts your PC in real mode and provides a command prompt. Or you can click **Start, Shut Down**, and then click **Restart Computer in MS-DOS mode**.

2. At the command prompt, type **C:\TOOLS\MSD.EXE** and press **Enter**. This command is how you run a program file located in a different directory from the one you're working in. You told the computer the exact path, called an "absolute path," to the file you wanted to run. At this point, your screen should look similar to Figure 15-1.

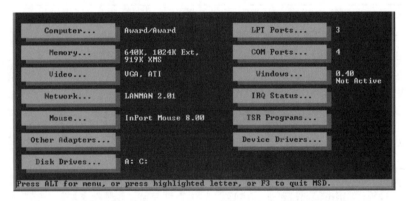

**Figure 15-1** The MSD utility

Study all the MSD menu options and answer the following questions about your system:

1. What categories of information are available in MSD?

   _____

   _____

2. What version of the operating system are you running?

   _____

3. What COM ports are available on the system?

   _____

4. What IRQ and port address are associated with COM1?

   _____

5. How far does the MEMORY map extend?

_____

6. What is the address range at 1024K?

_____

Save the information you noted so that you can compare it with the information you find with MSD in the next set of steps. Now you're ready to close MSD:

1. Click **File, Exit** from the MSD menu.

2. Remove the floppy disk and reboot your PC to the Windows desktop.

3. Open Windows Explorer, and double-click the **MSD.EXE** file to start it again.

With MSD open, answer the following questions again:

1. What categories of information are available in MSD?

_____

_____

2. What version of the operating system are you running?

_____

3. What COM ports are available on the system?

_____

4. What IRQ and port address are associated with COM1?

_____

5. How far does the MEMORY map extend?

_____

6. What is the address range at 1024K?

_____

Compare the information you gathered the first time you used MSD with the information you found the second time, and then answer these questions:

1. How does your first set of answers compare to your second set of answers?

_____

_____

2. How do you explain the differences?

_____

_____

3. What key can you press to exit MSD?

_____

You're finished with MSD now, so you can close it.

## REVIEW QUESTIONS

1. In what categories do you look to find information on COM ports?

   _____

2. What message did you see when you started MSD in Windows?

   _____

   _____

3. Which category gives information on the type of network installed?

   _____

4. What is an advantage of saving Msd.exe to the hard drive?

   _____

5. What is the absolute path to Msd.exe on the Windows 98 installation CD?

   _____

6. What Windows tool is similar to MSD?

   _____

7. As a PC repair technician, when would you use MSD?

   _____

   _____


# LAB 15.3 CREATE A WINDOWS 9X BOOT DISK WITHOUT USING WINDOWS 9X

## OBJECTIVES

The goal of this lab is to learn how to create a Windows 9x boot disk when you don't have access to a Windows 9x machine. After completing this lab, you will be able to:

◢ Create a Windows 98 boot disk

## MATERIALS REQUIRED

This lab requires the following:

◢ Windows 2000/XP or Windows 9x operating system
◢ Internet access
◢ A blank floppy disk

## LAB PREPARATION

Before the lab begins, the instructor or lab assistant needs to do the following:

◢ Verify that Internet access is available.
◢ For labs that don't have Internet access, download the Win98.exe file from *http://allbootdisks.com* to a file server or other storage media available to students in the lab.

## ACTIVITY BACKGROUND

At times, it isn't possible to access a running Windows 9x machine to create a boot disk (also called a startup disk). In this lab, you download a self-extracting boot image from the Internet. You'll be able to run the downloaded program and have it write all the necessary information to a floppy disk. Finally, you boot your machine with the new disk to verify that it's working correctly.

Web sites sometimes change, so as you follow the instructions in the lab, you might have to adjust for changes to the *http://allbootdisks.com* site. If your lab doesn't have Internet access, ask your instructor for the location of the Win98.exe file downloaded previously for your use. Write the path to that file here:

_____

**ESTIMATED COMPLETION TIME: 30 minutes**

 **Activity**

Follow these steps to create a Windows 98 boot disk:

1. To start Internet Explorer, click **Start, Run**. Type **iexplore.exe**, and click **OK**.

2. In the Address text box, type **http://allbootdisks.com** and press **Enter**.

3. At the left side of the Web page is a list of operating systems. Under the heading Windows 98, click **Download**. Near the center of the next Web page, click **Windows 98 Boot Disk**. On the next Web page, click **Download**. When the File Download dialog box opens, click **Save**. The Save As dialog box opens.

4. Pay special attention to the location in the Save in drop-down list box at the top. Select a location for the file you're about to save. A good choice is the desktop. Next, click the **Save** button in the lower-right corner. The Win98.exe file is then downloaded to the location you specified. After the file is saved, close the Download complete dialog box.

5. Double-click the **Win98.exe** file name on your desktop or at another location to run the file.

6. Follow the instructions on-screen to create your new boot disk.

7. To test the disk, after the disk creation process is finished, leave the disk in the floppy A drive and reboot the computer. Describe the screen that appears when you boot from your new boot disk:

_____

_____

_____

## REVIEW QUESTIONS

1. What is the advantage of knowing how to create a Windows 98 boot disk using files downloaded from the Internet instead of using Windows 98?

_____

2. What is the name of the executable file used to launch Internet Explorer?

_____

3. Were there any problems booting to the new boot disk?

4. Describe one situation when you might want to use the Windows 98 boot disk you created:

## LAB 15.4 LEARN TO WORK FROM THE COMMAND LINE

### OBJECTIVES

The goal of this lab is to introduce you to some commands used when working from the command line. You change and examine directories and drives, and then perform a copy operation. You also learn to use the command-line Help feature and how to read Help information. After completing this lab, you will be able to:

◢ Create a file and folder with Notepad and My Computer

◢ Examine directories

◢ Switch drives and directories

◢ Use various commands at the command prompt

### MATERIALS REQUIRED

This lab requires the following:

◢ Windows 2000/XP or Windows 9x operating system

◢ A blank formatted floppy disk

### LAB PREPARATION

Before the lab begins, the instructor or lab assistant needs to do the following:

◢ Verify that Windows starts with no errors.

### ACTIVITY BACKGROUND

In Lab 15.1, you used the DIR command to explore file structure. Experienced technicians can use the command line for tasks that just can't be done in a graphical interface, especially when troubleshooting a system. For most tasks, however, you'll rely on a graphical interface, such as My Computer. In this lab, you use My Computer to create a new folder and a new file. Then you use the command line to delete that file. In this lab, it's assumed that Windows is installed on the C drive. If your installation is on a different drive, substitute that drive letter in the following steps.

**ESTIMATED COMPLETION TIME: 30 minutes**

 **Activity**

To create a new folder and text file in My Computer, follow these steps:

1. On the Windows desktop, double-click **My Computer**, and then double-click the drive C: icon. In Windows XP, click **Start, My Computer** if the My Computer icon isn't on the desktop.

2. Right-click anywhere in the blank area of the drive C window, point to **New** on the shortcut menu, and then click **Folder**. A new folder icon appears with "New Folder" highlighted as the default name, ready for you to rename it.

3. To rename the folder Tools, type **Tools** and press **Enter**.

4. To create a file in the Tools folder, double-click the **Tools** folder icon, and then right-click anywhere in the blank area of the Tools window. Point to **New**, and then click **Text Document**. A new file icon appears in the Tools window with "New Text Document.txt" highlighted to indicate it's ready for renaming.

5. Double-click the **New Text Document.txt** icon to open the file in Notepad.

6. On the Notepad menu, click **File, Save As**.

7. In the Save As dialog box, name the file **Deleteme**, and make sure the selection in the Save as type drop-down list is **Text Documents**. Click the **Save** button.

8. Close Notepad.

9. In My Computer, right-click **New Text Document.txt** and click **Delete** in the shortcut menu. Click **Yes** to confirm the deletion.

10. Close all open windows.

To practice using the command-line environment, follow these steps:

1. To open a command prompt window, in Windows 2000/XP, click **Start, Run**, type **cmd**, and press **Enter**. In Windows 9x, click **Start, Run**, type **command**, and press **Enter**. The command prompt window opens, and the cursor is flashing at the command prompt.

2. The title bar of the command prompt window varies with different versions of Windows. Below the title bar, a command prompt like the following appears in Windows 2000:

   C:\>

   The Windows XP command prompt depends on the user name of the person currently logged in, for example:

   C:\Documents and Settings\Jean Andrews>

   The following command prompt appears in Windows 9x:

   C:\WINDOWS>

   The command prompt indicates the working drive (drive C) and working directory (the \Windows directory, the root directory indicated by the backslash, or the current user's Documents and Settings directory). Commands issued from this prompt apply to this folder unless you indicate otherwise.

3. Type **DIR** and press **Enter**. Remember that DIR is the command used to list a directory's contents. If the list of files and directories DIR displays is too large to fit on one screen, you see only the last few entries. Entries with the <DIR> label indicate that they are directories (folders), which can contain files or other directories. Also listed for each entry are the time and date it was created and the number of bytes it contains. (This information is displayed differently depending on which version of Windows you're using.) The last two lines in the list summarize the number of files and directories in the current directory, the space they consume, and the free space available on the drive.

As you'll see in the next set of steps, there are two ways to view any files that aren't displayed because of the length of the list and the window size. To learn more about displaying lists of files in the command-line environment, perform the following steps:

1. Type **DIR /?** and press **Enter** to display Help information for the directory command. You can view Help information for any command by entering the command followed by the /? parameter (also called a "switch").

2. Type **DIR /W** and press **Enter**. What happened?

_____

_____

3. Type **DIR /P** and press **Enter**. What happened?

_____

_____

4. Type **DIR /OS** and press **Enter**. What happened?

_____

_____

5. Type **DIR /O-S** and press **Enter**. What happened? What do you think the hyphen between O and S accomplishes?

_____

_____

6. Insert a blank disk in the floppy drive. Type **A:** and press **Enter**. The resulting prompt should look like this: A:\>. What does the A: indicate?

_____

_____

7. What do you think you would see if you issued the DIR command at this prompt?

_____

_____

8. Type **DIR** and press **Enter**. Did you see what you were expecting?

_____

_____

9. Change back to the C: drive by typing **C:** and pressing **Enter**.

10. Type **DIR C:\Tools** and press **Enter**. This command tells the computer to list the contents of a specific directory without actually changing to that directory. In the resulting file list, you should see the file you created earlier, Deleteme.txt.

File attributes are managed by using the Attrib command. Follow these steps to learn how to view and manage file attributes:

1. To make C:\Tools the default directory, type **CD C:\Tools** and press **Enter**.

2. To view the attributes of the Deleteme.txt file, type **Attrib Deleteme.txt** and press **Enter**.

3. To change the file to a hidden file, type **Attrib +H Deleteme.txt** and press **Enter**.

4. View the attributes of the Deleteme.txt file again.

◢ What command did you use?

_____

◢ How have the attributes changed?

_____

5. To view the contents of the C:\Tools directory, type **DIR** and press **Enter**. Why doesn't the Deleteme.txt file show in the directory list?

6. To change the attributes so that the file is a system file, type **Attrib +S Deleteme.txt** and press **Enter**. What error message did you get?

7. Because you can't change the attributes of a hidden file, first remove the hidden attribute by typing **Attrib -H Deleteme.txt** and pressing **Enter**.

8. Now try to make the file a system file. What command did you use?

9. Use the DIR command to list the contents of the C:\Tools directory. Are system files listed?

10. To remove the file's system attribute, type **Attrib -S Deleteme.txt** and press **Enter**.

11. To return to the root directory, type **CD C:\** and press **Enter**.

To learn how to delete a file from the command prompt, follow these steps:

1. Type **DEL Deleteme.txt** and press **Enter** to instruct the computer to delete that file. You'll see a message stating that the file couldn't be found because the system assumes that commands refer to the working directory unless a specific path is given. What command could you use to delete the file without changing to that directory?

2. Type **CD\** and press **Enter**. The resulting prompt is C:\>. The \ in the command you typed indicates the root directory.

3. Type **CD Tools** and press **Enter**. The prompt now ends with "Tools>" (indicating that Tools is the current working directory).

4. Now type **DEL Deleteme.txt /p** and press **Enter**. You're prompted to type **Y** for Yes or **N** for No to confirm the deletion. If you don't enter the /p switch (which means "prompt for verification"), the file is deleted automatically without a confirmation message. It's a good practice to use this /p switch, especially when deleting multiple files with wildcard characters. Also, when you delete a file from the command line, the file doesn't go to the Recycle Bin, as it would if you deleted it in Windows Explorer or My Computer. Because deletion from the command line bypasses the Recycle Bin, recovering accidentally deleted files is more difficult.

5. Type **Y** to delete the Deleteme.txt file. You're returned to the Tools directory.

To display certain files in a directory, you can use an asterisk (*) or a question mark (?) as wildcard characters. Wildcard characters are placeholders that represent other unspecified characters. The asterisk can represent one or more characters, and the question mark represents any single character. The asterisk is the most useful wildcard, so it's the one you'll encounter most often. To learn more, follow these steps:

1. Return to the root directory. What command did you use?

2. Type **DIR *.*** and press **Enter**. How many files are displayed?

3. Type **DIR C*.*** and press **Enter**. How many files are displayed?

_____

4. Explain why the results differed in the previous two commands:

_____

_____

## CRITICAL THINKING (ADDITIONAL 30 MINUTES)

Follow these steps to practice using additional commands at the command prompt:

1. Copy the program file **Notepad.exe** from the \Windows (in Windows XP or Windows 9x) or \WINNT directory (in Windows 2000) to the **\Tools** directory. What command did you use?

_____

2. Rename the file in the \Tools directory as **Newfile.exe**. What command did you use?

_____

3. Change the attributes of Newfile.exe to make it a hidden file. What command did you use?

_____

4. Type **DIR** and press **Enter**. Is the Newfile.exe file displayed?

_____

5. Unhide **Newfile.exe**. What command did you use?

_____

6. List all files in the \Windows or \WINNT directory that have an .exe file extension. What command did you use?

_____

_____

7. Create a new directory named **\New** in \Windows or \WINNT, and then copy **Newfile.exe** to the \New directory. What commands did you use?

_____

_____

8. Using the /p switch to prompt for verification, delete the **\New** directory. What commands did you use?

_____

_____

9. In Windows 2000/XP, open the Help and Support Center (Windows Help in Windows 9x). Use the Search text box to answer the following questions:

⊿ What is the purpose of the Recover command?

_____

_____

⊿ What is the purpose of the Assoc command?

_____

_____

## REVIEW QUESTIONS

1. What command/switch do you use to view Help information for the DIR command?

_____

2. What do you add to the DIR command to list the contents of a directory that's not the current working directory?

_____

3. What command do you use to change directories?

_____

4. What command do you use to delete a file?

_____

5. What command do you use to switch from drive A to drive C?

_____

# LAB 15.5 USE THE DISKCOPY AND XCOPY COMMANDS

## OBJECTIVES

The goal of this lab is to help you observe differences in the Diskcopy and Xcopy commands. After completing this lab, you will be able to:

⊿ Copy files and folders with the Xcopy command

⊿ Duplicate a disk with the Diskcopy command

⊿ Explain when to use Xcopy and when to use Diskcopy when copying files and folders

## MATERIALS REQUIRED

This lab requires the following:

⊿ Windows 98 operating system

⊿ Two blank floppy disks

▲ A safety pin

▲ *Optional*: Windows 2000/XP operating system

## LAB PREPARATION

Before the lab begins, the instructor or lab assistant needs to do the following:

▲ Verify that Windows starts with no errors.

## ACTIVITY BACKGROUND

The Copy command allows you to copy files from one folder to another folder. Using a single Xcopy command, you can copy files from multiple folders, duplicating an entire file structure in another location. The Diskcopy command enables you to make an exact copy of a floppy disk. In this lab, you learn to appreciate the differences between these commands.

**ESTIMATED COMPLETION TIME: 45 minutes**

 **Activity**

Before you begin using the Xcopy and Diskcopy commands, you need to create a test directory to use when copying files. Follow these steps:

1. Open a command prompt window, and make the root of drive C the current directory. The quickest way to change to the root of a drive is to type **X:** (*X* is the drive letter) and press **Enter**.

2. Make a directory in the drive C root called **copytest**.

Now you can begin experimenting with the Xcopy command. Follow these steps:

1. Type **Xcopy /?** and press **Enter**. Xcopy Help information is displayed. Notice all the switches you can use to modify the Xcopy command. In particular, you can use the /e switch to instruct Xcopy to copy all files and subdirectories in a directory, including any empty subdirectories, to a new location.

2. Type **Xcopy C:\"program files"\"internet explorer" C:\copytest /e** and press **Enter**. (You must use quotation marks in the command line to surround a folder name containing spaces.) You'll see a list of files scroll by as they are copied from the C:\program files\internet explorer folder to the C:\copytest folder.

3. When the copy operation is finished, check the copytest folder to see that the files have been copied and the subdirectories created.

4. Insert a blank floppy disk into drive A, type **md A:\copytest**, and then press **Enter**. This command creates a directory named copytest on the A drive.

5. To copy all files in the copytest directory on the hard drive to the copytest directory on drive A, type **Xcopy C:\"program files"\ "internet explorer" A:\copytest** and press **Enter**.

6. The system begins copying files, but the floppy disk lacks the capacity to hold the entire \internet explorer directory. As a result, the system displays a message stating that the disk is out of space and asking you to insert another disk. What is the exact error message?

_____

_____

7. In this case, you don't want to copy the entire directory to the floppy disk, so you need to stop the copying process. To do that, press **Ctrl + Pause/Break**. You're returned to the command prompt.

You have used the Xcopy command to copy some files to a floppy disk. Next, you use the Diskcopy command to make an exact copy of that floppy disk, which is referred to as the "source disk." (The disk you copy files to is known as the "target disk.") You begin by writing down a list of the files and directories on the source disk. Later, you compare this list to the list of files actually copied to the target disk. Follow these steps:

1. Display a directory listing for the A:\copytest directory.

2. Write the complete summary of files, directories, and space on the A drive:

_____

_____

_____

_____

3. Verify that the floppy disk you used in the preceding set of steps is inserted in the A drive. Then type **Diskcopy A: A:** and press **Enter**. This command instructs the system to copy files from one floppy disk to another using a single floppy disk drive. (If your system had a B drive, you could copy files from a disk in drive A to a disk in drive B, or vice versa.)

4. Press **Enter** to begin copying.

5. Because you're copying from drive A to drive A, the system prompts you to remove the source disk and insert the target disk. When prompted, insert a blank floppy disk and press **Enter**.

6. When the copy operation finishes, a message appears asking if you want to copy another disk. Type **n** and press **Enter** to confirm that you don't want to copy another disk. (When using Windows 98, you must also indicate that you don't want to make another duplicate.)

7. With the target disk still in drive A, use the **DIR** command to compare the newly copied files with the file list from the source disk, which you recorded in Step 2. The disks should be identical.

## CRITICAL THINKING (ADDITIONAL 30 MINUTES)

1. Format one floppy disk. Refer back to Lab 8.1 for a reminder on methods of formatting a disk.

2. Use a safety pin to damage one of the floppy disks created in this lab by sliding back the disk's protective guard and punching a small hole about half an inch from the disk's edge.

3. Attempt to copy files on the damaged disk to the newly formatted disk with the Xcopy command by first copying them to a folder on the hard drive. List the steps you used for this task and describe the outcome:

_____

_____

_____

4. Attempt to recover from the damaged disk the files that the system couldn't copy. Explain how you were able to do this:

_____

_____

## CRITICAL THINKING (ADDITIONAL 15 MINUTES)

Do the following to create and use a Windows 2000/XP bootable floppy disk:

1. Using Windows Explorer on a Windows 2000/XP computer, format a floppy disk.

2. Copy **Ntldr, Ntdetect.com**, and **Boot.ini** from the root of drive C to the root of the floppy disk.

3. Use the bootable floppy disk to boot the system. What appears on your screen after the boot?

_____

4. How might this bootable floppy disk be useful in troubleshooting?

_____

_____

## REVIEW QUESTIONS

1. Can a single Copy command copy files from more than one directory?

_____

2. What switch do you use with Xcopy to copy subdirectories?

_____

3. What is the complete Diskcopy command to copy files on a disk in drive A to a disk in drive B?

_____

4. What is one disadvantage of using the Diskcopy command with only one floppy disk drive?

_____

5. Which Xcopy switch suppresses overwrite confirmation?

_____

## LAB 15.6 INSTALL AND PARTITION A HARD DRIVE

### OBJECTIVES

The goal of this lab is to help you master the process of installing a hard drive in a computer. After completing this lab, you will be able to:

⬩ Physically install a drive

⬩ Set CMOS to recognize the drive

⬩ Partition the drive

### MATERIALS REQUIRED

This lab requires the following:

⬩ Windows 98 startup disk or the Windows 98 boot disk created in Lab 15.3

⬩ A hard drive with unpartitioned drive space

⬩ A PC toolkit and antistatic ground strap

### LAB PREPARATION

Before the lab begins, the instructor or lab assistant needs to do the following:

⬩ Verify that Windows starts with no errors.

### ACTIVITY BACKGROUND

As a technician, you definitely need to know how to install a hard drive in a computer. You might have to replace a failed drive with a new one, or if you have a hard drive that's running out of storage space, you might need to install an additional drive. In either situation, you need to know the steps for installing a new hard drive.

In this lab, you install and partition a new hard drive. Ideally, you would install a second hard drive in a system that already has a working drive. However, this lab also gives you the option of removing the hard drive from your system, trading your hard drive for another student's hard drive, and then installing the traded hard drive in your computer. Ask your instructor which procedure you should use. Because the steps in this lab allow for both possibilities, you need to read them carefully to make sure you're performing the right steps for your situation.

After you install the hard drive, you have to partition it. If you're installing a hard drive that has been used as a boot device, the drive already has a primary DOS partition. In that case, you need to verify that the drive contains at least some unpartitioned space. If it does, you can add an extended partition to the drive. Again, ask your instructor for specific directions.

**ESTIMATED COMPLETION TIME: 45 minutes**

 **Activity**

Do the following to physically install the drive in the computer case:

1. Remove the case cover. Remove the hard drive and exchange it for another student's hard drive. (If your instructor has provided a second hard drive to install in your system, simply open the case cover.)

2. Examine the case and decide where to place the drive. Consider whether to place the drive on the primary or secondary IDE channel and whether you need a bay kit to fit a 3.5-inch drive into a 5-inch drive bay. In most cases, you should use the primary channel for your hard drive and, if possible, it should be the only drive on that channel.

3. Place the drive in or near the bay to test its position. Make sure that all cables can reach in that position. If not, try a different bay or use longer cables.

4. When you're satisfied everything will fit, remove the drive and set the jumpers to their correct setting. If the drive is to be the only drive on an IDE channel, set it to single. If it's sharing the IDE cable with another drive, set it to master and set the other drive to slave. If the jumpers aren't marked on the drive, consult the drive documentation for jumper configuration. You might have to search the drive manufacturer's Web site for information on the drive.

5. Install the drive in the bay, and secure it with screws on each side of the drive.

6. Attach the power cord and data cable, and close the case.

Now that you have physically installed your hard drive, you need to configure CMOS to recognize the new hard drive. Follow these steps:

1. Attach the keyboard, monitor, and mouse.

2. Boot your computer and enter the CMOS setup utility.

3. If IDE hard drive autodetect isn't enabled, enable it now. In CMOS, what is the name of this entry? If you have just enabled autodetect, reboot the system so that the drive can be detected.

_____

4. Check the drive parameters set by autodetect, and change them if they weren't detected correctly. If your system doesn't have autodetect, set the drive parameters now. When in doubt, use Logical Block Addressing (LBA) or consult the drive documentation. What are the drive parameters in CMOS?

_____

5. Check the boot sequence to make sure the floppy disk is in the list of boot devices. This is important for the next set of steps.

6. Save and exit CMOS setup. The system reboots.

7. While the system boots, watch for the drive to appear during POST.

Now that the drive has been recognized, you can use the Fdisk (which stands for "fixed disk") utility to create or delete partitions. The following steps show you how to create and delete the primary partition, an extended partition, and a logical DOS drive.

Enter Fdisk by following these steps:

1. Insert a Windows 98 startup disk in drive A, and reboot the computer. This disk was created in Lab 15.3. If you don't have the disk, refer to that lab for instructions on creating a new one.

2. When you get a command prompt, type **Fdisk** and press **Enter**.

3. Select **Y** and press **Enter** to enable Large Disk Support, which uses FAT32 to enable partition sizes larger than 2 GB. The FDISK Options menu is displayed, as shown in Figure 15-2.

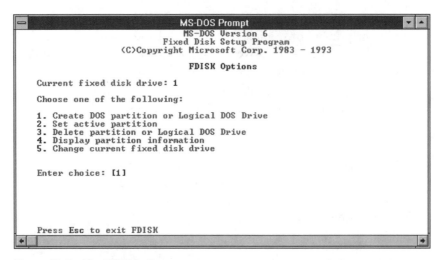

**Figure 15-2**    The FDISK Options menu

On the Fdisk screen, the current fixed disk drive is drive 1. If you're installing a second hard drive, you must first change to drive 2 by using the following steps. (If you're installing the only drive in the system, skip these steps and go to the next set of steps, where you determine what types of partition currently exist on your newly installed drive.)

1. Select option 5 in the menu and press **Enter**. A list of drives is displayed.

2. Select drive 2 and press **Enter**. You return to the FDISK Options menu shown previously in Figure 15-2.

Now that you have the correct drive selected, you need to find out what kinds of partition currently exist on the drive. Whether you're installing the only drive on the system or a second drive, follow these steps:

1. To display partition information, select option 4 in the menu and press **Enter**. Answer these questions about your drive:

   ◢ What is the total disk space reported?

   _____

   ◢ What is the available disk space reported?

   _____

   ◢ Do any partitions currently exist?

   _____

   ◢ If partitions exist, what kind of partitions are they?

   _____

2. Press **Esc** to return to the FDISK Options menu.

If the drive doesn't already have a primary DOS partition, the next step is to create one. If you're installing a second hard drive on your system, you need to create a primary DOS partition on the second hard drive by using the following steps. (If you have only one hard drive installed or if your second hard drive has a primary partition containing an operating system, skip these steps and move to the next set of steps, where you create an extended partition.)

1. To select the second hard drive, select option 5 in the FDISK Options menu and press **Enter**.

2. To select the second hard drive, select option **2** in the menu and press **Enter**. You return to the FDISK Options menu.

3. To create a DOS partition, select option **1** in the menu and press **Enter**. The Create DOS Partition or Logical DOS Drive menu is displayed.

4. To create a primary DOS partition, select option **1** in the FDISK Options menu and press **Enter**.

5. The system verifies disk space and displays a progress update. When space on the drive has been verified, Fdisk prompts you to use the maximum available space for the primary DOS partition. Type **N** and press **Enter**.

6. Fdisk again verifies disk space and prompts for the amount of disk space you want to use for the primary partition. Type a numerical value that's half the total available space and press **Enter**.

7. Fdisk tells you that the primary DOS partition has been created. It displays a summary of the new partition and assigns the partition a drive letter. Record the summary:

_____

_____

Note that Fdisk might slightly increase the partition size to accommodate the disk's geometry. You might also see an error message stating that you don't yet have an active partition.

8. Press **Esc** to return to the FDISK Options menu.

With a primary partition in place, you're ready to install an extended partition on the last part of the drive. Follow these steps to create an extended partition and one logical DOS drive within that extended partition:

1. In the FDISK Options Menu, select option **1** and press **Enter**.

2. To create an extended DOS partition, select option **2** and press **Enter**.

3. Fdisk verifies disk space and prompts you to enter the amount of disk space to use for the extended partition. Press **Enter** to use the remaining disk space to create the extended partition. Fdisk displays a summary of the extended partition. Note that the extended partition has no drive letter assigned.

4. Press **Esc**. A message is displayed indicating that no logical drives are defined, and Fdisk again verifies disk space.

5. Fdisk prompts you to enter the amount of space to use for a logical drive. Press **Enter** to use the maximum amount of disk space to create a logical drive.

6. Fdisk assigns a drive letter and displays a summary. Press **Esc** to return to the FDISK Options menu.

7. Select option **4** and press **Enter** to display the disk summary. Note that the system column displays Unknown because the drive hasn't been formatted.

8. Press **Esc** to return to the FDISK Options menu.

Next, you practice deleting partitions. Fdisk is particular about the order in which you create and delete partitions. To delete a primary partition, you must delete an extended partition; to delete an extended partition, you must delete all the logical DOS drives in the extended partition. A word of warning: If you have an operating system installed on the drive and you have only a single hard drive, *do not delete the primary partition*. Doing so destroys the operating system installed on the drive.

To delete the extended partition you just created, first you must delete the logical DOS drive in that partition. Follow these steps:

1. From the FDISK Options menu, select option **3** and press **Enter**.

2. On the next screen, select option **3** and press **Enter** to indicate that you're about to delete a logical DOS drive.

3. Type the drive letter assigned to the logical DOS drive, and then press **Enter** to confirm that you want to delete that drive.

4. Enter the volume label (or leave it blank), and then press **Enter**. Select **Y** and press **Enter** to confirm that you want to delete the drive. Fdisk confirms that the drive has been deleted.

5. Press **Esc** once. The No Logical Drive Defined message is displayed.

6. Press **Esc** to return to the FDISK Options menu.

Now that you have deleted the logical DOS drive, you can delete the extended partition by following these steps:

1. From the FDISK Options menu, select option **3** and press **Enter**.

2. On the next screen, select option **2** and press **Enter** to delete an extended partition.

3. Type **Y** and press **Enter** to confirm that you want to delete an extended partition. Fdisk confirms that the partition has been deleted.

4. Press **Esc** to return to the FDISK Options Menu.

If you're working with a second hard drive, you can now delete the primary partition. (Remember, don't delete the primary partition if you're working with a single hard drive.) Follow these steps:

1. From the FDISK Options menu, select option **3** and press **Enter**.

2. On the next screen, for the first partition, select option **1** and press **Enter**.

3. Enter the volume label (or leave it blank if there is no volume label) and press **Enter**.

4. Select **Y** and press **Enter** to confirm that you want to delete the partition. Fdisk confirms that the drive or partition has been deleted.

5. Press **Esc** to return to the FDISK Options menu.

Based on what you have learned, re-create a partition using half the total disk space. If you have only a single hard drive, create an extended partition. If you have a second hard drive, create only a primary partition, thus leaving half the drive space unused. Answer these questions:

⊿ What kind of partition did you create (primary or extended)?

_____

⊿ How much space did you use for your partition?

_____

⊿ What drive letter was assigned to the logical drive on the new partition?

_____

To exit the Fdisk utility, follow these steps:

1. With the FDISK Options menu displayed, press **Esc**.

2. A message is displayed indicating that the system must be rebooted for the changes to take effect. Reboot the system while pressing **Ctrl**.

3. Select **Command Prompt Only**.

4. To confirm that the drive is set up correctly, type the drive letter followed by a colon, and then press **Enter**. The command prompt now includes the drive's letter.

## REVIEW QUESTIONS

1. When physically installing a hard drive, what steps should you take before you fix the drive in place permanently with screws?

_____

_____

2. What CMOS setup tool can you use to recognize your hard drive?

_____

_____

3. What are two types of partitions?

_____

_____

4. What must you do before you can delete an extended partition?

_____

_____

5. What must you do before you can delete a primary partition?

_____

_____

6. What would prevent your partitions from being recognized after you exit Fdisk?

_____

_____

# LAB 15.7 FORMAT A DRIVE AND TEST IT WITH SCANDISK

## OBJECTIVES

The goal of this lab is to help you prepare a partitioned drive for use. After completing this lab, you will be able to:

◢ Format a drive

◢ Use ScanDisk to test the drive's condition

## MATERIALS REQUIRED

This lab requires the following:

◢ Windows 98 operating system

◢ A floppy disk containing no essential data

## LAB PREPARATION

Before the lab begins, the instructor or lab assistant needs to do the following:

◢ Verify that Windows starts with no errors.

## ACTIVITY BACKGROUND

Before your computer can read from and write to a drive, you must format the drive. It's also a good idea to test a drive to ensure that it's in working order before you put it to use. In this lab, you format and test your newly partitioned drive. You begin by creating a bootable floppy disk and adding some important utility files to it. Next, you use the disk to boot your computer, and then format and test your drive. The utility files you include are as follows:

◢ Scandisk.exe, used to detect and repair hard drive errors

◢ Himem.sys, used to manage memory larger than 1 MB

◢ Format.com, used to format a drive

You also include the system file Config.sys, which contains configuration settings.

**ESTIMATED COMPLETION TIME: 30 minutes**

 **Activity**

Follow these steps to create a bootable disk, and then copy the necessary files to it:

1. Create a bootable floppy disk. If you need help, see Lab 15.1.

2. Copy the **Scandisk.exe** file from **C:\Windows\Command** to the bootable floppy disk.

3. Copy the **Himem.sys** file from **C:\Windows** to the bootable floppy disk. Himem.sys is necessary to run Scandisk on a hard drive.

4. Copy the **Format.com** file from **C:\Windows\Command** to the bootable floppy disk.

5. Edit or create the **Config.sys** file on your floppy disk. Add the line **Device=A:\himem.sys**. (Note that if you fail to edit the Config.sys file on your boot disk, when you attempt to start ScanDisk, you'll get a message indicating that you must add this line.)

Now that you have prepared a bootable disk, follow these steps to format your new drive:

1. Boot your system from the floppy disk.

2. At the command prompt, type **Format** $x$: ($x$ is the drive letter assigned to the partition you created in Lab 15.6) and press **Enter**.

3. The system warns you that all data will be lost and prompts you to continue. Type **Y** and press **Enter** to confirm that you want to format this drive.

4. The system begins formatting the drive. When the formatting process is completed, you're prompted to enter a volume label. To name the volume New, type **New** and press **Enter**.

5. At the command prompt, type the drive letter followed by a colon, and then press **Enter**. The newly formatted drive is now the current directory.

6. Use the **DIR** command to view the drive summary. Record the summary information:

_____

_____

_____

_____

_____

Now that the drive has been formatted, you can use ScanDisk to check the drive's condition. Follow these steps:

1. Type **A:\Scandisk** *x*: (*x* is the drive letter of the New volume) and press **Enter**.

2. ScanDisk begins checking the following:

   ◢ Media descriptor
   ◢ File allocation table
   ◢ Directory structure
   ◢ File system
   ◢ Free space

3. If ScanDisk finds any file fragments or errors, it prompts you to correct the problem. If no errors are found (or after all errors are corrected), ScanDisk displays a summary and prompts you to run a surface scan.

4. A surface scan is a lengthy process in which the disk is scanned block by block until each platter's surface condition has been checked. Type **Y** and press **Enter** to begin a surface scan.

5. ScanDisk begins the surface scan and displays a graphic of the process. While the surface scan continues examining the disk, answer the following questions. ScanDisk can take a long time to complete. For the purposes of this lab, you can cancel the surface scan after you have answered the following questions:

   ◢ How many total clusters does the disk contain?

   _____

   ◢ How many clusters does each block represent?

   _____

   ◢ What symbol indicates a bad cluster?

   _____

## REVIEW QUESTIONS

1. Write the command you use to format the D drive:

   _____

2. When is Himem.sys required to run ScanDisk?

   _____

3. By default, does ScanDisk run a surface scan automatically?

4. Why should you run a surface scan?

5. What happens when ScanDisk finds errors during its automatic check?

# Supporting Windows 9x/Me

**Labs included in this chapter:**

- **Lab 16.1:** Perform a Custom Windows 98 Installation and Write Documentation
- **Lab 16.2:** Update Windows
- **Lab 16.3:** Update Drivers with Device Manager
- **Lab 16.4:** Optimize Windows
- **Lab 16.5:** Install Windows Components
- **Lab 16.6:** Modify System Configuration Files
- **Lab 16.7:** Modify Configuration Files and Observe the Results
- **Lab 16.8:** Save, Modify, and Restore the Registry

- **Lab 16.9:** Critical Thinking: Sabotage and Repair Windows 98

# LAB 16.1 PERFORM A CUSTOM WINDOWS 98 INSTALLATION AND WRITE DOCUMENTATION

## OBJECTIVES

The goal of this lab is to compare the differences between a typical and custom installation of Windows 98. After completing this lab, you will be able to:

▲ Perform a custom installation of Windows 98

▲ Explain the differences between typical and custom installations

▲ Explain when to use each type of installation

▲ Write documentation to install Windows 98

## MATERIALS REQUIRED

This lab requires the following:

▲ Windows 98 operating system

▲ Windows 98 installation CD or installation files

## LAB PREPARATION

Before the lab begins, the instructor or lab assistant needs to do the following:

▲ Verify that Windows starts with no errors.

▲ Provide each student with access to the Windows 98 installation files, if needed.

## ACTIVITY BACKGROUND

In Chapter 4's Case Project in A+ *Guide to Software: Managing, Maintaining, and Troubleshooting* or Chapter 13's Hands-On Project in A+ *Guide to Managing and Maintaining Your PC*, you performed a typical installation of Windows 98. In this lab, you perform a custom installation and note the differences.

**ESTIMATED COMPLETION TIME: 60 minutes**

 **Activity**

1. Prepare the hard drive for a clean install of Windows 98 by formatting the hard drive.

2. Copy files from the Windows 98 installation CD (or from the files your instructor has supplied) to a folder on the hard drive named **C:\WIN98CD**.

3. Perform a custom installation of Windows 98 using the clean install option. On a separate sheet of paper, record each decision you make and values you enter during the installation and setup process.

 **Notes**

This project erases everything on your hard drive. Don't do it if you have important data on the hard drive.

4. On another sheet of paper, as you're performing the installation, write user documentation that would guide someone step by step through a custom installation of Windows 98. Make the documentation as detailed as you think is necessary for a computer user who has never installed an operating system.

5. Give your user documentation to another student to critique it. Have the student enter the following information:

Student name:

Rate the documentation for:

⊿ Clarity of each step:

_____

⊿ What to do if problems occur:

_____

⊿ How to respond to questions asked by setup:

_____

⊿ Any other helpful comments:

_____

_____

_____

## REVIEW QUESTIONS

1. Compare your notes on the custom installation you performed in this lab to the typical installation you performed in Chapter 4's Case Project in *A+ Guide to Software: Managing, Maintaining, and Troubleshooting* or in Chapter 13's Hands-on Project in *A+ Guide to Managing and Maintaining Your PC*. What are the differences between a typical and custom installation? Be specific:

_____

_____

_____

_____

2. What added control do you have when performing a custom installation compared to a typical installation?

_____

_____

3. When would you recommend a custom rather than a typical installation?

_____

_____

# *LAB 16.2 UPDATE WINDOWS*

## OBJECTIVES

The goal of this lab is to show you how to update Windows to keep current with the latest fixes and features. After completing this lab, you will be able to:

⊿ Update Windows with the Critical Update Package

⊿ Upgrade Internet Explorer to the latest version

## MATERIALS REQUIRED

This lab requires the following:

⊿ Windows 9x/Me operating system

⊿ Internet access

---

**Notes**

Some educational institutions have Internet firewall policies that prevent you from downloading Microsoft updates. If you can't download updates from your lab PC, you might have to do this lab at home.

---

## LAB PREPARATION

Before the lab begins, the instructor or lab assistant needs to do the following:

⊿ Verify that Windows starts with no errors.

⊿ Verify that Internet access is available.

## ACTIVITY BACKGROUND

Microsoft updates many of its products continuously to provide enhancements or repair newly discovered problems. You can take advantage of these improvements by installing updates on your system. Keep in mind, however, that an update is not the same as an upgrade. Operating system updates typically make fairly minor changes to the existing Windows version, whereas an upgrade installs a new version of Windows. It's important to update Microsoft products regularly to ensure that they can make use of the most recent developments in technology. Updating is especially important with products such as Internet Explorer, which interact regularly with many computers and other software. These products don't work correctly without regular updates because they lack the technology required to interact with more current systems. In this lab, you update your current version of Windows 9x/Me to its most current state and upgrade Internet Explorer to the most recent version.

**ESTIMATED COMPLETION TIME: 45 minutes**

**Activity**

Use the following steps to update Windows:

1. Open your Web browser, go to **http://windowsupdate.microsoft.com**, and click the **Product Updates** link. You might see a security warning asking if you want to install and run Windows Update Control; click **Yes** to install it. The browser displays a message stating that Microsoft is examining your system and customizing the update selection for your system. Next, a list of available updates is displayed, with the Critical Updates Package selected.

2. Scroll through the available updates and notice that they're grouped into categories and include a brief description of each update's purpose.

16

3. Click the **Download** link. Depending on your update package and how you're connected to the Internet (28.8 modem, DSL, cable modem, and so forth), downloading might take considerable time.

4. When prompted, confirm the update files you selected.

5. Click the **View Instructions** link and make a note of any special instructions not included in this lab.

6. Close the View Instructions window, and then click the **Start Download** link.

7. If the update prompts you to accept an end user license agreement (EULA), click to accept it.

8. A window opens to indicate the download progress. When the installation process is finished, you're prompted to restart your computer. Click **Yes** to restart. When your system is in text mode, the message "setup will update configuration files" is displayed. Next, you might see a message indicating that the update is complete. Windows then continues to load to the desktop.

Follow these steps to upgrade to the latest version of Internet Explorer:

1. Open Internet Explorer, and click **Help, About Internet Explorer** from the menu. Record your current version of Internet Explorer:

_____

2. Go to **www.microsoft.com/windows/ie/default.asp** and click the **Download Now** link to download the most current version of Internet Explorer.

3. You see a page describing the most current version of Internet Explorer. Verify that the correct language is selected in the Select a Language list box, and then click **Go**.

4. Directions for downloading and installing the new version of Internet Explorer appear. Read the directions carefully. Note that you can choose to download the file to your hard drive and run the downloaded file later, or you can install the update from the Microsoft server. To save time, choose to install from the Microsoft server across the Internet.

5. Click the link for downloading the latest version of Internet Explorer—for example, **Internet Explorer 6 Service Pack 1**—and then follow the installation directions.

6. If you see a warning about receiving files, click the **Always trust content from Microsoft** check box, and then continue.

7. Windows asks whether you want to save to disk or run from the current location. To indicate that you want to install the file from its current location, click **Open**.

8. The installation wizard launches to guide you through the Internet Explorer upgrade. When the EULA appears, click the **Agree** button to continue.

9. Next, click the **Install Now** option button, and then click **Next**.

10. When you're asked if you want to accept additional files to be downloaded as necessary, click **Yes**. The download process begins, and you see a window indicating its progress. When the download is finished, the installation process begins.

11. When the installation is completed, click **Finish** to restart the computer.

12. Start Internet Explorer and verify that the new version has been installed.

13. Close Internet Explorer.

## CRITICAL THINKING (ADDITIONAL 15 MINUTES)

1. What version of Windows 9x/Me are you using?

   _____

2. Explain how you found your answer for Question 1:

   _____

3. Assign a new name for My Computer on your desktop that includes your version of Windows. List the steps to perform this task:

   _____

   _____

## REVIEW QUESTIONS

1. What types of change are normally associated with an operating system update? What types of change are associated with an operating system upgrade?

   _____

   _____

2. Why does Microsoft need to examine your system before displaying update files?

   _____

3. Can you still download an update if you don't accept the EULA?

   _____

4. What is the most current version of Internet Explorer?

   _____

5. Did you choose to save your new version of Internet Explorer to the hard drive before running it? Why did you choose this option?

   _____

   _____

# LAB 16.3 UPDATE DRIVERS WITH DEVICE MANAGER

## OBJECTIVES

The goal of this lab is to explore the functions of Device Manager. After completing this lab, you will be able to:

- Select your display adapter in Device Manager
- Update the driver for your display adapter from Device Manager

## MATERIALS REQUIRED

This lab requires the following:

- Windows 9x/Me operating system
- Windows 9x/Me installation CD or installation files

## LAB PREPARATION

Before the lab begins, the instructor or lab assistant needs to do the following:

- Verify that Windows starts with no errors.
- Provide each student with access to the Windows 9x/Me installation files, if needed.

## ACTIVITY BACKGROUND

With Device Manager, you can update device drivers as well as monitor resource use. If you find a new driver for a device, you can use Device Manager to select the device and update the driver. In this lab, you use Device Manager in Windows 9x/Me to update the driver for your display adapter.

> **ESTIMATED COMPLETION TIME: 30 minutes**

**Activity**

1. Open Device Manager, and click the **+** sign next to Display adapters to expand this category, and click your display adapter to select it.

2. Open the Properties dialog box for your display adapter, and then click the **Driver** tab.

3. Click the **Driver File Details** button. Record the path to the driver files, and then back up these files to a disk or another directory so that you can backtrack, if necessary.

4. Return to the Driver tab in Device Manager, and then click **Update Driver**. The Update Driver Wizard starts.

5. In the first window, click **Next**.

6. In the second window, click **Search for**, and then click **Next**.

7. In the next window, click the **Specify a location and CD** check box (if you're using the Windows 9x/Me CD), clear any other check boxes, and then click **Next**.

8. In the next window, type the location of the Windows CD installation file, or click the **Browse** button to select a location your instructor has designated. After you have specified a location, click **OK**. Windows searches the location and reports its findings.

9. If the wizard indicates it has found a file for the device you selected in Step 1 (the display adapter), click **Next** to continue. If the wizard reports that it can't find the file, verify that you have entered the installation file's location correctly.

10. After Windows locates the drivers, it copies the driver files. If a file being copied is older than the file the system is currently using, you're prompted to confirm that you want to use the older file. Usually, newer drivers are better than older drivers. However, you might want to use an older one if you've had problems after updating drivers recently. In this case, you might want to reinstall the old driver that wasn't causing problems.

11. When the files have been copied, click **Finish** to complete the installation.

12. Restart the computer if prompted to do so.

## CRITICAL THINKING (ADDITIONAL 30 MINUTES)

Use Device Manager to identify the installed display adapter. Search the device manufacturer's Web site for new video drivers for this adapter. If you find drivers newer than the one in use, install the updated drivers.

## REVIEW QUESTIONS

1. Describe the steps to access Device Manager:

   _____

   _____

2. How can you access a device's properties in Device Manager?

   _____

   _____

3. What tab in the Properties dialog box do you use to update a driver?

   _____

4. Besides typing the path, what other option do you have to specify a driver's location?

   _____

   _____

5. Why might you want to use an older driver?

   _____

   _____

# LAB 16.4 OPTIMIZE WINDOWS

## OBJECTIVES

The goal of this lab is to give you practice using common methods for optimizing Windows performance and security. After completing this lab, you will be able to:

◢ Enable and disable a screen saver with password protection

◢ Defragment a drive

◢ Improve the performance of Internet Explorer

## MATERIALS REQUIRED

This lab requires the following:

◢ Windows 9x/Me operating system

◢ Internet Explorer version 6 or later

## LAB PREPARATION

Before the lab begins, the instructor or lab assistant needs to do the following:

◢ Verify that Windows starts with no errors.

## ACTIVITY BACKGROUND

As a result of normal use, your computer's performance deteriorates gradually—perhaps not dramatically, but enough that you notice it eventually. This performance slowdown is caused by a number of factors. For example, as files are copied, moved, and deleted, a drive becomes fragmented, a condition in which segments of a file are scattered over the disk, prolonging read and write times.

Another potential problem relates to Internet Explorer caching (or storing) Web pages each time you visit them. Normally, this feature can speed up browsing if you return to the same pages often and the pages don't change much. (For example, if you go to a site you have visited previously, half the site's Web pages might already be stored in the browser's cache; as a result, only half the Web pages have to be downloaded over the Internet, thereby increasing the speed of displaying pages.) However, when this cache, called Temporary Internet Files, becomes large, caching can actually increase the time it takes to display Web pages. The reason is that your browser searches the cache every time you enter a URL (or click a link) to determine what Web pages it should get from the Internet and what's already in the cache. Searching a large cache takes more time than simply downloading all Web pages over the Internet.

> **Notes**
>
> For more information on defragmenting a drive, refer back to Lab 13.8.

You can prevent these problems stemming from normal use by optimizing your system, using Windows tools available for just that purpose. In this lab, you have a chance to practice using some of these tools. You start, however, by using a feature designed to protect your system from mischief—a special screen saver that activates password protection if you're away from your system for a specified amount of time. This feature doesn't completely prevent someone from accessing your system, but it does make unauthorized access more difficult.

**ESTIMATED COMPLETION TIME: 30 minutes**

 **Activity**

To enable a password-protected screen saver, follow these steps:

1. Right-click the desktop, and then click **Properties** in the shortcut menu. (You can also open Control Panel and then double-click the **Display** icon.) The Display Properties dialog box opens.

2. Click the **Screen Saver** tab.

3. Click the **Screen Saver** list arrow, and then click a screen saver. You see a preview at the top of the dialog box.

4. Try out several screen savers and choose one you like.

5. Click the **Settings** button, and customize the appearance of your selected screen saver. Then click **OK** to save the settings.

6. Click the **Preview** button. The screen saver is displayed on your monitor.

7. Press any key or move the mouse to return to the Display Properties dialog box.

Now that you have selected a screen saver, you can assign a password to it:

1. Click the **Password protected** check box, and then click **Change**. The Change Password dialog box opens, where you can specify a password.

2. Type the password, retype it to confirm it, and then click **OK**. This password can be, but doesn't have to be, the same as your Windows logon password. You return to the Display Properties dialog box.

3. In the **Wait** text box, you can specify how long the system is inactive before the screen saver appears. Change this setting to **1** minute.

4. Click **Apply** to save your settings, and then click **OK**.

5. Don't move your mouse or touch the keyboard, and wait one minute. The screen saver appears.

6. Move the mouse. A password dialog box opens.

7. Type your password, and then click **OK**. The Windows desktop is displayed.

8. Reopen the Display Properties dialog box, and list the steps to disable the screen saver:

_____

_____

Follow these steps to clear temporary Internet files:

1. Open Control Panel, and then double-click the **Internet Options** applet.

2. Click the **General** tab, and in the Temporary Internet files section, click **Settings**. The Settings dialog box opens.

3. In the Amount of disk space to use section, you can specify a size for the cache. The best size depends on your surfing habits, but for a multigigabyte hard drive, it should never exceed 1% of the drive size. Over time, you should experiment with this setting until you achieve the best performance for your system.

4. Click **View Files**. The Temporary Internet Files window opens, and you can see a list of files in the cache.

5. Drag this window to the side but don't close it. The cache might contain many types of files. Examine the cache and list four file types found there:

_____

_____

6. Click **OK**. The Settings dialog box closes and you return to the Internet Properties dialog box.

7. To delete most files in the cache, click **Delete Files**. Click **OK** to confirm deletion.

8. Click the Temporary Internet Files window, and press F5 to refresh the display. The list of files has been cleared except those with names similar to dave@abcnews.go(1).txt. These files, called "cookies," are created by Web servers when you visit a site. They are often used in a good way to help customize content to match your preferences when you revisit a page. However, cookies can also be used to invade your privacy and send private information secretly from your computer to another computer. Deleting cookies periodically is a good way to make sure your personal information stays private.

9. Click **Delete Cookies** in the Temporary Internet files section of the Internet Properties dialog box.

10. Again, click the Temporary Internet Files window, and press **F5** to refresh. There should be no files visible in your cache.

11. Click **OK** to close the Internet Properties dialog box and to close the window displaying the cache. Close Control Panel.

## REVIEW QUESTIONS

1. Why might a drive need defragmenting?

   _____

   _____

2. Which Control Panel applet do you use to enable password protection for a screen saver?

   _____

3. What is the name of the Internet Explorer cache containing content from Web sites you have viewed?

   _____

4. What factors can determine the size of your Internet cache?

   _____

   _____

# *LAB 16.5 INSTALL WINDOWS COMPONENTS*

## OBJECTIVES

The goal of this lab is to learn how to add an optional component to Windows. After completing this lab, you will be able to:

▲ Use the Add/Remove Programs applet

▲ Install desktop wallpaper

▲ Select a wallpaper for your desktop

## MATERIALS REQUIRED

This lab requires the following:

▲ Windows 98 operating system

▲ Windows 98 installation CD or installation files

## LAB PREPARATION

Before the lab begins, the instructor or lab assistant needs to do the following:

▲ Verify that Windows starts with no errors.

▲ Provide each student with access to the Windows 98 installation files, if needed.

## ACTIVITY BACKGROUND

Windows includes many optional features that can be installed when you install the operating system or at some later time. In this lab, you install optional desktop wallpapers on a computer that already has Windows 98 installed. You need the files stored on the Windows 98 installation CD. If you don't have this CD available, ask your instructor for the network path to these files. What is that path?

---

**ESTIMATED COMPLETION TIME: 30 minutes**

### Activity

1. Open Control Panel, and double-click the **Add/Remove Programs** icon.

2. Click the **Windows Setup** tab. In the Components section, you should see several categories of Windows components listed.

3. Click **Accessories,** and then click the **Details** button. The Accessories dialog box opens, displaying Windows components in the Accessories category.

4. Click to select the **Desktop Wallpaper** check box, and then click **OK** to close the dialog box.

5. In the Add/Remove Programs Properties dialog box, click **Apply**.

6. When prompted, click **OK**, type the path to the Windows 98 installation files, and then click **OK** again.

7. Windows installs the files containing the new desktop wallpaper. When the installation is finished, click **OK** to exit the Add/Remove Programs applet.

8. In Control Panel, double-click the **Display** icon to open the Display Properties dialog box.

9. Click the **Background** tab, and then browse through the available wallpapers. Experiment with the Tile, Center, and Stretch options in the drop-down list box, and observe the preview of your wallpaper selections.

10. Select a background combination you like, click **Apply**, and then click **OK** to close the Display Properties dialog box.

11. Close any other open windows, and observe your new desktop wallpaper.

12. Windows 98 includes four games: FreeCell, Hearts, Solitaire, and Minesweeper. Using what you have learned in this lab, list the steps to install these games as a Windows Accessories component:

_____

_____

_____

_____

## REVIEW QUESTIONS

1. What collection of files is necessary to install a new Windows component?

_____

2. Which Control Panel applet is used to install new Windows components?

_____

3. What category of components is desktop wallpaper part of?

_____

4. Which Control Panel applet did you use to select a wallpaper for your system?

_____

5. Is it necessary to apply the display properties before you see what a wallpaper will look like?

_____

## *LAB 16.6 MODIFY SYSTEM CONFIGURATION FILES*

### OBJECTIVES

The goal of this lab is to familiarize you with working with Windows configuration files. After completing this lab, you will be able to:

◢ Use the System Configuration Editor to modify configuration files

◢ Edit Msdos.sys

### MATERIALS REQUIRED

This lab requires the following:

◢ Windows 9x/Me operating system

◢ Location of the DOS utility Edit.com (provided by your instructor)

### LAB PREPARATION

Before the lab begins, the instructor or lab assistant needs to do the following:

◢ Verify that Windows starts with no errors.

### ACTIVITY BACKGROUND

Windows uses several configuration files when booting. In previous labs, you worked with two of these files, Autoexec.bat and Config.sys. In this lab, you work with the System Configuration Editor utility to examine and adjust several other configuration files. You also edit one configuration file, Msdos.sys, from the command line.

**ESTIMATED COMPLETION TIME: 30 minutes**

 **Activity**

Follow these steps to edit Msdos.sys with the text-editing utility Edit.com:

1. Open a command prompt window.

2. To remove the hidden, system, and read-only status from the Msdos.sys file, type **attrib -h -s -r C:\msdos.sys** and press **Enter**.

3. Type **edit C:\msdos.sys** and press **Enter**. The Msdos.sys configuration file opens in the command prompt window. Msdos.sys can be modified to control where Windows files are located and how Windows boots. The Paths section indicates on what drive and in which directory Windows system files can be found. The Options section controls how Window boots.

4. Notice the remarks (comment lines), which begin with a semicolon, indicating that extra characters have been added to ensure that Msdos.sys is larger than 1024 bytes.

5. Locate the line **Boot GUI=1**. You can think of the 1 as meaning yes and the 0 as meaning no. Therefore, this line tells the system to load a graphical user interface (GUI). Change the 1 to a 0 so that it reads **Boot GUI=0**. (Be sure to type a zero, not an uppercase "O.") What are you instructing the system to do the next time it boots?

_____

_____

6. Press and release **Alt**. This key activates the menu options in the edit utility you're using from the command prompt window.

7. Press **F**, which activates the File menu.

8. Press **S**. The file is saved.

9. Press and release **Alt** again, press **F** to access the File menu, and then press **X** to exit the edit utility.

10. Type **exit** and press **Enter**. The command prompt window closes.

11. Restart Windows, and describe what happens. Was your prediction in Step 5 accurate?

_____

_____

Next, you make another change to the Msdos.sys file and observe the change. Follow these steps:

1. Open a command prompt window, type **edit msdos.sys**, and press **Enter**.

2. Change the BootGUI entry to **=1**.

3. Save your changes, exit, close the command prompt window, and reboot, observing the boot process. What changed?

_____

Next, you make a third change to the Msdos.sys file and observe the change. Follow these steps:

1. Open the **msdos.sys** file for editing.

2. Place the cursor under the "D" in the Doublebuffer line and press **Enter**.

3. Press the up arrow to move the cursor to the new blank line and type **Logo=0** . (Again, be sure to type a zero, not an uppercase "O.") What do you think you just instructed the system to do?

_____

4. Save your changes, exit, close the command prompt window, and reboot, observing the boot process. What changed?

_____

_____

Next, you practice working with files by using the System Configuration Editor (Sysedit) utility, a Windows tool for editing system files. You start by creating a new user called Test1 on your system. Follow these steps:

1. Restart your PC and log on as **Test1**, entering a password. Windows creates a new user, Test1, making entries in the \Windows\System.ini file and creating a new password file in the Windows folder named Test1.pwl.

2. Log off as **Test1**, and then log back on as another authorized user on the computer (using your own name or whatever logon you were using on the computer previously).

3. Next, you use the System Configuration Editor utility to examine the Windows\System.ini file. Click **Start, Run**, type **sysedit**, and then click **OK**.

4. The System Configuration Editor utility opens, displaying five files. List these files here:

   _____

   _____

   _____

5. Click the title bar of the window showing the C:\Windows\System.ini file, bringing it to the front, and then scroll down to the Password Lists section, which has an entry for each user account on this computer.

6. Using the Delete or Backspace key, delete the entry for Test1. Do not delete anything else.

7. To save the changes to System.ini, with the Windows\System.ini window selected, click **File, Save** from the menu. Your changes are saved.

8. To examine the Win.ini file, which is also opened by Sysedit, click the **Windows\Win.ini file** window.

9. Click **Search, Find** from the menu.

10. In the Find dialog box, type **colors**, and then click **Next**.

11. The Windows\Win.ini file displays the [colors] section, with the word "colors" highlighted. After you specify a search item in the Find dialog box, you can use the F3 key to find the next instance of the search text.

12. Press **F3** to jump to the next instance of the word "colors." Was there another instance? What message do you see?

   _____

   _____

13. Exit the System Configuration Editor utility.

14. Log off and try to log back on as **Test1**.

15. Did you have to enter a password?

   _____

16. Did Test1 show up in the users list?

   _____

## REVIEW QUESTIONS

1. What was the purpose of the Test1 entry in System.ini?

   _____

2. What utility can you use to modify the Msdos.sys file?

   _____

3. What is the minimum size of Msdos.sys?

   _____

4. What are the five configuration files you can edit automatically with the System Configuration Editor?

   _____

   _____

5. Of the five files you listed in Question 4, which two are used by MS-DOS and Windows in real mode?

   _____

# LAB 16.7 MODIFY CONFIGURATION FILES AND OBSERVE THE RESULTS

## OBJECTIVES

The goal of this lab is to learn to use configuration files that affect the MS-DOS command-line environment. Specifically, you load drivers that make it possible to use a mouse in the command-line environment. You also learn to use utilities from the command line. After completing this lab, you will be able to:

- Create a bootable floppy disk
- Copy files to a floppy disk
- Modify configuration files

## MATERIALS REQUIRED

This lab requires the following:

- Windows 9x/Me operating system
- Windows 9x/Me installation CD or installation files
- The file to load a 16-bit generic mouse driver, such as Mouse.com or Mouse.sys (provided by your instructor)
- Location of the Windows and DOS utilities Msd.exe and Edit.com (provided by your instructor)
- A blank floppy disk

## LAB PREPARATION

Before the lab begins, the instructor or lab assistant needs to do the following:

◢ Verify that Windows starts with no errors.

◢ Gather the required system files, and make them available to students on CD, a file server, or other storage media.

## ACTIVITY BACKGROUND

In this lab, you boot to a command prompt by using a bootable floppy disk. As you'll see, a command prompt environment doesn't normally allow you to use the mouse. After the PC is booted, you use the Microsoft Diagnostics (MSD) utility, a program that displays information about the hardware environment, to verify that the PC doesn't provide mouse support. Then you add mouse support by adding a configuration file to your system that loads a mouse driver. The mouse driver file usually comes on a floppy disk bundled with the mouse, but your instructor might provide a different file location. Finally, you reboot the PC, run MSD again, and verify that mouse support has indeed been enabled.

> **ESTIMATED COMPLETION TIME: 30 minutes**

 **Activity**

Follow these steps on a Windows 9x/Me PC to create a bootable floppy disk from the command line and copy a file to the disk:

1. Click **Start, Run**. Type **command** and press **Enter** to open an MS-DOS command prompt window.

2. Insert a blank floppy disk.

3. Type **format A: /S** and press **Enter**.

4. The following prompt appears: "Insert new diskette for drive A: and press Enter when ready." Press **Enter** to start formatting the disk.

5. Watch as the floppy disk is formatted and system files are transferred to the floppy disk.

6. When prompted, type a volume name, if you like, and press **Enter** (or simply press **Enter** to bypass this step entirely).

7. When asked whether you want to format another disk, type **N** and press **Enter**. (If your disk was already formatted, you could have used the SYS A: command to copy system files to the disk.)

Now that you have created a boot disk, follow these steps to copy some configuration files to it:

1. Insert the Windows 9x/Me installation CD in the CD-ROM drive, type **copy D:\tools\oldmsdos\msd.exe A:\**, and then press **Enter**. (If you don't have access to the Windows CD, your instructor might give you another location for the file. If your CD-ROM drive has a drive letter other than D, substitute that letter in the command.)

2. Repeat Step 1 for the mouse driver file and the text editor, Edit.com, in the location your instructor specifies. The mouse driver file is named Mouse.com, Mouse.sys, or a similar name.

3. Close the command prompt window and shut down the system.

At this stage, the boot disk contains the necessary configuration files. Next, you boot the PC using the boot disk and verify that the mouse isn't available:

1. With the floppy disk still in the drive, boot the system. An A:\> prompt is displayed on your screen.

2. To use the Microsoft Diagnostics utility, type **msd.exe** and then press **Enter**.

3. Move the mouse around. Does it work as you would expect?

_____

4. Press **F3** to exit MSD.

Next, you use the Edit utility to create and edit an Autoexec.bat file:

1. At the A:\> prompt, type **edit Autoexec.bat**. The Edit window opens and the Autoexec.bat file is created.

2. Enter the command to load the mouse driver, using the driver's file name, such as Mouse.com.

3. To exit the editor and save your changes, press **Alt**, and use the arrow keys to select **Exit** from the Exit menu.

4. When asked whether you want to save your changes to the file, select **Yes**.

Next, you test your floppy disk to see whether it provides mouse support:

1. With the boot disk still in the floppy drive, reboot.

2. Run the MSD program. Did you observe any change when you moved the mouse?

_____

3. Click **File, Exit** from the menu to close MSD. Remove the floppy disk and reboot the PC.

## REVIEW QUESTIONS

1. When formatting a disk, what command can you use to make the floppy disk a boot disk?

_____

2. If you have a formatted floppy disk, what other command can you use to transfer system files to the floppy disk?

_____

3. Which configuration file did you modify to add automatic support for the mouse?

_____

4. Did you notice a difference in the boot process after you changed a configuration file?

_____

# LAB 16.8 SAVE, MODIFY, AND RESTORE THE REGISTRY

## OBJECTIVES

The goal of this lab is to learn how to save, modify, and restore the Windows 98 Registry. After completing this lab, you will be able to:

◢ Back up and modify the Registry

◢ Observe the effects of a damaged Registry

◢ Restore the Registry

## MATERIALS REQUIRED

This lab requires the following:

◢ Windows 98 operating system

## LAB PREPARATION

Before the lab begins, the instructor or lab assistant needs to do the following:

◢ Verify that Windows starts with no errors.

## ACTIVITY BACKGROUND

The Registry is a database of configuration information stored in two files: System.dat and User.dat. Each time Windows boots, it rebuilds the Registry from the configuration files and stores it in RAM. When you need to modify the behavior of Windows, you should consider editing the Registry as a last resort. Errors in the Registry can make your system inoperable, and there's no way for Windows to inform you that you have made a mistake. For this reason, many people are afraid to work with the Registry. If you follow the rule of backing up the Registry before you make any change, however, you can feel confident that even if you make a mistake, you can restore the Registry to its original condition. In this lab, you back up, change, and restore the Registry.

**ESTIMATED COMPLETION TIME: 45 minutes**

 **Activity**

Follow these directions to back up the Registry:

1. Click **Start, Run,** type **scanreg,** and then click **OK.**

2. The Windows Registry Checker utility opens. (You might see an MS-DOS prompt briefly and a message stating that the Registry has already been backed up. If so, it's because once a day, by default, the Registry is backed up the first time Windows starts successfully.)

3. Click **Yes** to back up the Registry again.

4. When the backup is completed, click **OK** to close the Windows Registry Checker. By default, Windows stores the five most recent copies of the Registry in the Windows\Backup folder. Backups are compressed in cabinet files, which have a .cab file extension.

5. Open Windows Explorer, click the **Windows\Sysbackup** folder, and determine the name of the backup you just created by checking the date and time the file was created. Record the name, date, and time of this file:

_____

As you know, you can use tools included with Windows to modify many of its features. Sometimes, however, the only way to make a modification is to edit the Registry. In these steps, you see examples of a feature you can modify by using a Windows shortcut menu and one you can modify only through the Registry. Follow these steps:

1. Right-click the **My Computer** icon on your desktop. Note that the shortcut menu gives you the option of renaming this icon.

2. Right-click the **Recycle Bin** icon. This shortcut menu doesn't give you the option of renaming. To rename it, you would have to install and use a Microsoft utility, TweekUI, that allows you to make special changes to Windows. Alternatively, you can change the Recycle Bin's name through the Registry.

3. Click **Start, Run**, type **regedit**, and then click **OK**. The Registry Editor opens, displaying the system's Registry hierarchy in the left pane and any entries for the selected Registry item in the right pane.

The Registry is large, and searching through it manually (by scrolling through all the entries) can be tedious even if you have a good idea of where to look. To save time, use the Registry Editor's search feature to find the section governing the Recycle Bin:

1. To make sure you're searching the entire Registry, if necessary, click to collapse **Registry Keys**, and then click **Edit, Find** from the menu.

2. Type **Recycle Bin** in the Search text box. You can narrow your search by limiting which items to search. What four ways can you further refine your search?

_____

_____

3. Click **Find Next** to begin searching the Registry. What is the first instance of Recycle Bin shown in the right pane?

4. Press **F3** to find the next instance. At this point, the right pane of your Registry Editor should display the two items shown in Figure 16-1.

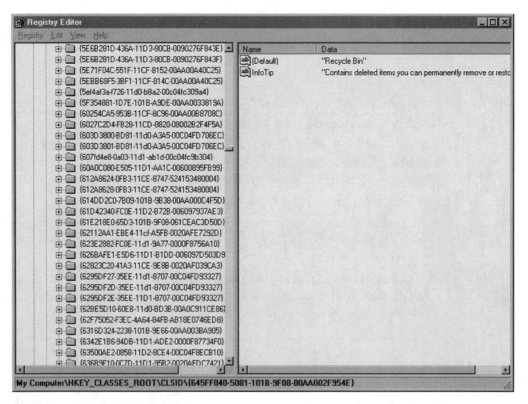

**Figure 16-1** The Windows Registry

5. Double-click the **Default** entry. The Edit String dialog box opens.

6. In the Value data text box, replace "Recycle Bin" with **Trash**, and then click **OK**.

7. Notice that "Trash" has replaced "Recycle Bin" in the right pane.

Next, you edit the Info Tip for the Recycle Bin. (The Info Tip is the pop-up text displayed when your mouse pointer hovers over a Windows item.)

1. Double-click the **Info Tip** entry, type **This used to be named Recycle Bin,** and then click **OK**. Note the change in the right pane.

2. Next, to close the Registry Editor, click **Registry, Exit** from the menu. You weren't prompted to save your changes to the Registry because they were saved the instant you made them. This is why editing the Registry is so unforgiving: There are no safeguards. You can't undo your work by choosing to exit without saving changes, as you can, for instance, in Microsoft Word.

3. Right-click the desktop, and then click **Refresh** in the shortcut menu. Note that the Recycle Bin icon is now named Trash.

4. Move the mouse pointer over the Trash icon. The new Info Tip appears.

Finally, you need to undo your changes to the Recycle Bin. Follow these steps to use the Registry Checker to restore the Registry's previous version:

1. Restart Windows. Hold down the **Ctrl** key during the boot process to activate the Startup Menu.

2. In the Startup Menu, select **Command Prompt Only**. A command prompt appears.

3. Type **scanreg** and then press **Enter**. The Microsoft Registry Checker starts.

4. Press **Enter** to start a scan that checks for a corrupted Registry. The Microsoft Registry Checker doesn't usually find errors if the Registry has been modified correctly with the Registry Editor. Assuming you performed the steps in this lab correctly, the Microsoft Registry Checker won't find any errors. However, if it detects any corruption in the Registry, it offers to repair the problem.

5. After the scan is completed, select **View Backups** and use your knowledge about the Registry to restore the most current saved state.

## REVIEW QUESTIONS

1. How often does Windows save the Registry automatically?

_____

2. Where are Registry backups usually stored?

_____

3. What type of safeguards does the Registry Editor have to keep you from making mistakes?

_____

4. What files constitute the Registry? What type of file are they saved as during backup?

_____

_____

5. In this lab, how did you check to make sure your Registry was restored?

_____

# LAB 16.9 CRITICAL THINKING: SABOTAGE AND REPAIR WINDOWS 98

## OBJECTIVES

The goal of this lab is to give you practice in troubleshooting Windows 98 by repairing a sabotaged system.

## MATERIALS REQUIRED

This lab requires the following:

◢ Windows 98 operating system installed on a PC designated for sabotage

◢ Windows 98 installation CD or installation files

◢ A workgroup of 2 to 4 students

## LAB PREPARATION

Before the lab begins, the instructor or lab assistant needs to do the following:

◢ Verify that Windows starts with no errors.

◢ Provide each student with access to the Windows 98 installation files, if needed.

## ACTIVITY BACKGROUND

You have learned about several tools and methods you can use to recover Windows 98 when it fails. This lab gives you the opportunity to use these skills in a troubleshooting situation. Your group works with another group to sabotage a system and then recover the failed system.

> ### ESTIMATED COMPLETION TIME: 60 minutes

 **Activity**

1. If the hard drive contains important data, back it up to another medium. Is there anything else you should back up before another group sabotages the system? Note that item here, and then back it up:

   _____

2. Trade systems with another group and sabotage the other group's system while it sabotages your system. Do one thing that will cause the system to fail to boot or to generate errors after booting. The following list offers some suggestions. You can choose one of these options, or do something else. Do *not*, however, alter the hardware.

   ◢ Rename a system file (in the root directory) that's required to boot the system (for example, Io.sys or Msdos.sys), or move one of these files to a different directory. Do *not* delete any system files.

   ◢ Using the Registry Editor, delete several important keys (or values) in the Registry.

   ◢ Rename important system files in the \Windows directory, or move one of these files to another directory.

   ◢ Put a corrupted program file in the folder that will cause the program to launch automatically at startup. Record the name of that folder here:

   _____

   ◢ Use display settings that aren't readable, such as black text on a black background.

3. What did you do to sabotage the system?

_____

_____

_____

4. Return to your system and troubleshoot it.

5. Describe the problem as a user would describe it to you if you were working at a help desk:

_____

_____

6. What is your first guess as to the source of the problem?

_____

7. List the steps you took in the troubleshooting process:

_____

_____

_____

_____

_____

8. What did you do that finally solved the problem and returned the system to good working order?

_____

_____

_____

## REVIEW QUESTIONS

1. Now that you have been through this troubleshooting experience, what would you do differently the next time you encounter the same symptoms?

_____

_____

2. What Windows utilities did you use or could you have used to solve the problem?

_____

_____

3. What third-party software utility might have been useful in solving this problem?

_____

_____

4. In a real-life situation, what might actually cause this problem to happen? List three possible causes:

_____

_____

_____

# CHAPTER 17

# PCs on a Network

**Labs included in this chapter:**

- **Lab 17.1:** Install and Test an Ethernet NIC
- **Lab 17.2:** Inspect Cables
- **Lab 17.3:** Compare Options for a Home LAN
- **Lab 17.4:** Troubleshoot with TCP/IP Utilities
- **Lab 17.5:** Practice Solving Network Connectivity Problems
- **Lab 17.6:** Share Resources on a Network
- **Lab 17.7:** Use NetBEUI Instead of TCP/IP
- **Lab 17.8:** Use a Parallel Port for a Direct Cable Connection
- **Lab 17.9:** Configure and Use Remote Access Service

# LAB 17.1 INSTALL AND TEST AN ETHERNET NIC

## OBJECTIVES

The goal of this lab is to install and configure an Ethernet network interface card (NIC). After completing this lab, you will be able to:

⬦ Remove a NIC (and network protocols, if necessary)

⬦ Install a NIC (and network protocols, if necessary)

⬦ Perform a loopback test

## MATERIALS REQUIRED

This lab requires the following:

⬦ Windows 2000/XP operating system or Windows 98 with no modem or dial-up networking installed

⬦ A NIC and drivers

⬦ Windows installation CD or installation files

⬦ A PC toolkit with antistatic ground strap

⬦ A crossover cable

⬦ A workgroup partner

## LAB PREPARATION

Before the lab begins, the instructor or lab assistant needs to do the following:

⬦ Verify that Windows starts with no errors.

⬦ Provide each student with access to the Windows installation files, if needed.

## ACTIVITY BACKGROUND

A computer connects to a wired network through a network interface card (NIC). In this lab, you install a NIC, configure necessary network settings, and verify that the NIC is functioning correctly. Working with a partner, you create a simple network of two PCs. By default, Windows 98 doesn't install network protocols needed to support a network, but Windows 2000/XP has these components installed, which makes installing a NIC much simpler in these operating systems.

**ESTIMATED COMPLETION TIME: 30 minutes**

**Activity**

In Windows 2000/XP, follow these steps to install and configure your NIC:

1. Physically install your NIC as you would other expansion cards. If you need a refresher on the process, review Lab 10.1.

2. Boot the system. The Found New Hardware Wizard detects the NIC and begins the driver installation process. In some cases, Windows XP doesn't allow using non-Microsoft drivers. If this option is available, however, click **Have Disk** and provide the manufacturer's drivers for the NIC. Reboot if prompted to do so.

Next, you give the computer an IP address, a computer name, and a workgroup name as shown in the following chart. Write your name and your partner's name in the chart, and then follow these steps to assign an IP address to the computer:

**Notes**

If you want to force Windows XP to use manufacturers' drivers, run the setup program on the CD or floppy disk that comes bundled with the NIC *before* you physically install the NIC. After you boot with the new card installed, Windows then finds the already installed manufacturers' drivers and uses them.

| Your names: | | |
|---|---|---|
| IP address: | 192.168.1.1 | 192.168.1.2 |
| Computer name: | Lab 1 | Lab 2 |
| Workgroup name: | NIC Lab | NIC Lab |

1. Right-click **My Network Places** and click **Properties** in the shortcut menu. The Network Connections window appears.

2. Right-click **Local Area Connection** and click **Properties** in the shortcut menu. The Local Area Connection Properties dialog box opens.

3. In the list of connection items, click **Internet Protocol (TCP/IP)**, and then click the **Properties** button. The Internet Protocol (TCP/IP) Properties dialog box opens. Click **Use the following IP address** and enter your IP address (192.168.1.1 or 192.168.1.2) and subnet mask (255.255.255.0). Click **OK** twice to close all open windows.

Next, you assign a computer name and workgroup name to your computer:

1. Right-click **My Computer** and click **Properties** in the shortcut menu. The System Properties dialog box opens.

2. In Windows XP, click the **Computer Name** tab, and then click the **Change** button. The Computer Name Changes dialog box opens (see Figure 17-1). In Windows 2000, click the **Network Identification** tab, and then click the **Properties** button. The Identification Changes dialog box opens.

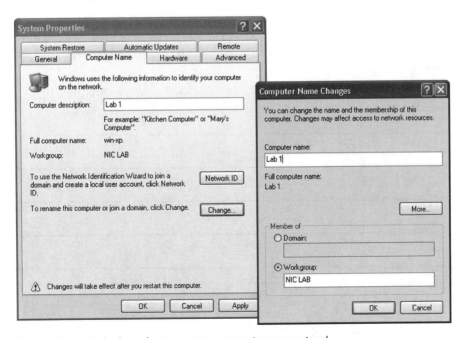

**Figure 17-1** Assigning a host name to a computer on a network

3. Enter the computer name (**Lab 1** in the example shown in Figure 17-1). Each computer name must be unique within a workgroup or domain.

4. Click **Workgroup** and enter the name of the workgroup (**NIC Lab** in this example).

5. Click **OK** twice to close all open windows. Restart your computer when prompted for changes to take effect.

For Windows 98, if your computer doesn't already have a NIC installed, skip to the next set of steps. Otherwise, follow these steps on your Windows 98 computer to remove the computer's networking components:

1. Right-click the **Network Neighborhood** icon and click **Properties** in the shortcut menu. The Network Properties dialog box opens.

2. If necessary, click the **Configuration** tab, click **Client for Microsoft Networks**, and then click **Properties**. The Client for Microsoft Networks Properties dialog box opens.

3. In the General section, make sure the **Log on to Windows NT domain** check box is not selected, and then click **OK** to close the Client for Microsoft Networks Properties dialog box. Close the Network Properties dialog box and reboot when prompted.

4. After the computer has rebooted, open the Network Properties dialog box again. If necessary, click the **Configuration** tab, click your NIC (indicated by an adapter symbol), and then click **Remove**. The NIC and any protocol associated with it are uninstalled; Client for Microsoft Networks is also uninstalled.

5. Click **OK** to close the Network Properties dialog box. You might see a message stating that the network is incomplete.

6. Click **Yes** to continue. When you're prompted to restart your computer, click **No**.

7. Shut down your computer, but do not reboot.

8. Remove your computer's NIC, or if your instructor directs you to do so, remove the network cable but leave the NIC in place.

In Windows 98, follow these steps to install and configure your NIC:

1. If your NIC isn't installed, physically install it as you would other expansion cards. If you need a refresher on the process, review Lab 10.1.

2. Boot the system. The Add New Hardware Wizard detects the NIC and begins the driver installation process. Step through the Add New Hardware Wizard as in previous labs. Reboot when prompted.

3. The Network Neighborhood icon is displayed on the desktop again. Right-click the **Network Neighborhood** icon and then click **Properties**. The Network Properties dialog box opens.

4. Click the **Configuration** tab, examine the installed network components that are listed, and record them here:

_____

_____

_____

_____

_____

5. Verify that your NIC is in the list and that TCP/IP is installed and bound to the NIC, as indicated by an item that includes TCP/IP with an arrow that points to the name of your NIC. Click this item and then click **Properties**. The TCP/IP dialog box opens.

6. Click the **IP Address** tab, if necessary, and then click the **Specify an IP Address** option button.

7. Next, you configure the network connection. You and your partner need an IP address, a computer name, and a workgroup name, which are listed in the following chart. Write your name and your partner's name in the chart.

| Your names: | | |
| --- | --- | --- |
| IP address: | 192.168.1.1 | 192.168.1.2 |
| Computer name: | Lab 1 | Lab 2 |
| Workgroup name: | NIC Lab | NIC Lab |

8. In the IP Address text box of the TCP/IP Properties dialog box, type **192.168.1.1** or **192.168.1.2**. (Your lab partner should use one and you the other.) In the Subnet Mask text box, type **255.255.255.0**. (Both you and your partner should enter this information.) Note that it's possible for a server (called a DHCP server) to assign these two values that enable TCP/IP communications, but in this lab, you don't assume this server is available.

9. Click **OK** to close the TCP/IP dialog box.

10. To identify each computer on the network, click the **Identification** tab in the Network Properties dialog box. Replace the computer name in the Computer Name text box with **Lab 1** or **Lab 2**. (Again, your partner should use one of these names while you use the other.) In the Workgroup text box, type **NIC Lab**. Although it's not necessary, you can type a description for your computer if you want. When you're browsing the network, this description is displayed in the computer's Properties dialog box (under the Comment heading). This description can help users determine what resources might be available on the computer. What description, if any, did you enter?

_____

11. Click **OK** to close the Network Properties dialog box and save your settings. Supply the Windows 98 CD or the location of the installation files, if prompted. If you see a message stating that a file being copied is older than the current file, click **Yes** to keep the current file. (This is usually the best practice, unless you suspect the newer file has been the source of an existing problem.)

12. Click **Yes** when prompted to restart the computer.

In Windows 2000/XP or Windows 98, follow these steps to test your NIC:

1. Open a command prompt window.

2. Type **ping 127.0.0.1** and press **Enter**. Ping is a TCP/IP utility used to test whether an address can be reached and is able to respond. Any 127.*x.x.x* address is a loopback address, which is essentially a stand-in for your computer's own address. When you use a loopback address in a ping test, the Ping utility sends packets to your local computer's NIC, thereby allowing you to verify that your computer's NIC has a functioning TCP/IP connection. If your computer is connected to a printer, take a screen shot of the results of the loopback Ping command and print it.

3. Examine the results of the loopback test and answer these questions:

◢ How many bytes were sent in each packet?

_____

◢ How many packets were sent with one Ping command?

_____

◢ How many responses were received from one Ping command?

_____

◢ Were any packets lost?

_____

In Windows 2000/XP, use the Ipconfig utility to verify your IP configuration. Do the following to check your NIC's configuration:

1. At the command prompt, type **ipconfig /all |more** and press **Enter**. An IP configuration report is displayed one screen at a time. If necessary, press **Enter** to see each new line. Answer the following:

◢ Is the configuration the same information you configured originally?

_____

◢ What is the physical address (MAC address) of your NIC?

_____

In Windows 98, use the Winipcfg utility to verify your IP configuration. Do the following to check your NIC's configuration:

1. At the command prompt, type **winipcfg** and press **Enter**.

2. Click your NIC in the drop-down list and examine your IP configuration. Answer the following:

◢ Is the configuration the same information you configured originally?

_____

◢ What is the MAC address of your NIC?

_____

In Windows 2000/XP or Windows 98, another way to test an NIC is to use its assigned IP address in a ping test:

1. Use the Ping command with the IP address you assigned to your computer. The results should be similar or identical to the loopback test results, except for the address listed in the Ping results.

2. Now ping your partner's IP address. Describe what happened to the request:

_____

_____

_____

Next, you connect the two PCs with the crossover cable, and then test your network:

1. Close the command prompt window, and shut down both computers.

2. Connect one end of the crossover cable to the NIC on your partner's computer and the other end to the NIC on your computer.

3. Reboot the computers, and open a command prompt window.

4. Ping your partner's IP address. If your computer is connected to a printer, take and print a screen shot of the results. How do these results differ from your earlier attempt to ping your partner's IP address?

_____

_____

## REVIEW QUESTIONS

1. Where do you configure network adapters and protocols?

_____

2. What two text boxes are used to identify a computer on a workgroup?

_____

_____

3. Other than the IP address, what information is required for TCP/IP communication?

_____

4. What are two ways to use the Ping utility to test a local computer's NIC?

_____

_____

5. What conclusion should you draw from a loopback test that reports dropped packets or an unreachable host?

_____

_____

## LAB 17.2 INSPECT CABLES

### OBJECTIVES

The goal of this lab is to help you visually inspect a set of cables and use a multimeter to test them. After completing this lab, you will be able to:

▲ Identify two Cat 5 wiring systems

▲ Test cables with a multimeter

▲ Draw pin-outs for cable connectors

◢ Determine whether a cable is a patch cable (also known as a straight-through cable) or a crossover cable

◢ Visually inspect cables and connectors

## MATERIALS REQUIRED

This lab requires the following:

◢ A variety of cables, including a patch cable and a crossover cable

◢ A multimeter

◢ Internet access

## LAB PREPARATION

Before the lab begins, the instructor or lab assistant needs to do the following:

◢ Verify that Internet access is available.

## ACTIVITY BACKGROUND

After you narrow down a problem to physical connectivity, you must inspect the connections to verify that they aren't loose. If you eliminate that possibility, you can assume the cable is the problem. In this lab, you physically inspect cables and the connector, and then test the cable for continuity and pin-outs using a multimeter.

**ESTIMATED COMPLETION TIME: 45 minutes**

 **Activity**

1. Open your browser, and go to **www.atcomservices.com/highlights/cat5notes.htm**. You can also search the Internet for information about a patch cable diagram, a crossover cable diagram, and a Cat 5 wiring diagram. List the two standards for Cat 5 wiring schemes. What Web site did you use?

2. For both wiring schemes, print a wiring diagram for a patch cable and a crossover cable. Follow these steps to visually inspect cables:

   1. Examine the length of the cable for obvious damage, such as a cut or abrasion in the outer sleeve with further damage to the twisted pairs inside. A completely cut strand is an obvious problem, but the conductor inside the cable might be broken even if the insulator is intact. Any visible copper is an indication you need a new cable.

   2. Inspect the RJ-45 connectors. In particular, look for exposed twisted pairs between the clear plastic connector and the cable sleeve. This indicates that the cable was assembled improperly or excessive force was used when pulling on the cable. The cable sleeve should be crimped inside the RJ-45 connector. Sometimes you can identify a nonconforming wiring scheme by noting the color of the insulation through the clear connector, but you should check the cable with a multimeter to verify its condition.

   3. Next, verify that the retaining clip on the connector is present. When an assembled cable is pulled, this clip often snags on carpet or other cables and breaks off. This results in a connector that's likely to become loose or fall out of the jack. Worse still, this connection might be intermittent. Some cables have hooded guards to prevent the clip from snagging when pulled, but these guards can cause problems when seating the connector in the jack if the guard has slid too far toward the end of the cable.

**4.** Test your cables with a multimeter, and fill in Table 17-1.

| | End A | | End B | | Questions About the Cable |
|---|---|---|---|---|---|
| Pin # | Insulator color | Pin tied to pin at End B | Insulator color | Pin tied to pin at End A | Is the cable good or bad? |
| 1 | | | | | |
| 2 | | | | | Wired with what scheme? |
| 3 | | | | | |
| 4 | | | | | |
| 5 | | | | | Is the cable a |
| 6 | | | | | crossover or |
| 7 | | | | | patch cable? |
| 8 | | | | | |
| Pin # | Insulator color | Pin tied to pin at End B | Insulator color | Pin tied to pin at End A | Is the cable good or bad? |
| 1 | | | | | |
| 2 | | | | | Wired with what scheme? |
| 3 | | | | | |
| 4 | | | | | |
| 5 | | | | | Is the cable a |
| 6 | | | | | crossover or |
| 7 | | | | | patch cable? |
| 8 | | | | | |
| Pin # | Insulator color | Pin tied to pin at End B | Insulator color | Pin tied to pin at End A | Is the cable good or bad? |
| 1 | | | | | |
| 2 | | | | | Wired with what scheme? |
| 3 | | | | | |
| 4 | | | | | |
| 5 | | | | | Is the cable a |
| 6 | | | | | crossover or |
| 7 | | | | | patch cable? |
| 8 | | | | | |

Cable 1 · Cable 2 · Cable 3

**Table 17-1**  Pin connections for selected cables

## REVIEW QUESTIONS

1. If you can see a copper conductor in a cable, what should you do with the cable?

2. What type of connector is used with Cat 5 cable?

3. Based on your research, what cabling scheme is more common?

4. On a patch cable, pin 3 on one end connects to pin _____ on the opposite end of the cable.

5. On a crossover cable, pin 2 on one end connects to pin _____ on the other end of the cable.

# LAB 17.3 COMPARE OPTIONS FOR A HOME LAN

## OBJECTIVES

The goal of this lab is to help you research the costs and capabilities of wired and wireless home LANs. After completing this lab, you will be able to:

◢ Research wired and wireless Ethernet

◢ Research 802.11 standards

◢ Identify the strengths and weaknesses of each option

## MATERIALS REQUIRED

This lab requires the following:

◢ Internet access

## LAB PREPARATION

Before the lab begins, the instructor or lab assistant needs to do the following:

◢ Verify that Internet access is available.

## ACTIVITY BACKGROUND

As the price of equipment and computers fall, installing a home LAN has become increasingly popular. In this lab, you research wired and wireless Ethernet and determine which option is best in certain situations.

**ESTIMATED COMPLETION TIME: 30 minutes**

**Activity**

Use your favorite search site to investigate and answer the following questions about wireless LAN standards:

1. List the 802.x standards for specifying wireless networks:

2. What industry name is associated with 802.11b?

_____

3. What is the simplest form of a wireless network? What devices are needed to create this type of network, and what mode does this type of network use?

_____

_____

_____

4. What device connects wireless users to a wired network?

_____

5. What standard speeds are supported by 802.11x?

_____

_____

_____

6. What kind of encryption is used with 802.11b?

_____

7. Give four examples of devices (besides PCs) that will probably eventually run on wireless LANs:

_____

_____

_____

_____

8. What does the acronym Wi-Fi stand for?

_____

9. What is the approximate maximum range for 802.11b technology?

_____

10. What inherent feature of 802.11b, seen as a major problem by businesses, might affect your decision to use Wi-Fi at home?

_____

_____

11. In the context of how they physically interface with a computer, what are the three basic types of wireless adapters?

_____

_____

_____

12. What mode requires a wireless access point?

_____

13. How many 802.11b devices can be used at one time with a single access point?

_____

14. What radio band and speed does 802.11a use?

_____

15. Which standard offers a faster transfer rate: 802.11a or 802.11b? List their transfer rates:

_____

_____

16. List the components required to connect four PCs in ad hoc mode and include their prices. List the device and extra expense needed to connect the same four PCs to a cable modem:

_____

_____

_____

_____

_____

Use the Internet to research and answer these questions on an Ethernet home LAN:

1. What is the maximum cable length for a 100BaseT Ethernet LAN?

_____

2. Must you use a hub to connect three PCs? Two PCs? Explain:

_____

_____

_____

3. What type of cabling is typically used for 100BaseT?

_____

4. Are special tools required when working with Cat 5 cabling to create patch or crossover cables?

_____

5. What feature of Windows 2000/XP or Windows 98 allows more than one computer to share a connection to the Internet?

_____

6. What type of cable connector is used for fast Ethernet?

_____

7. What standard supports a speed of 100 Mbps using two sets of Cat 3 cable?

_____

8. What is the name for a cable that connects a computer to a hub?

_____

9. Suppose you have a LAN consisting of a 100BaseT hub, two computers with 10BaseT NICs, and a computer with a 10/100BaseT NIC. At what speed would this LAN operate? Why?

_____

_____

10. Given a budget of $200 to connect five computers, would you choose 100BaseT or 10BaseT? Explain your choice:

_____

_____

_____

11. What is the name for a cable that connects a hub to a hub?

_____

12. In theory, if a file is transferred in 4.5 seconds on a fast Ethernet LAN, how long would the same file transfer take on a 10BaseT LAN?

_____

13. Give three examples of ways to physically interface a NIC to a computer:

_____

_____

_____

14. What device can you use to connect two or more PCs to a single cable modem?

_____

394 PCs on a Network

15. List the components, including cables, required to connect four PCs. Include the price of each component. List the changes and additional devices required to connect all four PCs to a cable modem and provide a hardware firewall:

_____

_____

_____

_____

_____

## REVIEW QUESTIONS

1. Based on your research, does wireless or 100BaseT offer the best performance for the money?

_____

_____

2. Is wireless or 100BaseT easier to configure in a home? Why?

_____

_____

3. What factors dictate the transmission range of 802.11x?

_____

_____

4. What determines the speed of a LAN that consists of both 10 Mbps and 100 Mbps devices?

_____

_____

5. Does a wired or wireless LAN offer better security?

_____

6. Could you combine a wireless and wired LAN in the same home? Why would you?

_____

_____

# *LAB 17.4 TROUBLESHOOT WITH TCP/IP UTILITIES*

## OBJECTIVES

The goal of this lab is to help you use Windows 2000/XP TCP/IP utilities to troubleshoot connectivity problems. After completing this lab, you will be able to:

◢ Use the Ipconfig utility

◢ Use the Ping utility

◢ Use the Tracert utility

◢ Identify the point at which your packets will no longer travel

## MATERIALS REQUIRED

This lab requires the following:

◢ Windows 2000/XP operating system

◢ A DHCP server

◢ Internet access

## LAB PREPARATION

Before the lab begins, the instructor or lab assistant needs to do the following:

◢ Verify that Windows starts with no errors.

◢ Verify that Internet access is available.

## ACTIVITY BACKGROUND

Perhaps nothing frustrates users more than a suddenly unavailable network connection. As a PC technician, you might be asked to restore these connections, and sometimes you even have to deal with several failed connections at one time. When troubleshooting network connections, it helps to know whether many users in one area of a network are having the same connection problem. That information can help you narrow down the source of the problem. After you have an idea of what machine is causing the problem, you can use a few TCP/IP utilities to test your theory without physically checking the system. In this lab, you learn to use TCP/IP utilities to isolate connection problems.

**ESTIMATED COMPLETION TIME: 30 minutes**

 **Activity**

Follow these steps to display IP settings in Windows 2000/XP:

1. Right-click **My Network Places** and click **Properties** in the shortcut menu. In, Windows XP, the Network Connections window opens; in Windows 2000, the Network and Dial-up Connections window opens.

2. Right-click **Local Area Connection** and click **Properties** in the shortcut menu. The Local Area Connection Properties dialog box opens.

3. Click **Internet Protocol (TCP/IP)**, and then click the **Properties** button. When the Internet Protocol (TCP/IP) dialog box opens, notice the different options. What two ways can you set up the IP configuration?

_____

_____

4. Verify that **Obtain an IP address automatically** is selected.

5. Click **OK** to close the Internet Protocol (TCP/IP) dialog box, and then close the Local Area Connection Properties dialog box. Close the Network and Dialup Connections window (Windows 2000) or the Network Connections window (Windows XP).

Follow these steps to adjust the command prompt so that you can view more information at a time:

1. Open a command prompt window.

2. Right-click the title bar of the command prompt window and click **Properties** in the shortcut menu. The Command Prompt Properties dialog box opens.

3. Click the **Layout** tab, if necessary. In the Screen Buffer Size section, type **150** for width and **300** for height. These settings enable you to scroll in the command prompt window and view the last 300 lines of 150 characters. If you want, you can adjust settings in the Window Size section, but generally, it's best to adjust a command prompt window after it opens so that you don't make the window too large for your monitor's display settings. Click **OK** to save the settings.

4. The Apply Properties to Shortcut dialog box opens. To specify that you want to apply the properties every time you open a command prompt window, click **Modify the shortcut that started this window**, and then click **OK**.

Follow these steps to learn how to display IP information from the command line:

1. Open a command prompt window.

2. Type **ipconfig** and press **Enter**. List the three types of information that are displayed:

_____

_____

_____

3. To get more information about your IP settings, type **ipconfig /all** and press **Enter**. Take a screen shot of these results, print the screen shot, and answer these questions:

◢ What is the purpose of DHCP?

_____

_____

◢ What is the address of the DHCP server?

_____

4. Because your system is using DHCP to obtain an IP address, type **ipconfig /renew** and press **Enter**. The command prompt window again displays IP information.

5. Again, type **ipconfig /all** and press **Enter**. Compare the current IP address lease information to the information in the screen shot. What information changed?

_____

_____

6. Next, type **ipconfig /release** and press **Enter**. What message is displayed? What implications do you predict this command will have on connectivity?

_____

_____

7. Using your screen shot as a reference, attempt to ping the DHCP server and the DNS server. What are the results?

_____

_____

8. Type **ipconfig** and press **Enter**. Note that your adapter has no IP address and no subnet mask. These two parameters are necessary to communicate with TCP/IP.

9. To get an IP address lease again, type **ipconfig /renew** and press **Enter**. New IP information, which might be the same address as before, is assigned.

10. Find your new IP address lease information. List the command you used to find this information and the lease information:

_____

_____

_____

11. In Windows XP, you can use the Network Connections window to release and renew the IP address. Right-click **My Network Places** and click **Properties** in the shortcut menu. The Network Connections window opens. Click the network connection you want to repair, and then click **Repair this connection**. You can also right-click the network connection you want to repair and click Repair in the shortcut menu.

If you're connected to the Internet, follow these steps to determine what route your packets take to reach an Internet address:

1. Open a command prompt window.

2. Type **tracert** followed by a single space and then a domain name on the Internet (for example, **tracert www.yahoo.com**). Press **Enter**.

3. The DNS server resolves the domain name to an IP address, and that address is listed, indicating you can reach at least one DNS server. This information tells you that your packets are traveling at least that far. Next, each hop (or router your packet passed through) is listed with the time in milliseconds the packet took to reach its destination. How many hops did the packet take to reach the domain you specified?

_____

4. Now use the Tracert command with an illegal name, such as **www.mydomain.c**. What are the results of this command?

_____

_____

When troubleshooting connectivity problems, always consider the number of users experiencing the problem. If many users have similar difficulties, it's unlikely the problem lies with any one user's computer. Therefore, you can probably eliminate the need to run extensive local tests on each computer. Instead, you can examine a device that all computers commonly use.

As a general rule, when troubleshooting, you should start by examining devices close to the computer exhibiting problems and then move farther away. The following steps show you how to apply this principle by examining the local computer first, and then moving outward to other devices on the network.

1. Verify that the computer is physically connected (that both ends of the cable are connected).

2. Verify that the NIC is installed and TCP/IP is bound to the NIC.

3. Perform a loopback test to verify that the NIC is functioning correctly.

4. Check the IP settings with the **ipconfig /all** command. Verify that an IP address is assigned.

5. Ping other computers on the local network. If you get no response, begin by examining a hub or punchdown panel (a panel where cables convene before connecting to a hub).

6. If you can ping other computers on the local network, ping the default gateway, which is the first stop for transmissions being sent to addresses that aren't on the local network.

7. Continue troubleshooting connections, beginning with nearby devices and working outward until you discover an IP address that returns no response. That device will be the source of the trouble.

8. If the device is under your supervision, take the necessary steps to repair it. If the device is out of your control, contact the appropriate administrator.

## REVIEW QUESTIONS

1. Name four additional pieces of information that the Ipconfig command with the /all switch provides that the Ipconfig command alone does not:

_____

_____

_____

_____

2. What type of server resolves a domain name to an IP address?

_____

3. In Windows 2000/XP, what command discards the IP address?

_____

4. What command do you use to determine whether you can reach another computer on the local network? Would this command work if the default gateway were down?

_____

_____

5. If many users suddenly encountered connection problems, would you suspect problems with their local computers or problems with other devices on the network? Explain:

_____

_____

_____

# LAB 17.5 PRACTICE SOLVING NETWORK CONNECTIVITY PROBLEMS

## OBJECTIVES

The goal of this lab is to troubleshoot and remedy common network connectivity problems. After completing this lab, you will be able to:

◢ Diagnose and solve connectivity problems

◢ Document the process

## MATERIALS REQUIRED

This lab requires the following:

◢ Windows 2000/XP or Windows 98 operating system

◢ A PC connected to a network and to the Internet

◢ Windows installation CD or installation files

◢ A PC toolkit with antistatic ground strap

◢ A workgroup partner

## LAB PREPARATION

Before the lab begins, the instructor or lab assistant needs to do the following:

◢ Verify that Windows starts with no errors.

◢ Provide each student with access to the Windows installation files, if needed.

## ACTIVITY BACKGROUND

To a casual user, Internet and network connections can be confusing. When users have a connectivity problem, they usually have no idea how to remedy the situation. In this lab, you introduce and solve common connectivity problems.

**ESTIMATED COMPLETION TIME: 30 minutes**

**Activity**

1. Verify that your network is working correctly by browsing the network and connecting to a Web site.

2. Do one of the following:

◢ Change your PC's IP address.

◢ Change your PC's subnet mask.

◢ Remove your PC's network cable.

- ◢ Remove TCP/IP from your PC.
- ◢ Remove your PC's adapter in the Network Properties dialog box.
- ◢ Unseat or remove your PC's NIC, but leave it installed in the Network Properties dialog box.
- ◢ Disable your PC's NIC in Device Manager.
- ◢ Release your PC's IP address (if DHCP is enabled).

3. Swap PCs with your partner and troubleshoot your partner's PC.

4. On a separate sheet of paper, answer these questions about the problem you solved:

   ◢ What is the initial symptom of the problem as user might describe it?

   _____

   _____

   ◢ What steps did you take to discover the source of the problem?

   _____

   _____

   _____

   _____

   ◢ What steps did you take to solve the problem?

   _____

   _____

   _____

   _____

5. Repeat Steps 1 through 4 until you and your partner have used all the options listed in Step 2. Be sure to answer the questions in Step 4 for each troubleshooting situation.

## REVIEW QUESTIONS

1. What problem could you solve by issuing only one command? What was the command you used?

   _____

   _____

2. Which problem (or problems) forced you to reboot the computer after repairing it?

   _____

   _____

   _____

3. What two pieces of information are necessary for TCP/IP communication on the local network?

_____

4. When using Windows 98, what problem (or problems) caused the Network Neighborhood icon to disappear?

_____

5. What TCP/IP utility was the most useful, in your opinion, for troubleshooting these problems? Why?

_____

_____

6. What situation doesn't necessarily cause a communication problem if a network protocol other than TCP/IP (such as NetBEUI) is installed on the local computer and other computers on the network?

_____

_____

## LAB 17.6 SHARE RESOURCES ON A NETWORK

### OBJECTIVES

The goal of this lab is to understand the process of sharing resources and using these shared resources on a remote computer on the network. After completing this lab, you will be able to:

▲ Share resources
▲ Control access to shared resources
▲ Connect to shared resources

### MATERIALS REQUIRED

This lab requires the following:

▲ Two or more Windows 2000/XP or Windows 98 computers on a network
▲ Windows installation CD or installation files
▲ A workgroup of 2 to 4 students

### LAB PREPARATION

Before the lab begins, the instructor or lab assistant needs to do the following:

▲ Verify that Windows starts with no errors.
▲ Provide each student with access to the Windows installation files, if needed.

### ACTIVITY BACKGROUND

The primary reason to network computers is to make it possible to share files, printers, Internet connections, and other resources. To share resources in a Windows workgroup, you need to make sure each computer has two Windows components installed: Client for

Microsoft Networks and File and Print Sharing. Those components are installed by default in Windows 2000/XP, and Client for Microsoft Networks is installed by default in Windows 98. In this lab, you install them on a Windows 98 computer (if they aren't already installed or have been uninstalled). Then you share resources and connect to these shared resources. Instructions are written for Windows 98, although they work about the same for Windows 2000/XP if you substitute My Network Places for Network Neighborhood in the instructions. Other differences between Windows 98 and Windows 2000/XP are noted.

**ESTIMATED COMPLETION TIME: 30 minutes**

 **Activity**

To share resources on a Windows peer-to-peer network, computers must belong to the same workgroup. Do the following to verify that all computers in your group belong to the same Windows workgroup:

1. To determine the workgroup name, right-click **Network Neighborhood**, click **Properties** in the shortcut menu, and then click the **Identification** tab. In Windows 2000/XP, right-click **My Computer**, click **Properties** in the shortcut menu, and then click the **Computer Name** tab (Windows XP) or **Network Identification** tab (Windows 2000). What is the workgroup name for this computer?

_____

2. Change the workgroup name, if necessary, so that all computers in your group belong to the same workgroup. If you're asked to reboot the PC, wait to do that until after you have installed the components in the next set of steps.

For each Windows 98 computer, follow these steps to see whether Client for Microsoft Networks and File and Print Sharing are installed, and if necessary, install those components:

1. Right-click the **Network Neighborhood** icon on the desktop and click **Properties** in the shortcut menu. The Network Properties dialog box opens.

2. If Client for Microsoft Networks is not listed as an installed component, you need to install it. To do that, click **Add**. The Add Network Component Type dialog box opens.

3. Click **Client**, and then click **Add**. The Select Network Client dialog box opens.

4. In the left pane of the Select Network Client dialog box, click **Microsoft**, and then click **Client for Microsoft Networks** in the right pane. Click **OK** to continue. The Add Network Component Type dialog box and the Select Network Client dialog box close. You return to the Network Properties dialog box.

5. If File and Print Sharing for Microsoft networks isn't listed as an installed component in the Network Properties dialog box, you need to install it. To do that, click **Add**. The Add Network Component Type dialog box opens again.

6. Click **Service**, and then click **Add**. The Select Network Service dialog box opens.

7. Click **File and printer sharing for Microsoft Networks**, and then click **OK**. Insert the Windows installation CD or point to the location of the installation files as instructed in the dialog box that opens. When the service is installed, you return to the Network Properties dialog box.

8. To enable File and Print Sharing, click **File and Print Sharing** in the Network dialog box. The File and Print Sharing dialog box opens.

9. Click the **I want to be able to give others access to my files** and **I want to be able to allow others to print to my printers** check boxes. Selecting these two options makes it possible for other computers on the network to access this computer's files and printers.

Click **OK** to close the File and Print Sharing dialog box. You return to the Network Properties dialog box.

10. Click **OK** to close the Network Properties dialog box and save your new settings. The Systems Settings Change message box opens and notifies you that before the settings take effect, the system must be restarted. Click **Yes** to reboot.

Now that you have enabled file and printer sharing, you're ready to set up folders or printers on your PC to be shared by others on the network. Follow these steps to share folders and control access to their contents:

1. Open Windows Explorer, and create three folders at the root of drive C named **Read, Full,** and **Depends**. Create a text file called **readtest.txt** in the Read folder, a text file called **fulltest.txt** in the Full folder, and a text file called **deptest.txt** in the Depends folder. Type a short sentence in each text file, save your changes, and close the files.

2. In the right pane of Windows Explorer, right-click the **Read** folder and click **Sharing** (**Sharing and Security** in Window XP) in the shortcut menu. The Read Properties dialog box opens, with the Sharing tab selected.

3. In the Access Type section, click **Read-Only**. This setting gives users on the network read-only access to all files in the Read folder.

4. In the Password section, type **read** in the Read-Only Password text box, and then click **OK**. The Password Confirmation dialog box opens.

5. Type **read** again in the Read-Only Password text box, and then click **OK**. The Confirm Password and Read Properties dialog boxes close.

6. Repeat Steps 2 through 5 for the other two folders you just created, selecting the access types associated with their names. For the Full folder, type **full** in the Full Access Type Password text box. For the Depends folder, supply both read-only and full access type passwords. Use passwords associated with the access type.

So far, you have verified that all computers sharing resources are in the same workgroup, have installed Windows components to share resources, and have set up the folders to be shared. Now you're ready to use shared resources over the network. Follow these steps to access shared folders:

1. In Windows Explorer, click the **Network Neighborhood** icon. The right pane of Windows Explorer displays a list of computers on the network.

2. In the right pane of Windows Explorer, double-click your partner's computer icon to display the shared resources available on that computer.

3. In the right pane of Windows Explorer, double-click the **Read** folder. The Enter Network Password dialog box opens, where you enter the password for this folder.

4. Type **Read** and click **OK**. The contents of the Read folder are displayed in Windows Explorer.

5. Double-click **readtest.txt**. The file opens in Notepad. Attempt to save the file, and record your results:

_____

_____

6. Now attempt to save the file in the My Documents folder on your computer. Record the results on the following lines. Why did your results in Step 5 differ from your results here?

_____

_____

_____

7. Close Notepad, click the **Network Neighborhood** icon in the left pane of Windows Explorer, and double-click the icon for your partner's computer in the right pane.

8. Double-click the **Full** folder in the right pane and, when prompted, enter the password and click **OK**. The contents of the Full folder are displayed in Windows Explorer.

9. Double-click **fulltest.txt**. The file opens in Notepad. Attempt to save the file, and record your results:

_____

_____

10. Attempt to save the file in the My Documents folder on your computer, and record the results on the following lines. Did you note any difference between the results of Steps 9 and 10? If so, explain the difference:

_____

_____

11. Close Notepad, return to the desktop, and open your **My Documents** folder.

12. Rename the fulltest.txt file with a new name of your choice. Attempt to copy, or drag and drop, this file into the Full folder on your partner's PC. Were you successful? Why or why not?

_____

_____

You have just seen how you can use Network Neighborhood to access shared folders on the network. You can make these shared folders appear to be a local drive on your PC, thereby making it more convenient to access these folders. When a shared folder on the network appears to be a local drive on your PC, the folder is called a network drive. Follow these steps to map a network drive and configure it to connect at logon:

1. In the left pane of Windows Explorer, click the **Network Neighborhood** icon. A list of computers on your network is listed in the right pane.

2. Double-click the icon for your partner's computer. A list of shared resources is displayed.

3. Right-click the **Full** folder and click **Map Network Drive** in the shortcut menu. The Map Network Drive dialog box opens.

4. In the Drive drop-down list box, click the drive letter you want to assign to this folder.

5. Click the **Reconnect at Logon** check box, and then click **OK**.

6. When prompted, enter the correct password, and then click **OK**. The drive is connected, and a window opens displaying the contents of the Full folder. The title bar includes the drive letter you assigned.

7. Check Windows Explorer and verify that the drive letter is now listed under My Computer.

8. Log off and then log back on to test that the drive reconnects. What did you have to do to reconnect when you logged back on?

_____

_____

**Alternate Activity**

To map a drive using a Windows 2000/XP computer, open Windows Explorer, right-click the **My Network Places** icon, and then click **Map Network Drive** in the shortcut menu. The Map Network Drive dialog box opens. Click **Browse** and locate the folder on the network that you want to map to the network drive. Then begin with Step 3 in the preceding set of steps.

## REVIEW QUESTIONS

1. What is the main advantage of connecting computers into networks?

   _____

   _____

2. What term refers to the process of allowing others to use resources on your computer?

   _____

3. What two Windows network components must be installed before you can grant others access to resources on your computer and use their resources?

   _____

4. How can you provide full access to some of your files while giving read-only access to other files shared on the network?

   _____

   _____

5. Explain how to allow some people to make changes to files in shared folders while allowing others to just view and read the contents of the same folder:

   _____

   _____

   _____

   _____

## *LAB 17.7 USE NETBEUI INSTEAD OF TCP/IP*

## OBJECTIVES

Most networks use the TCP/IP network protocol suite. The goal of this lab is to demonstrate how to replace TCP/IP with NetBEUI. After completing this lab, you will be able to:

◢ Install NetBEUI

◢ Remove TCP/IP

◢ Observe the results of using NetBEUI

## MATERIALS REQUIRED

This lab requires the following:

- Windows 2000/XP operating system
- A NIC configured to use only TCP/IP
- IP address information or a DHCP server on the network
- Internet access
- Windows 2000/XP Professional installation CD or installation files
- A network workgroup consisting of two computers
- A workgroup of 2 to 4 students

## LAB PREPARATION

Before the lab begins, the instructor or lab assistant needs to do the following:

- Verify that Windows starts with no errors.
- Provide each student with access to the Windows installation files, if needed.
- Verify that Internet access is available.

## ACTIVITY BACKGROUND

TCP/IP is probably the network protocol you're most familiar with, but it's not the only network protocol, nor is it the best for all situations. IBM originally developed NetBIOS Enhanced User Interface (NetBEUI) to make it possible to use NetBIOS names as official network addresses. NetBEUI is faster than TCP/IP and much easier to configure. Its main disadvantage is that it's nonroutable (meaning it can communicate only with computers on its network). In this lab, you configure one computer in your workgroup to use NetBEUI, and then observe the effect of this change on both computers in the workgroup. Then you use NetBEUI as the only network protocol in your workgroup.

**ESTIMATED COMPLETION TIME: 30 minutes**

Activity

First, you need to determine what the network looks like before you install NetBEUI and remove TCP/IP. Follow these steps:

1. On one of the two computers in the workgroup, open My Network Places via Windows Explorer. In Windows XP, click **View workgroup computers**. In Windows 2000, double-click **Computers Near Me**. A list of computers on your network is displayed. Take and print a screen shot of this list.

Notes

To take a screen shot, press **Alt+Print Screen**, which copies the window into the Clipboard. Open Windows Paint, and click **Edit, Paste** from the menu. To print the screen shot, click **File, Print** from the menu. Close Windows Paint without saving your work.

2. Repeat Step 1 for the other computer on your network.

Now follow these steps to install NetBEUI as the network protocol on one of the computers in your workgroup:

1. In Windows Explorer, right-click **My Network Places** and click **Properties** in the shortcut menu. The Network Connections (Windows XP) or Network and Dial-up Connections (Windows 2000) window opens.

2. Right-click the **Local Area Connection** icon and click **Properties** in the shortcut menu. The Local Area Connection Properties dialog box opens.

3. Click **Install**. The Select Network Component Type dialog box opens.

4. Click **Protocol**, and then click **Add**. The Select Network Protocol dialog box opens.

5. Click **NetBEUI Protocol**, and then click **OK**. The Select Network Protocol and Select Network Component Type dialog boxes close.

Your next job is to uninstall TCP/IP on the computer where you installed NetBEUI. You begin by recording the TCP/IP configuration information for that computer, and then uninstall TCP/IP. (You need this configuration information when you reinstall TCP/IP at the end of this lab.) Follow these steps:

1. Right-click **My Network Places** and click **Properties** in the shortcut menu. The Network Connections or Network and Dial-Up Connections window opens.

2. Right-click the **Local Area Connection** icon and click **Properties** in the shortcut menu. The Local Area Connection Properties dialog box opens.

3. Click **Internet Protocol (TCP/IP)** in the list of components, and then click **Properties**. The TCP/IP Properties dialog box opens.

4. Record the configuration information available in this window:

_____

_____

_____

_____

5. Click **Cancel** to close the TCP/IP Properties dialog box.

6. In the Local Area Connection Properties dialog box, click **Internet Protocol (TCP/IP)**, and then click **Uninstall**. A message appears informing you that you're about to remove the protocol from all connections.

7. Click **Yes** to continue. Internet Protocol (TCP/IP) is removed from the Local Area Connection Properties dialog box.

8. The Local Network dialog box opens and informs you that you must restart the computer before the changes can take effect.

9. Click **Yes** to restart the computer.

Follow these steps to observe the effects of using NetBEUI:

1. Go to the computer that you didn't alter (t the computer still running TCP/IP).

2. If it's not already open, open the **My Network Places** window. In Windows XP, click **View workgroup computers**. In Windows 2000, double-click **Computers Near Me**. (If Computers Near Me was already open, press **F5** to refresh the display.) Answer these questions:

◢ What computers are displayed?

_____

_____

_____

_____

◢ Compare the current screen to the screen shot you created earlier. What computers are missing?

_____

_____

◢ Why are they missing?

_____

_____

3. Go to the computer where you installed NetBEUI.

4. Open My Network Places, and then click **View workgroup computers** (Windows XP) or double-click **Computers Near Me** (Windows 2000). Answer the following questions:

◢ What computers are displayed?

_____

_____

_____

_____

◢ Compare the current screen to the screen shot you created earlier. What computers are missing?

_____

_____

◢ Why are they missing?

_____

_____

5. Press **F5** to refresh the list of computers on the network. Did any new ones appear? Why or why not?

_____

_____

_____

_____

6. On the computer where you installed NetBEUI, attempt to connect to the Internet, and then answer these questions:

◢ What message did you receive?

_____

_____

_____

_____

◢ Why do you think you were unable to connect to the Internet?

_____

_____

Next, you use some network utilities to test your network connections. You start by running a loopback ping test, as you did in Lab 17.1. Follow these steps:

1. On the computer running TCP/IP (the one you didn't change), open a command prompt window, type **ping 127.0.0.1**, and press **Enter**. Record the results of the loopback test:

_____

_____

_____

2. Next, you use the Ipconfig utility to test network configuration and connectivity. Type **ipconfig /all** and press **Enter**. Record the results of the command:

_____

_____

_____

3. On the computer where you installed NetBEUI, open a command prompt window, and then repeat Steps 1 and 2. Record the results. Why did you get these results?

_____

_____

_____

_____

Follow these steps to reinstall TCP/IP:

1. On the computer where you installed NetBEUI, right-click **My Network Places** and click **Properties** in the shortcut menu. The Network Connections or Network and Dial-up Connections window opens.

2. Right-click the **Local Area Connection** icon and click **Properties** in the shortcut menu. The Local Area Connection Properties dialog box opens.

3. Click **Install**. The Select Network Component Type dialog box opens.

4. Click **Protocol**, and then click **Add**. The Select Network Protocol dialog box opens.

5. Click **TCP/IP Protocol**, and then click **OK**. The Select Network Protocol and Select Network Component Type dialog boxes close.

6. The Local Network dialog box opens and informs you that you must restart the computer before the changes can take effect. Click **Yes** to restart the computer.

You've finished reinstalling TCP/IP. Now you need to reconfigure the necessary TCP/IP settings. Follow these steps:

1. Right-click **My Network Places** and click **Properties** in the shortcut menu. The Network Connections or Network and Dial-Up Connections window opens.

2. Right-click the **Local Area Connection** icon and click **Properties** in the shortcut menu. The Local Area Connection Properties dialog box opens.

3. Click **Internet Protocol (TCP/IP)**, and then click **Properties**. The Internet Protocol (TCP/IP) Properties dialog box opens.

4. Reconfigure the settings to match the ones you recorded earlier in this lab.

5. Click **OK** twice to close the Internet Protocol (TCP/IP) Properties and Local Area Connection Properties dialog boxes and save your settings.

6. Test your settings by connecting to another computer or the Internet.

## ADDITIONAL ACTIVITY (ADDITIONAL 20 MINUTES)

1. Install NetBEUI and remove TCP/IP on one more computer in your workgroup so that NetBEUI is the only network protocol installed on two computers.

2. Using NetBEUI, transfer files from one computer to the other.

3. Install TCP/IP and configure it, and then remove NetBEUI as an installed networking protocol.

## REVIEW QUESTIONS

1. Is it possible to have more than one network protocol installed on the same network? Explain how you arrived at your answer:

   _____

   _____

   _____

2. If you had to access the Internet from your computer, which protocol would you use?

   _____

3. What features of NetBEUI make it appealing for a small network that doesn't need Internet access?

   _____

   _____

4. Of the two network protocols covered in this lab, which is better suited for trouble-shooting problems? Why?

   _____

   _____

5. What type of computer name is used on a NetBEUI network?

   _____

# LAB 17.8 USE A PARALLEL PORT FOR DIRECT CABLE CONNECTION

## OBJECTIVES

The goal of this lab is to help you use the Direct Cable Connection feature of Windows 98 to connect two computers with a parallel port. After completing this lab, you will be able to:

◢ Install Direct Cable Connection

◢ Link two computers with a parallel cable

◢ Transfer files

## MATERIALS REQUIRED

This lab requires the following:

◢ Windows 98 operating system

◢ A standard parallel cable with a DB 25-pin connection at both ends (or a parallel printer cable with a 36-pin Centronics to DB 25-pin converter)

◢ Two computers that aren't connected to the network

◢ Windows 98 installation CD or installation files

◢ A workgroup of 2 to 4 students

## LAB PREPARATION

Before the lab begins, the instructor or lab assistant needs to do the following:

◢ Verify that Windows starts with no errors.

◢ Provide each student with access to the Windows 98 installation files, if needed.

## ACTIVITY BACKGROUND

Included with Windows 98, the Direct Cable Connection feature allows you to connect two computers without the benefit of a conventional network. Although this feature is slow in comparison to the typical LAN, it does enable you to transfer files by using a serial null-modem or parallel cable. The only other requirement is that the computers share a common communications protocol. NetBEUI is ideal for this type of connection because it's easy to configure and faster than other protocols. In this lab, you connect two computers by using the Direct Cable Connection feature.

**ESTIMATED COMPLETION TIME: 30 minutes**

### Activity

First, you need to install the Direct Cable Connection feature on both computers. Follow these steps:

1. Click **Start**, point to **Settings**, click **Control Panel**, and then double-click **Add/Remove Programs**.

2. Click the **Windows Setup** tab.

3. Click **Communications**, and then click **Details**. Click the **Direct Cable Connection** check box (if it's not already selected).

To use Direct Cable Connection, work with at least one partner to follow these steps:

1. Shut down both computers, connect the parallel cable to each computer, and reboot both computers.

2. Decide which computer will be the "host" and which will be the "guest." The guest computer will have access to files on the host computer.

3. On both computers, click **Start**, point to **Programs**, point to **Accessories**, point to **Communications**, and then click **Direct Cable Connection**. The Direct Cable Connection dialog box opens.

4. On the host computer, click **Host**. On the guest computer, click **Guest**. On both computers, click **Next**. If this is the first time Direct Cable Connection has been used, the Configuring Ports dialog box opens and closes, at which point you should continue with Step 5. If Direct Cable Connection has been run before, click **Change** in the Direct Cable Connection dialog box, and then continue with Step 5.

5. The Direct Cable Connection dialog box displays a list of possible ports to use for the cable. In the Select the port you want to use list box, click **Parallel cable on LPT1**, and then click **Next** to continue.

6. On the host computer, the Direct Cable Connection dialog box states that it will have access to shared files and lists the steps required to share a folder. Summarize these steps:

_____

_____

_____

_____

7. On the host computer, click **Next** to continue. On the guest computer, wait until the host computer completes Steps 8 and 9 and your partner gives you the go-ahead, and then skip to Step 10.

8. On the host computer, click the **Use Password Protection** check box, and then click **Set Password**. The Direct Cable Connection Password dialog box opens.

9. Type **dcclab** in the Password and Confirm Password text boxes, and then click **OK**. The Direct Cable Connection Password dialog box closes.

10. On the host computer, click **Finish**. The Direct Cable Connection dialog box displays "Status: Waiting to connect via parallel cable on LPT1." At this time, the host team should signal the guest team to proceed. The guest team should then click **Finish**. The Direct Cable Connection dialog box opens on the guest computer.

11. On the guest computer, enter the password when prompted. Click **OK** to establish the connection.

12. On the guest computer, test the connection by browsing to the host in Network Neighborhood and transferring files from a shared folder.

## REVIEW QUESTIONS

1. What kinds of cables could you use with the Direct Cable Connection feature?

_____

_____

2. In a direct cable connection, is it possible to share printers but not files? Is it possible to share files but not printers? Explain:

_____

_____

3. Would it make sense to use Direct Cable Connection to connect two computers that already have access to an existing network? Explain:

_____

_____

4. Why might you use Direct Cable Connection to connect two computers, even if one computer has access to a network?

_____

_____

_____

5. Of the two types of cable that can be used for a direct cable connection, which provides better transfer speeds?

_____

## LAB 17.9 CONFIGURE AND USE REMOTE ACCESS SERVICE

### OBJECTIVES

The goal of this lab is to give you practice using Remote Access Service to allow dial-up access to a computer. After completing this lab, you will be able to:

◢ Set up Remote Access Service

◢ Configure Remote Access Service

◢ Connect to a network through a dial-up connection

### MATERIALS REQUIRED

This lab requires the following:

◢ Two Windows XP computers

◢ A modem and telephone line for each computer

◢ A workgroup of 2 to 4 students

### LAB PREPARATION

Before the lab begins, the instructor or lab assistant needs to do the following:

◢ Verify that Windows starts with no errors.

◢ Provide students with the phone numbers of both machines.

## ACTIVITY BACKGROUND

You can set up your Windows computer to receive dial-up connections from other computers. You might want to do this if you travel and want to be able to transfer files to and from your home computer while away. In Windows 98, you need to install the Dial-Up Server component to use this feature. In Windows 2000/XP, you can allow incoming calls by default by using Remote Access Service (RAS). In this lab, you connect two Windows XP machines through a dial-up connection.

**ESTIMATED COMPLETION TIME: 45 minutes**

 **Activity**

Follow these steps to configure one machine to accept a remote connection:

1. Click **Start, Network Connections**. The New Connection Wizard starts.
2. Click **Create a new connection**, and then click **Next**.
3. Click **Set up an advanced connection**, and then click **Next**.
4. Click **Accept incoming connections**, and then click **Next** again.
5. Click to select the modem installed in your machine, and then click **Next**.
6. Click **Do not allow virtual private connections**, and then click **Next**.
7. Add a user name and password for a new user who's allowed to use this connection, and write that information here:

_____

8. Click **Next** to close the New Connection Wizard.
9. Click **Next** in the Networking Software window to accept the default settings.
10. Finally, click **Finish**.

Follow these steps to connect remotely to your first machine:

1. Click **Start, Network Connections**. The New Connection Wizard starts.
2. Click **Create a new connection**, and then click **Next**.
3. Click **Connect to the Network at my workplace**, and then click **Next**.
4. Click **Dial-up connection**, and then click **Next**.
5. Enter a name for this connection, and then click **Next**.
6. Next, enter the phone number of the machine accepting the remote connection.
7. Click **Anyone's use** to specify how this connection can be used, and then click **Next**.
8. Click **Finish** to complete the wizard. A window for the new connection should open automatically.
9. Enter the name and password of the new user account you created while configuring the first machine.
10. Finally, click **Dial** to connect to the remote machine.

## CRITICAL THINKING (ADDITIONAL 15 MINUTES)

Change the workgroup identity on one of the computers so that the two computers no longer belong to the same workgroup. Attempt to connect and transfer files. At what point did the process fail?

_____

_____

## REVIEW QUESTIONS

1. Which Windows 98 component allows a computer to receive an incoming call?

_____

2. Which Windows 2000/XP component handles dial-up connections?

_____

3. Is it possible to have more than one object in the Dial-up section of the Network Connections window? Why?

_____

_____

4. How does each computer disconnect from a Dial-Up Server session?

_____

_____

5. What is a disadvantage of connecting through RAS?

_____

_____

# PCs on the Internet

**Labs included in this chapter:**

- **Lab 18.1:** Use AT Commands to Control a Modem

- **Lab 18.2:** Simulate Modem Problems

- **Lab 18.3:** Install Software to Delete Cookies

- **Lab 18.4:** Use FTP to Download a Browser

- **Lab 18.5:** Download and Install Internet Explorer and Firefox

- **Lab 18.6:** Configure a Browser So That It Doesn't Download
  Images

- **Lab 18.7:** Use Remote Desktop

## LAB 18.1 USE AT COMMANDS TO CONTROL A MODEM

### OBJECTIVES

The goal of this lab is to help you use AT commands to initiate and receive modem calls. After completing this lab, you will be able to:

⊿ Install HyperTerminal

⊿ Use several modem commands to control a HyperTerminal session, dial a number, receive a call, and test your modem

### MATERIALS REQUIRED

This lab requires the following:

⊿ Windows 2000/XP or Windows 9x operating system

⊿ Windows installation CD or installation files

⊿ Access to a phone line that can send and receive calls

⊿ The line's telephone number

⊿ A lab partner to whom you can make modem calls

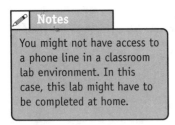

**Notes**

You might not have access to a phone line in a classroom lab environment. In this case, this lab might have to be completed at home.

### LAB PREPARATION

Before the lab begins, the instructor or lab assistant needs to do the following:

⊿ Verify that Windows starts with no errors.

⊿ Verify that the Internet connection has been configured for HyperTerminal.

⊿ Provide each student with access to the Windows installation files, if needed.

### ACTIVITY BACKGROUND

The AT command set is used for controlling modems. When a modem receives commands, each command line is prefaced with AT for "attention." A modem stays in command mode any time it's not connected to another modem. When a modem is in command mode and bits and bytes are sent to it from a PC, the modem interprets the bytes as commands to be followed instead of data to be sent over a phone line. It leaves command mode when it receives an incoming call or dials out, and returns to command mode when a call is completed or the computer sends a special escape sequence. A modem responds to a command with "OK" or gives the results after carrying out the command. With AT commands, you can control almost every aspect of modem behavior; these commands are also useful in troubleshooting modem hardware and connections. Table 18-1 lists a few of the core AT commands that most modems understand.

You can type a command from a communications software window to run immediately or enter a command from a dialog box for the modem configuration to run later when the modem makes a call. HyperTerminal is an excellent utility you can use to make a quick and easy phone call from a Windows PC. HyperTerminal is installed by default in Windows 2000/XP but isn't installed automatically in Windows 9x. By using HyperTerminal, you can test a newly installed modem with AT commands. In this lab, you use AT commands to make and receive calls and to adjust modem settings.

| Command | Description | Possible Values |
|---------|-------------|-----------------|
| AT | Get the modem's attention. | AT (Modem should respond with OK.) |
| *70 | Disable call waiting. | ATDT*70,4045551212 |
| +++ | Escape sequence: Tells the modem to return to command mode. You should pause at least 1 second before you start typing the sequence. After you end the sequence, wait another second before you send another command. Don't begin this command with AT. | +++ (Follow each + with a short pause. Use this command when trying to unlock a hung modem; don't begin the command with AT.) |
| On | Go online: Tells the modem to return to online data mode. This is the reverse command for the escape sequence. | ATO0 (Return online.) ATO1 (Return online and retrain; perform training or handshaking again with the remote system.) |
| A/ | Repeat last command: Repeat the last command the modem performed. Don't begin the command with AT, but do follow it with Enter. Useful when redialing a busy number. | |
| In | Identification: Instructs the modem to return to product identification information. | ATI0 (Return the product code.) ATI3 (Return the modem ROM version.) |
| Zn | Reset: Instructs the modem to reset and restore the configuration to what was defined at power on. | ATZ0 (Reset and return to user profile 0.) ATZ1 (Reset and return to user profile 1.) |
| &F | Factory default: Instructs the modem to reload the factory default profile. In most cases, use this command to reset the modem instead of using the Z command. | AT&F (This method is preferred to ATZ when trying to solve a modem problem.) |
| A | Answer the phone: Instructs the modem to answer the phone, transmit the answer tone, and wait for a carrier from the remote modem. | |
| Dn | Dial: Tells the modem to dial a number. Several parameters can be added to this command, as shown in the Possible Values column. | ATD5551212 (Dial the given number.) ATDD (Pause the dialing.) ATDP (Use pulse dialing.) ATDT (Use tone dialing.) ATDW (Wait for dial tone.) ATD& (Wait for the credit-card dialing tone before continuing with the remaining dial string.) |
| Hn | Hang up: Tells the modem to hang up. | ATH0 (Hang up.) ATH1 (Hang up and enter command mode.) |
| Mn | Speaker control: Instructs the modem on how to use the speaker. | ATM0 (Speaker always off.) ATM1 (Speaker on until carrier detect.) ATM2 (Speaker always on.) |
| Ln | Loudness: Sets the loudness of the modem's speaker. | ATL1 (Set to low volume.) ATL2 (Set to medium volume.) ATL3 (Set to high volume.) |
| Xn | Response: Tells the modem how to respond to a dial tone and busy signal. | ATX0 (Blind dialing; the modem doesn't need to hear the dial tone and won't hear a busy signal.) ATX4 (Default value; modem must first hear the dial tone, and it responds to a busy signal.) |

Table 18-1   AT commands for Hayes-compatible modems

**Activity**

In Windows 9x, follow these steps to install HyperTerminal:

1. Open Control Panel, double-click the **Add/Remove Programs** icon, and then click the **Windows Setup** tab.

2. In the Components list box, double-click the **Communications** group. The Communications dialog box opens.

3. Click the **HyperTerminal** check box, and then click **OK**. The Communications dialog box closes, and you return to the Add/Remove Programs Properties dialog box.

4. Click **OK** to close the Add/Remove Programs Properties dialog box. Supply Windows installation files as necessary.

In Windows 9x and Windows 2000/XP, follow these steps to use AT commands in HyperTerminal:

1. Click **Start**, point to **All Programs** (in Windows 2000 and 9x, **Programs**), point to **Accessories**, point to **Communications**, and then click **HyperTerminal**. If a message box opens, asking whether you want to make HyperTerminal the default Telnet program, click **Yes**.

2. HyperTerminal starts, with the Connection Description dialog box open.

3. Type **Test 1** in the Name text box, and then click **OK**. The Connect To dialog box opens.

4. Click your modem in the drop-down list, and then click **Cancel** to close the Connect To dialog box. The Connect To dialog box closes, and the main HyperTerminal window is active.

5. Click in a blank area of the HyperTerminal window to position the cursor.

At this point, if you start typing AT commands, the commands run but you might not be able to see them as you type in the HyperTerminal window. To be able to see AT commands as you type them (if displaying commands hasn't already been enabled), you must begin with the AT echo command, ATE1. To practice using this command, follow these steps:

1. Type **ATE1** and press **Enter**. The modem's response (OK) appears under the cursor. Although you couldn't see the command ATE1 as you typed it, from now on, you should be able to see commands as you type.

2. Type **ATE0** and press **Enter**. (Be sure to type a zero, not the letter "O.") The command ATE0 appears on the screen as you type. OK appears below ATE0 after you press Enter.

3. Type **AT** and press **Enter**. The AT command issued by itself should always return an OK response, and, in fact, OK does appear on the screen. However, this time the command you typed is not displayed on the screen. Which command caused the text not to appear as you typed (that is, caused the text not to "echo")?

_____

4. Issue the ATE1 command again to echo the commands as you type.

Now that you know how to make commands appear as you type, you're ready to test your modem by using HyperTerminal. Follow these steps:

1. To verify that a working phone line is connected to the modem, type **ATD** followed by your computer's telephone number (for example, ATD5551212) and press **Enter**. You should hear the modem dial. What message does HyperTerminal return?

_____

2. Type **ATL3**, press **Enter**, and then use the ATD command to dial your computer's number again.

◢ What difference do you notice from the first time you dialed the number?

_____

_____

◢ What does the L in the ATL command stand for?

_____

3. You can also control HyperTerminal by using menu commands. Click **Call, Wait for a Call** from the HyperTerminal menu.

4. Give your lab partner your computer's number and have him or her dial and connect to your computer. What messages does HyperTerminal display on your computer?

_____

_____

_____

5. Click the **Disconnect** button (the button with a phone handset over a phone cradle), shown in Figure 18-1 for Windows 9x. Your modem disconnects.

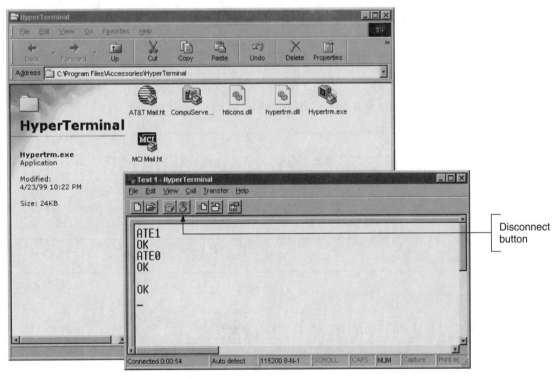

**Figure 18-1** The HyperTerminal window

6. Type **AT&T1** and press **Enter**. HyperTerminal runs a local analog loop to make sure the modem is working correctly. Record the results:

_____

_____

_____

_____

7. To end the test, type **AT&T0** and press **Enter**. (Ending the test might take a few moments.)

8. Click the **Disconnect** button again.

9. If you begin testing a working modem with AT commands and the modem begins to exhibit problems, you can use the AT&F command to reset the modem to factory settings. Type **AT&F** and press **Enter**. The modem's default settings are restored.

10. To close HyperTerminal, click **File, Exit** from the menu. When asked if you want to disconnect, click **Yes**. When asked if you want to save the session, click **No**.

## REVIEW QUESTIONS

1. What Windows application is commonly used for working with AT commands?

_____

2. What command turns on text echo so that you can see what you're typing?

_____

3. What command dials a number?

_____

4. What command returns the modem to its default settings?

_____

5. Look in Table 18-1 for additional AT commands. What AT commands not used in this lab would you find useful in debugging a modem?

_____

_____

_____

# LAB 18.2 SIMULATE MODEM PROBLEMS

## OBJECTIVES

The goal of this lab is to help you simulate, diagnose, and remedy common modem problems. After completing this lab, you will be able to:

◢ Diagnose problems with a modem

◢ Remedy problems with a modem

## MATERIALS REQUIRED

This lab requires the following:

▲ Windows 2000/XP or Windows 9x operating system

▲ A modem installed in a PC and connected to a phone line

▲ A PC toolkit with antistatic ground strap

▲ Modem installation drivers

▲ Windows installation CD or installation files

▲ A standard phone

▲ A lab partner with whom you can swap PCs

## LAB PREPARATION

Before the lab begins, the instructor or lab assistant needs to do the following:

▲ Verify that Windows starts with no errors.

▲ Provide each student with access to the Windows installation files, if needed.

## ACTIVITY BACKGROUND

Dial-up connections are notoriously unreliable. One of the challenges of troubleshooting these connections is determining whether a dial-up failure is related to a problem with the modem or the phone line. In this lab, you diagnose and remedy common modem problems. Mastering these skills makes it easier for you to determine when the modem is the source of trouble in a dial-up connection.

**ESTIMATED COMPLETION TIME: 90 minutes**

 **Activity**

1. To verify that your modem is working, start HyperTerminal, dial any reliable phone number, and listen for the sound of the modem dialing and attempting to connect. (The actual connection isn't necessary at this point.) Disconnect the call and close HyperTerminal.

2. Sabotage your modem by introducing one of these problems:

▲ If your modem has jumpers or DIP switches, record the original settings on the following lines, and then change the settings.

_____

_____

▲ In BIOS or Device Manager, disable the modem's COM port.

▲ Loosen the modem card in the expansion slot so that it doesn't make good contact.

▲ Unplug the phone cord from the wall.

▲ Change the port the phone line connects to on the back of the modem.

▲ Uninstall the modem in Device Manager.

▲ Change or disable the IRQ for the modem.

▲ Using Device Manager, disable the modem in the current hardware configuration.

3. Swap PCs with your partner, and then troubleshoot and repair your partner's PC.

4. Answer these questions:

◢ What is the initial symptom of a problem as a user would describe it?

_____

_____

◢ How did you discover the source of the problem?

_____

_____

_____

_____

◢ What did you do to solve the problem?

_____

_____

_____

_____

5. Introduce another problem from the list in Step 2, and swap again. Continue this process until you have introduced and remedied all the problems listed in Step 2.

## REVIEW QUESTIONS

1. What was the easiest problem to diagnose and why?

_____

_____

2. Which problems aren't apparent in Device Manager but would result in no dial tone when dialing?

_____

_____

3. Did all the problems listed in Step 2 actually prevent the modem from working? Which (if any) did not?

_____

_____

4. Which problem prevented the modem from being displayed in its Properties dialog box?

_____

_____

5. What was the simplest way to determine whether there was definitely a dial tone?

_____

_____

6. Suppose a user says, "I can't dial out using my modem." List the first three things you would check, in the order you would check them:

_____

_____

_____

# LAB 18.3 INSTALL SOFTWARE TO DELETE COOKIES

## OBJECTIVES

The goal of this lab is to help you install software that deletes cookies each time you boot your computer. After completing this lab, you will be able to:

- Locate, download, and install the software
- Delete cookies using the software you downloaded

## MATERIALS REQUIRED

This lab requires the following:

- Internet access
- Windows 2000/XP or Windows 9x operating system

## LAB PREPARATION

Before the lab begins, the instructor or lab assistant needs to do the following:

- Verify that Windows starts with no errors.
- Verify that Internet access is available.

## ACTIVITY BACKGROUND

When you visit certain Web sites, cookies are placed on your system to collect information about you, including what Web sites you visit. Although cookies can be useful by storing your preferences for when you revisit sites, they can also be a security risk, passing on information you don't want to make accessible to others. For example, this information could be passed on to companies that then sell it to a mailing list or use it for advertising purposes. Several utilities on the market can clean cookies from your computer. One is Webroot's Window Washer, which is available for trial download. In this lab, you install Window Washer and use it to delete cookies.

**Activity**

Follow these steps to download Webroot's Window Washer software. As you know, Web sites change often, so your steps might differ slightly from the following:

1. Open your browser, and go to **www.webroot.com**.

2. Find the Downloads section.

3. Scroll down and click the link to download Window Washer. (If this download site doesn't work, you might have to use one of the alternate links listed below it.)

4. The File Download dialog box opens, indicating that you have chosen to download the installation file for Window Washer. Click the **Run this program from its current location** option button, and then click **OK** (Windows 9x and 2000) or **Run** (Windows XP).

5. A dialog box opens indicating the progress of the installation. If necessary, click the **Close this dialog box when download completes** check box and wait for the download to finish. Depending on your connection speed, it could take a few minutes. While you're waiting, look on the Webroot site for information about Window Washer and record a short description of what it does:

_____

_____

_____

_____

6. When the download is finished, a security warning dialog box opens. Click **Yes** or **Run** to verify that you want to install and run the trial version of Window Washer.

7. If the Window Washer Setup dialog box opens, click **Yes** to continue.

8. The Window Washer installation program launches. In the first window, click **I Agree** to accept the license agreement.

9. Click the **Typical Installation** option, and then click **Next**. The Installation Status window shows the progress of the installation. When a completion message is displayed, click **Next**.

10. In the Custom Wash Item Detection window, leave the defaults selected, and then click **Next**. Leave the e-mail check box and text box blank, and then click **Next**.

11. In the Successful Installation window, click to clear **Run Window Washer**, and then click **Finished**.

Follow these steps to use Window Washer to delete cookies:

1. Open Internet Explorer, if necessary, and browse the Web for a couple of minutes, visiting a variety of sites, such as news sites and commercial sites. Click a few links and ads on those sites. Close Internet Explorer.

2. Open Windows Explorer, and then open the **Cookies** folder, which is usually located under C:\Windows (Windows 9x and 2000) or C:\Documents and Settings\*username* (Windows XP). Cookies are stored as text files.

◢ How many cookies are listed?

_____

◢ What sites appear to have stored cookies on your computer?

_____

_____

_____

3. Click **Start**, point to **All Programs** (**Programs** in Windows 2000 or 9x), point to **Web Root**, point to **Window Washer**, and then click **Window Washer**.

4. On the right side of the window, notice that no data is listed under Wash Statistics for the Last wash item. Click the **Wash My Computer Now** button.

5. In the Ready to Wash window that opens, click **Start**.

6. If the Internet Explorer Running dialog box opens, click **Yes** to close it. The Washing in progress window opens. When the Washing completed window opens, click **Finished**.

7. In Windows Explorer, open the **Cookies** folder again to verify that the cookies are gone.

If you still see cookies in the Cookies folder after you run Window Washer, you might need to verify that you selected all the options indicating which files you want to delete before running Window Washer again.

## REVIEW QUESTIONS

1. What other items can Window Washer clean besides cookies?

_____

_____

2. List some reasons you might not want cookies on your system, and explain why you might want to clear Internet Explorer form data as well as your document history:

_____

_____

_____

3. What information did the Webroot site provide about how Window Washer works?

_____

_____

4. Can you specify your own wash items—that is, items that aren't already listed in Window Washer? Explain:

_____

_____

5. How might cookies be useful?

_____

_____

# LAB 18.4 USE FTP TO DOWNLOAD A BROWSER

## OBJECTIVES

The goal of this lab is to help you use FTP from the command prompt to download a browser. After completing this lab, you will be able to:

▲ Use common FTP commands from a command prompt

▲ Download a browser via FTP

## MATERIALS REQUIRED

This lab requires the following:

▲ Windows 2000/XP or Windows 9x operating system

▲ Internet access

## LAB PREPARATION

Before the lab begins, the instructor or lab assistant needs to do the following:

▲ Verify that Windows starts with no errors.

▲ Verify that Internet access is available.

## ACTIVITY BACKGROUND

File Transfer Protocol (FTP) is a quick and easy way to transfer files over the Internet without converting them to ASCII text first. You might use FTP when transmitting files too large to be sent as e-mail attachments, for example. For this lab, imagine that your Web browser has been rendered inoperable by a virus or because you accidentally deleted some vital files, but you can still connect to the Internet. How can you get your browser back? If you're using a network, it might be possible for you to go to another computer on the network, use that computer's browser to download a new browser, and then transfer the downloaded browser file to your computer. Another option is to reinstall Windows on your computer, a process that installs Internet Explorer. However, if these options aren't available or practical, you can use FTP to download a browser. If you have no user-friendly GUI FTP software installed on your computer, you can use FTP from the command prompt. In this lab, you use FTP commands from the command prompt to locate and download the latest version of Netscape.

**Activity**

Follow these steps to connect to the Netscape FTP site from a command prompt and download the latest version of the Netscape browser:

1. When you download the browser, you should store the file in a location on your hard drive that's easy to find. In Windows Explorer, create a folder on your C drive called **Downloads**.

2. Leave Windows Explorer open, and open a command prompt window.

3. When the command prompt window opens, the C:\Windows (Windows 9x and 2000) or C:\Documents and Settings (Windows XP) directory is probably the active directory. When you use FTP, the files you download are stored in whatever directory was active when you began the session. To change to the Downloads directory, type **cd c:\downloads** and press **Enter**.

4. When the Downloads directory is active, type **ftp** and press **Enter**. How did the command prompt change?

   _____

5. To enter the Netscape FTP site, type **open ftp.netscape.com** and press **Enter**.

6. A message is displayed, stating that you're connected to the Netscape site and the server is ready, followed by a user prompt. Many sites, including this one, allow limited access to the site via an anonymous logon. Type **anonymous** at the user prompt and press **Enter**.

7. A message asks you to specify your password. Type **anonymous** and press **Enter**. What message do you see?

   _____

8. You now have access to certain files on the Netscape FTP site. Browse to the location of the latest version of the Netscape browser. Use the **dir** command to list the contents of various directories and the **cd** command to change directories as necessary. At the time of this writing, Netscape 8.1 was located in the path *ftp.netscape.com/pub/netscape8/english/8.1/windows/win32/nsb-setup.exe*. The names and locations of downloadable files can change as versions and site structure change, so you might find the file stored in a different directory. The exact file name might be different as well, depending on what the most current browser version is. If the location or name of the latest version of the browser setup file differs from the one mentioned earlier in this step, record the correct information here:

   _____

9. After you have located the file, type **bin** and press **Enter**. This command sets the download mode to specify that you want the file downloaded as a binary (not ASCII) file.

10. To download the file, type **get nsb-setup.exe** (substituting the correct file name if you noted a different one in Step 8). Remember that FTP commands are case sensitive.

11. Press **Enter**. What messages are displayed?

_____

_____

_____

12. Return to Windows Explorer, click **View, Refresh** from the menu, open the **Downloads** folder, and verify that the file was downloaded successfully.

13. To verify that the browser setup program you downloaded works, double-click the file you downloaded. The setup program opens.

14. Close the setup program because you're installing different browsers in Lab 18.5.

15. Return to the command prompt window. Type **bye** and press **Enter** to close the FTP session.

## REVIEW QUESTIONS

1. List all the FTP commands you used in this lab, with a short description of each:

_____

_____

_____

_____

_____

_____

_____

2. In what mode did you download the browser setup file? Why is using this mode necessary?

_____

_____

_____

_____

3. For what other operating systems and languages is Netscape available for download?

_____

_____

4. If you were using FTP to upload a text file that's too large to send as an e-mail attachment, which mode (ASCII or binary) should you choose to upload it and why?

_____

_____

5. You're downloading FileABC.txt from the FTP site of CompanyXYZ.com. The file is located in the /pub/documentation/ folder of that site. Your FTP client defaults to binary

mode for download. List in order all the commands you would use to open the FTP connection, download the file, and close the connection:

_____

_____

_____

_____

_____

# LAB 18.5 DOWNLOAD AND INSTALL INTERNET EXPLORER AND FIREFOX

## OBJECTIVES

The goal of this lab is to help you download and install the latest versions of Internet Explorer and Firefox. After completing this lab, you will be able to:

▲ Download the latest version of a browser from a company's Web site

▲ Install two downloaded browsers

## MATERIALS REQUIRED

This lab requires the following:

▲ Windows 2000/XP or Windows 9x operating system

▲ Internet access

## LAB PREPARATION

Before the lab begins, the instructor or lab assistant needs to do the following:

▲ Verify that Windows starts with no errors.

▲ Verify that Internet access is available.

## ACTIVITY BACKGROUND

Companies that make Web browsers periodically offer new versions of their products that incorporate new features or fix known bugs. In this lab, you download and install the Internet Explorer and Firefox browsers. Having more than one browser on your machine can be helpful if you want to test how a Web page is displayed in different browsers, for example.

**ESTIMATED COMPLETION TIME: 30 minutes**

 **Activity**

Follow these directions to download an update for Internet Explorer. As always, remember that Web sites change often, so your steps might differ slightly.

1. Open your browser, and go to **www.microsoft.com**. Locate the link to download the latest version of Internet Explorer. At the time of this writing, the link for downloading

the latest version was *www.microsoft.com/windows/ie/downloads/default.mspx*. If you find the link for the latest version at a different location, record it here:

_____

2. Click **English** and click **Go**. Click the link to begin downloading.

3. The File Download dialog box opens. Click the **Save this program to disk** option button, and then click **OK** (Windows 9x and 2000) or **Save** (Windows XP).

4. The Save As dialog box opens. Navigate to the C:\Downloads folder you created in Lab 18.4, and click **Save** to save the Internet Explorer setup file to that folder.

5. The File Download dialog box closes, and a dialog box indicating the progress of the download is displayed. If necessary, click the **Close this dialog box when download completes** check box. You know that the download is finished when the File Download dialog box closes. If you don't select this option, the progress indicator and the messages in the File Download dialog box change to indicate when the download is finished.

Follow these directions to install the version of Internet Explorer you downloaded:

1. Close all open windows.

2. Locate and double-click the **Internet Explorer** setup file in Windows Explorer in the C:\Downloads directory. If a security warning dialog box opens, click **Run.**

3. The Internet Explorer setup program starts. In the Welcome window, click **Next**. Accept the license agreement, and click **Validate** in the next window. Leave the option to install the latest updates selected, and then click **Next**.

4. In the next window, you can choose a typical or custom installation. Verify that the **Install now** option is selected to proceed with a typical installation, and then click **Next**.

5. A status window shows the progress of downloading and installing components. This process might take several minutes. When the status window closes and a message prompting you to restart your computer is displayed, click **Restart Now (Recommended)** to restart your computer and complete the installation.

Follow these steps to download and install Firefox:

1. Open your browser and go to **www.mozilla.com**. Click the link to download the latest version of Firefox.

2. The File Download dialog box opens. Click the **Save this program to disk** option button, and then click **OK** (Windows 9x and 2000) or **Save** (Windows XP).

3. The Save As dialog box opens. Navigate to the C:\Downloads folder you created in Lab 18.4, and click **Save** to save the Firefox setup file to that folder.

4. The File Download dialog box closes, and a dialog box indicating the progress of the download is displayed. If necessary, click the **Close this dialog box when download completes** check box. You know that the download is finished when the File Download dialog box closes. If you don't select this option, the progress indicator and the messages in the File Download dialog box change to indicate when the download is finished.

Follow these directions to install the version of Firefox you downloaded:

1. Close all open windows.

2. Locate and double-click the Firefox setup file in Windows Explorer in the C:\Downloads directory. If a security warning dialog box opens, click **Run.**

3. The Firefox setup program opens, showing the welcome window. Click **Next**.

4. The software license agreement window opens. Click **I accept the terms of the License Agreement,** and then click **Next**.

5. In the next window, you can choose a standard or custom installation. Verify that the **Standard** option is selected to proceed with a typical installation, and click **Next**.

6. A summary window is displayed to verify your downloading choices. If everything is correct, click **Next**.

7. A status window shows the progress of installing components. When the Install Complete dialog box opens, verify that the **Launch Mozilla Firefox now** check box is selected. Then click **Finish** to end the installation and launch Firefox.

## REVIEW QUESTIONS

1. Which installation took longer: Internet Explorer or Firefox?

   _____

2. Which installation offered more options for customization during the recommended/typical installation process?

   _____

   _____

3. List any other differences you noticed in the installations of Firefox and Internet Explorer:

   _____

   _____

   _____

   _____

4. List any differences you found between the procedures in this lab and the actual steps required to download and install the most current versions of the two browsers:

   _____

   _____

   _____

   _____

# LAB 18.6 CONFIGURE A BROWSER SO THAT IT DOESN'T DOWNLOAD IMAGES

## OBJECTIVES

The goal of this lab is to help you set up your browser so that it doesn't download images. After completing this lab, you will be able to:

▲ Configure Firefox so that it doesn't download images

▲ Configure Internet Explorer so that it doesn't download images

## MATERIALS REQUIRED

This lab requires the following:

▲ Windows 2000/XP or Windows 9x operating system

▲ Internet access

▲ Internet Explorer and Firefox installed on the same computer (as specified in Lab 18.5)

## LAB PREPARATION

Before the lab begins, the instructor or lab assistant needs to do the following:

▲ Verify that Windows starts with no errors.

▲ Verify that Internet access is available.

## ACTIVITY BACKGROUND

Slow browser performance can be caused by a variety of factors, such as a full cache, temporary files directory, or history file. It can also be caused by the size of the content in the Web page you're viewing. One way to improve browser performance is to set up your browser so that it downloads only text and not images. In this lab, you explore Firefox and Internet Explorer (which you installed in Lab 18.5) and find the options for selecting text-only downloads.

**ESTIMATED COMPLETION TIME: 30 minutes**

### Activity

Follow these steps to configure Firefox and Internet Explorer so that they don't download images:

1. Open Internet Explorer and browse the Web for a couple of minutes, recording the URLs of the sites you visit. (You need these URLs later in this lab.)

_____

_____

_____

_____

2. Click **Tools, Internet Options** from the menu. Explore the various options until you find the tab for configuring Internet Explorer so that it doesn't download images. Make that change and record your procedure here:

_____

_____

_____

3. Close the Internet Options dialog box, and click **View, Reload** from the browser menu. How does the current Web page change?

_____

4. Revisit the Web sites you recorded in Step 1. Do you notice any differences in how the pages are displayed or in how the browser performs? Record any differences in browser performance here:

_____

_____

5. Follow the same basic steps to configure Firefox so that it doesn't download images. Using the following lines, record the same information and answer the same questions for Firefox that you did for Internet Explorer, noting any differences in locations, names of menus, and procedures:

_____

_____

_____

_____

_____

_____

_____

_____

_____

## REVIEW QUESTIONS

1. Which browser was easier to configure? Explain your answer:

_____

_____

_____

2. For both browsers, was the option for not downloading images located where you expected it to be? If not, where would you have expected to find it?

_____

_____

3. Did you notice any other similar options in either browser that might also improve browser performance? If so, list them:

_____

_____

4. Did you notice any difference in how the two browsers performed before you blocked downloading images? After you blocked downloading images? Explain your answer:

_____

_____

_____

_____

5. Under what circumstances might you want to block image downloads?

_____

_____

_____

# LAB 18.7 USE REMOTE DESKTOP

## OBJECTIVES

The goal of this lab is to learn how to log on to another computer remotely by using Windows Remote Desktop. After completing this lab, you will be able to:

▲ Configure Remote Desktop

▲ Use Remote Desktop to log on to another computer remotely

## MATERIALS REQUIRED

This lab requires the following:

▲ Windows XP Professional operating system

▲ A network workgroup consisting of two computers

▲ A workgroup of 2 to 4 students

## LAB PREPARATION

Before the lab begins, the instructor or lab assistant needs to do the following:

▲ Verify that Windows starts with no errors.

▲ Verify that a network connection is available.

## ACTIVITY BACKGROUND

Windows XP Professional allows users to connect remotely from other Windows machines. The remote client software is installed automatically in Windows XP but is also available for Windows 2000 and 9x. With a remote connection, you can control a computer from another location, such as work or home. This feature might be useful if you need to access files or programs from another location, for example. In this lab, you configure one computer to accept a remote connection, and then connect to it from another machine.

**ESTIMATED COMPLETION TIME: 30 minutes**

**Activity**

To configure a computer to accept a remote connection, follow these steps:

1. Log on to an account with administrative privileges. Write down the account name and password:

   _____

2. To determine the computer name, open Control Panel, click **Performance and Maintenance**, and click **System**. In the System Properties dialog box, click the **Computer Name** tab. Write down the computer name:

   _____

3. Click the **Remote** tab, and then click the **Allow users to connect remotely to this computer** check box (see Figure 18-2).

4. Log off the system.

To establish a remote connection, follow these steps:

1. Move to another computer on the same network, and log on.

2. Click **Start**, point to **All Programs**, point to **Accessories**, point to **Communications**, and click **Remote Desktop Connection**.

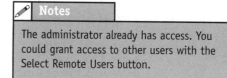

**Notes**

The administrator already has access. You could grant access to other users with the Select Remote Users button.

3. Enter the computer name (of the remote computer) or its IP address (which you learned how to determine in Lab 17.1), and then click **Connect**.

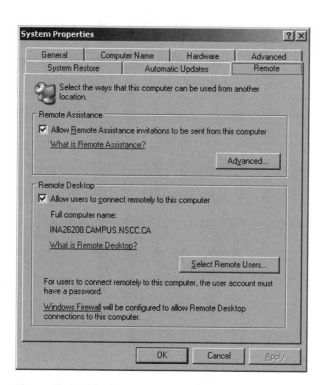

**Figure 18-2** Allowing users to connect remotely to a computer

**Notes**

Windows Firewall in SP2 blocks the port used by remote access if the Don't allow exceptions check box is selected when configuring firewall settings.

4. Log on to the other computer remotely with the account information you wrote down earlier.

5. When you're finished, log off to close the connection.

## REVIEW QUESTIONS

1. Describe two situations when you might want to use Remote Desktop Connection:

_____

_____

_____

_____

2. How can you tell if you are connected remotely to another computer?

_____

3. How can you determine the name of the remote computer before connecting?

_____

_____

4. How might other programs, such as firewalls, interfere with a remote connection?

_____

_____

_____

_____

# CHAPTER 19

# Securing Your PC and Network

**Labs included in this chapter:**

# LAB 19.1 PROTECT YOUR COMPUTER FROM VIRUSES AND ADWARE

## OBJECTIVES

The goal of this lab is to help you use antivirus and anti-adware software to protect your computer. After completing this lab, you will be able to:

▲ Install antivirus software

▲ Scan your system for viruses and adware

## MATERIALS REQUIRED

This lab requires the following:

▲ Windows 2000/XP operating system

▲ Internet access

▲ *Optional*: An installed antivirus program

## LAB PREPARATION

Before lab begins, the instructor or lab assistant needs to do the following:

▲ Verify that Windows starts with no errors.

▲ Verify that Internet access is available.

## ACTIVITY BACKGROUND

One of the best ways to protect your computer against malicious software is to always run current antivirus and antispyware software. Many excellent antivirus programs are available commercially, such as Norton AntiVirus or McAfee VirusScan. However, if you don't have an antivirus program installed but suspect your computer is infected, many Web-based programs are available to scan and disinfect your system. In this lab, you "infect" your computer with a fake virus, and then use a Web-based antivirus program to disinfect your system.

**ESTIMATED COMPLETION TIME: 60 minutes**

 **Activity**

1. Open your browser, and go to **www.eicar.org**. Attempt to download the **eicar.com** antivirus test file. If you're already running an antivirus program, you'll probably be alerted that the file is infected and the download will be blocked or isolated.

2. What alert or warning does your antivirus program display when you try to download this file?

_____

3. Next, go to **http://housecall.trendmicro.com** and click **Scan Now. It's Free!** On the next page, click **Scan Now. It's Free!** again.

4. Follow the instructions to launch the program, and then click the appropriate button to do a complete scan of the computer. Depending on your system, this process might take some time.

5. When the scan is finished, you can choose to delete any infected files. How many infections did HouseCall find?

_____

6. Exit the program and close your browser.

Occasionally, some infected files, particularly adware, manage to avoid detection by one program or another. For this reason, running several anti-adware programs on your computer is often useful. Follow these steps to download and run two anti-adware programs:

1. Open your Web browser, if necessary, and go to **www.lavasoft.com**. Click to download **Ad-Aware SE Personal**, and install it on your system. Leave your Web browser open.

2. Use this program to perform a system scan of your computer, which could take several minutes. How many critical objects were recognized?

   _____

3. Next, go to **www.spybot.info**. Click **English,** click to download **Spybot Search and Destroy** by PepiMK, and install it on your system.

4. Use the program to check your computer for problems. Did Spybot find any adware that the first program missed?

   _____

5. Exit the program.

## REVIEW QUESTIONS

1. List some ways your computer might become infected with a virus:

   _____

2. Why is it important to allow your antivirus program to update its virus definition files automatically?

   _____

3. Why do some companies bundle adware with their programs?

   _____

4. Why does scanning your hard drive for viruses take so long?

   _____

5. What can you do if you aren't running antivirus software and suspect your computer is infected?

   _____

## *LAB 19.2 USE ENCRYPTION*

### OBJECTIVES

The goal of this lab is to help you work with encryption and observe the effects of trying to use an encrypted file without permission. After completing this lab, you will be able to:

◢ Encrypt a directory

◢ Save files to the encrypted directory

◢ Access the encrypted files as a different user

## MATERIALS REQUIRED

This lab requires the following:

◢ Windows XP Professional operating system installed on an NTFS partition

◢ A blank floppy disk

## LAB PREPARATION

Before the lab begins, the instructor or lab assistant needs to do the following:

◢ Verify that Windows starts with no errors.

## ACTIVITY BACKGROUND

Despite your best efforts, unauthorized users might gain access to sensitive files. To protect these files from this type of security breach, you can use file encryption, which prevents unauthorized users from being able to view files, even if they do manage to gain access to them. You can encrypt individual files or entire directories. As with disk quotas, you can use file encryption only on NTFS drives. FAT file systems don't support file encryption. In this lab, you create and encrypt an entire directory, and then create a test file in that encrypted directory.

**ESTIMATED COMPLETION TIME: 30 minutes**

 **Activity**

Follow these steps to create an encrypted directory and a test file in that directory:

1. Log on as an administrator.

2. In Windows Explorer, create two new directories in the NTFS root called **Encrypt** and **Normal**.

3. Right-click the **Encrypt** folder, and then click **Properties**. The Encrypt Properties dialog box opens.

4. Click the **Advanced** button to open the Advanced Attributes dialog box.

5. Click the **Encrypt contents to secure data** check box to encrypt the contents of the Encrypt folder.

6. Click **OK** to apply the settings and close the Advanced Attributes dialog box. You return to the Encrypt Properties dialog box.

7. Click **OK** to apply encryption.

8. In Windows Explorer, double-click the **Encrypt** folder to open it.

9. From the Windows Explorer menu, click **File**, point to **New**, and click **Text Document**. Double-click **New Text Document** and type **This file is encrypted**. Close the file, saving it as **Secure.txt**.

Follow these steps to see the effects of encrypting a file in Windows:

1. Double-click **Secure.txt** in the Encrypt folder and record what happens:

_____

2. Log off as an administrator, and log on again as a different user.

3. Double-click **Secure.txt** in the Encrypt folder and record the results:

_____

4. Copy **Secure.txt** to the Normal folder and record the results:

_____

5. Log off, and then log on again as an administrator.
6. Copy **Secure.txt** to the Normal folder and record the results:

_____

7. Insert a blank, formatted floppy disk. Copy **Secure.txt** to drive A, and record the results:

_____

8. Log off, and then log on again as the previous user.
9. Double-click **Secure.txt** in the Normal folder and record the results:

_____

10. Double-click **Secure.txt** in drive A and record the results:

_____

_____

11. Right-click the **Secure.txt** file in drive A, and then click **Properties**. The file's Properties dialog box opens. Is there an Advanced button?

_____

12. Right-click the **Secure.txt** file in the Normal folder, and then click **Properties**. The file's Properties dialog box opens.
13. Click the **Advanced** button, click to clear the **Encrypt contents to secure data** check box, and then click **OK**. Record the results:

_____

_____

## REVIEW QUESTIONS

1. Which file system must be used to enable encryption?

_____

2. How do you encrypt a single file?

_____

3. What happens when an unauthorized user tries to open an encrypted file?

_____

_____

4. What happens when an unauthorized user tries to unencrypt a file?

_____

_____

5. What happens to an encrypted file that's removed from an NTFS partition?

_____

_____

## *LAB 19.3 SECURE A WIRELESS LAN*

### OBJECTIVES

The goal of this lab is to learn how to set up and configure security options on your wireless router. After completing this lab, you will be able to:

◢ Download a manual for a wireless router

◢ Explain how to improve wireless security

◢ Describe some methods of securing a wireless LAN

### MATERIALS REQUIRED

This lab requires the following:

◢ Windows XP Professional operating system

◢ Internet access

◢ Adobe Acrobat Reader installed for viewing .pdf files

### LAB PREPARATION

Before the lab begins, the instructor or lab assistant needs to do the following:

◢ Verify that Windows starts with no errors.

◢ Verify that Internet access is available.

### ACTIVITY BACKGROUND

Wireless networks have become common in recent years and are a simple way to include a laptop in your home network. Without adequate security, however, you can open up your network to a wide range of threats. In this lab, you learn how to enable and configure some security features of your wireless router.

**ESTIMATED COMPLETION TIME: 45 minutes**

 Activity

1. Open your Web browser, and go to **www.linksys.com**.

2. Click **Downloads**.

3. In the drop-down list of products, click **WRT54G V1.0**, and then click the **Downloads For This Product** button.

 Notes

Your instructor might choose to substitute the manual for another wireless router instead of having you download the Linksys user guide.

4. Click the **User Guide** link. The manual opens in a separate window in .pdf format. Use it to answer the following questions:

◢ Most wireless routers can be configured with a Web-based utility by entering the router's IP address in the browser's Address text box. What's the default IP address of this router?

_____

◢ Describe how you would log in to the router for the first time:

_____

_____

_____

Most routers are easily configured with a setup utility that asks a series of questions about your network and Internet service provider. The default settings, however, might not enable all your router's security features. These are the four most important steps in securing your LAN:

◢ Setting a password on the router itself so that other people can't change its configuration

◢ Not broadcasting your network's name (called a service set identifier—SSID) to anyone who's listening

◢ Using some kind of encryption

◢ Enabling MAC filtering so that you can limit access to only your computers

Now continue to use the manual to answer the following additional questions:

◢ Which window in the router's Web-based utility do you use to change the user name and password?

_____

◢ List the steps for changing the router's SSID:

_____

_____

_____

_____

◢ How many hexadecimal characters must be used for 64-bit Wired Equivalent Privacy (WEP) encryption?

_____

◢ Describe the steps to limit access to everything but your laptop through MAC filtering:

_____

_____

_____

_____

## REVIEW QUESTIONS

1. How are most wireless routers configured?

2. Why should you change your router's password before making any other security changes?

3. Why don't "password" and "linksys" make strong passwords?

4. Why might you choose to enter a WEP key manually instead of using a passphrase?

# LAB 19.4 INVESTIGATE STARTUP PROCESSES

## OBJECTIVES

The goal of this lab is to help you identify malicious software running on your computer by examining all running processes. After completing this lab, you will be able to:

- Identify all processes running on your computer at startup
- Use the Internet to determine the function of each process

## MATERIALS REQUIRED

This lab requires the following:

- Windows 2000/XP Professional operating system
- Internet access

## LAB PREPARATION

Before the lab begins, the instructor or lab assistant needs to do the following:

- Verify that Windows starts with no errors.
- Verify that Internet access is available.

## ACTIVITY BACKGROUND

There's an old saying that a rose is a weed in the vegetable garden. Malicious software, for the same reason, is any software you don't want using up valuable resources on your computer. The first step in removing it is realizing it's there. In this lab, you learn to investigate all the startup processes on your computer and identify any you want to remove.

**Activity**

1. Use Task Manager to list all the running processes on your machine. (You might want to refer to Lab 12.5 for a review of this process.)

2. On a separate piece of paper, make a list of each process running on the computer. How many processes are running?

   _____

3. Now reboot the computer in Safe Mode, and use Task Manager to list the running processes again. How many processes are running now?

4. Which processes didn't load when the system was running in Safe Mode?

   _____

   _____

   _____

   _____

5. Use the Internet to research each process identified in Step 4, and write a one-sentence explanation of each process on a separate piece of paper.

6. Did you find any malicious processes running? If so, list them:

   _____

   _____

   _____

7. Suppose one of the processes running on your computer is named whAgent.exe. What program is associated with this process?

   _____

8. List the steps you could take to remove this program from your computer:

   _____

   _____

   _____

   _____

## REVIEW QUESTIONS

1. Why might antivirus and antispyware software not detect malicious software?

   _____

   _____

2. Why would you expect fewer processes to be running in Safe Mode?

_____

_____

3. How might a malicious process get onto your computer?

_____

_____

4. Why isn't disabling the Lsass.exe process a good idea?

_____

# Notebooks, Tablet PCs, and PDAs

**Labs included in this chapter:**

- **Lab 20.1:** Examine Notebook Documentation
- **Lab 20.2:** Compare Notebooks and Desktops
- **Lab 20.3:** Replace a Notebook Hard Drive
- **Lab 20.4:** Research Software Available for PDAs
- **Lab 20.5:** Battery Calibration and Power Management

# *LAB 20.1 EXAMINE NOTEBOOK DOCUMENTATION*

## OBJECTIVES

The goal of this lab is to help you find documentation for a notebook on a manufacturer's Web site and become familiar with it. After completing this lab, you will be able to:

◢ Locate documentation for specific notebook computer models

◢ Download the documentation

◢ Use the documentation to find critical information

## MATERIALS REQUIRED

This lab requires the following:

◢ Internet access

## LAB PREPARATION

Before the lab begins, the instructor or lab assistant needs to do the following:

◢ Verify that Internet access is available.

## ACTIVITY BACKGROUND

Notebooks are designed for portability, compactness, and energy conservation, and their designs are often highly proprietary. Therefore, establishing general procedures for supporting notebooks is more difficult than for desktop computers. Often, consulting the documentation for a particular model is necessary to get information on technical specifications and support procedures. In this lab, you locate and download documentation for two different notebook computers, and then use that documentation to answer questions about each model.

| ESTIMATED COMPLETION TIME: 30 minutes |
| --- |

 **Activity**

Follow these steps to locate and download documentation:

1. Choose two notebook manufacturers listed in Table 20-1, go to their Web sites, and select one model from each to research. List your two choices here:

_____

_____

| Manufacturer | Web Site |
| --- | --- |
| Acer America | *http://global.acer.com* |
| ARM Computer | *www.armcomputer.com* |
| Compaq Computer | *www.hp.com* |
| Dell Computer | *www.dell.com* |
| Gateway | *www.gateway.com* |
| Hewlett-Packard | *www.hp.com* |

**Table 20-1**   Notebook manufacturers

| Manufacturer | Web Site |
|---|---|
| IBM | www.ibm.com |
| Micron PC | www.buympc.com |
| PC Notebook | www.pcnotebook.com |
| Sony | www.sonystyle.com/vaio |
| Toshiba America | www.csd.toshiba.com |
| WinBook | www.winbook.com |

**Table 20-1**   Notebook manufacturers (continued)

2. In the Support section of each Web site, search for documentation on both models you chose and follow the directions to download it. Were you able to find documentation for both models? If not, list the models for which you were unable to find documentation. Try other models until you have located documentation for two.

_____

_____

3. Using the documentation you found, answer the following questions for your first model. If you can't answer a question because the information isn't included in the documentation, write "information unavailable."

▲ What type of processor does the notebook use and how much RAM is installed?

_____

▲ What operating system does the notebook support?

_____

▲ Could you download or save the documentation locally, or did you have to view it on the company's Web site?

_____

▲ Does the notebook offer Quick Launch keys for commonly used applications? If so, can you customize them? How? If they can't be customized, what buttons are offered, and which applications do they launch?

_____

_____

_____

▲ List the functions assigned to keys F1 through F4:

_____

_____

_____

_____

◢ Does the notebook have a sleep or hibernation mode? If so, how do you activate it? How does activating this mode differ from shutting down the computer?

_____

_____

_____

◢ What other types of downloads are offered besides the manual?

_____

_____

◢ What type of optical storage (CD, CD-RW, DVD, and so forth) does the notebook offer?

_____

_____

◢ What type of networking (modem, NIC, infrared port, wireless LAN port, and so forth) comes built in?

_____

_____

_____

**4.** Using the documentation you found, answer the following questions for your second model. If you can't answer a question because the information isn't included in the documentation, write "information unavailable."

◢ What type of processor does the notebook use and how much RAM is installed?

_____

_____

◢ What operating system does the notebook support?

_____

_____

◢ Could you download or save the documentation locally, or did you have to view it on the company's Web site?

_____

_____

◢ Does the notebook offer Quick Launch keys for commonly used applications? If so, can you customize them? How? If they can't be customized, what buttons are offered, and which applications do they launch?

_____

_____

_____

◢ List the functions assigned to keys F1 through F4:

_____

_____

_____

_____

◢ Does the notebook have a sleep or hibernation mode? If so, how do you activate it? How does activating this mode differ from shutting down the computer?

_____

_____

_____

◢ What other types of downloads are offered besides the manual?

_____

_____

◢ What type of optical storage (CD, CD-RW, DVD, and so forth) does the notebook offer?

_____

◢ What type of networking (modem, NIC, infrared port, wireless LAN port, and so forth) comes built in?

_____

_____

### Alternate Activity

If you have access to a notebook computer, do the following:

1. Go to the manufacturer's Web site for your notebook computer and download the user manual, if available. List other downloads that are available:

_____

_____

_____

2. From the list of available downloads, choose a device driver or system update for your notebook. Download and install it following the instructions on the site. List the driver or update and the steps you took to install it on your notebook:

_____

_____

_____

_____

_____

## REVIEW QUESTIONS

1. On a manufacturer's Web site, where do you usually find support and documentation information?

_____

2. For which model was it easiest to find documentation? Which manufacturer site did you think was most user friendly and, in general, offered the best support?

_____

_____

3. Besides the questions you researched in the lab, what other type of information is available in the manuals you reviewed?

_____

_____

4. Of the notebooks you researched, which one would you purchase? Explain your answer:

_____

_____

# LAB 20.2 COMPARE NOTEBOOKS AND DESKTOPS

## OBJECTIVES

The goal of this lab is to help you compare the specifications and costs for notebook and desktop computers. After completing this lab, you will be able to:

▲ Compile a list of specifications for a computer according to its purpose

▲ Locate a desktop computer and a notebook computer with similar specifications

▲ Compare the price of a desktop computer to a similar notebook computer and decide which you would purchase

## MATERIALS REQUIRED

This lab requires the following:

▲ Internet access

## LAB PREPARATION

Before the lab begins, the instructor or lab assistant needs to do the following:

▲ Verify that Internet access is available.

## ACTIVITY BACKGROUND

When you shop for a computer, your purchasing decisions are generally driven by questions such as: What will the computer be used for? What features are required to accomplish your goals? What features would be nice to have but aren't essential? What features are you willing to compromise on to gain others?

One of the most basic decisions is whether to choose a notebook computer or a desktop. Unlike desktops, notebooks are portable; however, to make notebooks portable, manufacturers often sacrifice performance or other features. In addition, you usually pay more for a notebook than for a desktop computer with comparable features. In this lab, you compile a list of requirements for a computer, locate a notebook and desktop computer with those features, and compare the two systems.

**ESTIMATED COMPLETION TIME: 30 minutes**

### Activity

1. Determine your requirements by answering the following questions:

   ◢ What will the computer mainly be used for? (Possible uses include office applications, graphics and multimedia, gaming, and software development.)

   _____

   ◢ Based on the purpose, what features are required? Include in your list the amount of memory and hard drive space you want. (Some features you might consider include wireless support, display or screen type, software packages supported, PC card support, and external device support.)

   _____

   _____

   _____

   _____

   _____

   ◢ List any additional features you would like but don't require:

   _____

   _____

   _____

   _____

2. Use computer manufacturer Web sites (such as the ones listed in Table 20-1) or comparison Web sites (such as *www.cnet.com* or *www.pricewatch.com*) to find one notebook and one desktop computer that fulfill as many of your requirements as possible and are as similar to each other as possible. Summarize your findings by filling in Table 20-2. Print the Web pages supporting this information.

| Features | Desktop Computer | Notebook Computer |
|---|---|---|
| Manufacturer and model | | |
| Processor type and frequency | | |
| Memory installed | | |
| Hard drive space | | |
| Operating system | | |
| Drive 1 | | |
| Drive 2 | | |
| Drive 3 | | |
| External ports | | |
| Preinstalled applications | | |
| Cost | | |

**Table 20-2**   Desktop and notebook computer specifications

3. Based on your research and the requirements you listed in Step 1, would you purchase a desktop computer or a notebook? Explain your answer:

_____

_____

_____

## REVIEW QUESTIONS

1. Which computer was more expensive: the desktop or the notebook? What was the price difference?

_____

_____

2. What features, if any, were you unable to find information for?

_____

_____

3. What features, if any, were missing from the desktop and notebook? How did this information influence your purchasing decision?

_____

_____

4. Did you change your requirements or expectations based on the available products? Explain your answer:

_____

_____

_____

5. Was it easier to find a comparable desktop and notebook from the same manufacturer or from a different manufacturer? Why or why not?

_____

_____

_____

# LAB 20.3 REPLACE A NOTEBOOK HARD DRIVE

## OBJECTIVES

The goal of this lab is to show you the process of replacing a hard drive in a notebook computer. After completing this lab, you will be able to:

◢ Locate the hard drive in a notebook computer

◢ Remove the hard drive from a notebook computer

◢ Replace the hard drive in a notebook computer

## MATERIALS REQUIRED

This lab requires the following:

◢ A notebook computer or Internet access

◢ Printer access

◢ A PC toolkit with antistatic ground strap

◢ Additional smaller screwdrivers, if necessary

## LAB PREPARATION

Before the lab begins, the instructor or lab assistant needs to do the following:

◢ Verify that Internet access is available.

## ACTIVITY BACKGROUND

Hard disk drives are by nature delicate devices. Dropping one, even a few inches, can cause permanent damage to the read/write heads, platter surfaces, or both. Notebook systems are, of course, often moved and commonly subjected to forces that most other hard drives never encounter. Although drives intended for notebook systems are designed to be resistant to movement and shock, they are still more likely to fail than any other notebook component. In this lab, you remove a hard drive from a notebook computer, and then reinstall the same hard drive. If you don't have access to a notebook, skip to the alternate activity at the end of this lab.

Hard drives designed for notebook computers tend to be 75% to 100% more expensive than the standard 3.5-inch drives of comparable capacity for desktop computers. Also, the majority of newer notebooks support most 2.5-inch drives designed for notebooks, but sometimes a notebook computer requires a proprietary hard drive. For these reasons, researching your replacement options carefully is important. Read the documentation that came with your notebook to determine what drives it supports. If this information isn't available in the documentation, search the manufacturer's Web site. For the purpose of this lab, you remove the existing drive, and then reinstall the same drive. The steps for your notebook might be slightly different from the procedures in this lab, so make sure you study the documentation before you begin.

**ESTIMATED COMPLETION TIME: 30 minutes**

**Activity**

1. What are the manufacturer and model of your notebook computer?

   _____

2. Based on the notebook's documentation or information on the manufacturer's Web site, what type of hard drive can be used to replace the existing hard drive? Be as specific as the documentation or the Web site:

   _____

   _____

3. Search the Internet for a replacement hard drive that meets your notebook's requirements. Print the Web page showing the specifications and cost for the drive. How much space does the hard drive have?

   _____

4. Look for specific directions (in the documentation or on the Web site) for removing and replacing your notebook's hard drive. If you find any, summarize those directions here. (If you're using the Web site as your source of information, print any relevant Web pages.)

   _____

   _____

   _____

   _____

Follow these general steps to remove the hard drive from a notebook computer. Note that these directions might not list every step necessary for your model. Refer to specific directions in the documentation or the manufacturer's Web site, as needed.

1. Remove the main battery or batteries and, if necessary, unplug the computer from the AC adapter. Close the screen and turn the computer so that the bottom is facing up.

2. Locate and remove the access panel or component enclosing the drive bay. In many notebooks, the hard drive is located beneath a floppy drive or other removable device, as shown in Figure 20-1.

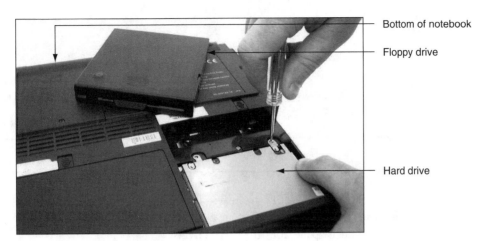

Figure 20-1   Remove the floppy drive first to reveal the hard drive cavity

3. After you have accessed the drive, determine how it's secured in the system. It's commonly attached to a frame or "cradle" with small screws, and the cradle is often attached directly to the system chassis. This cradle helps locate and support the drive inside the drive bay. Remove the screws securing the cradle.

4. In most notebooks, data cables don't connect the hard drive to the motherboard, as in desktop computers. Instead, a hard drive connects to the notebook's motherboard by way of an edge connector, similar to those on expansion cards in desktop computers. This type of direct connection has two advantages. First, it improves reliability because it reduces the total number of connection points; fewer connection points mean fewer connections that could shake loose as the notebook is moved around in daily use. The second advantage is that the lack of data cables reduces the notebook's overall size and weight. To remove the drive-cradle assembly, slide the cradle away from the connector. Slide the assembly back until all pins are clear of the connector. When the pins are clear, lift the assembly straight up out of the drive bay.

5. Note the orientation of the drive in the cradle so that when you reinstall the drive, you can mount it in the same direction. Remove the screws securing the drive in the cradle, and then remove the drive.

Follow these general steps to reinstall the hard drive in the notebook computer. Note that these directions might not list every step necessary for your model. Refer to specific directions in the documentation or the manufacturer's Web site, as needed.

1. If necessary, configure the jumper settings to indicate master or slave. Place the drive in the cradle so that the pins are oriented correctly, and then secure it with screws.

2. Set the drive-cradle assembly straight down into the drive bay. Gently slide the assembly to the connector, and verify that the pins are aligned correctly with the connector. Slide the assembly until the drive is fully seated in the connector. The cradle should now align with the holes in the chassis. If the holes don't align, you should remove the assembly, loosen the drive-retaining screws, and adjust the drive's position in the cradle. Repeat this process until the drive is fully seated so that there's no room for it to move after the cradle is secured. When the assembly is seated, secure it with screws.

3. Replace any drives or access covers you removed to get at the hard drive.

4. Reinstall any batteries and reconnect to AC power, if necessary. As with any other hard drive, a notebook drive must be recognized by BIOS correctly, and then partitioned and formatted before it can be used. This process isn't necessary in this lab because you haven't installed a new hard drive.

**⚙ Alternate Activity**

If you don't have access to a notebook computer, follow these steps:

1. Using the documentation for one of the notebooks you selected in Lab 20.1 as your source, what are its requirements for a replacement hard drive? Be as specific as the documentation:

   _____

   _____

2. Search the Internet for information on replacement hard drives, and print the Web page showing the correct specifications for a replacement hard drive. What is the cost of the drive? How much space does the drive have?

   _____

3. Locate the steps for replacing the hard drive. To find this information, use the manuals you downloaded in Lab 20.1, the manufacturers' Web sites, and other Internet resources (such as Web sites for manufacturers of replacement notebook hard drives).

4. How do the steps you found differ from the steps in this lab? Note the differences here:

   _____

   _____

   _____

   _____

   _____

   _____

   _____

   _____

## REVIEW QUESTIONS

1. Why should you research hard drives thoroughly when replacing one in a notebook computer?

   _____

   _____

2. Why is cabling commonly not included in notebook systems?

   _____

   _____

3. How was the installation procedure for your computer different from the one in this lab?

_____

_____

_____

4. Suppose you need to install a hard drive in a notebook that doesn't include an access panel for the hard drive. Where should you look for the hard drive inside the notebook?

_____

_____

5. What do you have to do in CMOS setup before a new hard drive can be used?

_____

_____

# LAB 20.4 RESEARCH SOFTWARE AVAILABLE FOR PDAS

## OBJECTIVES

The goal of this lab is to help you research and compare personal digital assistants (PDAs). After completing this lab, you will be able to:

▲ Locate and compare information on available PDAs

## MATERIALS REQUIRED

This lab requires the following:

▲ Internet access

## LAB PREPARATION

Before the lab begins, the instructor or lab assistant needs to do the following:

▲ Verify that Internet access is available.

## ACTIVITY BACKGROUND

One common problem with PDAs is finding compatible software (in addition to preinstalled software). There are two basic choices for a PDA operating system: Windows Mobile and Palm OS. Earlier handheld OSs by Microsoft are PocketPC and Windows CE. Before you can install additional software, you must verify that the software is compatible with the PDA's operating system and with the specific PDA model. On some basic models, you can't add any software. You must also make sure the software is compatible with the desktop PC that you want to synchronize with the PDA. Finally, some business organizations don't allow certain PDAs to synchronize with the business network. You learn more about these issues in this lab as you research software availability for two different PDA models.

**ESTIMATED COMPLETION TIME: 30 minutes**

**Activity**

1. Using the manufacturer sites listed in Tables 20-3 and 20-4, select one Palm OS PDA and one Windows Mobile PDA. Record the name and model number of your choices here:

   _____

   _____

| Manufacturer | Web Site |
|---|---|
| HandEra | *www.handera.com* |
| Handspring | *www.handspring.com* |
| IBM | *www.ibm.com* |
| Palm | *www.palm.com* |
| Sony | *www.sonystyle.com* |

**Table 20-3**   Manufacturers of Palm OS PDAs

| Manufacturer | Web Site |
|---|---|
| Casio | *www.casio.com* |
| Compaq | *www.hp.com* |
| Hewlett-Packard | *www.hp.com* |
| Toshiba | *www.toshiba.com* |

**Table 20-4**   Manufacturers of Windows Mobile and PocketPC PDAs

2. On the manufacturers' Web sites, search for technical specifications and lists of installed software for the first model you selected. Then answer the following questions for this model. Download and search user manuals if necessary.

   ◢ What version of the operating system is installed?

   _____

   ◢ What software comes installed on the PDA?

   _____

   _____

   _____

   _____

   ◢ Can you install other software? If so, list some available programs:

   _____

   _____

   _____

   _____

▲ Can the applications on the PDA synchronize with common office applications on a desktop PC or notebook? List the applications on the PDA and the applications on the desktop PC or notebook with which they can synchronize:

_____

_____

_____

_____

_____

▲ Does the PDA support upgrades to the OS? Why would you want to have this capability?

_____

_____

▲ What add-on devices are available for the PDA, such as recharger cradles, cameras, and so forth?

_____

_____

_____

3. Answer the following questions for the second model PDA:

   ▲ What version of the operating system is installed?

   _____

   ▲ What software comes installed on the PDA?

   _____

   _____

   _____

   ▲ Can you install other software? If so, list some available programs:

   _____

   _____

_____

_____

_____

_____

▴ Can the applications on the PDA synchronize with common office applications on a desktop PC or notebook? List the applications on the PDA and the applications on the desktop PC or notebook with which they can synchronize:

_____

_____

_____

_____

_____

_____

▴ Does the PDA support upgrades to the OS? Why would you want to have this capability?

_____

_____

▴ What add-on devices are available for the PDA, such as recharger cradles, cameras, and so forth?

_____

_____

_____

### Alternate Activity

If you have access to a PDA, perform the research suggested in this lab for your model. Try to locate, download, and install a trial version of an add-on software program for your PDA. Record the steps and the name of the program you installed:

_____

_____

_____

_____

_____

_____

_____

_____

_____

## REVIEW QUESTIONS

1. Was add-on software available for both PDA models you researched?

   _____

2. How easy was it to find the information you needed? List the Web sites you visited, ranking them from most user friendly to least user friendly:

   _____

   _____

   _____

   _____

3. Which PDA OS supports the most PDA applications? Explain your answer:

   _____

   _____

   _____

4. Are more or fewer software options available for the higher priced PDAs? Explain your answer:

   _____

   _____

   _____

5. Would you consider purchasing either PDA you researched in this lab? Why or why not?

   _____

   _____

   _____

   _____

6. List three questions on software availability you should research carefully before selecting a PDA:

   _____

   _____

   _____

# LAB 20.5 BATTERY CALIBRATION AND POWER MANAGEMENT

## OBJECTIVES

The goal of this lab is to demonstrate the effect battery calibration has on the power-management features of a notebook PC. After completing this lab, you will be able to:

- Explain the calibration process
- Discuss how a battery might drift from calibration
- Explain how battery calibration affects some power-management features

## MATERIALS REQUIRED

This lab requires the following:

- A Windows desktop computer
- A Windows notebook computer
- Internet access

## LAB PREPARATION

Before the lab begins, the instructor or lab assistant needs to do the following:

- Verify that Windows starts with no errors.
- Verify that Internet access is available.

## ACTIVITY BACKGROUND

Many factors affect the battery life of a notebook PC. Two common types of notebook batteries are nickel metalhydride (NiMH) and lithium ion (LiION). Lithium batteries, the most common, are more expensive and last longer. A fully charged lithium battery in good condition can provide about 3 hours of normal use. By contrast, a healthy, fully charged NiMH battery can provide about 2 hours of normal use.

As you might expect, however, "normal use" is a subjective term. The actual way you use your notebook can affect battery life dramatically. For instance, editing text in a word processor doesn't require much power compared with playing a DVD. The word processor uses only a little processor time and occasionally reads or writes to the hard drive. Playing a DVD is processor intensive and requires powering the laser in the drive, thus requiring more power than the word processor.

What the notebook does when you stop using it for a time also affects battery life. For instance, if you don't use the notebook for 10 minutes, it might go into hibernation mode automatically to conserve power. Notebooks also have a few additional power-management features to extend battery life during inactivity and protect data when the battery charge becomes low. Some of these features depend on the notebook being able to accurately judge how much life is left in the battery. If the battery is calibrated accurately, the notebook can make better power-management decisions. In this lab, you explore how power management and battery life are related.

**ESTIMATED COMPLETION TIME: 30 minutes**

**Activity**

1. Examine your desktop computer's CMOS setup utility and the Power Management applet in Control Panel. Usually, a computer's BIOS offers a wider range of options for defining a power-management profile than in Windows. Fill in the following chart to compare the power-management options offered in BIOS and Windows:

| Power-Management Options and Settings | In BIOS | In Windows |
|---|---|---|
| | | |
| | | |
| | | |
| | | |
| | | |
| | | |
| | | |
| | | |
| | | |

Although the two power-management systems might work together, to avoid possible conflict, Microsoft recommends using BIOS power management as the preferred method if BIOS power management conforms to ACPI standards. These standards have been set by a group of manufacturers, including Microsoft, Intel, and Compaq.

In addition to the BIOS features you just explored, notebooks often have features or settings that allow the computer to shut down or suspend activity if the battery is about to run out of power. But how does the computer know when power is about to run out? Electronically programmable read-only memory (EPROM) is often included in the battery assembly to inform the computer about remaining battery life. The following steps explain the basic procedure for calibrating a battery's EPROM. For specific steps for your notebook, consult its documentation or search the manufacturer's Web site.

1. Verify that your notebook has a fully charged battery attached to AC power.

2. Enter the CMOS setup utility and select the **Power Management** section.

3. In the Power Management section, disable the **Power Savings** option so that the computer doesn't attempt to save power during the calibration process.

4. In the Power Management section, disable any **Suspend on Low Battery** options to prevent interference with calibration.

5. In the Power Management section, select the **Battery Calibration** option. A warning message indicates that the calibration should be carried out only with a fully charged battery and prompts you to confirm that you want to continue.

6. Remove the AC power, and then immediately press **Y** or **Enter** to continue. A message displays the estimated remaining battery life. In a real-life situation, when you actually need to calibrate your notebook's battery, this information would likely be incorrect.

7. Wait for the battery to drain, which might take more than an hour.

8. The manufacturer might specify that the battery should be left to cool for a period after it's drained and the notebook switches off. When appropriate, reattach AC power, boot the laptop, and enter CMOS setup.

9. Select the **Power Management** section, and then select the **Battery Reset** option. This option tells the EPROM that the battery is at (or very near) zero charge and takes you back to the Power Management section of CMOS.

10. Reapply your preferred power management settings, and then save and exit CMOS setup. The battery is now calibrated so that the related power-management and suspend features will work correctly.

If you have access to a notebook and the permission of your instructor, do the following to calibrate the battery:

1. Locate documentation (in the user manual or on the Web) that explains how to calibrate the battery. Note how these steps differ from the ones listed previously:

   _____

   _____

   _____

   _____

   _____

2. Follow the specific steps for your notebook to calibrate the battery. (Do *not* attempt this procedure unless you have the specific steps because you might do damage to the notebook or battery.)

Some factors can prevent power management from functioning as intended. For instance, word-processing programs often include an auto-save feature that continually saves changes to a document at specific intervals. This feature is intended to safeguard against lost work but tends to interfere with hard disk power-down settings. Many screen savers cause similar effects and can prevent a computer from entering or exiting standby or suspend modes.

## REVIEW QUESTIONS

1. What types of activity might decrease the battery life of a fully charged battery more quickly than reading a document or spreadsheet? Give three examples:

   _____

   _____

   _____

2. In your opinion, is aggressive power management more important on a desktop computer or a notebook computer? Explain why:

   _____

   _____

   _____

3. Should BIOS power management always be used with Windows Power Management? Why or why not?

_____

_____

4. What types of programs might prevent a hard drive power-down setting from saving power as intended? Why?

_____

_____

_____

_____

5. What are two possible consequences of an incorrectly calibrated battery? Explain:

_____

_____

_____

_____

**CHAPTER**
# 21

# Supporting Printers and Scanners

**Labs included in this chapter:**

- **Lab 21.1:** Install and Share a Printer
- **Lab 21.2:** Install a Network Printer
- **Lab 21.3:** Update Printer Drivers
- **Lab 21.4:** Install and Test a Scanner
- **Lab 21.5:** Printer Maintenance and Troubleshooting
- **Lab 21.6:** Critical Thinking: Sabotage and Repair a Network Printer

# LAB 21.1 INSTALL AND SHARE A PRINTER

## OBJECTIVES

The goal of this lab is to help you install and share a printer. After completing this lab, you will be able to:

- Install a local printer on a computer
- Share a local printer with other users on the network
- Using another computer on the network, install and use the shared network printer

## MATERIALS REQUIRED

This lab requires the following:

- A printer and its printer drivers
- Two or more Windows 2000/XP or Windows 9x computers connected to a network
- Windows installation CD or installation files
- A workgroup of 3 to 4 students

## LAB PREPARATION

Before the lab begins, the instructor or lab assistant needs to do the following:

- Verify that Windows starts with no errors.
- Provide each student with access to the Windows installation files, if needed.

## ACTIVITY BACKGROUND

A printer can be connected to and dedicated to one PC (called a local printer), or it can be shared with other PCs on the network (called a network printer). For a printer to be shared on a Windows operating system, it must be physically connected to and installed on one computer and then shared with others in the same Windows workgroup. The computer with the printer physically connected to it must have the File and Printer Sharing component installed, and computers on the network using this printer must have the Client for Microsoft Networks component installed. In most cases, installing both components on all computers is easier. In this lab, you install and share a printer in a workgroup, and then use the shared printer on the network.

**ESTIMATED COMPLETION TIME: 45 minutes**

### Activity

First, you must install Client for Microsoft Networks and File and Printer Sharing (if they aren't already installed). Both components are installed on Windows 2000/XP computers by default. Client for Microsoft Networks is installed in Windows 9x by default. To install both components on Windows 9x computers (if necessary), use these steps:

1. Open Control Panel, and double-click the **Network** applet. The Network dialog box opens.
2. Click **Add**. The Select Network Component Type dialog box opens.
3. In the list box, click **Client**, and then click **Add**.

4. In the Select Network Client dialog box that opens, click **Microsoft** on the left and **Client for Microsoft Networks** on the right. Click **OK** twice, and then insert the Windows installation CD. Reboot the computer when prompted.

5. Return to the Network dialog box. Repeat Steps 2 and 3, this time clicking **Service** instead of Client. The Select Network Service dialog box opens.

6. Click **File and printer sharing for Microsoft Networks**, and then click **OK**. Click **OK** to close the Network dialog box, and then insert the Windows installation CD. Reboot the computer when prompted.

7. Return to the Network dialog box, and then click **File and Print Sharing**. The File and Print Sharing dialog box opens.

8. Verify that the **I want to be able to give others access to my files** and **I want to be able to allow others to print to my printer(s)** check boxes are selected, and then click **OK**. (You aren't practicing file sharing in this lab, but as a general rule, you usually set up file sharing and print sharing at the same time so that remote computers have access to printer drivers already installed on the host machine.) Click **OK** to close the Network dialog box.

Next, you need to verify that all computers that need to use the printer are in the same workgroup. Follow these steps:

1. Ask your instructor for the name of the workgroup you should use for this lab, and record the name here:

   _____

2. In Windows 9x, right-click the **Network Neighborhood** desktop icon and click **Properties** in the shortcut menu. The network's Properties dialog box opens. Click the **Identification** tab. In Windows 2000/XP, right-click **My Computer** and click **Properties** in the shortcut menu. In the Windows 2000 System Properties dialog box, click the **Network Identification** tab, and then click the **Properties** button. The Identification Changes dialog box opens. In the Windows XP System Properties dialog box, click the **Computer Name** tab and then click **Change**. The Computer Name Changes dialog box opens.

3. To what workgroup does this computer belong?

   _____

4. If necessary, change the workgroup assignment to match the one you wrote down in Step 1.

Now you're ready to install and share the printer. On a Windows 2000/XP computer that will be physically connected to the printer, follow these steps. The steps for Windows 9x differ slightly, but you can use these steps as a guide.

1. With the computer off, connect the printer cable to the parallel port or USB port on your computer, turn on the printer, and then boot the computer.

2. If the Add Printer Wizard starts, click **Next** and then skip to Step 4.

3. If the wizard doesn't start, in Windows XP, click **Start, Printers and Faxes**. In Windows 2000, click **Start**, point to **Settings**, and then click **Printers**. In the Printers and Faxes window (Printers in Windows 2000) that opens, click the **Add a printer** link (in Windows 2000, double-click the **Add Printer** icon). When the Add Printer Wizard starts, click **Next**.

4. Click **Local printer** (Windows 2000) or **Local printer attached to this computer** (Windows XP), verify that the **Automatically detect and install my Plug and Play printer** check box is selected, and then click **Next**.

5. If a warning dialog box is displayed, click **Next**. A list of ports is displayed. Click **Use the following port**, click **LPT1**, and then click **Next**.

6. A list of manufacturers and printer models is displayed. Select the manufacturer and the model from the list, and then click **Next**. If your printer isn't listed and you have the correct printer driver on disk or CD, click **Have Disk**. Keep in mind that drivers designed for one Windows operating system might not work for a later version of Windows, so you need to make sure you have the correct drivers for your computer's version of Windows. (You can download printer driver files from the printer manufacturer's Web site.) If you select a manufacturer and model from the Windows list, a dialog box might open where you can specify the location of the Windows setup files. In that case, insert the Windows setup CD or select another location for the files.

7. The next window in the Add Printer Wizard asks for a name for the printer. This name appears later in the list of available printers. Accept the default name Windows provides or enter your own, and then click **Next** to continue.

8. Click **Share as** (Windows 2000) or **Share name** (Windows XP) to indicate that this printer will be shared with others on a network, and then click **Next** to continue.

9. If the Location and Comment window is displayed, you can describe the location of the printer, or leave it blank and click **Next**. Click **Yes** to print the test page, and then click **Next**.

10. Windows displays the printer settings you selected. Click **Finish** to complete the installation.

After the printer is installed, you need to make it possible for other computers in the network to access it. Follow these directions to share the printer with other computers in the workgroup:

1. On the computer with a locally installed printer, in Windows 2000 click **Start**, point to **Settings**, and click **Printers**. In Windows XP, click **Start, Printers and Faxes**.

2. The Printers and Faxes window (Printers window in Windows 2000) opens, showing the printer you just installed. Right-click the printer and click **Sharing** in the shortcut menu.

3. The Properties dialog box for the printer opens with the Sharing tab selected. Click the **Shared as** option button (Windows 2000) or **Share this printer** option button (Windows XP), type a share name for the printer.

4. For Windows 2000/XP computers, click **Additional Drivers**, and select the operating systems that remote computers use. Windows can then provide remote computers with the necessary driver files when they first attempt to connect to the shared printer. (Windows 9x doesn't provide this service.) Click **OK**, and then click **OK** to close the Properties dialog box, if necessary.

The printer is now listed in the My Network Places window (Network Neighborhood window in Windows 9x) on all other computers on the network. However, before a remote computer can use the printer, printer drivers must be installed on it.

There are two approaches to installing a shared network printer on a remote PC. You can perform the installation using the printer drivers installed on the host PC or using the drivers on CD (the Windows CD or printer manufacturer's CD). If you need to install the printer on several remote PCs, it's faster to use the drivers installed on the host PC. The disadvantage of this method is that you must share the C:\Windows folder on the host PC, which is considered a security risk. For this reason, as soon as the printer is installed on all remote PCs, you should unshare the C:\Windows folder on the host PC to protect that critical folder.

Follow these steps to install the shared printer on the other PCs:

1. On the computer with the printer connected locally, you need to share the C:\Windows folder so that the drivers in this folder are available to the other computers. To do this, right-click the **C:\Windows** folder in Windows Explorer, click **Properties** in the shortcut menu, click the **Sharing** tab, and click the **Shared as** (Windows 2000) or **Share this folder** (Windows XP) option to share the folder. Don't require a password to access the folder unless you want to prevent some users from accessing the printer. Click **OK**.

2. On remote PCs, open My Network Places or Network Neighborhood, and find the printer. Right-click the printer and click **Connect** (in Windows 2000/XP) or **Install** (in Windows 9x) on the shortcut menu.

3. Enter a name for the printer and print a test page to complete the installation.

4. After all remote computers have installed the printer, you should remove the shared option on the local computer's C:\Windows folder to protect this important folder. To do this, right-click the folder in Windows Explorer, click **Properties**, click the **Sharing** tab, and click **Not Shared** (Windows 2000) or **Do not share this folder** (Windows XP). Click **OK**.

## REVIEW QUESTIONS

1. What two Windows components must be installed before you can share a printer in a workgroup?

   _____

   _____

2. What would happen if the C:\Windows folder on the host PC wasn't shared when you tried to install the printer on remote PCs? How could you have installed the printer on a remote computer if you didn't have access to the C:\Windows folder on the host computer?

   _____

   _____

3. Name an advantage of setting up file sharing at the same time as printer sharing:

   _____

   _____

4. Suppose you want to stop some people on the network from using a shared printer, but you still want the printer to be available to the local computer to which it's connected. What's the easiest way to do this?

   _____

   _____

# LAB 21.2 INSTALL A NETWORK PRINTER

## OBJECTIVES

The goal of this lab is to give you more practice installing a local printer on a computer, sharing it, and then printing to it from a remote computer on the network. After completing this lab, you will be able to:

◢ Install a local printer

◢ Share a printer on the network

◢ Test the printer across the network

## MATERIALS REQUIRED

This lab requires the following:

◢ Windows 2000/XP or Windows 9x operating system

◢ Printer, printer cable, and printer driver files

◢ A functioning network

◢ A workgroup of 2 to 4 students

## LAB PREPARATION

Before the lab begins, the instructor or lab assistant needs to do the following:

◢ Verify that Windows starts with no errors.

## ACTIVITY BACKGROUND

A local printer is connected to a PC by way of a serial, parallel infrared, or USB connection. Usually, it's not available to the network for general printing jobs, but allowing other computers to print from your local printer can be useful sometimes. For example, if you have an expensive photo-quality printer installed locally on your computer, you might want to let users who need to print photos access your printer through the network. In this lab, you install a local printer and a network printer. Instructions in this lab are written for Windows XP/2000 but work much the same for Windows 9x if you substitute Network Neighborhood for My Network Places.

**ESTIMATED COMPLETION TIME: 30 minutes**

 **Activity**

The following steps describe the default method for installing a printer in Windows XP. (The steps differ slightly in Windows 2000 and 9x.) However, printer manufacturers often provide specialized steps for installing their devices. In that case, you should follow the steps your printer manufacturer prescribes rather than the steps listed here.

1. With the computer off, attach the printer cable to the computer and the printer. Attach the power cable to the printer, and then plug it in. Turn on the printer and then the computer. After the computer starts, insert the installation disk if you have one.

2. Click **Start, Printers and Faxes**. The Printers and Faxes window opens, displaying any installed printers.

3. Click the **Add a printer** link to open the Add Printer Wizard.

4. In the Add Printer Wizard, click **Next** to begin the installation process.

5. What two printer options do you see in the Add Printer Wizard?

_____

_____

6. In the Add Printer Wizard, click **Local printer attached to this computer**, and then click **Next** to continue.

7. Select the appropriate port, and then click **Next** to continue. If the New Printer Detection window opens with a warning that Windows couldn't detect the device, click **Next**.

8. In the left pane, click to select your printer manufacturer. A list of printers for that manufacturer is displayed in the right pane. Scroll down the list to locate your printer.

9. If you can locate your printer, click it in the right pane, click **Next**, and then skip to Step 12. If you can't locate your printer, click **Have Disk**. The Install From Disk dialog box opens.

10. Click **Browse**, and then locate and select the installation file for your operating system. This file has an .inf file extension and is most likely in a folder named after your operating system (such as \WinXP\install.inf, \WindowsXP\oem.inf, or something similar). Click **OK** to tell the wizard to use the selected file.

11. Click **OK** in the Install From Disk dialog box to close it. The Add Printer Wizard identifies your printer. Click **Next** to continue.

12. In the Printer name text box, type a name for the printer (or leave the default name).

13. When asked if you want this printer to be your Windows default printer, click **Yes**, and then click **Next**. When asked if you would like to print a test page, click **No**, and then click **Finish**. The necessary files are copied to your computer, and in some cases (if the printer has fax capabilities, for instance) a new wizard launches. If it does, complete the wizard or follow instructions from your instructor. When the installation process is finished, an icon for the newly installed printer appears in the Printers window.

Follow these steps to test the printer:

1. In the Printers and Faxes window, right-click the icon for your printer and click **Properties** in the shortcut menu. The printer's Properties dialog box opens.

2. Click the **General** tab, and then click **Print Test Page**. A test print job is sent to the printer, and a dialog box opens asking you whether the page printed correctly.

3. Verify that your test page printed correctly (without any gibberish), and then click **OK** to close the dialog box.

4. Open Windows Explorer and arrange it so that you can still see your printer's icon in the Printers window. In Windows Explorer, locate a .txt or .bat file and drag the file to the printer's icon in the Printers window. What happens?

_____

_____

Now that you have tested your printer, share it (using Lab 21.1 as a guide). Then go to the other computer and follow these steps to install a network printer:

1. Open the Printers and Faxes window and launch the Add Printer Wizard as you did previously. Click **Next** in the first wizard window.

2. Click **A network printer or a printer attached to another computer**, and then click **Next** to continue.

3. Click **Browse for a printer** and click **Next** to locate the printer you'll install. The Browse for Printer window appears, which displays the network in a similar way to Windows Explorer.

4. Locate your printer by expanding the computer on which you installed and shared it. When you have found the correct printer, click to select it, and then click **Next**.

5. In the Add Printer Wizard, verify that the path is correct, and then click **Next** to continue. If a warning dialog box opens, click **Yes** to continue.

6. If necessary, select the manufacturer and model or click **Have Disk**, depending on your printer and operating system.

7. Select whether to make this printer the default, and click **Next**. Complete the Add Printer Wizard.

8. Test your printer.

## REVIEW QUESTIONS

1. A printer is connected to the parallel port on computer A but is shared on the network. Computer B installs the shared computer and connects to it. Computer A considers it a(n) ___ printer, and computer B considers it a(n) ___ printer.

2. If a manufacturer's prescribed method for installing its printer differs from the default Windows method, which method should you use?

   _____

3. When installing a local printer attached through a parallel cable, what port should you specify?

   _____

4. Is it possible for a single printer to be both a local and a network printer? Why or why not?

   _____

   _____

   _____

5. Explain how to print a document without opening it:

   _____

   _____

# LAB 21.3 UPDATE PRINTER DRIVERS

## OBJECTIVES

The goal of this lab is to give you experience in upgrading printer drivers. After completing this lab, you will be able to:

◢ Identify driver information

◢ Locate new drivers

◢ Install new drivers

◢ Test printer drivers for functionality

## MATERIALS REQUIRED

This lab requires the following:

◢ Windows 2000/XP or Windows 9x operating system

◢ Windows installation CD or installation files

◢ Administrator account and password, if applicable

◢ *Optional*: A file compression utility

◢ Internet access

◢ A local printer

## LAB PREPARATION

Before the lab begins, the instructor or lab assistant needs to do the following:

◢ Verify that Windows starts with no errors.

◢ Provide each student with access to the Windows installation files, if needed.

◢ Verify that Internet access is available.

## ACTIVITY BACKGROUND

Printer manufacturers often release new drivers for their existing printers to fix problems with earlier drivers, add new functions, support new applications, and accommodate new operating system features. A PC support technician needs to know how to update printer drivers as they become available. The process of updating printer drivers is similar to that for other devices. You must gather information about the device and the currently installed drivers, download the new drivers, and install them. Like other devices, after the drivers are installed, you should test the printer to be certain it's functioning correctly before turning it over to end users. Unlike many other devices, it's easy to verify that a printer is working correctly. You also learn that the process of updating printer drivers is similar across different Windows platforms and printer manufacturers. This lab gives you general instructions for updating printer drivers. Modify these instructions to fit your situation and printer.

**ESTIMATED COMPLETION TIME: 30 minutes**

 **Activity**

The first step in updating printer drivers is to gather information about your current printer and drivers. Use Printers and Faxes (Device Manager in Windows 9x) to research and answer the following questions:

1. How is your printer generally used (for example, text, photographs, or graphics)?

   _____

2. What operating system are you using?

   _____

3. Who is the printer manufacturer?

   _____

4. What is the model of the printer?

   _____

5. What is the printer interface (USB, parallel, other)?

   _____

6. Printers typically have many setup options that deal with print quality and paper handling. Right-click the printer in Printers and Faxes (Device Manager in Windows 9x) and click **Properties** in the shortcut menu. Note any important settings because you'll probably need to reapply them after the driver is updated:

   _____

   _____

   _____

In Windows 9x, follow these instructions to view driver details:

1. Open Device Manager, click the **+** (plus sign) next to the printer to expand the heading, and then right-click your printer in the list. Click **Properties**, and a dialog box with both General and Driver tabs should open.

2. Click the **Driver** tab, and then click the **Driver File Details** button to open the Driver File Details dialog box shown in Figure 21-1. List all drivers displayed in the Driver files section:

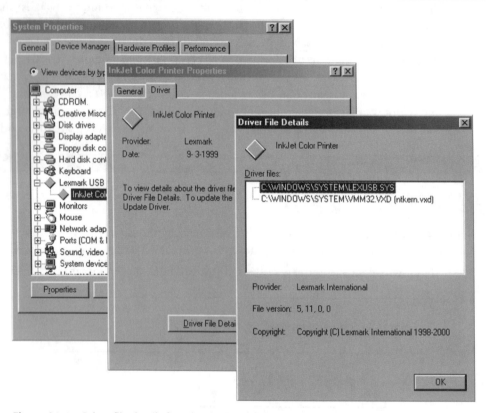

**Figure 21-1**    Driver file details for a local printer

3. In addition to the previous information, list all driver information shown in the dialog box that can help you identify the current driver later. Include the provider, file version, and copyright information. This information gives you a starting point in locating new drivers for your printer.

In Windows 2000/XP, follow these instructions to identify the printer driver:

1. Open the Printers and Faxes (or Printers in Windows 2000) window.

2. Right-click your printer icon, and click **Properties** in the shortcut menu. The printer's Properties dialog box opens.

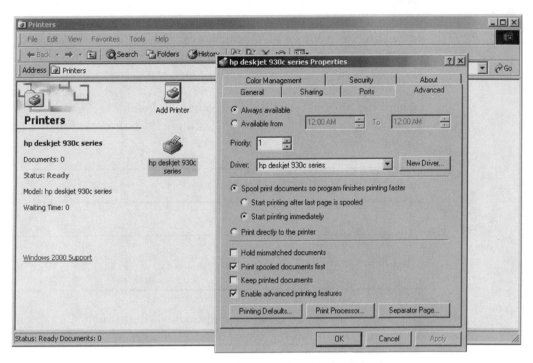

**Figure 21-2** Identifying the printer driver in the printer's Properties dialog box

3. Click the **Advanced** tab (see Figure 21-2). Note that tabs might differ from one printer to another.

4. What's the name of the driver listed in the Driver text box?

Follow these general directions to locate available driver updates:

1. Go to the printer manufacturer's Web site and locate the driver download section. Use Table 21-1 to help you find a Web site. What's the URL of the driver download page?

| Printer Manufacturer | Web Site |
|---|---|
| Brother | *www.brother.com* |
| Canon | *www.canon.com* |
| Hewlett-Packard | *www.hp.com* |
| IBM | *www.ibm.com* |
| Lexmark | *www.lexmark.com* |
| Okidata | *www.okidata.com* |
| SATO | *www.satoamerica.com* |
| Seiko Epson | *www.epson.com* |
| TallyGenicom | *www.tally.com* |
| Xerox | *www.xerox.com* |

**Table 21-1** Printer manufacturers

2. When you search for the correct driver on the Web site, you might find more than one driver that will work for your printer, operating system, or application. Generally, you should select the most recent version that matches your printer and operating system. There are exceptions, however. For instance, if a driver is listed as beta, it's still in development and has been released for evaluation. Usually, but not always, the manufacturer has most of the kinks worked out. To be on the safe side, don't download a beta release driver. List all drivers, with brief descriptions, for your printer and operating system:

_____

_____

_____

3. What driver have you selected to download?

_____

4. Find and list any special installation instructions the manufacturer recommends:

_____

_____

5. Create a folder on your C drive named **Downloads**, if necessary, and then create a subfolder named for the manufacturer, such as C:\Downloads\Lexmark. What's your folder name?

_____

6. Download the driver you intend to install to that folder.

With any device, it's best to follow the manufacturer's recommended method of installation instead of the Windows approach. A good manufacturer tests the driver as well as the installation process. The exception is when you have several printers installed on a system and you think one set of drivers might overwrite files another printer needs. In this case, use the Windows method to update the drivers. Do the following to install the new driver using the manufacturer's installation process:

1. Print an example—a document or a digital picture—of the printer's main use. This printout verifies that your printer is working before you make any changes and is used for comparison later to verify that the new drivers are working.

2. In Windows Explorer, double-click the file you downloaded. If it's a compressed file, it self-extracts files or uses file compression software on your PC to extract the files. If an installation wizard starts, exit it.

3. Were any files extracted? List them here:

_____

4. Locate any Readme.txt files for late-breaking information about installation.

5. Double-click the setup or install program. Document the process you used to install the new drivers:

_____

_____

_____

Do the following to test the printer and new drivers:

1. Open the Printers and Faxes (Windows XP) or Printers (Windows 2000) window.

2. Right-click the printer icon and click **Properties** in the shortcut menu. Click the **Print Test Page** button and verify that the test page is legible.

3. Apply the correct printer settings you recorded in Step 6 at the beginning of this lab.

4. Reprint the typical document or photograph and compare it to the one printed before the driver update. List any differences you see:

_____

## REVIEW QUESTIONS

1. List four reasons you might want to update a printer's drivers:

_____

_____

_____

_____

2. List four things you should know before you start searching the Web for updated drivers:

_____

_____

_____

_____

3. What does a driver being in beta release indicate about that driver?

_____

4. List the steps to print a test page in Windows:

_____

_____

## LAB 21.4 INSTALL AND TEST A SCANNER

## OBJECTIVES

The goal of this lab is to give you experience installing and testing a scanner. After completing this lab, you will be able to:

▲ Install a scanner on a computer

▲ Test the scanner for functionality

## MATERIALS REQUIRED

This lab requires the following:

◢ Windows 2000/XP operating system

◢ Windows installation CD or installation files

◢ An administrator account and password, if applicable

◢ A USB scanner

◢ Any necessary installation software or drivers for the scanner

## LAB PREPARATION

Before the lab begins, the instructor or lab assistant needs to do the following:

◢ Verify that Windows starts with no errors.

◢ Provide each student with access to the Windows installation files, if needed.

## ACTIVITY BACKGROUND

A scanner is a popular peripheral device used to digitize images, such as pages from a book or photographs. The images can be saved as an uncompressed bitmap or, because the files are often quite large, saved in a compressed file format, such as .jpg or .gif. Scanners can be purchased separately or combined with a printer in a single device that prints, scans, and copies. Most scanners use a USB connection, but other interface types, such as FireWire, parallel, and SCSI, are available. In this lab, you install and then test a scanner.

**ESTIMATED COMPLETION TIME: 30 minutes**

 **Activity**

It's best to follow the manufacturer's directions when installing a scanner. You can get the directions and any required software from the CD that comes with the scanner or from the manufacturer's Web site. If the instructions tell you to use the Scanner and Camera Installation Wizard, you can use the following steps:

> **Notes**
>
> Most USB scanners come bundled with their own installation software. It's important to run this software *before* attaching the scanner.

1. Log on to an administrative account in Windows, and make sure all unnecessary programs are closed.

2. Attach the scanner to your computer, and then power on the scanner.

3. Because most scanners are Plug and Play, the Scanner and Camera Installation Wizard should launch automatically. If it doesn't, click **Start, Control Panel, Printers and Other Hardware**, and **Scanners and Cameras**. In the Scanners and Cameras window, click the **Add an imaging device** link.

4. Click **Next** in the Scanner and Camera Installation Wizard.

5. Click to select the manufacturer and model of your scanner (or click **Have Disk** if your scanner came with separate drivers), and then click **Next**.

6. Click to select the correct port, and then click **Next**.

7. Enter a name for your scanner, and then click **Next**. Write the name of your scanner in the following space:

8. Finally, click **Finish** to begin installing the drivers.

To test that your scanner is working correctly, do the following:

1. Click **Start, Control Panel, Printers and Other Hardware,** and **Scanners and Cameras.**
2. Right-click the scanner you want to test and click **Properties.**
3. Click the **General** tab and click the **Test Scanner** button.
4. What message did you get after the test was completed?

_____

_____

5. What message do you get if you turn off the scanner and then go through Steps 1 through 3 again?

_____

_____

## REVIEW QUESTIONS

1. What are some advantages and disadvantages of combining your printer and scanner into a single device?

_____

_____

2. Why does the Scanner and Camera Installation Wizard usually launch automatically the first time a scanner is attached to a computer?

_____

3. When might you want to save images as .jpg files?

_____

_____

4. What are some reasons that a scanner might not work correctly after it has been installed?

_____

_____

_____

# LAB 21.5 PRINTER MAINTENANCE AND TROUBLESHOOTING

## OBJECTIVES

The goal of this lab is to give you experience supporting printers. After completing this lab, you will be able to:

◢ Use the Web to help with printer maintenance
◢ Correct common printer problems

## MATERIALS REQUIRED

This lab requires the following:

◢ Internet access

◢ A printer

## LAB PREPARATION

Before the lab begins, the instructor or lab assistant needs to do the following:

◢ Verify that Internet access is available.

## ACTIVITY BACKGROUND

Printers require more maintenance than most other peripheral devices. Paper gets jammed, the ink cartridge or toner runs out, and image or document quality is degraded by dust and misalignment. Most manufacturers and many models have specific instructions for maintaining ink and toner cartridges that apply exclusively to their printers, so you must rely on the printer manufacturer for instructions when maintaining a printer. In this lab, you investigate maintenance and troubleshooting instructions for several types of printers.

**ESTIMATED COMPLETION TIME: 30 minutes**

 **Activity**

Use the Internet to research how to solve the following problems. The printer is a high-end color laser printer by Hewlett-Packard (*www.hp.com*), the LaserJet 9500. Answer these questions about routine maintenance for this printer:

1. Everything needed for routine maintenance of the LaserJet 9500 can be purchased in a printer maintenance kit. List the printer components included in this kit:

_____

_____

_____

2. On the HP Web site, find the instructions for using the kit to perform routine maintenance. What should you wear while you do the maintenance?

_____

3. How many pages can be printed before maintenance should be performed?

_____

The next printer is an inkjet printer, the HP Deskjet 930c. Answer these questions:

1. Your computer displays a message to replace the ink cartridge. You replace the cartridge, but the message is still displayed. Also, you notice that the resume light on the printer is blinking. Search the HP Web site and locate the troubleshooting steps to solve the problem.

2. What is the first thing HP suggests you do when you see these errors?

_____

**3.** One thing HP suggests is that you clean the cartridge contacts. List the steps:

_____

_____

_____

_____

_____

**4.** If the problem isn't fixed, HP suggests you reclean the cartridge contacts, this time using a cotton swab dipped in what?

_____

Next, follow these steps to learn how to perform routine maintenance or troubleshoot problems on your local printer:

**1.** List the following information to identify your local printer:

◢ Printer manufacturer:

_____

◢ Printer model:

_____

◢ Printer interface (parallel, USB, other):

_____

**2.** Search the manufacturer's Web site for troubleshooting and maintenance procedures and answer the following questions:

◢ What types of problems are addressed for your printer?

_____

_____

◢ Does the manufacturer offer a printer maintenance kit? If so, what components are included and how much does the kit cost?

_____

_____

_____

◢ What maintenance tips for your printer can you find on the Web site?

_____

_____

## REVIEW QUESTIONS

1. When a printer isn't working correctly, what are two ways the problem is communicated to users?

_____

_____

2. Why do printers require more maintenance than other peripherals?

_____

3. How often should you perform printer maintenance using a maintenance kit purchased from the manufacturer?

_____

4. After you replace an ink cartridge in an inkjet printer, an error message is displayed. What's the first thing you should do?

_____

# LAB 21.6 CRITICAL THINKING: SABOTAGE AND REPAIR A NETWORK PRINTER

## OBJECTIVES

The goal of this lab is to learn how to troubleshoot problems with a network printer.

## MATERIALS REQUIRED

This lab requires the following:

- ◢ Two or more computers connected to a network, one with a local printer attached
- ◢ Windows installation CD or installation files
- ◢ A workgroup of 2 to 4 students

## LAB PREPARATION

Before the lab begins, the instructor or lab assistant needs to do the following:

- ◢ Verify that Windows starts with no errors.
- ◢ Provide each student with access to the Windows installation files, if needed.

## ACTIVITY BACKGROUND

Problems with a network printer are common, and a PC support technician is often called on to solve them. This lab gives you practice solving these types of problems.

**ESTIMATED COMPLETION TIME: 45 minutes**

 Activity

1. Using the steps in Lab 21.1, verify that each computer in a workgroup is able to print to a network printer that's locally installed on one of the computers in the workgroup.

2. Trade systems with another group, and sabotage the other group's system while that group sabotages your system. The following list has some suggestions for preventing a computer from using the network printer. Do something in this list, or think of another option.

   ◢ On the host computer, remove the sharing option for the printer.

   ◢ Uninstall the printer on a remote computer.

   ◢ Pause printing on one or more computers.

   ◢ Turn the printer off or offline.

   ◢ Disconnect the printer cable from the host computer.

   ◢ Remove paper from the printer.

   ◢ Introduce an error in the printer configuration on the host computer or a remote computer.

3. What did you do to sabotage the other team's system?

   _____

   _____

   _____

4. Return to your system and troubleshoot it.

5. Describe the problem as a user would describe it to you if you were working at a help desk:

   _____

   _____

6. What is your first guess as to the source of the problem?

   _____

7. List the steps you took in the troubleshooting process:

   _____

   _____

   _____

   _____

8. How did you solve the problem and return the printing system to working order?

   _____

   _____

## REVIEW QUESTIONS

1. What would you do differently the next time you encounter the same symptoms?

   _____

2. What are three easy things you could ask a user to check that don't require experience with Windows?

_____

_____

_____

3. What might cause this problem to happen? List three possible causes:

_____

_____

_____

# CHAPTER 22

# The Professional PC Technician

**Labs included in this chapter:**

- **Lab 22.1:** Produce Help Desk Procedures
- **Lab 22.2:** Troubleshoot General Computer Problems
- **Lab 22.3:** Troubleshoot Hypothetical Situations
- **Lab 22.4:** Customer Service
- **Lab 22.5:** Critical Thinking: Update Motherboard Drivers

## *LAB 22.1 PRODUCE HELP DESK PROCEDURES*

### OBJECTIVES

The goal of this lab is to demonstrate the process of setting up help desk troubleshooting procedures. After completing this lab, you will be able to:

◢ Identify problems that would prevent users from browsing the network

◢ Decide which problems can be solved over the telephone

◢ Decide which problems require administrative intervention

◢ Create a support matrix for telephone instruction

### MATERIALS REQUIRED

This lab requires the following:

◢ Windows 2000/XP or Windows 9x operating system

◢ A PC connected to a working TCP/IP network

◢ Two workgroups with 2 to 4 students in each group

### LAB PREPARATION

Before the lab begins, the instructor or lab assistant needs to do the following:

◢ Verify that Windows starts with no errors.

◢ Verify that the network connection is available.

### ACTIVITY BACKGROUND

When a company sets up a help desk for computer users, it establishes a set of procedures to address common troubleshooting situations. These procedures should include instructions that the average user can be expected to carry out with telephone support. In this lab, you design and create help desk procedures for a common problem: the inability to connect to a network. Assume you're working at the company help desk. If you can't solve the problem, you escalate it to the network administrator or another technician who actually goes to the computer to fix the problem.

> **ESTIMATED COMPLETION TIME: 60 minutes**

 **Activity**

1. Assume that your company network is designed according to the following parameters. (Note that your instructor might alter these parameters so that they more closely resemble your network's parameters.)

   ◢ Ethernet LAN is using only a single subnet.

   ◢ TCP/IP is the only protocol.

   ◢ Workgroup name is ATLGA.

   ◢ DHCP server assigns IP information.

2. Assume that all users on your company network use computers with the following parameters. (Note that your instructor might alter these parameters so that they more closely resemble your PC.)

▲ Pentium IV 1.2 GHz

▲ Windows XP operating system

▲ Internal NIC

▲ Category 5 cabling with RJ-45 connectors

3. As a group, discuss the reasons a user might not be able to connect to the network, and then make a list of the four most common reasons. List the source of these problems, both hardware and software, on the following lines. In your list, include at least one problem that's difficult to solve over the phone and requires the network administrator or another technician to go to the computer to solve the problem. Order the four problems from the least difficult to solve to the most difficult to solve. Write the one problem that requires administrator intervention at the bottom of the list.

▲ Source of Problem 1:

_____

▲ Source of Problem 2:

_____

▲ Source of Problem 3:

_____

▲ Source of Problem 4 (requires an administrator or another technician to get involved):

_____

For each problem, describe the symptoms as a user would describe them:

▲ Symptoms of Problem 1:

_____

_____

▲ Symptoms of Problem 2:

_____

_____

▲ Symptoms of Problem 3:

_____

_____

▲ Symptoms of Problem 4 (requires an administrator or another technician to get involved):

_____

_____

As a group, decide how to solve each problem. On separate sheets of paper, list the steps to verify and solve the problems. (This list of steps is sometimes referred to as a procedure, support matrix, or job aid.) Double-check the steps by testing them on your computer. (In real life, you would test the steps using a computer attached to the network you're supporting.) When making your list of steps, allow for alternatives, based on how the user responds to your questions. For example, you might include one list of steps for situations in which the user says others on the network are visible in My Network Places and another list of steps for situations in which the user says no remote computers can be seen in My Network Places. Well-written help desk procedures ensure that help desk workers know exactly what steps to perform, which results in quicker support and users feeling more confident about getting help. For any problem that can't be solved by the procedure, the last step should be for help desk personnel to notify the administrator. In your procedure, include questions to the user when appropriate. As you work, you might find it helpful to use a diagram or flowchart of the questions asked and decisions made.

Here's an example of one step that involves a question:

▲ **Question:** Is your computer on?

▲ **Answer:** Yes, go to Step 3; No, go to Step 2.

Now test your help desk procedures by using them on another workgroup. Follow these steps:

1. Introduce one of your four problems on a PC connected to a network.

2. Have someone from another workgroup sit at your PC. The remainder of these steps refer to this person as "the user."

3. Sit with your back to this person so that you can't see what he or she is doing. Place your step-by-step procedures in front of you, on paper or on-screen. (It's helpful if you can sit at a PC connected to the network so that you can perform the same steps you ask the user to perform. However, make sure you can't see the other PC or see what the user is doing.)

4. The user should attempt to access the network and then "call" your help desk for assistance.

5. Follow your procedure to solve the problem.

6. Revise your procedure as necessary.

7. Test all four help desk procedures.

## REVIEW QUESTIONS

1. Can all users' computer problems be solved with help desk support? Explain:

   _____

   _____

2. After you design and write your help desk procedures to solve problems, what should you do next?

   _____

   _____

3. How should help desk procedures address complex problems that require administrative intervention?

   _____

   _____

4. How should you alter your procedures based on your users' technical experience? Explain:

_____

_____

_____

_____

5. Why do you need to consider what the network and computer are like when creating your procedures?

_____

_____

_____

6. What has been your experience when calling a help desk? How well did the technician walk you through the process of solving your problem?

_____

_____

## _LAB 22.2 TROUBLESHOOT GENERAL COMPUTER PROBLEMS_

### OBJECTIVES

The goal of this lab is to troubleshoot and remedy general computer problems. After completing this lab, you will be able to:

▲ Diagnose and solve problems with various hardware devices

▲ Document the troubleshooting process

### MATERIALS REQUIRED

This lab requires the following:

▲ Windows 2000/XP or Windows 9x operating system

▲ Windows 2000/XP or Windows 9x installation CD or installation files

▲ Drivers for all devices

▲ A PC toolkit with antistatic ground strap

▲ A workgroup partner

### LAB PREPARATION

Before the lab begins, the instructor or lab assistant needs to do the following:

▲ Verify that Windows starts with no errors.

▲ Provide each student with access to the Windows installation files, if needed.

## ACTIVITY BACKGROUND

In previous labs, you have learned to troubleshoot problems in specific subsystems of a PC. This lab takes a comprehensive approach to troubleshooting an entire system, so the problem might relate to any subsystem. Troubleshooting a general problem is no different from troubleshooting a specific subsystem. You simply apply your troubleshooting techniques to a wider range of possibilities.

**ESTIMATED COMPLETION TIME: 120 minutes**

 **Activity**

1. Verify that your computer and your partner's computer are working by checking that the system runs smoothly and all drives are accessible. Browse the network and connect to a Web site.

2. Randomly pick one of the following hardware or software problems and introduce it on your PC:

   ◢ Change the boot sequence to boot from a nonexistent device.

   ◢ If both the mouse and the keyboard have PS/2 connectors, switch the connectors at the case.

   ◢ Using Add or Remove Programs (Add/Remove Hardware in Windows 9x), install a nonexistent device.

   ◢ Remove the data cable from the primary master hard drive.

   ◢ Change the display settings to two colors that are hard to read.

   ◢ Remove the RAM from the system. (Be sure to store all memory modules in an antistatic bag while they're outside the case.)

   ◢ Unplug the monitor from the video adapter.

   ◢ Use Control Panel to switch the primary and secondary buttons on the mouse.

   ◢ In BIOS, manually add information for a fictitious hard drive.

   ◢ Unplug the network cable from the wall or hub.

   ◢ Use Network Connections to disable your current network connection.

3. Troubleshoot your partner's PC while your partner troubleshoots your computer. Verify that you can accomplish all the tasks you could before the computer was sabotaged.

4. On a separate sheet of paper, answer these questions:

   ◢ What is the initial symptom of the problem as a user would describe it?

   ◢ How did you discover the source of the problem?

   ◢ How did you solve the problem?

   ◢ If you were working at a help desk and someone called with this problem, could the problem have been solved over the phone, or would it have required a visit from a technician? Explain your answer.

5. Return to your computer and repeat Steps 2 through 4. Continue until you have solved all the problems listed in Step 2. For each problem, make sure to answer the questions in Step 4.

## REVIEW QUESTIONS

1. Which problems caused the computer to halt during the boot process?

_____

_____

_____

2. Which problem was the most difficult to repair? Why?

_____

_____

_____

3. Of those problems that *allowed* the computer to boot, which problem was easiest to detect? Why?

_____

_____

_____

4. Of those problems that *prevented* the computer from booting, which problem was easiest to detect? Why?

_____

_____

_____

# LAB 22.3 TROUBLESHOOT HYPOTHETICAL SITUATIONS

## OBJECTIVES

The goal of this lab is to help you think through the troubleshooting process using hypothetical situations. After completing this lab, you will be able to:

▲ Evaluate a troubleshooting situation

▲ Determine the likely source of a problem

▲ Explain how to verify the source of a problem

▲ Briefly explain a problem and the procedure required to remedy it

## MATERIALS REQUIRED

This lab requires the following:

▲ A workgroup of 2 to 4 students

## LAB PREPARATION

Before the lab begins, the instructor or lab assistant needs to do the following:

▲ Read through the hypothetical problems and be prepared to discuss them with each group.

## ACTIVITY BACKGROUND

One way to sharpen your troubleshooting skills is to think through the process of solving hypothetical problems. This lab presents situations that, although common, should pose a challenge for your workgroup.

To complete this lab, imagine that you're in charge of repairs at a small computer shop. As part of your job, first you need to describe the problem's symptoms on the repair work order, and then explain your initial guess or opinion as to the source of the problem. Next, you must write a short summary on the work order explaining what you did to repair the computer. Your explanations should be as clear and precise as possible. Customers who know something about computers appreciate careful explanations. Even if the customer doesn't fully understand, a detailed work order helps assure the customer that you did a thorough job.

**ESTIMATED COMPLETION TIME: 60 minutes**

 **Activity**

1. A customer installed a new 20 GB hard drive and complains that it doesn't work. He claims he called the manufacturer's technical support, who walked him through BIOS setup. When he rebooted, POST did recognize the hard drive, but Windows still didn't. The customer became frustrated and decided to bring the computer to you.

   ▲ What are the possible sources of the problem?

   _____

   _____

   _____

   _____

   ▲ What would you do to find out how to solve the problem?

   _____

   _____

   _____

   _____

2. A customer brings in a computer and says that when she turns it on, it doesn't boot. She says a screen appears with an error message about the operating system. The customer claims she has never modified the system, but she does have children who use the computer and might have changed something inadvertently.

When you boot the system, you get an invalid system disk error, and you can hear the hard drive spin when power is applied. You suspect the BIOS settings are incorrect and the hard drive isn't being recognized. You detect the hard drive successfully by using the BIOS autodetection feature. In standard CMOS setup, you notice that the date and time are also incorrect, so you reset them. You save your changes and reboot. The system reboots to Windows. You test the system for 10 minutes, leave it on, and come back to it after an hour, and it's still functioning correctly. You call the customer and tell her that you have fixed the problem and she can come and pick it up the next day. Then you shut the system off and eventually leave work.

The next day the customer comes in, and when you demonstrate that you have fixed the problem, you see the invalid system disk message again.

◢ What do you suspect the problem is?

_____

_____

◢ How long will it probably take you to fix it?

_____

3. A customer brings in a computer. She complains that she can no longer update her antivirus program, and the problem began shortly after she reinstalled her operating system. You ask her if she downloaded the latest Windows updates, and she says she did that just before installing her antivirus program.

◢ What is the source of the problem?

_____

_____

◢ What steps would you take to correct the problem?

_____

_____

4. A customer brings in a computer and a popular video game. He says that the game appeared to install properly, but when it runs, the screen goes blank and he only hears sound. He installed it again with the same results and then decided to bring it in to you. You check the documentation that came with the game and determine that his computer meets all the suggested hardware requirements.

◢ What is likely the problem?

_____

◢ What will you do to correct it?

_____

_____

5. A customer brings in a system and claims it hasn't worked since a recent thunderstorm. You open the case and immediately notice a burned smell. You test each component in a test system and find no functional components. You call and report the sad news to the

customer. He's upset about the system but even more concerned about the loss of important information on the hard drive for which he has no backup.

▲ What information or recommendation can you give the customer about what he can do now and what he should do in the future to safeguard important data?

_____

_____

_____

_____

▲ What advice can you give the customer about protecting his hardware?

_____

_____

_____

6. A customer wanted to upgrade her processor to a faster one. She checked with the motherboard manufacturer and discovered that her motherboard supports a faster processor. When she installed the new processor, the system booted, and the POST reported that the processor is running at only two thirds of its potential. Windows works, and the computer functions normally but at a slower clock speed.

▲ What is the likely problem?

_____

▲ How would you solve the problem?

_____

## REVIEW QUESTIONS

1. How could a properly functioning hard drive that's recognized by BIOS fail to show up in Windows?

_____

_____

2. What device maintains CMOS settings even if the computer is totally unplugged from AC power?

_____

3. How can you avoid infecting your computer before installing an antivirus program?

_____

4. Why is it important to periodically download the latest drivers from the hardware manufacturer's Web site?

_____

_____

5. How might lightning destroy a computer, besides coming in through the roof and striking the computer directly?

_____

_____

# LAB 22.4 CUSTOMER SERVICE

## OBJECTIVES

The goal of this lab is to help you appreciate some of the issues involved in providing excellent customer service. After completing this lab, you will be able to:

▲ Evaluate the service needs of your customers

▲ Plan for good customer service

▲ Respond to customer complaints

## MATERIALS REQUIRED

This lab requires the following:

▲ A workgroup of 2 to 4 students

## LAB PREPARATION

Before the lab begins, the instructor or lab assistant needs to do the following:

▲ Read through the customer service scenarios and be prepared to discuss them with each group.

## ACTIVITY BACKGROUND

A PC technician needs to be not only technically competent, but also skilled at providing excellent customer service. Acting in a helpful, dependable, and, above all, professional manner is a must, whether you deal directly with customers or work with other employees as part of a team.

To complete this lab, work through the following customer service scenarios. When you are done, compare your answers with the rest of your group and see whether you can arrive at a consensus. Keep in mind that there might not be a single right answer to each question.

**ESTIMATED COMPLETION TIME: 60 minutes**

### Activity

1. A customer returns to your store complaining that the upgraded computer he just picked up doesn't boot. You remember testing the computer yourself before the pickup, and everything was fine.

   ▲ What can you do to remedy the situation?

   _____

   _____

◢ How can you avoid this kind of problem in the future?

_____

_____

2. You're working in a call center that provides support to customers who are trying to install your product at home. While working with an inexperienced customer over the telephone, you realize that she's having trouble following your directions.

　◢ What are some ways you can help customers even though they can't see you?

_____

_____

_____

_____

_____

　◢ How can you communicate clearly with your customers while avoiding the impression that you're talking down to them?

_____

_____

_____

3. You arrive on a service call, and the overly confident office supervisor shows you the malfunctioning computer. She begins to explain what she thinks is the problem, but you can tell from the computer's operation that it's something else. You suspect that she might have caused the malfunction.

　◢ How can you troubleshoot the problem without offending your customer?

_____

_____

_____

　◢ Would it be a mistake to accuse the customer of causing the problem?

_____

_____

4. An irate customer calls to complain that he's not satisfied with service he has received from your company and tells you he plans to take his future business elsewhere.

　◢ Should you apologize if you don't think your company acted improperly?

_____

_____

⊿ How can you give the customer the impression that you and your company are listening to his complaints?

_____

_____

## REVIEW QUESTIONS

1. Did the other members of your group come up with any viewpoints you hadn't considered?

_____

2. Did you have any trouble coming to a consensus about how to deal with each situation?

_____

3. Why is good customer service important for a technician who doesn't work directly with the public?

_____

_____

4. How could you go about improving your listening skills with customers?

_____

_____

_____

# *LAB 22.5 CRITICAL THINKING: UPDATE MOTHERBOARD DRIVERS*

## OBJECTIVES

The goal of this lab is to help you update drivers for motherboard components. After completing this lab, you will be able to:

⊿ Identify a motherboard and its embedded devices

⊿ Search a motherboard manufacturer's Web site for updated drivers

⊿ Download all applicable drivers for a motherboard

⊿ Install drivers

⊿ Document the process of updating motherboard drivers

## MATERIALS REQUIRED

This lab requires the following:

⊿ Windows 2000/XP or Windows 9x operating system

⊿ Motherboard documentation or SiSoftware Sandra (installed in Lab 1.3)

⊿ Internet access

⊿ A PC toolkit with antistatic ground strap (if necessary)

⊿ A blank floppy disk (if necessary)

## LAB PREPARATION

Before the lab begins, the instructor or lab assistant needs to do the following:

◢ Verify that Windows starts with no errors.

◢ Verify that Internet access is available.

## ACTIVITY BACKGROUND

Like other devices, components on the motherboard use drivers to interact with the operating system. These drivers might be updated from time to time to fix newly discovered bugs or to conform to new industry standards. However, if the motherboard is working correctly and performance is acceptable, you shouldn't update drivers because you might introduce new problems. In this lab, you use your experience in researching and installing drivers to install all available drivers for the components embedded on your motherboard.

---

**ESTIMATED COMPLETION TIME: 90 minutes**

---

### Activity

1. Using procedures you've learned in previous labs, provide the following information:

    ◢ Motherboard manufacturer:

    _____

    ◢ Motherboard model:

    _____

2. Using procedures you've learned in previous labs, identify the components on your motherboard, and record the information in the following chart. In the Included? column, enter Yes or No to indicate whether a component is included on the motherboard. Enter the version number of each component, if you have that information.

| Component | Included? | Version Number (If Available) |
|---|---|---|
| CPU type | | |
| Chip set | | |
| IDE controller | | |
| AGP controller | | |
| Embedded audio | | |
| Embedded NIC/LAN | | |
| Embedded modem | | |
| Embedded video | | |
| Other | | |
| Other | | |

3. Research the motherboard manufacturer's Web site for driver updates and documentation for performing the updates.

4. Download any necessary files, including any documentation. List the files you downloaded and the purpose of each file in the following chart:

| Downloaded File | Purpose of the File |
| --- | --- |
| | |
| | |
| | |
| | |
| | |
| | |

5. Print any documentation describing how to perform the updates.

6. Update the drivers.

7. Briefly explain how you updated the drivers:

_____

_____

_____

_____

_____

## REVIEW QUESTIONS

1. What is an embedded device?

_____

_____

2. If your motherboard documentation covers different models of motherboards, some with more embedded components than others, how can you definitely determine which model is installed in your computer?

_____

_____

3. What embedded device controls most hard drives?

_____

4. If you connect your monitor to a PCI video card in an expansion slot, would downloading and installing drivers for embedded video or for an AGP controller solve any problems related to video performance? Explain:

_____

_____

_____

5. Why would you want to update motherboard drivers? Give two reasons:

_____

_____

6. When would you *not* want to update motherboard drivers?

_____

_____

# GLOSSARY

This glossary defines terms related to managing and maintaining a personal computer.

**100BaseT** An Ethernet standard that operates at 100 Mbps and uses STP cabling. *Also called* Fast Ethernet. Variations of 100BaseT are 100BaseTX and 100BaseFX.

**10Base2** An Ethernet standard that operates at 10 Mbps and uses small coaxial cable up to 200 meters long. *Also called* ThinNet.

**10Base5** An Ethernet standard that operates at 10 Mbps and uses thick coaxial cable up to 500 meters long. *Also called* ThickNet.

**80 conductor IDE cable** An IDE cable that has 40 pins but uses 80 wires, 40 of which are ground wires designed to reduce crosstalk on the cable. The cable is used by ATA/66, ATA/100, and ATA/133 IDE drives.

**802.11a/b/g** *See* IEEE 802.11a/b/g.

**A (ampere or amp)** A unit of measurement for electrical current. One volt across a resistance of one ohm produces a flow of one amp.

**access point (AP)** A device connected to a LAN that provides wireless communication so that computers, printers, and other wireless devices can communicate with devices on the LAN.

**ACPI (Advanced Configuration and Power Interface)** Specification developed by Intel, Compaq, Phoenix, Microsoft, and Toshiba to control power on notebooks and other devices. Windows 98 and Windows 2000/XP support ACPI.

**active matrix** A type of video display that amplifies the signal at every intersection in the grid of electrodes, which enhances the pixel quality over that of a dual-scan passive matrix display.

**active partition** The primary partition on the hard drive that boots the OS. Windows 2000/XP calls the active partition the "system partition."

**adapter address** *See* MAC (Media Access Control) address.

**adapter card** A small circuit board inserted in an expansion slot used to communicate between the system bus and a peripheral device. *Also called* interface card.

**administrator account** In Windows 2000/XP, an account that grants the administrator rights and permissions to all hardware and software resources, such as the right to add, delete, and change accounts and change hardware configurations.

**Advanced Options menu** A Windows 2000/XP menu that appears when you press F8 when Windows starts. The menu can be used to troubleshoot problems when loading Windows 2000/XP.

**Advanced Transfer Cache (ATC)** A type of L2 cache in the Pentium processor housing that's embedded on the same core processor die as the CPU itself.

**AirPort** The term Apple uses to describe the IEEE 802.11b standard.

**alternating current (AC)** Current that cycles back and forth rather than traveling in only one direction. In the United States, the AC voltage from a standard wall outlet is normally between 110 and 115 V. In Europe, the standard AC voltage from a wall outlet is 220 V.

**ammeter** A meter that measures electrical current in amps.

**antivirus software** Utility programs that prevent infection or scan a system to detect and remove viruses. McAfee Associates VirusScan and Norton AntiVirus are two popular antivirus packages.

**APIPA (Automatic Private IP Address)** An IP address in the address range 169.254.x.x, used by a computer when it can't successfully lease an IP address from a DHCP server.

**ASCII (American Standard Code for Information Interchange)** A popular standard for writing letters and other characters in binary code. Originally, ASCII characters were 7 bits, so there were 127 possible values. ASCII has been expanded to an 8-bit version, allowing 128 additional values.

**ASR (Automated System Recovery)** The Windows XP process that allows you to restore an entire hard drive volume or logical drive to its state at the time the backup of the volume was made.

**AT** A form factor, generally no longer produced, in which the motherboard requires a full-size case. Because of their dimensions and configuration, AT systems are difficult to install, service, and upgrade. *Also called* full AT.

**AT command set** A set of commands that a PC uses to control a modem and a user can enter to troubleshoot the modem.

**ATAPI (Advanced Technology Attachment Packet Interface)** An interface standard, part of the IDE/ATA standards, that allows tape drives, CD-ROM drives, and other drives to be treated like an IDE hard drive by the system.

**ATX** The most common form factor for current PCs, originally introduced by Intel in 1995. ATX motherboards and cases make better use of space and resources than did the AT form factor.

**autodetection** A feature on newer system BIOS and hard drives that automatically identifies and configures a new drive in CMOS setup.

**Autoexec.bat** A startup text file once used by DOS and used by Windows to provide backward compatibility. It runs commands automatically during the boot process and is used to create a 16-bit environment.

**autorange meter** A multimeter that senses the quantity of input and sets the range accordingly.

**Baby AT** An improved and more flexible version of the AT form factor. Baby AT was the industry standard from approximately 1993 to 1997 and can fit into some ATX cases.

**backup** An extra copy of a file, used if the original becomes damaged or destroyed.

**bandwidth** In relation to analog communication, the range of frequencies a communications channel or cable can carry. In general use, the term refers to the volume of data that can travel on a bus or over a cable stated in bits per second (bps), kilobits per second (Kbps), or megabits per second (Mbps). *Also called* data throughput *or* line speed.

**bank** An area on the motherboard that contains slots for memory modules (typically labeled bank 0, 1, 2, and 3).

**baseline** The level of performance expected from a system, which can be compared to current measurements to determine what needs upgrading or tuning.

**basic disk** A way to partition a hard drive, used by DOS and all versions of Windows, that stores information about the drive in a partition table at the beginning of the drive. *Compare to* dynamic disk.

**batch file** A text file containing a series of OS commands. Autoexec.bat is a batch file.

**binary numbering system** The numbering system used by computers; it has only two numbers, 0 and 1, called binary digits, or bits.

**binding** The process by which a protocol is associated with a network card or a modem card.

**BIOS (basic input/output system)** Firmware that can control much of a computer's I/O functions, such as communication with the floppy drive and the monitor. *Also called* ROM BIOS.

**bit (binary digit)** A 0 or 1 used by the binary numbering system.

**blue screen** A Windows 2000/XP error displayed on a blue screen that causes the system to halt. *Also called* stop error.

**Bluetooth** A standard for wireless communication and data synchronization between devices, developed by a group of electronics manufacturers and overseen by the Bluetooth Special Interest Group. Bluetooth uses the same frequency range as IEEE 802.11b but doesn't have as wide a range.

**BNC connector** A connector used with thin coaxial cable. Some BNC connectors are T-shaped and called T-connectors. One end of the T connects to the NIC, and the other two ends can connect to cables or end a bus formation with a terminator.

**boot loader menu** A startup menu that gives users the choice of which operating system to load, such as Windows 98 or Windows XP, which are both installed on the same system, creating a dual-boot system.

**boot partition** The hard drive partition where the Windows 2000/XP OS is stored. The system partition and boot partition can be different partitions.

**boot record** The first sector of a floppy disk or logical drive in a partition; it contains information about the disk or logical drive. On a hard drive, if the boot record is in the active partition, it's used to boot the OS. *Also called* boot sector.

**boot sector** *See* boot record.

**boot sector virus** An infected program that can replace the boot program with a modified, infected version of the boot command utilities, often causing boot and data retrieval problems.

**Boot.ini** A Windows 2000/XP hidden text file that contains information needed to build the boot loader menu.

**bootable disk** For DOS and Windows, a floppy disk that can upload the OS files necessary for computer startup. For DOS or Windows 9x, it must contain the files Io.sys, Msdos.sys, and Command.com.

**bootstrap loader** A small program at the end of the boot record that can be used to boot an OS from the disk or logical drive.

**(bps) bits per second** A measure of data transmission speed. For example, a common modem speed is 56,000 bps, or 56 Kbps.

**broadband** A transmission technique that carries more than one type of transmission on the same medium, such as cable modem or DSL.

**brownouts** Temporary reductions in voltage, which can sometimes cause data loss. *Also called* sags.

**BTX (Balanced Technology Extended)** The latest form factor expected to replace ATX. It has higher quality fans, is designed for better air flow, and has improved structural support for the motherboard.

**buffer** A temporary memory area where data is kept before being written to a hard drive or sent to a printer, thus reducing the number of writes to devices.

**bus** The paths, or lines, on the motherboard on which data, instructions, and electrical power move from component to component.

**bus speed** The speed, or frequency, at which the data on the motherboard moves.

**byte** A collection of 8 bits that's equivalent to a single character. When referring to system memory, an additional error-checking bit might be added, making the total 9 bits.

**cabinet file** A file with a .cab extension that contains one or more compressed files and is often used to distribute software on disk. The Extract command is used to extract files from a cabinet file.

**cable modem** A technology that uses cable TV lines for data transmission, requiring a modem at each end. From the modem, a network cable connects to a NIC in the user's PC.

**capacitor** An electronic device that can maintain an electrical charge for a period of time and is used to smooth out the flow of electrical current. Capacitors are often found in computer power supplies.

**CardBus** The latest PCMCIA specification. It improves I/O speed, increases the bus width to 32 bits, and supports lower-voltage PC Cards, while maintaining backward compatibility with earlier standards.

**cards** Adapter boards or interface cards placed into expansion slots to expand the functions of a computer, allowing it to communicate with external devices, such as monitors or speakers.

**carrier**   A signal used to activate a phone line to confirm a continuous frequency; used to indicate that two computers are ready to receive or transmit data through modems.

**CCITT (Comité Consultatif International Télégraphique et Téléphonique)**   An international organization that was responsible for developing standards for international communications. This organization has been incorporated into the ITU. *See also* ITU (International Telecommunications Union).

**CD (change directory) command**   A command given at the command prompt that changes the default directory, such as CD \Windows.

**CDFS (Compact Disk File System)**   The 32-bit file system for CDs and some CD-Rs and CD-RWs that replaced the older 16-bit mscdex file system used by DOS. *See also* UDF (Universal Disk Format) file system.

**CD-R (CD-recordable)**   A CD drive that can record or write data to a CD. The drive may or may not be multisession, but the data can't be erased after it's written.

**CD-RW (CD-rewritable)**   A CD drive that can record or write data to a CD. The data can be erased and overwritten. The drive may or may not be multisession.

**chain**   A group of clusters used to hold a single file.

**child directory**   *See* subdirectory.

**chip creep**   A condition in which chips loosen because of thermal changes.

**chipset**   A group of chips on the motherboard that control the timing and flow of data and instructions to and from the CPU.

**CHS (cylinder, head, sector) mode**   The traditional method by which BIOS reads from and writes to hard drives by addressing the correct cylinder, head, and sector. *Also called* normal mode.

**circuit board**   A computer component, such as the main motherboard or an adapter board, that has electronic circuits and chips.

**clean install**   An installation of an OS on a new hard drive or a hard drive that has a previous OS installed, but it's performed without carrying forward any settings kept by the old OS, including information about hardware, software, or user preferences. *Also called* fresh installation.

**client/server**   A computer concept whereby one computer (the client) requests information from another computer (the server).

**client/server application**   An application that has two components. The client software requests data from the server software on the same or another computer.

**clock speed**   The speed, or frequency, expressed in MHz, that controls activity on the motherboard and is generated by a crystal or oscillator located on the motherboard.

**clone**   A computer that's a no-name Intel- and Microsoft-compatible PC.

**cluster**   One or more sectors that constitute the smallest unit of space on a disk for storing data. Files are written to a disk as groups of whole clusters. *Also called* file allocation unit.

**CMOS (complementary metal-oxide semiconductor)**   The technology used to manufacture microchips. CMOS chips require less electricity, hold data longer after the electricity is turned off, are slower, and produce less heat than TTL chips. The configuration, or setup, chip is a CMOS chip.

**CMOS configuration chip**   A chip on the motherboard that contains a very small amount of memory, or RAM, enough to hold configuration, or setup, information about the computer. The chip is powered by a battery when the PC is turned off. *Also called* CMOS setup chip *or* CMOS RAM chip.

**CMOS setup**   The CMOS configuration chip, or the program in system BIOS that can change the values in the CMOS RAM.

**CMOS setup chip**   *See* CMOS configuration chip.

**coaxial cable**   Networking cable used with 10 Mbps Ethernet ThinNet or ThickNet.

**cold boot**   *See* hard boot.

**combo card**   An Ethernet card that contains more than one transceiver, each with a different port on the back of the card, to accommodate different cabling media.

**Command.com**    Along with Msdos.sys and Io.sys, one of the three files that are the core components of the real-mode portion of Windows 9x. Command.com provides a command prompt and interprets commands.

**comment**    A line or part of a line in a program that's intended as a remark or comment and is ignored when the program runs. A semi-colon or "REM" is often used to mark a line as a comment.

**compact case**    A type of case used in low-end desktop systems. Compact cases follow the NLX, LPX, or Mini LPX form factor. They are likely to have fewer drive bays, but they generally still provide for some expansion. *Also called* low-profile *or* slimline cases.

**compressed drive**    A drive whose format has been reorganized to store more data. A compressed drive is really not a drive at all; it's actually a type of file, typically with a host drive called H.

**computer name**    Character-based host name or NetBIOS name assigned to a computer.

**Config.sys**    A text file used by DOS and supported by Windows 9x that lists device drivers to be loaded at startup. It can also set system variables to be used by DOS and Windows.

**console**    A centralized location from which to run commonly used tools.

**continuity**    A continuous, unbroken path for the flow of electricity. A continuity test can determine whether internal wiring is still intact or whether a fuse is good or bad.

**conventional memory**    Memory addresses between 0 and 640 K. *Also called* base memory.

**cooler**    A combination cooling fan and heat sink mounted on the top or side of a processor to keep it cool.

**(CPU) central processing unit**    The heart and brain of the computer, which receives data input, processes information, and carries out instructions. *Also called* microprocessor *or* processor.

**C-RIMM (Continuity RIMM)**    A placeholder RIMM module that provides continuity so that every RIMM slot is filled.

**cross-linked clusters**    Errors caused when more than one file points to a cluster and the files appear to share the same disk space, according to the file allocation table.

**crossover cable**    A cable used to connect two PCs into the simplest network possible. Also used to connect two hubs.

**CVF (compressed volume file)**    The file on the host drive of a compressed drive that holds all compressed data.

**data bus**    The lines on the system bus that the CPU uses to send and receive data.

**data cartridge**    A type of tape medium typically used for backups. Full-sized data cartridges are $4 \times 6 \times \frac{5}{8}$ inches. A minicartridge is only $3\frac{1}{4} \times 2\frac{1}{2} \times \frac{3}{5}$ inches.

**data line protector**    A surge protector designed to work with the telephone line to a modem.

**data path size**    The number of lines on a bus that can hold data, for example, 8, 16, 32, and 64 lines, which can accommodate 8, 16, 32, and 64 bits at a time.

**data throughput**    *See* bandwidth.

**DC (direct current)**    Current that travels in only one direction (the type of electricity provided by batteries). Computer power supplies transform AC to low DC.

**DC controller**    A card inside a notebook that converts voltage to CPU voltage. Some notebook manufacturers consider the card to be a field replaceable unit (FRU).

**DCE (data communications equipment)**    The hardware, usually a dial-up modem, that provides the connection between a data terminal and a communications line. *See also* DTE (data terminal equipment).

**DDR SDRAM (Double Data Rate SDRAM)**    A type of memory technology used on DIMMs that runs at twice the speed of the system clock.

**DDR2 SDRAM**    A version of SDRAM that's faster than DDR and uses less power.

**default gateway**   The gateway a computer on a network uses to access another network unless it knows to specifically use another gateway for quicker access to that network.

**default printer**   The printer Windows prints to unless another printer is selected.

**defragment**   To "optimize" or rewrite a file to a disk in one contiguous chain of clusters, thus speeding up data retrieval.

**desktop**   The initial screen displayed when an OS has a GUI interface loaded.

**device driver**   A program stored on the hard drive that tells the computer how to communicate with an I/O device, such as a printer or modem.

**DHCP (Dynamic Host Configuration Protocol) server**   A service that assigns dynamic IP addresses to computers on a network when they first access the network.

**diagnostic cards**   Adapter cards designed to discover and report computer errors and conflicts at POST time (before the computer boots up), often by displaying a number on the card.

**diagnostic software**   Utility programs that help troubleshoot computer systems. Some Windows diagnostic utilities are Chkdsk and Scandisk. PC-Technician is an example of a third-party diagnostic program.

**dial-up networking**   A Windows 9x and Windows 2000/XP utility that uses a modem and telephone line to connect to a network.

**differential cable**   A SCSI cable in which a signal is carried on two wires, each carrying voltage, and the signal is the difference between the two. Differential signaling provides for error checking and improved data integrity. *Compare to* SE (single-ended) cable.

**digital certificate**   A code used to authenticate the source of a file or document or to identify and authenticate a person or organization sending data over the Internet. The code is assigned by a certificate authority, such as VeriSign, and includes a public key for encryption. *Also called* digital ID *or* digital signature.

**digital ID**   *See* digital certificate.

**digital signature**   *See* digital certificate.

**DIMM (dual inline memory module)**   A miniature circuit board used in newer computers to hold memory. DIMMs can hold up to 2 GB RAM on a single module.

**DIP (dual inline package) switch**   A switch on a circuit board or other device that can be set on or off to hold configuration or setup information.

**Direct Rambus DRAM**   A memory technology by Rambus and Intel that uses a narrow, very fast network-type system bus. Memory is stored on a RIMM module. *Also called* RDRAM *or* Direct RDRAM.

**Direct RDRAM**   *See* Direct Rambus DRAM.

**directory table**   An OS table that contains file information such as the name, size, time, and date of last modification, and cluster number of the file's beginning location.

**disk cache**   A method whereby recently retrieved data and adjacent data are read into memory in advance, anticipating the next CPU request.

**disk cloning**   *See* drive imaging.

**disk compression**   Compressing data on a hard drive to allow more data to be written to the drive.

**disk imaging**   *See* drive imaging.

**Disk Management**   A Windows 2000/XP utility used to display, create, and format partitions on basic disks and volumes on dynamic disks.

**disk quota**   A limit placed on the amount of disk space that's available to users. Requires a Windows 2000/XP NTFS volume.

**disk thrashing**   A condition that results when the hard drive is excessively used for virtual memory because RAM is full. It dramatically slows down processing and can cause premature hard drive failure.

**DMA (direct memory access) channel**   A number identifying a channel whereby a device can pass data to memory without involving the CPU. Think of a DMA channel as a shortcut for data moving to and from the device and memory.

**DMA transfer mode**   A transfer mode used by devices, including the hard drive, to transfer data to memory without involving the CPU.

**DNS server**   A computer that can find an IP address for another computer when only the domain name is known.

**docking station**   A device that receives a notebook computer and provides additional secondary storage and easy connection to peripheral devices.

**domain**   In Windows 2000/XP, a logical group of networked computers, such as those on a college campus, that share a centralized directory database of user account information and security for the entire domain.

**domain controller**   A Windows 2000 computer that holds and controls a database of user accounts, group accounts, and computer accounts used to manage access to the network.

**domain name**   A unique text-based name that identifies a network.

**DOS box**   A command window.

**Dosstart.bat**   A type of Autoexec.bat file that Windows 9x run in two situations: when you select Restart the computer in MS-DOS mode from the shutdown menu or when you run a program in MS-DOS mode.

**dot pitch**   The distance between the dots that the electronic beam hits on a monitor screen.

**doze time**   The time before an Energy Star® or "green" system reduces 80% of its activity.

**DPMS (Display Power Management Signaling)**   Energy Star standard specifications that allow for the video card and monitor to go into sleep mode simultaneously. *See also* Energy Star.

**DRAM (dynamic RAM)**   The most common type of system memory, it requires refreshing every few milliseconds.

**Dr. Watson**   A Windows utility that can record detailed information about the system, errors that occur, and the programs that caused them in a log file. Windows 9x names the log file \Windows\Drwatson\WatsonXX.wlg (*XX* is an incrementing number). Windows 2000 names the file \Documents and Settings\user\Documents\DrWatson\Drwtsn32 .log. Windows XP calls the file Drwatson.log.

**drive imaging**   Making an exact image of a hard drive, including partition information, boot sectors, operating system installation, and application software, to replicate the hard drive on another system or recover from a hard drive crash. *Also called* disk cloning *and* disk imaging.

**drop height**   The height from which a manufacturer states that its drive can be dropped without making the drive unusable.

**DSL (Digital Subscriber Line)**   A telephone line that carries digital data from end to end and can be leased from the telephone company for individual use. DSL lines are rated at 5 Mbps, about 50 times faster than regular telephone lines.

**DTE (data terminal equipment)**   Both the computer and a remote terminal or other computer to which it's attached. *See also* DCE (data communications equipment).

**dual boot**   The ability to boot using either of two different OSs, such as Windows 98 and Windows XP.

**dual channel**   A motherboard feature that improves memory performance by providing two 64-bit channels between memory and the chipset. DDR and DDR2 memory can use dual channels.

**dual-scan passive matrix**   A type of video display that's less expensive than an active-matrix display and does not provide as high-quality an image. With dual-scan display, two columns of electrodes are activated at the same time.

**dual-voltage CPU**   A CPU that requires two different voltages, one for internal processing and the other for I/O processing.

**DVD (digital video disk** or **digital versatile disk)**   A faster, larger CD format that can read older CDs, store more than 8 GB of data, and hold full-length motion picture videos.

**dynamic disk**   A way to partition one or more hard drives, introduced with Windows 2000, in which information about the drive is stored in a database at the end of the drive. *Compare to* basic disk.

**dynamic IP address**   An assigned IP address used for the current session only. When the session is terminated, the IP address is returned to the list of available addresses.

**dynamic volume**   A volume type used with dynamic disks for which you can change the size of the volume after you have created it.

**ECC (error-correcting code)**   A chipset feature on a motherboard that checks the integrity of data stored on DIMMs or RIMMs and can correct single-bit errors in a byte. More advanced ECC schemas can detect, but not correct, double-bit errors in a byte.

**ECHS (extended CHS) mode**   *See* large mode.

**ECP (Extended Capabilities Port)**   A bidirectional parallel port mode that uses a DMA channel to speed up data flow.

**EDO (extended data out)**   A type of RAM that can be 10% to 20% faster than conventional RAM because it eliminates the delay before it issues the next memory address.

**EEPROM (electrically erasable programmable ROM)**   A type of chip in which higher voltage can be applied to one of the pins to erase its previous memory before a new instruction set is electronically written.

**EFS (Encrypted File System)**   A way to use a key to encode a file or folder on an NTFS volume to protect sensitive data. Because it's an integrated system service, EFS is transparent to users and applications and difficult to attack.

**EIDE (Enhanced IDE)**   A standard for managing the interface between secondary storage devices and a computer system. A system can support up to six serial ATA and parallel ATA EIDE devices or up to four parallel ATA IDE devices, such as hard drives, CD-ROM drives, and Zip drives.

**Emergency Repair Process**   A Windows 2000 process that restores the OS to its state at the completion of a successful installation.

**emergency startup disk (ESD)**   *See* rescue disk.

**EMI (electromagnetic interference)**   A magnetic field produced as a side effect from the flow of electricity. EMI can cause corrupted data in data lines that aren't properly shielded.

**Emm386.exe**   A DOS and Windows 9x utility that provides access to upper memory for 16-bit device drivers and other software.

**encryption**   The process of putting readable data into an encoded form that can be decoded (or decrypted) only through use of a key.

**Energy Star**   "Green" systems that satisfy the EPA requirements to decrease the overall consumption of electricity. *See also* Green Standards.

**enhanced BIOS**   A system BIOS that has been written to accommodate large-capacity drives (more than 504 MB, usually in the gigabyte range).

**EPP (Enhanced Parallel Port)**   A parallel port that allows data to flow in both directions (bidirectional port) and is faster than original parallel ports on PCs that allowed communication only in one direction.

**EPROM (erasable programmable ROM)**   A type of chip with a special window that allows the current memory contents to be erased with special ultraviolet light so that the chip can be reprogrammed. Many BIOS chips are EPROMs.

**error correction**   The capability of a modem to identify transmission errors and then automatically request another transmission.

**ESD (electrostatic discharge)**   Another name for static electricity, which can damage chips and destroy motherboards, even though it might not be felt or seen with the naked eye.

**ESD (emergency startup disk)**   *See* rescue disk.

**Ethernet**   The most popular LAN architecture that can run at 10 Mbps (ThinNet or ThickNet), 100 Mbps (Fast Ethernet), or 1 Gbps (Gigabit Ethernet).

**expansion bus**   A bus that doesn't run in sync with the system clock.

**expansion card**   A circuit board inserted into a slot on the motherboard to enhance the computer's capability.

**expansion slot** A narrow slot on the motherboard where an expansion card can be inserted. Expansion slots connect to a bus on the motherboard.

**extended memory** Memory above 1024 K used in a DOS or Windows 9x system.

**extended partition** The only partition on a hard drive that can contain more than one logical drive.

**external command** Commands that have their own program files.

**faceplate** A metal plate that comes with the motherboard and fits over the ports to create a well-fitted enclosure around them.

**Fast Ethernet** *See* 100BaseT.

**FAT (file allocation table)** A table on a hard drive or floppy disk that tracks the clusters used to contain a file.

**FAT12** The 12-bit-wide, one-column file allocation table for a floppy disk, containing information about how each cluster or file allocation unit on the disk is currently used.

**fault tolerance** The degree to which a system can tolerate failures. Adding redundant components, such as disk mirroring or disk duplexing, is a way to build in fault tolerance.

**file allocation unit** *See* cluster.

**file extension** A three-character portion of the file name used to identify the file type. In command lines, the file extension follows the file name and is separated from it by a period, such as Msd.exe, with exe being the file extension.

**file system** The overall structure that an OS uses to name, store, and organize files on a disk. Examples of file systems are FAT32 and NTFS.

**file virus** A virus that inserts virus code into an executable program file and can spread wherever that program runs.

**file name** The first part of the name assigned to a file. In DOS, the file name can be no more than eight characters and is followed by the file extension. In Windows, a file name can be up to 255 characters.

**firewall** Hardware or software that protects a computer or network from unauthorized access.

**FireWire** *See* IEEE 1394.

**firmware** Software permanently stored in a chip. The BIOS on a motherboard is an example of firmware.

**flash ROM** ROM that can be reprogrammed or changed without replacing chips.

**flat panel monitor** A desktop monitor that uses an LCD panel.

**FlexATX** A version of the ATX form factor that allows for maximum flexibility in the size and shape of cases and motherboards. FlexATX is ideal for custom systems.

**flow control** When using modems, a method of controlling the flow of data to adjust for problems with data transmission. Xon/Xoff is an example of a flow control protocol.

**folder** *See* subdirectory.

**forgotten password floppy disk** A Windows XP disk created to be used in case the user forgets the user account password to the system.

**form factor** A set of specifications on the size, shape, and configuration of a computer hardware component, such as a case, power supply, or motherboard.

**formatting** Preparing a hard drive volume or floppy disk for use by placing tracks and sectors on its surface to store information (for example, the FORMAT A: command).

**FPT (forced perfect terminator)** A type of SCSI active terminator that includes a mechanism to force signal termination to the correct voltage, eliminating most signal echoes and interference.

**FQDN (fully qualified domain name)** A host name and a domain name, such as *jsmith.amazon.com*. Sometimes loosely referred to as a domain name.

**fragmentation** The distribution of data files on a hard drive or floppy disk so that they are stored in noncontiguous clusters.

**fragmented file** A file that has been written to different portions of the disk so that it's not in contiguous clusters.

**FRU (field replaceable unit)** A component in a computer or device that can be replaced with a new component without sending the computer or device back to the manufacturer. Examples: power supply, DIMM, motherboard, floppy disk drive.

**FTP (File Transfer Protocol)** The protocol used to transfer files over a TCP/IP network so that the file doesn't need to be converted to ASCII format before transferring it.

**full AT** *See* AT.

**gateway** A computer or other device that connects networks.

**GDI (Graphics Device Interface)** A Windows 9x component that controls screens, graphics, and printing.

**GHz (gigahertz)** 1000 MHz, or one billion cycles per second.

**Gigabit Ethernet** The newest version of Ethernet. Gigabit Ethernet supports rates of data transfer up to 1 gigabit per second but isn't widely used yet.

**global user account** Sometimes called a domain user account, the account is used at the domain level, created by an administrator, and stored in the SAM (Security Accounts Manager) database on a Windows 2000 or Windows 2003 domain controller.

**GPF (General Protection Fault)** A Windows error that occurs when a program attempts to access a memory address that isn't available or is no longer assigned to it.

**graphics accelerator** A type of video card with an on-board processor that can substantially increase speed and boost graphical and video performance.

**graphics DDR (G-DDR), graphics DDR2, graphics DDR3** Types of DDR, DDR2, and DDR3 memory specifically designed to be used in graphics cards.

**Green Standards** A computer or device that conforms to these standards can go into sleep or doze mode when not in use, thus saving energy and helping the environment. Devices that carry the Green Star or Energy Star comply with these standards.

**ground bracelet** An antistatic strap you wear around your wrist that's attached to the computer case, grounding mat, or another ground so that ESD is discharged from your body before you touch sensitive components inside a computer. *Also called* antistatic strap, ground strap, *or* ESD bracelet.

**group profile** A group of user profiles. All profiles in the group can be changed by changing the group profile.

**guard tone** A tone that an answering modem sends when it first answers the phone to tell the calling modem that a modem is on the other end of the line.

**Guest user** A user who has limited permissions on a system and can't make changes to it. Guest user accounts are intended for one-time or infrequent users of a workstation.

**handshaking** When two modems begin to communicate, the initial agreement made as to how to send and receive data.

**hard boot** Restart the computer by turning off the power or by pressing the Reset button. *Also called* cold boot.

**hard copy** Output from a printer to paper.

**hard drive** The main secondary storage device of a PC is a small case containing magnetic coated platters that rotate at high speed.

**hard drive controller** The firmware on a circuit board mounted on or inside the hard drive housing that controls access to a hard drive. Older hard drives used firmware on a controller card that connected to the drive by way of two cables, one for data and one for control.

**hard drive standby time** The amount of time before a hard drive shuts down to conserve energy.

**hardware** The physical components that constitute the computer system, such as the monitor, keyboard, motherboard, and printer.

**hardware address** *See* MAC (Media Access Control) address.

**hardware cache** A disk cache contained in RAM chips built right on the disk controller. *Also called* buffer.

**hardware interrupt** An event caused by a hardware device signaling the CPU that it requires service.

**hardware profile** A set of hardware configuration information that Windows keeps in the Registry. Windows can maintain more than one hardware profile for the same PC.

**HCL (Hardware Compatibility List)** The list of all computers and peripheral devices that have been tested and are officially supported by Windows 2000/XP (see *www.microsoft.com/whdc/hcl/default.mspx*).

**head** The top or bottom surface of one platter on a hard drive. Each platter has two heads.

**heat sink** A piece of metal, with cooling fans, that can be attached to or mounted on an integrated chip (such as the CPU) to dissipate heat.

**hexadecimal (hex) notation** A numbering system that uses 16 digits, the numerals 0 to 9, and the letters A to F. Hexadecimal notation is often used to display memory addresses.

**hibernation** A notebook OS feature that conserves power by using a small trickle of electricity. Before the notebook begins to hibernate, everything currently stored in memory is saved to the hard drive. When the notebook is brought out of hibernation, open applications and their data are returned to their state before hibernation.

**hidden file** A file that isn't displayed in a directory list. Whether to hide or display a file is one of the file's attributes the OS keeps.

**high-level formatting** Formatting performed by means of the DOS or Windows Format command (for example, FORMAT C:/S creates the boot record, FAT, and root directory on drive C and makes the drive bootable). *Also called* operating system formatting.

**Himem.sys** The DOS and Windows 9x memory manager extension that allows access to memory addresses above 1 MB.

**hive** Physical segment of the Windows 2000/XP Registry that's stored in a file.

**HMA (high memory area)** The first 64K of extended memory.

**host** Any computer or other device on a network that has been assigned an IP address. *Also called* node.

**host adapter** The circuit board that controls a SCSI bus supporting as many as 7 or 15 separate devices. The host adapter controls communication between the SCSI bus and the PC.

**host bus** *See* system bus.

**host drive** Typically drive H on a compressed drive. *See* compressed drive.

**host name** A name that identifies a computer, printer, or other device on a network.

**hot-pluggable** *See* hot-swappable.

**hot-swappable** A device that can be plugged into a computer while it's turned on and the computer senses the device and configures it without rebooting, or the device can be removed without an OS error. *Also called* hot-pluggable.

**HTML (Hypertext Markup Language)** A markup language used for hypertext documents on the World Wide Web. This language uses tags to format the document, create hyperlinks, and mark locations for graphics.

**HTTP (Hypertext Transfer Protocol)** The protocol used by the World Wide Web.

**HTTPS (HTTP secure)** A version of HTTP that includes data encryption for security.

**hub** A network device or box that provides a central location to connect cables.

**HVD (High Voltage Differential)** A type of SCSI differential signaling requiring more expensive hardware to handle the higher voltage.

**hypertext** Text that contains links to remote points in the document or to other files, documents, or graphics. Hypertext is created by using HTML and is commonly used on Web sites.

**Hz (hertz)** Unit of measurement for frequency, calculated in terms of vibrations, or cycles per second. For example, for 16-bit stereo sound, a frequency of 44,000 Hz is used. *See also* MHz (megahertz).

**i.Link** *See* IEEE 1394.

**I/O addresses** Numbers used by devices and the CPU to manage communication between them. *Also called* ports *or* port addresses.

**I/O controller card** An older card that can contain serial, parallel, and game ports and floppy drive and IDE connectors.

**IBM-compatible PC** A computer that uses an Intel (or compatible) processor and can run DOS and Windows.

**ICF (Internet Connection Firewall)** Windows XP software designed to protect a PC from unauthorized access from the Internet; updated to Windows Firewall in Service Pack 2.

**ICS (Internet Connection Sharing)** A Windows 98/XP utility that uses Network Address Translation (NAT) and acts as a proxy server to manage two or more computers connected to the Internet.

**IDE (Integrated Drive Electronics or Integrated Device Electronics)** A hard drive with a disk controller integrated into the drive, eliminating the need for a controller cable and thus increasing speed and reducing price. *See also* EIDE (Enhanced IDE).

**IEEE (Institute of Electrical and Electronics Engineers)** A nonprofit organization that develops standards for the computer and electronics industries.

**IEEE 1284** A standard for parallel ports and cables developed by the Institute for Electrical and Electronics Engineers and supported by many hardware manufacturers.

**IEEE 1394** Standards for an expansion bus that can also be configured to work as a local bus. It's expected to replace the SCSI bus, providing an easy method to install and configure fast I/O devices. *Also called* FireWire *and* i.Link.

**IEEE 1394.3** A standard, developed by the 1394 Trade Association, designed for peer-to-peer data transmission. It allows imaging devices to send images and photos directly to printers without involving a computer.

**IEEE 802.11a/b/g** IEEE specifications for wireless communication and data synchronization. *Also called* Wi-Fi. Apple Computer's versions of 802.11a/b/g are called AirPort and AirPort Extreme.

**infestation** Any unwanted program that's transmitted to a computer without the user's knowledge and designed to do varying degrees of damage to data and software. There are a number of different types of infestations, including viruses, Trojan horses, worms, and logic bombs.

**information (.inf) file** Text file with an .inf file extension, such as Msbatch.inf, that contains information about a hardware or software installation.

**infrared transceiver** A wireless transceiver that uses infrared technology to support wireless devices, such as keyboards, mice, and printers. A motherboard might have an embedded infrared transceiver, or the transceiver might plug into a USB or serial port. The technology is defined by the Infrared Data Association (IrDA). *Also called* IrDA transceiver *or* infrared port.

**initialization files** Configuration information files for Windows. System.ini is one of the most important Windows 9x initialization files.

**inkjet printer** A type of ink dispersion printer that uses cartridges of ink. The ink is heated to a boiling point and then ejected onto the paper through tiny nozzles.

**internal command** A command embedded in the Command.com file.

**intranet** A private network that uses TCP/IP protocols.

**Io.sys** Along with Msdos.sys and Command.com, one of the three files that are the core components of the real mode portion of Windows 9x. It's the first program file of the OS.

**IP address** A 32-bit address consisting of four numbers separated by periods, used to uniquely identify a device on a network that uses TCP/IP protocols. The first numbers identify the network; the last numbers identify a host. An example of an IP address is 206.96.103s.114.

**IrDA transceiver** *See* infrared transceiver.

**IRQ (interrupt request) line** A line on a bus assigned to a device that's used to signal the CPU for servicing. These lines are assigned a reference number (for example, the normal IRQ for a printer is IRQ 7).

**ISA (Industry Standard Architecture) slot** An older slot on the motherboard used for slower I/O devices, which can support an 8-bit or a 16-bit data path. ISA slots have mostly been replaced by PCI slots.

**ISDN (Integrated Services Digital Network)** A digital telephone line that can carry data at about five times the speed of regular telephone lines. Two channels (telephone numbers) share a single pair of wires.

**ISP (Internet service provider)** A commercial group that provides Internet access for a monthly fee. AOL, Earthlink, and CompuServe are large ISPs.

**ITU (International Telecommunications Union)** The international organization responsible for developing international standards of communication. Formerly CCITT.

**JPEG (Joint Photographic Experts Group)** A graphical compression scheme that allows users to control the amount of data that's averaged and sacrificed as file size is reduced. It's a common Internet file format. Most JPEG files have a .jpg extension.

**jumper** Two wires that stick up side by side on the motherboard and are used to hold configuration information. The jumper is considered closed if a cover is over the wires and open if the cover is missing.

**key** In encryption, a secret number or code used to encode and decode data. In Windows, a section name of the Windows Registry.

**keyboard** A common input device through which data and instructions can be typed into computer memory.

**LAN (local area network)** A computer network that covers only a small area, usually within one building.

**laptop computer** *See* notebook.

**large mode** A mode of addressing information on hard drives that range from 504 MB to 8.4 GB by translating cylinder, head, and sector information to break the 528 MB hard drive barrier. *Also called* ECHS (extended CHS) mode.

**large-capacity drive** A hard drive larger than 504 MB.

**Last Known Good Configuration** In Windows 2000/XP, Registry settings and device drivers that were in effect when the computer last booted successfully. These settings can be restored during the startup process to recover from errors during the previous boot.

**LBA (logical block addressing) mode** A mode of addressing information on hard drives in which the BIOS and operating system view the drive as one long linear list of LBAs or addressable sectors, permitting drives to be larger than 8.4 GB. (LBA 0 is cylinder 0, head 0, and sector 1.)

**LIF (low insertion force) socket** A socket that requires the installer to manually apply an even force over the microchip when inserting the chip into the socket.

**Limited users** Windows XP user accounts known as Users in Windows 2000; they have read-write access only on their own folders, read-only access to most system folders, and no access to other users' data.

**line speed** *See* bandwidth *or* modem speed.

**Lmhosts** A text file in the Windows folder that contains NetBIOS names and their associated IP addresses. This file is used for name resolution on a NetBEUI network.

**local bus** A bus that operates at a speed synchronized with the CPU frequency. The system bus is a local bus.

**local I/O bus** A local bus that provides I/O devices with fast access to the CPU.

**local printer** A printer connected to a computer by way of a port on the computer. *Compare to* network printer.

**local profile** A user profile stored on a local computer that can't be accessed from another computer on the network.

**local user account** A user account that applies only to a local computer and can't be used to access resources from other computers on the network.

**logical drive**   A portion or all of a hard drive partition that the operating system treats as though it were a physical drive. Each logical drive is assigned a drive letter, such as C, and contains a file system. *Also called* volume.

**logical geometry**   The number of heads, tracks, and sectors that the BIOS on the hard drive controller presents to the system BIOS and the OS. The logical geometry doesn't consist of the same values as the physical geometry, although calculations of drive capacity yield the same results.

**lost allocation units**   *See* lost clusters.

**lost clusters**   File fragments that, according to the file allocation table, contain data that doesn't belong to any file. The CHKDSK/F command can free these fragments. *Also called* lost allocation units.

**low-level formatting**   A process (usually performed at the factory) that electronically creates the hard drive tracks and sectors and tests for bad spots on the disk surface.

**low-profile case**   *See* compact case.

**LPX**   A form factor in which expansion cards are mounted on a riser card that plugs into a motherboard. The expansion cards in LPX systems are mounted parallel to the motherboard instead of perpendicular to it, as in AT and ATX systems.

**LVD (Low Voltage Differential)**   A type of differential signaling that uses lower voltage than does HVD, is less expensive, and can be compatible with single-ended signaling on the same SCSI bus.

**MAC (Media Access Control) address**   A 6-byte hexadecimal hardware address unique to each NIC card and assigned by the manufacturer. The address is often printed on the adapter. An example is 00 00 0C 08 2F 35. *Also called* physical address, adapter address, *or* hardware address.

**main board**   *See* motherboard.

**MBR (Master Boot Record)**   The first sector on a hard drive, which contains the partition table and a program BIOS uses to boot an OS from the drive.

**MDRAM (MultiBank DRAM)**   A type of video memory that's faster than VRAM and WRAM but can be more economical because it can be installed on a video card in smaller increments.

**memory**   Physical microchips that can hold data and programming, located on the motherboard or expansion cards.

**memory address**   A number assigned to each byte in memory. The CPU can use memory addresses to track where information is stored in RAM. Memory addresses are usually displayed as hexadecimal numbers in segment/offset form.

**memory bus**   *See* system bus.

**memory dump**   The contents of memory saved to a file at the time an event halted the system. Support technicians can analyze the dump file to help understand the source of the problem.

**memory extender**   For DOS and Windows 9x, a device driver named Himem.sys that manages RAM, giving access to memory addresses above 1 MB.

**memory paging**   In Windows, swapping blocks of RAM memory to an area of the hard drive to serve as virtual memory when RAM is low.

**memory-resident virus**   A virus that can stay lurking in memory even after its host program is terminated.

**MHz (megahertz)**   One million Hz, or one million cycles per second. *See also* Hz (hertz).

**microATX**   A recent version of the ATX form factor. MicroATX addresses some new technologies that have been developed since the original introduction of ATX.

**MicroDIMM**   A type of memory module used on notebooks that has 144 pins and uses a 64-bit data path.

**microprocessor**   *See* CPU (central processing unit).

**Mini PCI**   The PCI industry standard for desktop computer expansion cards, applied to a much smaller form factor for notebook expansion cards.

**Mini-ATX** A smaller ATX board that can be used with regular ATX cases and power supplies.

**minicartridge** A tape drive cartridge that is only $3\frac{1}{4}$ x $2\frac{1}{2}$ x $\frac{3}{5}$ inches. It's small enough to allow two drives to fit into a standard $5\frac{1}{2}$-inch drive bay of a PC case.

**Mini-LPX** A smaller version of the LPX motherboard.

**MMC (Microsoft Management Console)** A utility to build customized consoles. These consoles can be saved to a file with an .msc file extension.

**MMX (Multimedia Extensions)** Multimedia instructions built into Intel processors to add functionality such as better processing of multimedia, SIMD support, and increased cache.

**modem** From the words "modulate-demodulate," a device that modulates digital data from a computer to an analog format that can be sent over telephone lines, and then demodulates it back into digital form.

**modem eliminator** *See* null modem cable.

**modem speed** The speed at which a modem can transmit data along a phone line, measured in bits per second (bps). *Also called* bandwidth *or* line speed.

**monitor** The most commonly used output device for displaying text and graphics on a computer.

**motherboard** The main board in the computer. The CPU, ROM chips, SIMMs, DIMMs, RIMMs, and interface cards are plugged into the motherboard. *Also called* the main board *or* system board.

**motherboard bus** *See* system bus.

**motherboard mouse** *See* PS/2-compatible mouse.

**mouse** A pointing and input device that allows users to move a cursor around a screen and select programs with the click of a button.

**MP3** A method to compress audio files that uses MPEG level 1. It can reduce sound files as low as a 1:24 ratio without losing much sound quality.

**MPEG (Moving Pictures Experts Group)** A processing-intensive standard for data compression for motion pictures that tracks movement from one frame to the next and stores only the data that has changed.

**Msdos.sys** In Windows 9x, a text file containing settings used by Io.sys during booting. In DOS, the Msdos.sys file was a program file that contained part of the DOS core.

**MSDS (material safety data sheet)** A document that explains how to handle substances such as chemical solvents; it includes information such as physical data, toxicity, health effects, first aid, storage, disposal, and spill procedures.

**multicasting** A process in which a message is sent by one host to multiple hosts, such as when a video conference is broadcast to several hosts on the Internet.

**multimeter** A device used to measure the components of an electrical circuit. The most common measurements are voltage, current, and resistance.

**multiplier** The factor by which the bus speed or frequency is multiplied to get the CPU clock speed.

**multiscan monitor** A monitor that can work within a range of frequencies and, therefore, can work with different standards and video cards. It offers a variety of refresh rates.

**name resolution** The process of associating a NetBIOS name or host name to an IP address.

**NAT (Network Address Translation)** A process that converts private IP addresses on a LAN to the proxy server's IP address before a data packet is sent over the Internet.

**NetBEUI (NetBIOS Extended User Interface)** A fast Microsoft networking protocol used only by Windows-based systems and limited to LANs because it doesn't support routing.

**NetBIOS (Network Basic Input/Output System)** An API protocol used by some applications to communicate over a NetBEUI network.

NetBIOS has largely been replaced by Windows Sockets over a TCP/IP network.

**network adapter** *See* NIC (network interface card).

**network drive map** Mounting a drive, such as drive E, to a computer that's actually hard drive space on another host computer on the network.

**network printer** A printer that any user on the network can access, through its own network card and connection to the network, through a connection to a standalone print server, or through a connection to a computer as a local printer, which is shared on the network. *Compare to* local printer.

**NIC (network interface card)** An expansion card that plugs into a computer's motherboard and provides a port on the back of the card to connect a PC to a network. *Also called* network adapter.

**NLX** A low-end form factor that's similar to LPX but provides more support for current and emerging processor technologies. NLX was designed for flexibility and efficiency of space.

**node** *See* host.

**noise** An extraneous, unwanted signal, often over an analog phone line, that can cause communication interference or transmission errors. Possible sources are fluorescent lighting, radios, TVs, lightning, or bad wiring.

**nonparity memory** Eight-bit memory without error checking. A SIMM part number with a 32 in it (4 x 8 bits) is nonparity.

**nonvolatile** Refers to a kind of RAM that's stable and can hold data as long as electricity is powering the memory.

**normal mode** *See* CHS (cylinder, head, sector) mode.

**NOS (network operating system)** An operating system that resides on the controlling computer in the network. The NOS controls what software, data, and devices users on the network can access. Examples of an NOS are Novell NetWare and Windows 2000 Server.

**notebook** A portable computer designed for travel and mobility. Notebooks use the same technology as desktop PCs, with modifications for conserving voltage, taking up less space, and operating while on the move. *Also called* laptop computer.

**NTFS (NT File System)** The file system for the Windows 2000/XP operating systems. NTFS can't be accessed by other operating systems, such as DOS. It provides increased reliability and security compared with other methods of organizing and accessing files. There are several versions of NTFS that might be compatible.

**Ntldr (NT Loader)** In Windows 2000/XP, the OS loader used on Intel systems.

**NTVDM (NT virtual DOS machine)** An emulated environment in which a 16-bit DOS application resides in Windows 2000/XP with its own memory space or WOW (Win16 on Win32).

**null modem cable** A cable that allows two data terminal equipment (DTE) devices to communicate; the transmit and receive wires are cross-connected, and no modems are necessary.

**octet** Term for each of the four 8-bit numbers that make up an IP address. For example, the IP address 206.96.103.114 has four octets.

**ohm ($\Omega$)** The standard unit of measurement for electrical resistance. Resistors are rated in ohms.

**on-board ports** Ports that are directly on the motherboard, such as a built-in keyboard port or on-board serial port.

**operating system formatting** *See* high-level formatting.

**OS (operating system)** Software that controls a computer. An OS controls how system resources are used and provides a user interface, a way of managing hardware and software, and ways to work with files.

**P1 connector** Power connection on an ATX motherboard.

**P8 connector** One of two power connectors on an AT motherboard.

**P9 connector** One of two power connectors on an AT motherboard.

**page fault** An OS interrupt that occurs when the OS is forced to access the hard drive to satisfy the demands for virtual memory.

**page file** *See* swap file.

**Pagefile.sys** The Windows 2000/XP swap file.

**page-in** The process in which the memory manager goes to the hard drive to return the data from a swap file to RAM.

**page-out** The process in which, when RAM is full, the memory manager moves a page to the swap file.

**pages** 4 KB segments in which Windows 2000/XP allocates memory.

**parallel port** A female 25-pin port on a computer that can transmit data in parallel, 8 bits at a time, and is usually used with a printer. The names for parallel ports are LPT1 and LPT2.

**parity** An error-checking scheme in which a ninth, or "parity," bit is added. The value of the parity bit is set to 0 or 1 to provide an even number of 1s for even parity and an odd number of 1s for odd parity.

**parity error** An error that occurs when the number of 1s in the byte isn't in agreement with the expected number.

**parity memory** Nine-bit memory in which the ninth bit is used for error checking. A SIMM part number with 36 in it (4 x 9 bits) is parity. Older PCs almost always use parity chips.

**partition** A division of a hard drive that can be used to hold logical drives.

**partition table** A table at the beginning of the hard drive that contains information about each partition on the drive. The partition table is contained in the Master Boot Record.

**passive terminator** A type of terminator for single-ended SCSI cables. Simple resistors provide termination of a signal. Passive termination isn't reliable over long distances and should be used only with narrow SCSI.

**PATA (parallel ATA)** An older IDE cabling method that uses a 40-pin flat data cable or an 80-conductor cable and a 40-pin IDE connector. *See also* SATA (serial ATA).

**patch** An update to software that corrects an error, adds a feature, or addresses security issues. *Also called* update *or* service pack.

**patch cable** A network cable used to connect a PC to a hub.

**path** A drive and list of directories pointing to a file, such as C:\Windows\command. Also the OS command to provide a list of paths to the system for finding program files to run.

**PC Card** A credit-card-size adapter card that can be slid into a slot in the side of many notebook computers and is used for connecting to modems, networks, and CD-ROM drives. *Also called* PCMCIA Card.

**PC Card slot** An expansion slot on a notebook computer into which a PC Card is inserted. *Also called* PCMCIA Card slot.

**PCI (Peripheral Component Interconnect) bus** A bus common on Pentium computers that runs at speeds up to 33 MHz or 66 MHz, with a 32-bit-wide or 64-bit-wide data path. PCI-X, released in September 1999, enables PCI to run at 133 MHz. For some chipsets, it serves as the middle layer between the memory bus and expansion buses.

**PCMCIA (Personal Computer Memory Card International Association) Card** *See* PC Card.

**PCMCIA Card slot** *See* PC Card slot.

**PDA (personal digital assistant)** A small handheld computer that has its own operating system and applications.

**peer-to-peer network** A network of computers that are all equals, or peers. Each computer has the same amount of authority, and each can act as a server to the other computers.

**peripheral devices** Devices that communicate with the CPU but aren't located directly on the motherboard, such as the monitor, floppy drive, printer, and mouse.

**PGA (pin grid array)** A feature of a CPU socket whereby the pins are aligned in uniform rows around the socket.

**physical address**   *See* MAC (Media Access Control) address.

**physical geometry**   The actual layout of heads, tracks, and sectors on a hard drive. *See also* logical geometry.

**PIF (program information file)**   A file used by Windows to describe the environment for a DOS program to use.

**Ping (Packet Internet Groper)**   A Windows and UNIX command used to troubleshoot network connections. It verifies that the host can communicate with another host on the network.

**pinout**   A description of how each pin on a bus, connection, plug, slot, or socket is used.

**PIO (Programmed I/O) transfer mode**   A transfer mode that uses the CPU to transfer data from the hard drive to memory. PIO mode is slower than DMA mode.

**pixel**   A small spot on a fine horizontal scan line. Pixels are illuminated to create an image on the monitor.

**polling**   A process by which the CPU checks the status of connected devices to determine whether they are ready to send or receive data.

**port**   As applied to services running on a computer, a number assigned to a process on a computer so that the process can be found by TCP/IP. *Also called* a port address *or* port number. Another name for an I/O address. *See also* I/O address. A physical connector, usually at the back of a computer, that allows a cable from a peripheral device, such as a printer, mouse, or modem, to be attached.

**port address**   *See* port *or* I/O addresses.

**port number**   *See* port.

**port replicator**   A device designed to connect to a notebook computer to make it easy to connect the notebook to peripheral devices.

**port settings**   The configuration parameters of communication devices such as COM1, COM2, or COM3, including IRQ settings.

**port speed**   The communication speed between a DTE (computer) and a DCE (modem). As a general rule, the port speed should be at least four times as fast as the modem speed.

**POST (power-on self test)**   A self-diagnostic program used to conduct a simple test of the CPU, RAM, and I/O devices. The POST is performed by startup BIOS when the computer is first turned on and is stored in ROM-BIOS.

**power scheme**   A feature of Windows XP support for notebooks that allows users to create groups of power settings for specific sets of conditions.

**power supply**   A box inside the computer case that supplies power to the motherboard and other installed devices. Power supplies provide 3.3, 5, and 12 volts DC.

**power-on password**   A password that a computer uses to control access during the boot process.

**PnP (Plug and Play)**   A standard designed to make installing new hardware devices easier by automatically configuring them to eliminate system resource conflicts (such as IRQ or I/O address conflicts). PnP is supported by Windows9x, Windows 2000, and Windows XP.

**primary partition**   A hard disk partition that can contain only one logical drive.

**primary storage**   Temporary storage on the motherboard used by the CPU to process data and instructions. Memory is considered primary storage.

**printer**   A peripheral output device that produces printed output to paper. Different types include dot matrix, inkjet, and laser printers.

**printer maintenance kit**   A kit purchased from a printer manufacturer that contains the parts, tools, and instructions needed to perform routine printer maintenance.

**private IP address**   An IP address used on a private TCP/IP network that's isolated from the Internet.

**process**   A running instance of a program together with the program resources. More than one process can be running for a program at the same time. One process for a program happens each time the program is loaded into memory or runs.

**processor**   *See* CPU (central processing unit).

**processor speed**   The speed, or frequency, at which the CPU operates. Usually expressed in GHz.

**product activation**   The process that Microsoft uses to prevent software piracy. For example, after Windows XP is activated for a particular computer, it can't be installed on another computer.

**program**   A set of step-by-step instructions to a computer. Some are burned directly into chips, whereas others are stored as program files. Programs are written in languages such as BASIC and C++.

**program file**   A file containing instructions designed to be carried out by the CPU.

**protected mode**   An operating mode that supports preemptive multitasking. The OS manages memory and other hardware devices, and programs can use a 32-bit data path. *Also called* 32-bit mode.

**protocol**   A set of rules and standards that two entities use for communication.

**Protocol.ini**   A Windows initialization file containing network configuration information.

**proxy server**   A server that acts as an intermediary between another computer and the Internet. The proxy server substitutes its own IP address for the IP address of the network computer making a request so that all traffic over the Internet appears to be coming from only the proxy server's IP address.

**PS/2-compatible mouse**   A mouse that plugs into a round mouse PS/2 port on the motherboard. *Also called* motherboard mouse.

**public IP address**   An IP address available to the Internet.

**RAID (redundant array of independent disks)**   Several methods of configuring multiple hard drives to store data to increase logical volume size and improve performance or to ensure that if one hard drive fails, the data is still available from another hard drive.

**RAM (random access memory)**   Memory modules on the motherboard containing microchips used to temporarily hold data and programs while the CPU processes both. Information in RAM is lost when the PC is turned off.

**RAM drive**   An area of memory treated as though it were a hard drive, but it works much faster than a hard drive. The Windows 9x startup disk uses a RAM drive. *Compare to* virtual memory.

**RDRAM**   *See* Direct Rambus DRAM.

**read/write head**   A sealed, magnetic coil device that moves across the surface of a disk reading data from or writing data to the disk.

**real mode**   A single-tasking operating mode whereby a program has 1024 K of memory addresses, has direct access to RAM, and uses a 16-bit data path. Using a memory extender (Himem.sys), a program in real mode can access memory above 1024 K. *Also called* 16-bit mode.

**Recovery Console**   A Windows 2000/XP command-line utility and OS that can be used to solve problems when Windows can't load from the hard drive.

**Registry**   A database that Windows uses to store hardware and software configuration information, user preferences, and setup information.

**remarked chips**   Chips that have been used and returned to the factory, marked again, and resold. The surface of the chips might be dull or scratched.

**rescue disk**   A floppy disk that can be used to start a computer when the hard drive fails to boot. *Also called* ESD (emergency startup disk) *or* startup disk.

**resistance**   The degree to which a device opposes or resists the flow of electricity. As the electrical resistance increases, the current decreases. *See* ohm *and* resistor.

**resistor**   An electronic device that resists or opposes the flow of electricity. A resistor can be used to reduce the amount of electricity supplied to an electronic component.

**resolution**   The number of pixels on a monitor screen that can be addressed by software (for example, 1024 x 768 pixels).

**restore point** A snapshot of the Windows XP system state, usually made before installing new hardware or applications.

**RIMM** A type of memory module developed by Rambus, Inc.

**RJ-11** A phone line connection found on modems, telephones, and house phone outlets.

**RJ-45 connector** A connector used with twisted-pair cable that connects the cable to the NIC.

**ROM (read-only memory)** Chips that contain programming code and can't be erased.

**ROM BIOS** *See* BIOS (basic input/output system).

**root directory** The main directory created when a hard drive or disk is first formatted. In Linux, it's indicated by a forward slash (\). In DOS and Windows, it's indicated by a backward slash (/).

**routable protocol** A protocol that can be routed to interconnected networks on the basis of a network address. TCP/IP is a routable protocol, but NetBEUI is not.

**sags** *See* brownouts.

**SATA (serial ATA)** An ATAPI cabling method that uses a narrower and more reliable cable than the 80-conductor cable. *See also* PATA (parallel ATA).

**SCSI (Small Computer System Interface)** A fast interface between a host adapter and the CPU that can daisy-chain as many as 7 or 15 devices on a single bus.

**SCSI ID** A number from 0 to 15 assigned to each SCSI device attached to the daisy chain.

**SDRAM (synchronous DRAM)** A type of memory stored on DIMMs that runs in sync with the system clock, at the same speed as the motherboard.

**SDRAM II** *See* DDR SDRAM (Double Data Rate SDRAM).

**SE (single-ended) cable** A type of SCSI cable in which two wires are used to carry a signal. One carries the signal, and the other is a ground for the signal. *Compare to* differential cable.

**secondary storage** Storage that's remote to the CPU and permanently holds data, even when the PC is turned off, such as a hard drive.

**sector** On a disk surface, it's one segment of a track, which almost always contains 512 bytes of data.

**sequential access** A method of data access used by tape drives, whereby data is written or read sequentially from the beginning to the end of the tape or until the data is found.

**serial ATA cable** An IDE cable that's narrower and has fewer pins than the parallel IDE 80-conductor cable.

**serial mouse** A mouse that uses a serial port and has a female 9-pin DB-9 connector.

**serial port** A male 9-pin or 25-pin port on a computer system used by slower I/O devices, such as a mouse or modem. Data travels serially, one bit at a time, through the port. Serial ports are sometimes configured as COM1, COM2, COM3, or COM4.

**service pack** *See* patch.

**SFC (System File Checker)** A Windows tool that checks to make sure Windows is using the correct versions of system files.

**shadow RAM or shadowing ROM** ROM programming code copied into RAM to speed up the system operation because of the faster access speed of RAM.

**shortcut** An icon on the desktop that points to a program that can be run or to a file or folder.

**SIMM (single inline memory module)** A miniature circuit board used in older computers to hold RAM. SIMMs hold 8, 16, 32, or 64 MB on a single module.

**simple volume** A type of dynamic volume used on a single hard drive that corresponds to a primary partition on a basic disk.

**single-voltage CPU** A CPU that requires one voltage for both internal and I/O operations.

**slack** Wasted space on a hard drive caused by not using all available space at the end of clusters.

**sleep mode** A mode used in many "green" systems that allows them to be configured through CMOS to suspend the monitor or even the drive, if the keyboard and/or CPU have been inactive for a set number of minutes. *See also* Green Standards.

**slimline case** *See* compact case.

**snap-ins** Components added to a console by using the Microsoft Management Console.

**SO-DIMM (small outline DIMM)** A type of memory module used in notebook computers that uses DIMM technology and can have 72 pins or 144 pins.

**soft boot** To restart a PC without turning off the power, for example, in Windows XP by clicking Start, Turn Off Computer, Restart. *Also called* warm boot.

**soft power** *See* soft switch.

**soft switch** A feature on an ATX system that allows an OS to power down the system and allows for activity, such as a keystroke or network activity, to power up the system. *Also called* soft power.

**software** Computer programs, or instructions to perform a specific task. Software can be BIOS, OSs, or application software, such as a word-processing or spreadsheet program.

**software cache** Cache controlled by software, whereby the cache is stored in RAM.

**SO-RIMM (small outline RIMM)** A 160-pin memory module in notebooks that uses Rambus technology.

**spacers** *See* standoffs.

**SPGA (staggered pin grid array)** A feature of a CPU socket whereby the pins are staggered over the socket to squeeze more pins into a small space.

**SPI (SCSI Parallel Interface)** The part of the SCSI-3 standard that specifies how SCSI devices are connected.

**spooling** Placing print jobs in a print queue so that an application can be released from the printing process before printing is completed. "Spooling" is an acronym for "simultaneous peripheral operations online."

**SRAM (static RAM)** RAM chips that retain information without the need for refreshing, as long as the computer's power is on. They are more expensive than traditional DRAM.

**standby time** The time before a "green" system reduce 92% of its activity. *See also* Green Standards.

**standoffs** Round plastic or metal pegs that separate the motherboard from the case so that components on the back of the motherboard don't touch the case. *Also called* spacers.

**startup BIOS** The part of system BIOS responsible for controlling the PC when it's first turned on. Startup BIOS gives control over to the OS after it's loaded.

**startup disk** *See* rescue disk.

**startup password** *See* power-on password.

**static electricity** *See* ESD (electrostatic discharge).

**static IP address** An IP address permanently assigned to a workstation.

**stop error** An error severe enough to cause the operating system to stop all processes. *See also* blue screen.

**STP (shielded twisted-pair) cable** A cable made of one or more twisted pairs of wires and surrounded by a metal shield.

**streaming audio** Downloading audio data from the Internet in a continuous stream of data without downloading an entire audio file first.

**subdirectory** A directory or folder contained in another directory or folder. *Also called* child directory *or* folder.

**subnet mask** A group of four numbers (dotted decimal numbers) that tell TCP/IP whether a remote computer is on the same or a different network.

**surge suppressor or surge protector** A device or power strip designed to protect electronic equipment from power surges and spikes.

**suspend time** The time before a "Green" system reduces 99% of its activity. After this time, the system needs a warm-up time so that the CPU, monitor, and hard drive can reach full activity.

**swap file** A file on the hard drive used by the OS for virtual memory. *Also called* page file.

**synchronous SRAM**   SRAM that's faster and more expensive than asynchronous SRAM. It requires a clock signal to validate its control signals, enabling the cache to run in step with the CPU.

**Sysedit**   The Windows System Configuration Editor, a text editor generally used to edit system files.

**system BIOS**   BIOS located on the motherboard.

**system board**   *See* motherboard.

**system bus**   The bus between the CPU and memory on the motherboard. The bus frequency in documentation is called the system speed, such as 400 MHz. *Also called* memory bus, motherboard bus, front-side bus, local bus, *or* host bus.

**system clock**   A line on a bus dedicated to timing the activities of components connected to it. The system clock provides a continuous pulse that other devices use to time themselves.

**system disk**   Windows terminology for a bootable disk.

**system partition**   The active partition of the hard drive containing the boot record and the specific files required to load Windows 2000/XP.

**system resource**   A channel, line, or address on the motherboard that can be used by the CPU or a device for communication. The four system resources are IRQ, I/O address, DMA channel, and memory address.

**System Restore**   A Windows XP utility, similar to the ScanReg tool in earlier versions of Windows, used to restore the system to a restore point. Unlike ScanReg, System Restore can't be run from a command prompt.

**system state data**   In Windows 2000/XP, files that are necessary for a successful load of the operating system.

**System.ini**   A text configuration file used by Windows 3.x and supported by Windows 9x for backward compatibility.

**TAPI (Telephony Application Programming Interface)**   A standard developed by Intel and Microsoft that can be used by 32-bit Windows communication programs for communicating over phone lines.

**TCP/IP (Transmission Control Protocol/Internet Protocol)**   The suite of protocols that support communication on the Internet. TCP is responsible for error checking, and IP is responsible for routing.

**telephony**   A term describing the technology of converting sound to signals that can travel over telephone lines.

**terminating resistor**   The resistor added at the end of a SCSI chain to dampen the voltage at the end of the chain.

**termination**   A process necessary to prevent an echo effect of power at the end of a SCSI chain, resulting in interference with the data transmission.

**ThickNet**   *See* 10Base5.

**ThinNet**   *See* 10Base2.

**TIFF (Tagged Image File Format)**   A bitmapped file format used to hold photographs, graphics, and screen captures. TIFF files can be rather large and have a .tif file extension.

**top-level domain**   The highest level of domain names, indicated by a suffix that tells something about the host. For example, .com is for commercial use and .edu is for educational institutions.

**tower case**   The largest type of personal computer case. Tower cases stand vertically and can be as tall as two feet. They have more drive bays and are a good choice for computer users who anticipate making major upgrades.

**trace**   A wire on a circuit board that connects two components or devices.

**track**   One of many concentric circles on the surface of a hard drive or floppy disk.

**training**   *See* handshaking.

**translation**   A technique used by system BIOS and hard drive controller BIOS to break the 504 MB hard drive barrier, whereby a different set of drive parameters are communicated to the OS and other software than that used by the hard drive controller BIOS.

**TSR (terminate-and-stay-resident)** A program loaded into memory that remains dormant until called on, such as a screen saver or a memory-resident antivirus program.

**UART (universal asynchronous receiver-transmitter) chip** A chip that controls serial ports. It sets protocol and converts parallel data bits received from the system bus into serial bits.

**UDF (Universal Disk Format) file system** A file system for optical media used by all DVDs and some CD-Rs and CD-RWs.

**UMB (upper memory block)** In DOS and Windows 9x, a group of consecutive memory addresses in RAM from 640 K to 1MB that can be used by 16-bit device drivers and TSRs.

**unattended installation** A Windows 2000/XP installation done by storing the answers to installation questions in a text file or script that Windows calls an answer file. With this installation type, answers don't have to be typed in during the installation.

**upgrade install** The installation of an OS on a hard drive that already has an OS installed in such a way that settings kept by the old OS are carried forward into the upgrade, including information about hardware, software, and user preferences.

**upper memory** In DOS and Windows 9x, the memory addresses from 640 K up to 1024 K, originally reserved for BIOS, device drivers, and TSRs.

**URL (Uniform Resource Locator)** An address for a resource on the Internet. A URL can contain the protocol used by the resource, the name of the computer and its network, and the path and name of a file on the computer.

**USB (universal serial bus) port** A type of port designed to make installation and configuration of I/O devices easy, providing room for as many as 127 devices daisy-chained together.

**USB host controller** Manages the USB bus. If the motherboard contains on-board USB ports, the USB host controller is part of the chipset. The USB uses only a single set of resources for all devices on the bus.

**user account** The information, stored in the SAM database, that defines a Windows 2000/XP user, including user name, password, memberships, and rights.

**user profile** A personal profile about a user that enables the user's desktop settings and other operating parameters to be retained from one session to another.

**USMT (User State Migration Tool)** A Windows XP utility that helps you migrate user files and preferences from one computer to another to help users make a smooth transition from one computer to another.

**UTP (unshielded twisted-pair) cable** A cable made of one or more twisted pairs of wires that is not surrounded by a metal shield.

**V (volt)** A measure of potential difference in an electrical circuit. A computer ATX power supply usually provides five separate voltages: +12 V, -12 V, +5 V, -5 V, and +3.3 V.

**V.92** The latest standard for data transmission over phone lines that can attain a speed of 56 Kbps.

**value data** In Windows, the name and value of a setting in the Registry.

**VCACHE** A built-in Windows 9x 32-bit software cache that doesn't take up conventional memory space or upper memory space, as SMARTDrive did.

**video card** An interface card installed in the computer to control visual output on a monitor. *Also called* display adapter.

**virtual device driver (VxD or VDD)** A Windows device driver that can have direct access to a device. It might depend on a Windows component to communicate with the device itself.

**virtual memory** A method whereby the OS uses the hard drive as though it were RAM. *Compare to* RAM drive.

**virtual real mode** An operating mode that works similarly to real mode provided by a 32-bit OS for a 16-bit program to work.

**virus** A program that often has an incubation period, can infect other computers, and is intended to cause damage. A virus program might destroy data and programs or damage a disk drive's boot sector.

**virus signature** A set of distinguishing characteristics of a virus used by antivirus software to identify the virus.

**volatile** Refers to a kind of RAM that's temporary, can't hold data very long, and must be refreshed frequently.

**voltage** Electrical differential that causes current to flow, measured in volts. *See also* V (volt).

**voltmeter** A device for measuring electrical AC or DC voltage.

**volume** *See* logical drive.

**VRAM (video RAM)** RAM on video cards that holds the data being passed from the computer to the monitor and can be accessed by two devices simultaneously. Higher resolutions often require more video memory.

**VRM (voltage regulator module)** A device embedded or installed on the motherboard that regulates voltage to the processor.

**VxD** *See* virtual device driver.

**W (watt)** The unit used to measure power. A typical computer can use a power supply that provides 200W.

**wait state** A clock tick in which nothing happens, used to ensure that the microprocessor isn't getting ahead of slower components. A 0-wait state is preferable to a 1-wait state. Too many wait states can slow down a system.

**WAN (wide area network)** A network or group of networks that span a large geographical area.

**warm boot** *See* soft boot.

**wattage** Electrical power measured in watts.

**WFP (Windows File Protection)** A Windows 2000/XP tool that protects system files from modification.

**Wi-Fi** *See* IEEE 802.11b.

**wildcard** A * or ? character used in a command line that represents a character or group of characters in a file name or extension.

**Win.ini** The Windows initialization file that contains program configuration information needed for running the Windows operating environment. Its functions were replaced by the Registry beginning with Windows 9x, which still supports it for backward compatibility with Windows 3.x.

**Win386.swp** The name of the Windows 9x swap file. Its default location is C:\Windows.

**WLAN (wireless LAN)** A type of LAN that doesn't use wires or cables to create connections; instead, it transmits data over radio or infrared waves.

**workgroup** In Windows, a logical group of computers and users in which administration, resources, and security are distributed throughout the network, without centralized management or security.

**worm** An infestation designed to copy itself repeatedly to memory, on drive space or on a network, until little memory or disk space remains.

**WRAM (window RAM)** Dual-ported video RAM that's faster and less expensive than VRAM. It has its own internal bus on the chip with a 256-bit-wide data path.

**ZIF (zero insertion force) socket** A socket that uses a small lever to apply even force when you install the microchip into the socket.

**zone bit recording** A method of storing data on a hard drive whereby the drive can have more sectors per track near the outside of the platter.